Androscoggin River

Mouth of the brook   Log Cabin

Olivet

Cemetery

Pinkham Brook

Holland Cottage   To Brunswick

Street Called Straight   Higgins Cottage

John Douglas Barn   Hephzibah

Neighborhood Cemetery

Shiloh Post Office

Shiloh and Environs

— AROUND 1904 —

FAIR
CLEAR
AND
TERRIBLE

**BRITISH
AMERICAN
PUBLISHING**

FAIR
CLEAR
AND
TERRIBLE

The Story of Shiloh, Maine

Shirley Nelson

British American Publishing

Published by British American Publishing
3 Cornell Road
Latham, NY 12110

A portion of this book was written at Yaddo.

Manufactured in the United States of America

93 92 91 90 89   5 4 3 2 1

Library of Congress Cataloging in Publication Data

Nelson, Shirley.
    Fair clear and terrible

    1. Sandford, Frank W., 1862–1948. 2. Evangelists—
United States—Biography. 3. Shiloh (Me.)—History.
4. Nelson, Shirley—Family. I. Title.
BV3785.S18N45 1989 269'.2'0924 [B] 88–34083
ISBN 0-945167-17-2

For Leander,
who almost got away.

Fair as the moon,
Clear as the sun,
And terrible as an army
with banners.

Song of Solomon 6:10

Contents

Illustrations

The Search Begins

Three years after Olive Mills was raised from the dead, my father's family moved to Shiloh—he, his parents, and his three sisters. He was twelve years old. My mother was already there, her family in fragments. She was fifteen.

That was in 1902. Nine years had gone by since Frank Weston Sandford had launched his movement in southern Maine, and five since he had laid the foundation for the first towering building on the Douglas sandhill just off the River Road in the town of Durham. It would be eighteen months until his first manslaughter trial, and another nine years until the second.

The world was fairly quiet in 1902, if we discount the concluding skirmishes of the Boer War, an earthquake in Russian Turkestan, and the explosion of Mt. Pelee in the West Indies. By the same dubious standard things were quiet at Shiloh as well—clear through to the middle of December, when the smallpox broke out. Even so, we must move across a snowy New Year and include the whole winter of 1903 before events take on their true significance. And then they do so only in distant retrospect, for not one of the four hundred persons living at Shiloh during those months could have identified that time then for what it really was—the Black Winter, the year when things began to go wrong. The people who told me Shiloh stories were not historians. Dates were seldom given, if remembered at all. The past was recorded much as it is in the Old Testament: "In the year that King Uzziah died. . . ." In the year that Olive Mills did not.

Long before Shiloh was a reality in my life it was a sound, a word that began with a hush. Even now it echoes back into the depths of pre-memory, carrying the overtones of many other Scriptural names—

1

Manasseh, Shechem, Baal Shalisha—war cries hidden in their soft syllables. In time I learned that the sound was a place, and then that there were other places in the world called Shiloh. My Shiloh was somewhere in the state of Maine. Yet at the same time it was nowhere. It was less a place than a thing that had happened, like a private volcano in the vague past, its ashes, decades later, still sifting down.

That was how it came to me, in fact, a speck at a time, isolated stories told as the occasion arose. More often than not, these were stories of hunger or cold: scores of families with nothing to eat for days on end, or only carrots, or only cornbread; my father splitting green wood in the snow; my mother washing down six flights of stairs in an unheated building; and a laundry of overwhelming proportions—underwear, sheets, and shirts turning to ice even as they were hung on the line, flapping like cardboard in the wind.

My brain held no spaces for these scenes to settle into. I could not imagine a house that could hold so many people. They jammed themselves around the table in our own small dining room and slept in layers on our beds. I had never seen six flights of stairs. In my mind's eye they shot right out through the rooftop into a wintry sky, and my mother was up there crying, her hands so cold she could scarcely wring out the rag.

Yet there were the "good times," my mother insisted, invariably describing the gingerbread as evidence, great sheets of it—"as big as this table," she would say—served warm from the enormous brick ovens. So the images gathered, full of odd surprises. In the midst of hunger two matched trotting horses pulled a gold and white "chariot" over country roads, a luxury yacht sailed around the world, and—dinner or not—my father played a horn at sunset from the window of a tower, the notes echoing brightly over the valley of the river.

The river was the Androscoggin, the tower "David's." There were other towers as well, and buildings with graceful, feminine names like Olivet and Bethesda. Bethesda was a hospital, minus doctors and medication. Sickness also pervaded Shiloh stories, sometimes in detail. Yet on the whole, references to dying were rueful and brief. My mother spoke of her brother's death almost cryptically. His name was Leander. He died of diphtheria at age fourteen. Diphtheria, to me, was one of the things you got a needle for in the second grade. It left a red-hot welt on your upper arm. No one explained that Leander had been the focus of one of the more anomalous court trials in the country. I never heard my grandmother talk about her son or so much as say his name, though she lived with us for months in New England.

We moved north from New Jersey when I was six, in 1931. I had no idea we were moving geographically closer to Shiloh, and certainly that was not the intention. We rented an old farmhouse on Underwood Street in Holliston, Massachusetts. The house was heated by a wood range and a parlor stove. There was no electricity. All our water came from a pump in the iron kitchen sink. I learned how to prime that pump, how to light a kerosene lamp, and how to carry a load of wood heaped up to just under my eyes.

If I was proud of all that, I was also worried. The move seemed to have replanted us in an earlier time, as if we had slipped backwards. Our house in New Jersey had been "modern." But it was not just the kitchen pump that troubled me, nor the fact that we were quite suddenly and obviously poor. It was people, relatives and old friends of my parents whom I had now begun to meet, and their unmistakable threads to an earlier generation and place. They had all been "there."

Furthermore, our Grammy Bartlett, my mother's mother, who had only visited before, was now an integral part of each day, sometimes as an extra adult, sometimes as a petulent child. She prayed in her bedroom, a hanky (produced from her bosom) on her head, kneeling on a little cushion that smelled of balsam. That kneeling pad was all she owned, along with her Bible and a magnifying glass to read it by. I think I have never since known anyone so free of possessions and human bonds. A sister in New Hampshire and her daughter, my mother, were her only family, all that anchored her safely to earth. God provided for her needs from day to day, she told us cheerfully. I have a strong memory of the sense of magic her declaration provoked in me—that people could actually live that way, their ties held loosely, or not at all, without ownership or income.

I loved her, there was no question of that. She was affectionate and brave, but she was a road that led directly into the past, and the past, I had learned, meant trouble. At supper time amazing words flew across the table. A tool of the devil, Grammy called my father one night—a traitor and a quitter. He, the mildest of men, grew red and dismissed her from the dining room. She left, with a parting shot. "God will strike you dead!" she whispered fiercely at the door. "You see if He don't!"

By now I had begun to realize that there were people who were still "in" Shiloh and those who were "out." Grammy Bartlett was in. My parents were out. Some who were out were really still in, and some who were out were *actively* out—that is, being out was the centrality of their lives. My father was in a class by himself. He was *aggressively* out. He was so out he was out with most of the others who were out.

To confuse matters more, the White grandparents, on my father's side, seemed neither to be in nor wholly out. Our real reason for moving to New England was to be close to them in their aging years. They lived in Framingham, along with some cousins and aunts, about a block from the Dennison factory, a neighborhood of Italians and Jews and Irish—from whom my relatives held themselves distinctly apart.

They needn't have gone to the trouble. Their apartness was unavoidably clear. It showed in their speech, their clothing, and their habits. They did not approve of movies, dancing, permanent waves, playing cards, or too much skin showing anywhere.

What was I to do about this? I saw myself in their faces. Their freckles were mine, their extravagant grins, and the way they walked, swinging their arms and bent on duty. They welcomed us, the young tribe of Whites, kissed us hard on the mouth, and laughed when we showed off. I wanted to belong to them, but the present was too alluring. I had just found out about nail polish and Hollywood. Our three-holed backhouse had been papered by a former tenant with old rotogravure photos of movie stars, and Douglas Fairbanks, omniscient in eye-makeup, watched me pee.

The local movie theatre was in Framingham. We slipped in and out of the matinee, then stopped to see the relatives on Freeman Street. That house, soot-gray and ugly, was the only place I ever knew as home to my grandparents, yet I could tell it was not their real home. It was an outpost between life and death. They had come to Framingham after Shiloh, penniless and in their mid-sixties. The purchase of the ugly house was an economic triumph I could not appreciate, and the frugality of their lives within in it merely strange. If we arrived after dark, we would find them sitting in an unlighted living room, saving electricity. Two of the rooms were shut off in the winter, the shade-drawn bedroom cold and musty, a place to collapse in at the end of the day.

The steely rod of principle that ran down their lives—owe no man anything and share all you can—set them off from Grammy Bartlett, who was dependent on other people for her very survival. Yet she and they both, in their opposite ways, represented what I understood of Shiloh. There was a hard reality to their religion which repelled me.

If you gave yourself to it an inch, it would take all of you. Yet that very quality was magnetic.

Over the years we lived in five different houses in Holliston, and in each the words about Shiloh increased, for my father had begun a book about the place and the more he wrote, the more he seemed to talk— the more everyone talked, all those relatives and old friends. Children were snared into hearing this by the simple requirement of being polite to adults. Whole days of vacation might erode away while people talked. Plans could be cancelled, dinner postponed unbearably. We would stand in somebody's front hall, itchy in coats and scarves, while hope vanished that a last goodbye would ever be spoken. The Talk, we called it, tyranny in an otherwise happy and free existence, the ambiguities of those Shiloh years examined again and again, the name Frank Sandford slipping in and out, never neutrally spoken, always in tones of either bitterness or adoration. He was hated or he was loved. And where was he now, people asked each other? In hiding? Still alive? He was responsible for the deaths of many people, someone said, but he himself was not supposed to die. Did I hear that right? It didn't matter. He had nothing to do with me.

I was eighteen when I visited Shiloh—the place where it had been, that is—for the first time. Let me locate it specifically. The Androscoggin River, plunging out of the Teutonic Range of the White Mountains, hooks north just short of the Atlantic and joins the Kennebec in the waters above Casco Bay. The land between the rivers is hill country. The Androscoggin, rock-strewn, breaking often into falls and rapids and other burly business, offers water power for the mills of the towns that crowd its edges: Lewiston and Auburn, Brunswick and Topsham. Durham, quite in the middle of these, untouched by industry, spreads out just across the river from Lisbon Falls. Here Shiloh settled and grew until its "Scattering" in 1920.

Following that event, close relatives of my family stayed on to farm Durham's sandy soil and harvest its woodlands. So in the natural course of things I had been to Shiloh at least once before the visit I refer to, which to me was the first with any meaning. Only mildly interested in going, once there I was captured by a familiarity that seemed to entail more than memory. Though the whole back portion of that enormous structure had become a sagging shell, two levels of veranda wrapped around it like loose string, I had no trouble imagining it as it once had been, a giant triple-decker river boat caught on a lofty sandbar, flags snapping from its turrets, people moving back and forth across the stretches of sandy waste between the buildings. And there was my mother (so I imagined) on her way from Olivet with her friends, toeing out like the good nineteenth-century girl she was, her dark ankle-length skirt blowing in the wind.

But that moment of intrigue was short-lived. For a long time yet I would struggle to keep the place a safe distance behind me. Let my father write his book if he must, or rather, the first chapter, the introduction, the prologue, epilogue, and summaries that he seemed to be rewriting again and again, fiddling with file-folders under tortuous labels ("Mythical Nonsense Foisted Upon Modern Believers"). I was still not asking the most basic questions—how it could happen, why people went there and why they stayed, why it took a war to release my father, or why my mother had to leave twice before she was really gone.

It was two decades before I saw the place once more. By that time the "river boat" had disappeared altogether and Olivet was a hollow of granite. Bethesda's upstairs floors lay crumpled in its cellar, the ground outside scattered with veranda spokes and bricks. Shiloh Proper, the original building, was the only remaining structure, its golden crown still perched at the top of its tower.

I walked with my father down to the private cemetery, on a trapezoid of land between two dry river gullies. There, two hundred graves were sprawled with no apparent plan, most of them designated by wooden or cement slabs. Some of these bore touching and dignified tributes: "Papa Dear," "Marjorie—A White Heart," and "More Than A Conqueror." Leander, my mother's brother, was buried at the back, so closely bound by others there seemed scarcely room enough for him to lie. Perhaps there wasn't. He had been buried in a hurry and graves are hard to dig by hand in the dead of winter. There was nothing on his marker except his name and the dates. "He had planned to run away," said my father.

I had heard that before, but no one had ever explained what it meant. Now, out of the dozens of questions still unanswered and unasked, it was essential to know one thing—why this boy had died. So it was for Leander that the search first began.

I found him with surprising ease—in the basement of the Bowdoin College library, at the end of a mile of microfilm. His story hit the screen like a clap of thunder on the front page of the six o'clock edition of the *Lewiston Saturday Journal,* January 23, 1904: THE CHARGE IS MANSLAUGHTER! To the left of the page a Bath schooner tilted into the Atlantic, the *Augustus Hunt* wrecked in a storm, and on the right flames raged at the windows of the Masonic Temple in Chicago. Between them sat a well-groomed gentleman with a short beard and intelligent eyes which looked directly into mine. This was Frank Sandford. It was he who had been charged in the death of the boy, and he— though he had nothing to do with me—who had pervaded and shaped my own life.

For almost two weeks the *Journal* carried the entire proceedings of the trial at the courthouse in Auburn, Maine. On February 5 the headline announced that the mother of Leander Bartlett, in sworn testimony, had given "important evidence for the defense." My grand-mother. For an instant I thought her picture had been included. In a nearby column a sketch of a buxom woman looked just like her. Instead, it was an ad, a "prominent society woman" of Boston with her own sworn testimony, cured within twenty-four hours by TO-NI-TA, which would "heal any case of grippe or influenza if taken as ordered, as well as catarrh of the head, throat, lungs, stomach, kidneys, bladder and female organs."

Back at my cousin's farmhouse in Durham I scanned the microfilm prints again, then escaped outdoors to work in the garden, in my ignorance hoeing a crop gone by. Kittens crouched, watching, while brown hens sat in a square of sunlight on the shed floor, wary of my presence.

I needed to see the place again, I thought, to come upon it suddenly and with surprise. I set out walking toward the village of Lisbon Falls, two miles on the other side of the river, waiting to be startled by the first glimmer of the Shiloh dome and crown through the trees. There it was, a flash of light in that rural context, then gone. At the entrance to the River Road I could see it again.

The road had been graded and surfaced, and new little houses with lawns and straight driveways occupied its edges, where once there had been open fields. But it was still the same road. This was where you walked, to and from Shiloh. If you ran away, this is where you turned, at this corner, on the way to Lisbon Falls, while over your right shoulder—where you might frequently glance—the gold crown appeared and reappeared between the houses and the trees.

Charles Lindbergh, I had been told, flying over Durham in 1927, saw the gold dome below him and thought it was the capitol of Maine. How long did it take him, I wondered, to catch on? How many second looks did he need to realize that the city of Augusta was not there, and that farmland encompassed the imposing white structure below him for acres and acres, save for the red brick mills of Lisbon Falls?

Imagined from above like that, the story took on new breadth. It was clear to me now why my father had grown paralyzed, standing at the end of his first chapter like a stunt man at the tip of an airplane wing, staring into that beguiling vista. For fully as important as the event of Shiloh itself was the wider world that contained it and made it possible, from a nineteenth-century sky clear of machinery—clear of anything but crows and circling hawks—down to chickens in sunlight on a shed floor and that society woman in Boston who was cured of all that ailed her by a dose of TO-NI-TA.

It was the danger that took your breath away. I had never really seen it. It was hard to see, so softly focused in the background of safety and innocence and heroic intentions. It must have been now that I recognized the story (and the danger) as my inheritance, and knew that equal to it or not, when the time was right I would go after it.

Not that I nurtured any illusions of ownership—not then or now. The Shiloh story has always belonged to many people, a thousand stories in one. It belongs to Frank Sandford, above all. Without him there would be no story, and his becomes everyone else's. But for me, the story belongs first to the members of my family who lived it—to my grandparents, my mother and Leander, and to my father, surely, who completed his memoirs after all, and saw them published. My relatives were not among the principals in the wider sweep of the Shiloh drama, or even witnesses to all that took place, but they are my authentic access to the history. More, they help to tell it, whenever they have lent their eyes and ears and voices.

Rid of Scrofula

's Sarsaparilla

FIFTEEN OF CREW LOST!

Big Bath Schooner in Kindling Wood.

Strewn Along the Shore of Long Island.

Only Two Men Rescued in Terrific Sea and Fog.

The Augustus Hunt Wrecked Off West Hampton, To-Day.

Was the Pioneer of the Big Four Masters Built by Morse Co. and Called "Jumbo."

NEW YORK, Jan. 23.—Fifteen lives were lost in the wreck of the four-masted schooner Augustus Hunt, of West Hampton. Long Island. Two others who were on board were saved.

Through the dense fog, the cries of the doomed crew appealed for help and the life-savers tried repeatedly to reach the wreck but without success. They were flinging back the life boat, while the thick fog veiled the schooner from sight and prevented the use of any lines to reach the wreck.

The schooner went ashore one and one-half miles east of Quogue life saving station soon after midnight and during the early morning hours the cries of the crew attracted attention.

Soon after daylight, the wreck began to go to pieces. Fragments reached shore bore the name of the vessel.

Within a few hours the schooner had broken up completely and of her crew of seventeen, only two survived. These were the second mate and one other who reached the shore on a piece of wreckage.

Captain Blair was not on board the schooner being at Boston, his mate Captain Conary, having the command. [The August Hunt was built in 1901 at Bath, Me., her home port. She is 1,258 tons gross, 285 feet long, 45.7 feet deep, 36.5 feet wide and carries a crew of nine.]

BOSTON, Jan. 23.—It was learned here to-day that Captain Blair was not in command of the Schooner Augustus Hunt, which is reported as having been wrecked off West Hampton, L. I. Captain Blair is in this city, having stayed at home during the present trip of the vessel and he states that his mate, Captain Conary, was in command of the Hunt.

The schooner carried a cargo of 1718 tons of bituminous coal valued at $5,400 and insured, consigned to A. Gore & Son, of East Boston. The vessel is valued at $60,000 with partial insurance.

BATH, Me., Jan. 23.—The four-masted schooner Augustus Hunt, reported wrecked off West Hampton, L. I., to-day, was the largest vessel built by the G. M. Morse of this city in 1901 and for many years was known as "the Jumbo" because of her unusually large proportions for a schooner at that time. She was of 143 gross tons, 26 feet in length, 46.7 feet beam and 36.5 feet depth of hold.

NEW YORK, Jan. 23.—A little later in the day a private dispatch reported that the brig Alena a British schooner under command of Capt. Durham from Hantsport for New York, had gone ashore at Rockaway, L. I.

French creek has overflowed the Erie railroad tracks and blocked traffic between Oil City and Meadville.

A gorge in Oil Creek near Rouseville has passed out, breaking a gas main and shutting off the fuel supply from towns along the stream.

BOSTON, Jan 23.—Greater Boston was snowbound in a thick and misty fog to-day, which was so impenetrable and blinding that the train service, especially that connected with the South Terminal station was much delayed. The great trouble developed at the South station where the fog interfered with the usually expeditious handling of the scores of trains to arrive during the forenoon. To avoid the possibility of a collision in the train shed many suburban trains were detained outside. All transportation in the city stood on the Boston Elevated Railway had to be directed with utmost caution to prevent accident. During the morning it was necessary to provide light in the business district buildings as dark was the atmosphere.

THE CHARGE IS MANSLAUGHTER!

REV. FRANK W. SANDFORD.

Rev. Frank W. Sandford Indicted on Six Counts and Arrested.

FOR CRUELTY TO CHILDREN

Five of the Indictments Are Held Over Him—He Will Be Arraigned at Once.

Rev. Frank W. Sandford, identified for years with the Shiloh and the Holy Ghost and Us movement at Durham, Maine, known as a leader of the world-wide crusade for evangelization, self-announced as Elijah II, prominent in leading the Jerusalem party, a traveler in many lands, recently at the head of an established movement at Lewiston, was indicted on six counts by the Grand Jury of Androscoggin county on Saturday at 11 A. M. and at 1 P. M. Saturday was arrested on one of them a charge of manslaughter in the case of Leander Bartlett, a fourteen-year-old boy, inmate of Shiloh.

Five other specific indictments are also returned by the Grand Jury, all for cruelty to children. Mr. Sandford's arrest was made by Sheriff Cummings and Deputy Sheriff Hurley. He took it calmly. The offense is bailable and Rev. Mr. Sandford will probably secure bail.

The Grand Jury of Androscoggin county rose at 11 A. M. Saturday and put its list of 65 indictments into the hands of County Attorney Shelton.

"Is there an indictment in the Sandford-Shiloh case?" was the first question asked.

County Attorney Shelton declined to say. He gave out the usual list of indictments, in which the parties are to custody and offered nothing more.

Less than twenty minutes after this, Sheriff Cummings and Deputy Sheriff Hurley bundled into a sleigh and drove off through the storm of hail and rain towards Durham. At 1 P. M and came to County Attorney Shelton that Mr. Frank W. Sandford had been arrested at Shiloh on Beulah Hill in Durham and that him with manslaughter and that law officers were on their way to Auburn with their charge.

months old child of John Scott of Auburn.

CRUELTY TO CHILD in case of LEANDER BARTLETT, aged 14

CRUELTY TO CHILD in case of 7-year-old child of John Scott of Auburn.

CRUELTY TO CHILD in case of 2-year-old son of John Swart of Auburn.

FORM OF INDICTMENT

We give herewith the form of indictment in case of manslaughter and the form in one of the cases alleging cruelty to children

INDICTMENT FOR MANSLAUGHTER

STATE OF MAINE
ANDROSCOGGIN, ss.

AT THE SUPREME JUDICIAL COURT, begun and holden at Auburn, within and for the county of Androscoggin on the third day of January in the year of our Lord one thousand nine hundred and four.

THE JURORS FOR SAID STATE upon their oath present that heretofore to wit on the third day of January...

STUCTURE BURNING.

Masonic Temple in Chicago, Scene of a Panic.

Over 2000 People in the Giant Office Building.

An Explosion in a Doctor's Office Caused the Blare.

Corridors and Elevator Shafts Soon Filled With Smoke.

Firemen Handicapped and Many People Injured—Near Iroquois Scene

CHICAGO, Jan. 23.—Fire broke out this afternoon in the Masonic Temple, a twenty-story sky scraper, one square east of the Iroquois theatre. Owing to the fact that upwards of 2000 people occupy the offices and stores in the giant structure, the fire caused much excitement.

The series of sprinklers surrounding the rotunda in the centre of the building continued to run while the smoke and flames issued from the windows in the fourth story where the fire originated. The people were removed from the upper floors as rapidly as possible.

Great crowds of spectators quickly surrounded the temple, being drawn from the fashionable shopping district of State street and adjoining thoroughfares. The sight of the majestic structure through the clouds of smoke and flame was one long to be remembered.

Firemen were summoned by an alarm automatically sent in from the rooms in which the fire began. The firemen quickly made connections with the stationary stand-pipe in the building. Immediately tons of water flooded the floors where the blaze had its base and therefrom.

When the smoke and flames was increasing by the suspected presence of a gas, a chemicals which occupants declared were stored near the place where the fire originated.

Occupants of the building, warned by the suffocating clouds of smoke that rose through its many stuffed rooms and penetrated every corridor, lost no time in making efforts for safe exit. Guards were stationed at each entrance leading on every floor and the panic-stricken people were hurried from the building.

The origin of the fire was an explosion of chemicals in a doctor's office on the fifth floor. The explosion was a sudden one and threw all of the occupants of the neighbors of the floors immediately above and below but the uproar was heard by hundreds of other persons in the structure who received their warning more suddenly combined with walls of smoke.

Flames followed the explosion and quickly spread to the floors above. Men and women rushed wildly for the stairs and elevators. So rapidly did the immense sky-scraper fill with smoke that the firemen found it almost impossible to work within the walls.

In a short time the fire was raging on three floors containing many chemical and laboratories and doctors offices. Further explosions were momentarily feared. The Marshal Marsh on was soon on hand and he quickly warned the men of the danger.

MASSAR BOUND OVER.

Held in $1000 Bail in Brunswick Burglary Case—Taken to Portland Jail.

BRUNSWICK, Me., Jan. 23.—Antonio Nassar, the young Syrian who escaped from a cell in the local police station and later was captured at Yarmouth, was arraigned in police court late Friday afternoon charged with burglary and was held for the grand jury. He was unable to furnish bail in the sum of $1,000 and was taken to the county jail at Portland. It has been the intention of the Brunswick officers to bring a charge of highway robbery against Nassar, but as John Foster, the man who was held up and robbed of $5 on Pleasant street early Friday morning, was unable to identify the prisoner as his assailant, it was decided not to press the charge.

FOR ELECTORS AT LARGE.

WS 25,000 UT OF WORK.

urg Industries Are ded and Water Still Rising.

eet of Heavy Barges wept Down River.

from Other Places of ge—Boston in an Impenetrable Fog.

BRO., Pa., Jan. 23.—At 4 morning the gauges showed highway stood at 29.6 feet six and rising at the rate of a foot an hour. The Mononongahela wharf stood at 37.2, rising 1 foot an hour. The Ohio at Davis Island and rising at 3 feet per

A fears of the manufacturers Pittsburg side of the Allegheny the Sharpsburg bridge down, and shortly after midnight waters swept over the banks have and inundated the sawmilleries.

r union mill of the U. S. Steel was about the first plant to business temporarily throwing men out of work until next Tuesday. The lower union 800 employes and the Black Works of the Crucible Steel be nearer. At the latter place men are now idle.

very mill and factory between meny Valley railroad tracks or is more or less flooded and stood that 25,000 men will be Monday or Tuesday.

clock this morning two barges a fifty thousand bushels of of the coal fleet moored close he ice gorge is forming in the ais were caught by the current a mass of ice and sunk.

ntire Coal Co. sent three coal the river consigned to New end of the flood yesterday Late last night they passed e in safety. The tows carried twenty barges with 500,000 coal.

f forty barges loaded by the

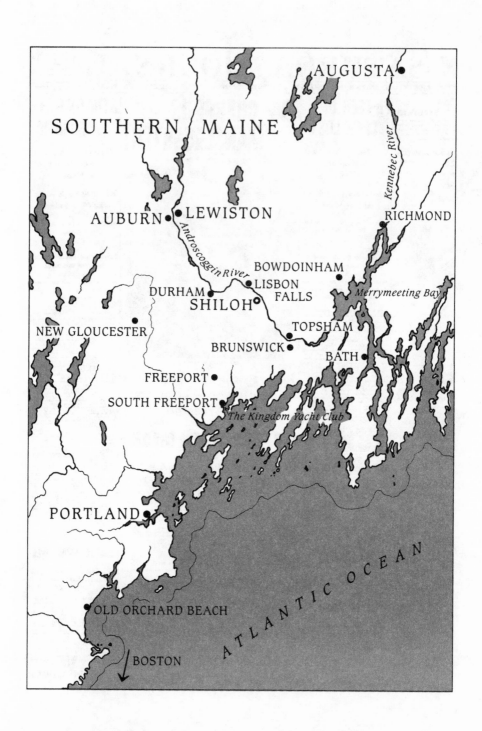

2

First Steps

My father was brought to Shiloh slowly, just sidling into it, you could say, in a kind of shuffling dance. The moment at which he was finally there, or there to stay, is lost in a series of small, tentative decisions. My mother arrived suddenly, and all at once—sent, not brought. She came alone on a cool May morning in 1900, Merlyn Salome Bartlett, a girl of thirteen, wearing a plaid tam with a ridiculously tall red feather. She had spent the night on the packet boat from Boston to Bath, where she caught the electrics to Lisbon Falls and climbed aboard the mail wagon headed over the river to the Bible school at Durham. Her trip had been hastily planned, and her own mother, who had been a student at the school for a year, had not been told when to expect her.

What Merlyn remembered later was the feeling of being perched high on the wagon seat beside the mailman, shivering in the spring air. Steam from the mills had turned the trees along the river white with frost, and ice still stretched across the fields. But clear water ran freely in the ditches, and acres of newly turned earth shown moist and brown. She had been awake most of the night, too excited to sleep. Now, with the turn of the iron wheel rims on the dirt road, she began to relax.

My mother was sent to Shiloh to die, though she had no suspicion of that. She had been told that the doctor recommended country as the cure for a cough that would not go away, and she knew nothing of a whispered conversation in which he had given her three months to live. She did not think of herself as ill, and made no connection between her own persistent cough and the one she had listened to day after day years before.

They were living in Bangor then. She was six. On the night her

11

father died of "consumption" she had lain awake listening to the wind off the Penobscot River wailing around the house, her instincts alive with impending trouble. Her younger brother Leander had already been sent to Boston to live with relatives, and her mother was leaving soon too, going away to rest. "Elvira has never been strong," people were saying, and now she was "close to prostration."

For the next two years Merlyn shuttled from one family to another in the Bangor area, a few months at a time in each place, at the home of the doctor who had treated her father, at the home of the minister who had buried him, at the home of a cousin, all the while growing more disheveled, her hair cropped short and sticking out of a round comb—an old-fashioned urchin much in need of a parent.

At last she was sent to join Leander in Boston. The aunt and uncle who cared for them were generous and loving, but their mother, renting dressmakers' rooms close by, visited only on occasion, like a guest, kissing them a lot and crying when she left. She was working very hard, the children understood, as a seamstress, as a housekeeper, as a salesgirl, paying off old medical bills and providing for their expenses. Someday the three of them would be a "regular family" again with their own house, she promised. That was the goal, or it was until she went away to the Bible School in Maine.

Elvira Bartlett had first learned of Shiloh two years before. Selling the new Worcester Salt door to door in Boston, she met a woman whose daughter had been healed of brain fever by a Shiloh evangelist. There were "meetings" in the parlors of a grand house on Massachusetts Avenue, which Merlyn and Leander sometimes attended and where they heard frequent references to a Mr. Sandford, who was seldom present. Merlyn met him only once—a kind and funny man who skipped with her down the sidewalk one day on the way to a meeting, teasing her about her witch's name, and renaming her on the spot as "Leah, the tender-eyed."

The meetings themselves had not meant much to Merlyn, and Leander had hated them. They were long and made his legs restless and jumpy. One of the leaders said that it was Satan who got into children and made them disruptive, and all the way home that day Leander threatened to touch Merlyn and give her the devil.

Whatever Shiloh was, it had restored their mother's spirits, and that had made it more bearable when she took the "big step of faith" which carried her away to the Durham school. She had moved to a mansion in the country, the children were told.

"I expect you shan't lack for anything," Aunt May said, as she helped Merlyn gather her things. "There will even be ponies to ride!"

But it was said with a heartiness Merlyn had learned to distrust. So she anticipated very little on the morning of her arrival, and was overwhelmed by the sight that greeted her as the mail wagon turned a corner and approached Shiloh hill. Not a mansion, but a castle, she thought with a gasp, a magnificent gold and white building with windows afire in the morning sun. It rose above them on the hill, growing taller and more imposing as they pulled up the long straight driveway.

At the top, the wagon stopped alongside another ascent of wide, white steps leading to a veranda. Merlyn climbed these at the mailman's bidding, her heart pounding, pushed open the double front door, also immaculately white, and stepped into a hall full of people and the warm homey smell of breakfast. Instantly a bell began to ring, as if to announce her presence, and somewhere nearby a piano began to play. She stood quietly in a corner of the hall, trying hard not to cough, or to be noticed at all by the astonishing number of young men and women who rushed past her into a room on her right.

Then, there was her mother, her face flushed with surprise and pleasure, running down the stairs to greet her, and Merlyn entered the happiest summer she could remember in what seemed like a lifetime.

My father was Wendell and Annie White's second child and only son among three daughters. His name was Arnold. An easy-going redhead, he grew up favored by the notion that the world had been created for his personal good. Until he was taken to Shiloh, that world consisted almost entirely of two localities, the Growstown farm outside Brunswick where he lived, and his mother's childhood home in the city of Lewiston, where he visited. In his earliest recollections the farm blurred into a hundred sensual pleasures, while the house at Lewiston always stood out crisp and clean. Even the barn there seemed strangely citified, Old Dick, its one occupant, smelling less horsey than he might.

If in these agreeable circumstances, a slight edge of disapproval cut the air, it was lost on Arnold. The ambiguity with which the Wood grandparents viewed Wendell White, the man who had married their youngest daughter Annie, was far too elusive for a small boy to identify.

Grandpa Wood had very definite ideas about success. He had built up an empire in lumber and real estate and put two sons through college. The youngest, Will, who graduated from Bates and went on to Yale for a Ph.D., was a member of the bar in both Massachusetts and Maine, and now owned the *Lewiston Daily Sun,* the new local paper. In terms of advancement, Wendell could not have been more Will's opposite. Wendell was a farmer, and yet he was not. Said to be a good teacher, he had earned only enough credentials to place him in a one-room country schoolhouse. Even now, with a family to feed, he spoke longingly of going back to college.

Politically, too, Wendell seemed confused. Though he professed to be a Republican, he had voted recently for the squabbling Prohibitionists, a party that drew under its skirts vagabond issues, such as labor reform and women's suffrage. As for religion, his approach was rather too earnest and explicit, and it was best not to raise the subject, his in-laws had learned, for he would debate with tenacity, proving his points with an arsenal of quoted Scripture. The Woods, members of the Main Street Free Baptist Church in Lewiston, readily agreed that the church as a whole had lost its zeal, but they saw no reason to take so personally something that was clearly not their fault.

Arnold never heard his mother take part in these discussions. Maybe Annie thought her own performance was in question. She had been raised to keep a spotless house, but dirt on a dairy farm was a different matter than dirt in the city. Mud got tracked in daily from ankle depths in the barnyard, scraps of bark cluttered the floor by the wood box, and scarves and mittens dried on a line behind the stove, fogging the windows with moisture. Yet Annie seldom complained and often pulled on a pair of old boots to help in the barn or the hay field. Arnold was aware of how hard his parents worked. Though tensions between them were not well masked (the simplest conversation could turn into a long run of sarcasm on his father's part and tight-lipped silence on his mother's), a tender concern prevailed for the load of work they each carried.

"Father insisted that mother sleep until 6:00 in the morning. He arose at 4:00, stirred the kitchen fire, carried water from the well in the yard (we had no indoor pump), and left the kettle to simmer while he did the earliest chores. By the time the rest of us were awake, he had finished stripping fifteen cows, had set the cream to rise and loaded the milk cans onto the wagon for the morning delivery route in Bruns-wick." At noon he returned to face everything else on the farm still waiting to be done. For periods of time neighboring men hired on as help, but it was hard to match in wages what they could earn at the local mills.

The children were frightened one day to see their father throw a milking stool at one of the cows. They were accustomed to his quick changes in mood. One moment he was patient and jolly, then suddenly they would find themselves cringing under a reprimand, or he would shout at a horse and jerk hard on its bit. But they had never seen him strike an animal.

Sometime in the spring of 1899 Arnold heard his father tell Grandpa Wood that the farm was "killing" him. He said it with his usual note of irony and Arnold thought he was joking—and maybe Wendell, too, was startled to be taken at face-value. Grandpa Wood was a fixer. He had once offered Arnold an unbelievable dollar to stop twisting a calf's tail. Now, by some simple manipulation, he managed to completely alter their lives. After the calves had been weaned and the gardens set in, the farm and the milk business were rented and the family moved into one of Grandpa Wood's houses in Lewiston. Wendell was transformed from a farmer into a businessman with clean fingernails. Each morning he walked out the door in a suit, his moustache combed and trimmed, to spend the day in the circulation department of Uncle Will's newspaper.

Then, in hardly more than a year, that was over. He had quit the job without warning and had enrolled at a school over in the town of Durham, where he was gone from Monday to Friday of each week. Now he was not working at all. The revenue from the farm met their needs.

The purpose of the school, Arnold had been told, was the training of missionaries, but he had never known that his father had any such aspirations. The school was run by a man named Frank Sandford, who had once been a local baseball star. If anything else was explained, Arnold was not listening. Later, he recalled two remarks that might have been made at this time. Uncle George, his father's brother, stopping by at the Lewiston house one day, announced that in his opinion "Frank Sandford had more life in his little finger than most men have in their whole bodies." But Grammy Wood, on hearing the name, slid her dental plates back and forth in her mouth and muttered, "There has been more deviltry concocted under the name of religion than in any other disguise."

Arnold preserved only one other impression of his father's days as a student. It was on a particular evening early in November of 1900, when Wendell returned home for the weekend with a weary and sober face. As he sat at the kitchen table, eating the supper Annie had kept warm on the back of the stove, Arnold heard him say that he was "quite discouraged" about his chances of being able to continue at the school. Something special was taking place over there, a "cleaning-out time," he said, his words emerging in little spurts between forkfuls of food which he hardly seemed to chew. "A sifting-out process," he said. Annie sat quietly, watching him eat. "Only those who pass muster," murmured Wendell. "Only the fair, clear, and terrible."

It came out as one multi-syllabled word, and he was forced to repeat it slowly for Annie's ears.

"Fair, clear, and terrible," she echoed in wonder.

"From the Song of Solomon," said Wendell.

Arnold, doing his homework at the other end of the table, rehearsed the words silently to himself. They stuck in his head, in their right order, for all the years it would take him to fathom what they were supposed to mean.

3

Survival Training

Wendell White had met Frank Sandford for the first time in 1882, when they were both young men at Bates College in Lewiston—Frank an entering student and Wendell a sophomore, a returning dropout. They knew each other because it was difficult not to in the small community of that school. Yet there was little about Wendell to draw Frank's attention, and to Wendell, who was twenty-five and felt much older, Frank was just a good-looking farm boy who spent too much time playing ball.

They had grown up twenty miles from each other, on either side of the land between the rivers where so much of the Shiloh story unfolds. What they held in common is striking, though that would not have impressed either of them in the year that they met. Most Bates students at the time emerged out of the same history and environment, the same Republican, agrarian confines. Many had come from large families whose lives were dominated by work, and many had already assumed adult responsibilities before entering college. It was not unusual in the hill country of New England, even that late in the century, to be catapulated out of childhood by the early death of a parent, as both Frank and Wendell had been.

But the similarities went even deeper than that. For in a remarkably fateful way, these two shared the origin of their destinies, the same heartfelt propensities that would also foster Shiloh and make it necessary to them both. If we reach back in time for a beginning to the story, this is it.

My grandfather was born and raised in the town of New Gloucester, just west of the Androscoggin. He was named for Wendell Phillips, the famous abolitionist, in a day when the subject of slavery was on everyone's tongue. At home he was Wen and abroad he was known as Whitey, as most of his forebears had been. Actually, there were too many Whites in New Gloucester for all to carry the nickname at once, seventeen living males in 1857, the year Wendell was born, to say nothing of the White women who had married and stocked the town with cousins. Altogether they occupied close to a dozen pews in the Freewill Baptist Meeting House and filled many of the singer's seats in the gallery. They were the choir, as it were, to a sanctuary full of themselves. The church, an unadorned clapboard rectangle, stood just a stone's throw from White's Corner at the top of Gloucester Hill, where Wendell's father was blacksmith and farrier.

In the middle of the nineteenth century, New Gloucester still felt like a frontier, with the help of a boy's imagination. The wolves and the Indians were long gone, but the wilderness hovered only a few rods away on every hand, pushing against the cleared acreage, a place where a child might get lost or a sheep fall prey to the bloody work of a lynx. Awe for the wild had not diminished. As you fell into sleep at night after the barn had gone silent, it was the sounds of the forest that thrilled you, the bark of a fox or the quaver of a raccoon. For all that these were enemies who robbed the henhouse and the garden, their presence kept alive the belief that something remained to be conquered.

So it did. For Wendell it was the beast within, a roaring, unpredictable temper. At age sixteen he chased his mother around the kitchen table with a knife. I insert that scrap of intelligence not for its sensational quality, or its absurdity perhaps, but because it is the single most revealing thing I know about my grandfather's early life. The fact was offered, without embellishment, by someone who had heard Wendell admit to explosions of rage, huge thunderheads that had engulfed him as a child and left him trembling and ashamed.

Not that he used the knife, you understand, or ever pulled it on anyone else at any other time. That is not the issue, and it can be said that his anger, healthy or otherwise, is not important either, or not nearly so much as how he viewed it—until he got to Shiloh, where anger, breaking the surface of daily life, would be given more glorious labels.

Whatever the cause of Wendell's volatile temper, it would be foolish to divorce it from his expectation of himself, which was to make his life the conduit for something terribly hard and unquestionably splendid. Throughout his young manhood he lived in that hope, as if on any given day an unseen door would burst open before him, and he would step across into the clear wide space where he belonged.

Such high ambition was due in part to his heritage, which meant the distinct absence of any trace of aristocracy. He was not the patrician for whom he was named. The Whites were not New England Brahmins, and to pretend that they were, to "take on airs," would have been unforgivable. They were as much old family as the Adamses or the Brewsters, but so was nearly everyone else they knew. Neither rich nor poor, they kept no servants, not even a "girl," except when Delphine Humphrey came to help with the wash. The tradition that counted was to be a person of principle and influence, someone who knew how to set the world to rights. That, among other things, was what it meant to be a Freewill Baptist.

The Freewillers were a product of another movement with an equally intriguing name—the New Light Stir—and the Stir, a localized movement in the hills of New England, had caught its spark from the First Great Awakening, which had fueled itself up and down the entire eastern seaboard of the country.

The Awakening was a pivotal occasion in the American colonies, the first uprising—a revolution, really—or it did the work of one. Preceding the Revolution we all understand, the one with guns, this more subjective protest fostered a break with the past that still affects us profoundly, for it introduced new possibilities of power to the ordinary citizen.

Puritan Calvinism, with its stress on salvation for the chosen and an elitist style of church membership, had cast a century-long shadow over personal autonomy in the colonies. With one hand it beckoned a wandering people back to a vital faith and with the other it held them away. When the population at last turned to God, it did so not by conceding to the religious hierarchy, but by leaping over its walls. What the Awakening offered, to all practical purposes, was the right to choose to be chosen.

It was the wrapping around this package that alarmed the Puritans— the easy facility of salvation—and more, the emotion, the display of high feeling so often released in public gatherings. All that joyful singing, the astonished laughter following tears of repentance, the vulgar shouting and swooning and hysteria, were feared to be substitutes for the true work of God. But to the newly converted it seemed a natural response to the overwhelming news that God was not mad at them after all, a theological insight so astute as to render any propriety meaningless.

All this was happening within the world-shaking context of the

Englightenment, with its insistence on the reliability of individual experience. So on the eve of the American Revolution both the intellect and the emotions were freed for the adventures of self-determination.

As one consequence, thousands of "Separatists" cut away from the established church community. The more cautious now watched with despair as a reckless profusion of nonconformists exposed themselves to heresies and hazards—including one in particular with a name like a virulent disease: antinomianism.

The word, in its most generalized sense, meant simply the claim to private revelation, a higher inner law. The Puritan position had been that when God spoke, it was in a way that could be safely examined by an enlightened corporate body. Once the privilege of special revelation—through Scripture or visions or simple instinct—was claimed by single individuals without checks and balances, chaos was inevitable. Antinomianism was not a disease, but dangerous it was, and it had come to stay. Dozens of parties began to leap into life, all spawned with a purifying mission, and all with the brash assurance of the chosen people, a quality they were soon to share with just about everyone else in the country.

The New Light Stir was part of that revival of dissent. It lasted five years, throughout the Revolutionary War. By the time it died down separatists of various stripes had organized in many parts of Maine. In New Gloucester a group of radicals, tossed out of the Congregational Church for disrupting worship, immersed their members in the millpond (the most concrete statement they could make to the infant-sprinkling Congregationalists), and soon began to call themselves the Freewill Baptists.

In one of Sarah Orne Jewett's stories of nineteenth-century Maine, a conversation occurs among three women passengers on a stage coach. "I ain't orthodox," declares one, with pride. "I was brought up amongst the Freewill Baptists."

"We're well acquainted with several of that denomination in our place," answers another lady, with a sniff. "They've never built 'em no church; there ain't but a scattered few."

"They prevail where I come from," claims the first woman, undaunted, knowing perhaps the strength of the "gathered" (voluntary or uncoerced) church, for whom architecture is merely a matter of convenience.

Prevail they did throughout the hill country of Maine for the next one hundred years, featuring in their name the key to the most momentous changes of the day. Far more than a "scattered few," they finally built themselves churches, modest structures which became the center of life—on Gloucester Hill, as well as at Bowdoinham Ridge, where the Sandford family had settled.

Two generations later, when my grandfather was a boy, the Freewillers had entered the mainstream. Since the optimistic presidency of Andrew Jackson and the influence of the famous preacher Charles Finney (in what some called a Second Great Awakening), the word "evangelical" had become almost synonymous with the word "American." And though the Free Baptists would have howled in protest at an official union of church and state, they embraced along with most other Protestants a civil religion—the hope of a perfect democracy, America as the Kingdom of God.

No circumstance is more important as a forerunner to this story. The word "perfect" is crucial. It settled deep in the nation's consciousness. To the right of private revelation it added the dream of unlimited potential. Like yeasts that would not stop working, these two awesome possibilities were to spread themselves down to the end of the century, where Shiloh lay waiting, like a sponge at the end of a long spill.

All this was part of my grandfather's sense of identity as he grew up. Wendell was the third child in a large family of noisy, talkative children, full of wry humor and unrelenting arguments, which no one ever lost. Their mother, a disciple of Wendell Phillips, had passed on to her offspring a skill in debate that their friends learned not to challenge. The Whites loved words—too often their own—and loved books, reading everything in print on Gloucester Hill. Any subject would do. They read the way they ate, swallowing what was set before them without complaint and looking around for more. Yet formal education beyond the roadside school was hardly considered for most hill country children of the area, until the Freewill Baptists established Bates College in nearby Lewiston. Wendell's older brother George was the first in the family to attend, preparing at Nichols Latin, a "fitting school," and enrolling at Bates in the fall of 1872.

The year was a key one for Wendell as well. It marked the first postponement of his personal ambitions. He had gone as far as he could with the available rural instruction and was ready for Nichols himself. But he was obliged to wait. It was not only a matter of money. His father had injured his hip, and as the oldest son at home, Wendell was needed in the barn and at the smithy.

There is no record of how he coped. I know only that this was the winter of the knife, that moment of rage when he chased his mother around the kitchen table. It appears the whole matter was quickly forgotten, except by Wendell. The incident preceded two others, and the three put together altered his life for all time.

That March of 1873 revival meetings were held at the church, the speaker George's twenty-year-old roommate at Bates. George and Wendell and their sister Louella all made "personal decisions" to become Christians, followed by seventeen other young people from Gloucester Hill.

I want to be careful not to imply that Wendell responded out of an exaggerated sense of guilt, even though he had glanced over the edge into "original sin," that pit of the worst possibilities. Nor was the fear of hell and death necessarily a motivation. While the White children were aware of how quickly death could snatch, as yet they had not endured the awful moment when somebody's chair and plate were removed forever from the kitchen table. The solemnity of the decision was more in having learned so well the Freewill lesson of their own accountability, for there was no salvation through the church itself or through any sacrament (baptism was a public witness only, a symbol of death and resurrection) or across the bridge of their parents. God's grace was available to all, but the transaction was not complete until a person voluntarily sealed it, and there was no one who could do that in your place. In short, nothing stood between you and God, and it was with God only that you dealt, facing all that unconditional love alone, yet knowing (and here was where the terror lay) the freedom was yours to reject it.

The custom among Freewillers at the time was to open the meeting, at the end of the service, to those who wished to "start." The term meant exactly what it said, to take the first step in a life-long journey. You got to your feet and as bravely as possible made that declaration to the surrounding group. More than likely you would then be asked to "come forward" to the front pew, to kneel on the floor in a mixture of embarrassment and elation, while the congregation sang behind you.

> Just as I am, without one plea
> But that Thy blood was shed for me. . . .

The Whites had seen this happen dozens of times to others. They knew the humility required was not meant to be humiliation, and that the courage entailed was no cause for self-glory.

Less than a year after Wendell's conversion, in the midst of a raging

February storm, his mother died in the miscarriage of her ninth baby. During the months that followed, the three older children assumed the role of parents, desperately trying to keep life normal, lighting the fire for breakfast, finding clean underwear for the little ones (the youngest of whom was three), and snuggling into bed with them at night when they cried. Yet nothing would ever be quite the same again, as every child in the family understood.

That spring their father, still disabled, sold the farm and the smithy and rented a house in Lewiston, finding light work for himself in a brother's shoe shop. Wendell, with his sister Louella in charge at home, entered the senior year at Lewiston High School and then enrolled at Bates College at last, eager to prepare for some form of ministry. He was an excellent student. But he did not return to college again for five years. Dropping out to earn his tuition for another semester, he found himself trapped by a state of affairs far beyond the reach of his own determination.

The decade of 1870 was a frightening one. In a nation still recovering from the anguish of the Civil War, new evils aroused pervasive shame and anger: political corruption—bribery, fraud—as well as organized crime and another kind of slavery, the exploitation of paid labor. With the value of money shifting constantly, many were homeless and hungry. The dream of a perfect republic had gone sour. Like a reflection of this wider turmoil, the Whites fell into a malaise. Diphtheria swept through the family and took a seven-year-old sister.

Weakened and grieving, they headed back to the country. It was a strange time to return. Farmers, unable to make ends meet and feeling abandoned by the political process, were giving up. The state was losing its rural population in great numbers as people fled to the cities for their livelihood, leaving their farms to fall into disarray. But that in itself made the purchase of property possible. George and Wendell found one hundred acres of cleared and wooded land with a large house and barn in Growstown, on the outskirts of Brunswick, and there they transported their family—a crippled father and a flock of half-grown children.

With cash money more than ever a problem, Wendell shelved his educational plans once again in order to teach in the country schools. He went wherever the pay was best, moving term by term, and growing more discontented every year—not only with his circumstances, but with himself. One winter night at Machias, on the easternmost shore of the

state, working late in his room at the home where he boarded, he made
the following notation in a copy book:

> When, at the age of 16 years, I finally determined to give up my
> selfishness, when I determined to deny myself the indulgence of my
> passions and give myself and all my powers to God, then He came
> into my heart and a beautiful life opened up before me. For nearly
> two years I enjoyed peace and love, but the slow insidious workings
> of sin had begun within me. I have commenced to sow the seed from
> which I have reaped an abundant harvest of sorrow and misery which
> has prostrated me upon my face for hours at a time. . . . My Father,
> I shall never be able to resist temptation till I become changed by
> beholding Thee.

This Storm and Stress was written with a quill in flowing penmanship,
which suggests self-dramatization, but not insincerity. The temptation
he spoke of may have been no more than a healthy farmboy libido. Or
it may have been the old choler, the old black mood. Either one
represented loss of control, which meant failure.

Wendell was twenty-two by now. In the next several years a pattern
developed. Work varied between intense labor on the farm and teaching
terms of school, and his moods swung from serenity to depression. The
only rest he got, he wrote to his brother George, was when by excessive
bodily labor his mind was stupified. "Haying deadens my faculties so
that for much of the fall I go about without much thought. . . . Then
begins again the war of the members."

He should stop worrying about himself, answered George, and just
get ready for the "work." No, returned Wendell. He deplored his lack
of "manliness," he said. "When self is brought under, when my will
can control all the powers of the body and mind—in a word, when I
am filled with the Holy Spirit, then and not till then I'll make ready
for the work." Or, "in a word," when he had reached perfection.

He made two more stabs at college. The first was at Bates again,
in 1882, the year he met Frank Sandford. Wendell was gone before the
term was over. A few years later he repeated the same abortive process
at Bowdoin College in Brunswick. Nor did he ever finish college
anywhere. In September of 1887, still teaching, still farming, still acting
as a parent to his younger siblings, he married quiet, auburn-haired
Annie Wood, whom he had met at Lewiston High School years before,
and brought her to Growstown to live with the family. At the prospect

of becoming a real father with new obligations, he changed the nature of the farm. The demand for fresh milk in the cities had been growing along with an interest in nutrition, so he invested in a dairy herd—twenty cows—and established a milk route in Brunswick, where he traveled every morning in a canvas-covered wagon.

Returning home at noon, the empty milk cans rattling behind him, he would give the horse its head, unroll the *Lewiston Journal* across his lap and try to catch up with the rest of the world. Other than that he had little time to think about anything. He had settled into the concreteness of farming. That, at least, was dependable. It gave no quarter and allowed no room for doubt.

Yet this life was not what he had intended. He could hardly say what had happened, except that it was bad. The nation itself had changed, the political system stripped of its honor. Even the hills around him were different. The abandoned, overgrown farms he passed in his wagon signaled the end of something unreplaceable. He lived in a depleted state, belonged to a depleted church. He himself was an anomaly, a believer without a home, a Christian servant without a ministry, over-educated for what he was doing, under-equipped for the work he longed to do. Yet he also knew what he had learned to be good at, and at times it seemed like a lot. He had learned to keep going, to accept disappointment and the inevitability of back-breaking labor.

Actually, Wendell had passed with honors a long course in survival training, which would yet stand him in good stead. Years ahead he would not be overwhelmed by the hardships and discipline of Shiloh, where only those with the fortitude to "stick" would make it through. But though the idea of Shiloh was already at hand, growing up beside him in the same hills, trailing the same history behind it, another decade would pass before he and Annie would exchange the words "fair, clear, and terrible" in the kitchen at Lewiston.

4

A Cry for the Best

Not long after the death of Wendell's mother in 1874, Frank Sandford's father began to notice the first nagging symptoms of the disease that would eventually take his life. James and Mary Jane Sandford were the parents of twelve children, eight of whom had lived. By the year James became too sick to pretend otherwise, the four older children were grown up and gone. It was Frank, who was fourteen, and his brother Charles, eighteen, who took over the work of the farm.

The Sandfords were known and respected for miles around as gallant, indomitable people, their farm on Bowdoinham Ridge a place that could seem like the center of the universe. With its three hundred acres divided among sheep pasture, hay fields, and orchards, the work had moved throughout the years from crisis to crisis, each a race against time— lambing, shearing, picking, mowing. Sons and hired men filled the kitchen table at the noontime meal, while half-grown daughters served doughnuts and pies baked that morning, and an elderly grandmother rocked the babies by the stove.

Frank Weston Sandford was the tenth child, born on October 2, 1862, at the height of the Civil War. The earliest war stories he heard came from his older brother Thomas, a mere boy in the First Maine Cavalry, who told of foraging food alone in enemy territory and singing at the top of his lungs as he rode back to camp. Heroic stories were not new in the family. Frank's grandfather, who had fought in the War of 1812, held an annual celebration of thanksgiving for his rescue as a young sailor, shipwrecked and adrift in the Atlantic for twenty-four days.

Such legends were cherished throughout the vicinity, particularly as they related to the sea. With easy access to the bay via the Kennebec, Bowdoinham considered itself a port. Ocean-going vessels—the great four-masters, and after the Civil War, the steamers—sailed up the river as far as Gardiner, fifteen miles above Bowdoinham, delivering goods and passengers. Bath, just to the south, was known the world around as a shipbuilding center. Even up on the Ridge, overlooking Merrymeeting Bay, a wind from the southeast could bring the taste of salt to your lips, always with the faint flavor of peril.

So with crisis and heroism romanticized, yet undeniably real parts of life, Frank Sandford faced the death of his father. The extended siege of James's illness was almost more than the family could endure. Adding together Mary Jane's twelve deliveries, the confinement to bed of two grandparents, the illnesses and deaths of four children, and finally the drawn-out months of James's struggle with abdominal cancer, the sickroom had been the focus of the home for much of the thirty-eight years of the marriage. What that could mean on an active farm is hard to imagine. To be quiet, to wait on the patient, to change linen, to watch endlessly by the bed or gallop miles for the doctor—these roles were shared by all the well, while the daily work of the farm went on as if nothing was wrong.

James died in 1876. For the next two years the family's future continued to hang in jeopardy, while prices for products dropped and the cost of help soared. To meet property taxes the boys chored at nearby farms as well as at home, and during the winter sawed ice on the Kennebec, a business which for years had employed hundreds of men in the coldest months. In spite of this Frank "kept to school" without missed time, his stamina an amazement to those who were watching.

I should explain that the record of Frank Sandford's early years comes largely out of his own recollection and telling. None of these accounts explore the early family relationships which shaped his adult concept of himself. His two biographies, one by his namesake, Frank Sandford Murray, and the other an academic dissertation by William C. Hiss, also have little to say on the subject. Hiss does suggest that Frank might have been one of the nineteenth-century figures "for whom the loss of and subsequent search for the Father became the obsession which eventually propelled them into a hero's and martyr's role."

If a case can be made for that view, it may have had less to do with James's premature death than with his undemonstrative nature. Frank often spoke of his father as a devout and gentle man, one who "looked ahead" and "rarely raised his voice." The fact that he said little else about him is revealing in itself. By contrast, his mother, Mary Jane, with a fiery personality and a knack for making swift and unshrinking decisions, predominated in her children's memories. She had married young, at age sixteen, assuming the management of the Sandford home and the care of James's ailing parents. Within a decade she had borne six of her babies and buried two and was famous in the town for her strength and buoyancy.

Yet there is no reason to think that Mary Jane Sandford ever questioned her belief in the ultimate authority of men, either in her home or in the Ridge Freewill Baptist Church down the road. She could have run that whole outfit by herself, but she knew her place there, too, and carried it out in style and dignity for twenty-five years as secretary of the missionary society. If she fostered guilt in her children, that was also just part of a mother's duty. Mary Jane found it easier than most people to talk about her religious beliefs, and she did it with a natural enthusiasm that disarmed her listeners. It was not unusual for the Sandford children to go shouting through the house after their mother and find her on her knees in her room, praying, quite possibly, for *them.* They were right. Mary Jane ardently counseled her children in the faith, with uneven results, and Frank seemed the most impervious of all, growing more independent and headstrong with each year.

Whatever ambiguities strong women imposed on Frank later in life (and they did, with devastating importance), from boyhood he was open and verbal in his admiration of his mother. He loved to surprise her with gifts and gestures of affection, or when away at college, with unexpected visits home, elaborately staged. As he remembered later:

> It was my delight to send no word of my coming, to walk the four miles from the depot. . . . I usually skirted the house and approached from the backside of the building, gliding in at the back porch door when open, or if I found that locked, opening a window and crawling noiselessly within . . . . I found the stove, the mending work in the chair, or the apron thrown hastily aside. . . . But never once do I recall sitting down and enjoying the evidences of my mother's existence. No, I carried my research from room to room until at last I found *her*—the object of my affections, the one that gave me life.

Well into adulthood he signed his letters to her, "Your boy, Frank," and he *was* her boy, like her in both energy and imagination, often to her despair. Among his friends he was the one who made things happen, a show-off for sure, and maybe an exhibitionist (as a close relative called him), but an unfaltering one, comical and a little vulnerable. He seemed to walk into adventure with his chin out, if not fearlessly, then acting as if he were, which he knew was just as important.

He was the one who drove the horse and steered the boat, remembered a companion from those days. If they played ball, he was always a captain. By the end of the Civil War, baseball—popular earlier as "round-ball"—had become a madness in the country, following close on the heels of revival as a legitimate reason to gather a noisy crowd. Play for its own sake still carried a whiff of hell-smoke, but "pasture-ball" became an obsession of rural children, with rocks and dried cow flops as bases. Frank played it with a passion from the time he was big enough to swing a bat, fascinated by its endless tests of instinct and reflex. It was as if he and the game had discovered each other by some marvelous stroke of fate. From the start, winning was an overwhelming requirement, even in the casual circumstances of a back-forty field. Team orchestration aside, he felt privately accountable for both victory and loss, and defeat sent him home to evening chores in a somber and moody silence, running the plays through his mind again and again, figuring out the failure.

He was quite aware of his importance, that if he were removed from the game, or from almost any scene in which he had a part, things would not go as well. This was more a matter of responsibility than conceit, though as he grew older he worried about the difference, for he hated conceit. Yet it was not that he loved himself, he thought, but rather loved to put himself to the test. Often this seemed like the real measurement of life. It was what a person lived to do.

At age sixteen he was considered mature enough to teach—or brave enough, perhaps. His first job was at the school he had attended himself for a decade. The next was on Barter's Island in Casco Bay, where he was told by the superintendent that if the pupils "knew more than the clams at the end of the term" he could congratulate himself.

In the Maine hills the teacher who could truly master was admired and respected. Few questioned the need for strong discipline, though stories abounded of injuries and injustices. With no enforced age limit for students, boys in men's bodies, too big to fit at the desks, grouped themselves on a bench at the back, chewing tobacco and inventing trouble. Frank Sandford's first "hard school" was at Ham's Hill, on the Bath-to-Brunswick Road. The man who hired him was careful to reveal that the last two masters had been "carried out" of the classroom. Frank's response to this (unspoken) was, "That's just the place for me."

On the first day he walked in to face a back bench full of "great gawking fellows." Before the morning was over he had licked one in a fist fight. Another he threw out the door and ordered never to return, and a third, the superintendent's son, he dealt with through the father.

Those were the easy ones. There was still Richie Garrison, six feet to Frank's five feet nine inches, and forty pounds heavier. One morning Frank came in to school with his hand in a sling, having injured it in a skating accident. When Richie balked at a direction, Frank threatened to "shake him out of his buttons." "Ye can't do it!" jeered Richie, pointing to the sling. In a matter of seconds the hand was out of the sling, Richie hung horizontal to the floor, and buttons were rolling everywhere. The boy ran home in disgrace but returned to become a cooperative student.

Years later, newspapers happy for any anecdote about Sandford's past circulated rumors that he had been a bully of a teacher, that he had "thrown" a boy out of a window (which would have been about four feet off the ground in a one-room school), and that he had used the ferrule on a student's hands until they were swollen to "twice their size." If, as the papers meant to indicate, Frank exercised a sadistic streak in these episodes, it would be hard to prove. I have no evidence that as a young man he ever spun off into one of Wendell White's blue-hot rages. But at some point in his life, probably very early, Frank had learned to get boiling mad with effect—to use his anger to control his circumstances. It worked in a total of seven schools. "He straightened things out in about fifteen minutes," a former student told Murray. "It was rule or ruin with Frank Sandford! He had a wonderful personality."

The odd ambivalence of that remark anticipates the two images as teacher he would wear in the future: swift anger and judgment side by side with gentleness and humor. Work was more fun when he was in charge. His pupils adored him for that. If he was angry, his voice roaring, they did what he said in a hurry. The result was diligence— and immense pride and elation when they pleased him.

Looking back, Frank claimed that in those years as a young teacher he was "in danger of drifting off into a wild life." In Maine in 1880 wild was a wonderful word that left much to the fancy. While in Frank's knowledge of himself he may have put no limits on the outer edge of the term, debauchery was not likely. For sure, though, "wild" meant cigars and fast horses and girls from Lewiston, money to spend on a flashy rig and well-tailored clothes. It meant an awareness of his own multiple charms. He was uniquely handsome, hair and moustaches a gold blond, skin clear and high-colored. His eyes were remarkable, piercing like his mother's, the irises a transparent blue and the pupils large. He carried his body with athletic sureness and seemed to look good in anything he wore.

As for horses, he was apt to be hard on them, as befits a wild youth. He loved to tear on country roads, feet braced, leaving a trail of dust behind him. Alton Lancaster, his nephew, twelve years younger, sometimes rode along to the depot when Frank had somewhere to go. They seldom left the house on time. Frank would wait until it was almost impossible to catch the train, then make a dash for it—four miles or so to Bowdoinham or Richmond. He never missed.

In later life Lancaster had little good to say about his uncle and liked to tell another story with a certain amount of derision. One day, sent on an errand for his mother with the buggy and Kate, the family's old mare, Frank "touched up" the horse with abandon on the down side of a hill. Kate fell and broke her neck. It was akin to smashing the family car, only worse in the sense that Kate was as beloved as a cross old servant. But in a few months Mary Jane replaced the horse with a flourish, paying the astounding price of $250 (worth many times that today) for a beautiful gray gelding sired by General Knox, a famous Maine stallion.

Soon after the purchase, as Lancaster told it, Frank masterminded an elaborate charade with a friend, Will Whitmore. Having destroyed one horse, perhaps Frank wanted to "save" the next to make restitution and regain his mother's approval. Horse thieves were thought to be prowling the area, so Frank began to sleep in the barn with a hunting dog and a gun. Late one night Will sneaked into the barnyard with his father's horse. The two boys let the gelding out of the stall, Will galloped off on his own horse, the dog began to bark, Frank fired the gun into the air and charged into the house yelling for help. He and his brother Charles chased the "thief" with a lantern until they lost the tracks. The story of Frank's heroism appeared in the next issue of the local paper.

Two years afterward, said Lancaster, when "Frank had got more pious," he decided to confess the truth and told the whole story. That would have happened sometime after February of 1880, when Frank was in his second year of teaching.

Late that month, home for a visit, he walked into unexpected circumstances—a revival in full swing at the Ridge Free Baptist Church. His brother Charles and his sisters Josie and Annie, both in their teens, had all been converted and were quick to tell him so, with an air of joy Frank found irritating. He adamantly refused to attend the services, until his mother burst into tears in front of him.

That day he went to church simply to please her and sat sullenly in the pew, untouched by the testimonies or the music until an elderly man, a person who seldom appeared in church, stood up during a period of prayer and said quietly, "Lord, you know we have no promise of the morrow."

"That sentence lay upon my soul like a fallen tree across one's pathway," Frank wrote later. The "morrow" hung bright and full of promise. To become a Christian would mean giving up selfish pursuit. The breadth of the sacrifice held a thousand uncertainties as he looked down the years ahead. If he made this decision, there would be no reneging—he knew that about himself. Once he had "started" he would never go back on his word. As he saw it, a commitment to Christ would be the end of every personal dream, and he thought he would smother at the thought.

For a week he vacillated, and that in itself with its indication of pride and cowardice, disgusted him. Had he actually sunk too low to take the step? "Hurling such contemptible suggestions" behind him, as he later put it, he stood to his feet at the next meeting and blurted out his intentions to become a Christian. It humbled him even more than he had predicted, though a cheer went up from the friends around him. Inwardly laughing at himself, outwardly in tears, hours passed before the turmoil ceased and, invaded by peace, he knew "some change had come." The date was February 29, 1880.

As the weeks progressed, he was swept off his feet by one realization after another. What he had feared as boring and lifeless gripped him with its challenge. No previous test of inner strength had counted like this. Now it was he whose buttons had been shaken loose. There was no place for bravado—God would see right through that. The old take-ahold confidence and the vigorous drive to win were no longer dependable as platforms for behavior. Those qualities needed to be reshaped, but he had no idea how.

He began with simpler changes. First, away with the smokes—not because the use of tobacco, chewed or smoked, was recognized then as specifically injurious, but because it was considered sinful in its addictive pleasure, an idol. The decision was made one day that summer on a

river excursion boat chartered by the church. If it was God who gave
the orders, the word was conveyed through a young woman playing the
organ for a hymn-sing on the cruise. "Shame on you, Frank Sandford!"
she admonished him. "You know very well Christians don't smoke!"
So overboard went his last cigar, symbol of his old vanity and willfulness,
shot—along with its brand new holder—in a long arc into the waters
of the Kennebec.

There was grace in that gesture, at least. What followed was harder
and performed with some clumsiness. Within a month he had enrolled
for the spring term at Nichols Latin, which now shared the Bates
campus, where he made it a point to announce his new birth in Christ
before the entire school. Granted, to do that at Nichols was not as
hard as it might have been elsewhere, with easily half the student body
Freewill Baptists. But the occasion was Frank's first public confession
outside the little church on the Ridge and it took a strength of will.
It happened at the all-school prayer meeting, where students were invited
to participate informally—to give prayer requests or present some matter
of concern. Few gave testimonies about their personal faith, and those
who did set themselves apart as a little too devout to be wholly regular.
Frank, with a strong social sensitivity, understood that very well.

Later he considered the experience important enough to be included
in his autobiography, along with another story. Immediately after he
arrived at school the entire student body joined in a prank, "to cut up
some trick" on a particular professor. For success it required the cooperation of every scholar at both Nichols and Bates. Frank, who loved
a practical joke, saw it as an act "unworthy of a Christian" and refused
to take part. He was the only person who openly disapproved, though
as a green entering student it took "more courage than Wellington had
at Waterloo." The prank was abandoned, and he found himself suddenly
classified as a self-righteous humbug, the lowest of human forms. Burning
with humiliation, he saw the moment as a crossroads, proof of his
willingness to be the one who was different, if that was what God
required.

He was probably not exaggerating the reaction of the school. In spite
of the churchy emphasis on the Bates-Nichols campus, many students
went out of their way to strike a cosmopolitan pose, with canes,
meerschaums, and poker games merely the tamer manifestations. To be
good at "shines" was a measure of acceptability. *The Bates Student*
reports drinking bouts and vandalism as not uncommon, with door panels
kicked in and iron woodstoves tossed down the stairs.

In the end, Frank's failure to endorse the prank had little effect on his popularity. Two years later, entering Bates on a general scholarship, he was elected class president and both coach and catcher of the freshman baseball team. That feisty "boy's team," as they were called, signed up from a total class count of twenty-six students, beat the sophomores (historically, a first) and went on to be the "finest nine of any class in college."

Lewiston was as crazy for baseball as the rest of the country. When the team returned from an out-of-town victory over Colby, a crowd met the train at the station and escorted the boys through the streets, with the City Band playing and roman candles bursting over their heads. Frank, frequently carried off the field on his teammates' shoulders, got considerable attention in the local and college papers. "Sandford has caught several perfect games. His remarkably accurate throwing to second . . . has rendered stealing second well-nigh an impossibility." From his position behind home plate he seemed to preside over the games, his huge voice carrying above all others. Throughout the winters he coached his men in the tiny gym, an area hardly suitable for Indian clubs and ten pins. The hard work paid off in his senior year. Bates tied with Colby for the state championship, beating out Bowdoin—a supreme joy, since Bowdoin had a reputation for snobbery among Bates men.

In June of 1886, at age twenty-four, Frank graduated from college with honors and was chosen to give a commencement address. In the future he would be able to remember only one appropriately purple line: "Hypocrisy is but the crescent of the waning moon, but the sun of Truth is rising, with God behind it."

That summer he agreed to captain a semi-pro baseball team with men chosen from the four leading Maine colleges: Bates, Bowdoin, Colby, and the University of Maine. A prospect he had never dared to take seriously dangled for the picking—a career in professional sports. But before the season was over, he knew that was not where he belonged. For a long time he had been certain he would study law, with one eye on political prospects. Now that ambition too chafed under a new awareness. He was seeing in both politics and sports a potential for worldly compromise that repelled him.

He could always teach. A few of his classmates were accepting positions as principals of the new free local high schools. Others, even some of the rakes (all at once steady young men), were going into the ministry. Two years back, representing Bates at a YMCA conference, Frank had responded to an appeal to give his life to "full-time" Christian service. Yet what that could mean had never been clear to him. What would he do? He certainly had no interest in pastoring a dry little country church, as he told his friends, "talking to old women about their spiritual condition."

That fall, still uncertain, he enrolled in the Theological Department at Bates, newly named Cobb Divinity, and was immediately sorry. The courses were dull and wooden, head work that had no connection to the rest of his life. If this was what serving God was all about, it was not worth the sacrifice of worldly ambition. But something else was wrong as well. He sensed a disturbing loss of direction in the seminary. It followed him out of the classroom and cast a shadow over his days. At one point that fall, exasperated and more than a little scared, he climbed the steep bank behind the school and implored, "Oh God, is this the best you've got for a Christian?"

He might not have felt any better if he had understood what was happening. Cobb Divinity, says William Hiss, was probably making an effort to "trim [its] academic sails to the confusing theological cross-currents of the day. . . ." Put more drastically, the school was drifting in a storm, one that had finally overtaken most seminaries and colleges. The winds of Darwinism and the German Higher Criticism had been blowing for a long time; now they were invading course work and the thinking of the average student.

To adopt Hiss's metaphor, the sailing ship of the nineteenth-century American Christian, a vessel that had freighted so much of the country's meaning, was being snapped in two. Both sections were desperately seeking ways to stay afloat, for if the ship went down, it would surely take America with it, along with the hope of worldwide civilization. Those on the deck of one half were determined to ride out the storm by dialoguing with science and scholarship. The other half saw in that compromise nothing less than a trip to the bottom of the sea. And Cobb was splashing about, unsettled about which half of the endangered boat it belonged to.

It is hard to know how to label those two halves of the split, because both still considered themselves evangelical, as the larger portion of the American church did, and both were destined for further splits. The words conservative and liberal were not in common use in a religious context—or fundamentalism or modernism—and it would be many years yet before such terms had meaning. For the sake of convenience, I am going to call only one half of the boat "evangelical," with an eye to where it was going, which was all the way to the various seas of twentieth-century evangelicalism. Frank was about to step onto that part of the deck, into a criss-cross of ideas and ideals, a network as interlaced and complicated as a ship's rigging, halyards, lifelines, and stays. He would soon wrap himself up in that inviting web, then spin free and sail off, figuratively (and literally, one day), in a ship of his own.

Just now, climbing the bank behind the Divinity School building, he felt only despair. But to his wonder, once again he was answered. The words, "Blessed are they that hunger and thirst after righteousness, for they shall be filled," flashed into his mind. It was a verse of Scripture he had been hearing all his life, but it came to him with a startling difference, almost as if the words had been audibly spoken. Later on he looked back at this moment as the first in which God addressed him directly.

What happened next hardly seemed like delivery on the promise. Practice-preaching was required of all Cobb students. Maine offered plentiful opportunity for this, as scores of rural pulpits had remained unfilled since the Civil War. At many churches the door weeds were cut and the stale little sanctuaries aired out only when a seminary student was available.

Frank was given his first assignment at the Free Baptist Church in Harrison, thirty miles west of Lewiston. He was not only nervous, but chagrined at the assumption that he, a twenty-five-year-old student, had anything to say to these "grey-haired farmers." He spent hours writing the message out in longhand, then read it word for word from the pulpit, plunging through it, utterly wretched. Apparently his listeners felt the same, for they shook his hand at the door in courteous silence.

Quitting seminary altogether might have appeared to someone else as the next logical step. To Frank, that fell into a category with failure. If he must quit, it would be *after* he had preached a good sermon. The following Sunday he was expected at Topsham, just across the Androscoggin River from Brunswick and Bowdoin College. That week he beat his way to solid ground. First, his youth must make no difference. College sports had taught him a "disgust for every artificial way," as he said later. He must state only what he could with the integrity of his own limited experience, and say it to please God and not to make an impression.

Topsham loved him and immediately called him to be their permanent pastor. He was ordained by the local church itself, a process legitimate by Baptist regulations, though he had not completed seminary. Seminary, in fact, seemed gratuitous. In another term he dropped out of school and never returned.

For the next three years the Topsham Freewill Church, a white wooden structure sitting with the great sea captains' houses on the hill overlooking the falls, was the liveliest place in town. In a revival spirit, close to a hundred people made "decisions for Christ," according to church records, many of them students from Bowdoin.

George White, Wendell's brother, who had been Sandford's classmate at Cobb, was now the pastor of the Brunswick Freewill Church, and the two cooperated in various functions. George was a good steady pastor, not destined to set the world on fire. Frank was all over town, acting as principal of the Topsham schools, organizing a sports program for children and a baseball team at the paper mill, visiting the town's poor, and more than once roaming the streets at night by the foggy river, searching for somebody's drunken father or brother. No one doubted he could carry a man home bodily if that was required. Brash and witty, he said exactly what he thought, in or out of the pulpit, and if he acted a bit too self-confident, he was young enough to be forgiven.

Topsham, then, appeared to be part of the answer to his plea for God's best. Frank knew it was not the whole answer. He was waiting for more, and it came quickly, in a complex series of inner adventures. At the very time that Wendell White was cashing in his dreams, Frank Sandford was just beginning to recognize the shadowy shape of his own. It began with a book, one which brought a rush of tears to his eyes. Opening it one day under the pine trees at Topsham, he had not read three minutes before he came to the words: "But *is* this all?"—a disarming echo of his own earnest question.

Lewiston Me. Nov. 4 1886

Mother, dear Please accept these slippers to make more comfortable those poor, tired, aching feet which have been made so by hugging + toiling for your children

Your Boy Frank.

Sandford homestead, Bowdoinham Ridge.

Sandford family, about 1887. Mary Jane, seated center. Frank, seated second right; Charles, seated second left.

Frank Sandford as a Bates College student.

Bates College baseball team, 1886. Frank Sandford stands at far left. Courtesy Batesiana.

5
Armageddon
1887–1892

The author of the book, Hannah Whitall Smith, had been raised in a Quaker family in Philadelphia. A well-bred woman with wide connections (she was acquainted with Walt Whitman and William James and would become mother-in-law to both Bertrand Russell and Bernard Berenson), she and her husband, Robert Pearsall Smith, were popular in England and America as lecturers on the "Higher Life"— sometimes called the "victorious life" or the "deeper life." It was, in fact, one more version of Christian perfectionism, the impulse that had enchanted and befuddled Wendell White not long before.

Throughout the nineteenth century the idea of perfection had become as familiar to the American public as an old housedress. Dozens of perfectionist social experiments, such as Brook Farm and the Oneida Community, had come and gone. "Hygienic utopianism" and faddist diet reform had begun their undying quest for the perfected body and mind. Yet none of these spells carried more magic than personal sanctification, the transcendence of the sinful, recalcitrant self.

As Wendell White had discovered, while conversion delivered a person from past sins, it did not guarantee a sinless life. Many in the church never thought it would. They saw the Christian experience as a long, uphill trek, full of nosedives and misjudgments. While the "war of the members," as Wendell had called it, raged on throughout life, one grew *toward* perfection, a goal that might not be reached. The word "perfect" in Scripture, some thought, indicated adulthood or wholeness, rather than the absence of error.

Other groups sought more radical changes, offshoots of the teachings of John Wesley and evangelist Charles Finney, both of whom, with differences, had seemed to propose "sinless perfection" or "entire sanctification" as a viable goal for daily living. This cluster of ideals, commonly called the holiness movement, had poured healthy amounts of initiative and dedication into the reform measures that had occupied many Americans since early in the nineteenth century: the abolition of slavery, aid to the poor, temperance, and women's rights. Yet in its more extreme forms it had left a trail of bodies behind it, sick with guilt or killed off by failure. The noblest of intentions could get snarled, sometimes to the point of serious disorientation. Old questions kept surfacing. Where do you tuck original sin? How perfect is perfection? How do you know when you're there? And the most worrisome of all: What does it mean if you fail?

New teachings popped up constantly, supplementing and clarifying the old ones. One of the most attractive appeared in the generation just preceding the Civil War. The clue to overcoming sin was to "yield" to the control of the Holy Spirit. A person "placed all on the altar" in what purported to be a private day of Pentecost and received a "second blessing" (a second experience of grace beyond redemption). No tongues of fire appeared on the head or strange tongues on the lips. Glossalalia, "speaking in tongues," was virtually unknown by mainstream evangelicals as a modern spiritual experience. But semantically the stress began to shift from being "perfect" to being endowed (or "endued") by the Holy Spirit with the power to live a life of winsome and effective service, even miraculously effective, as the early disciples had done.

The mellowness of this idiom softened up Protestantism almost across the board. Hymns changed. Many of what have become Gospel classics were written in the new romantic mood, resembling love songs in their melodies and words—"O, Love That Wilt Not Let Me Go," "Safe in the Arms of Jesus," "I Need Thee Every Hour"—though those who sang them would have been shocked at such a suggestion.

In 1857 and 1858, the movement merged into the "Businessmen's Revival," a quite respectable "stir" concentrated in the cities among the urban middle class. Touted by some as a third "awakening," its effect carried over to the other side of the war, offering a substitute for failed national dreams. The Republic might go corrupt, the institutional church might compromise and lose power, greed might pervade all society, but nothing could argue away the reality of God operating in the private life.

It was not quite so easy, of course. The reality of God, always hard to define, became even less clear cut after the war. The wave of revival broke into and out of the spirit of free enterprise and capitalism. The drive behind Horatio Alger's rags-to-riches stories had by now penetrated American self-consciousness—self-improvement for the sake of self-advancement—a kind of vulgarization of Emerson's "Self-Reliance," as some thought. The line between God's potential and human potential had been badly smudged, particularly because human potential, as it related to material progress, was perceived as a masculine affair. Could you "yield," be "submissive," even to God, and still be a man? So along with the new style of tenderness, seen as feminine, spiritual life began to be translated into terms with more masculine personality. Effective Christianity had always meant strength and courage. Now it also meant dignity and control, even military discipline.

The Higher life, born at about the time of the Businessmen's Revival, incorporated this mix of feminine and masculine traits, especially as it was shaped by Hannah Whitall Smith. Her lectures were collected into a book, called *The Christian's Secret of a Happy Life*. When it fell into Frank Sandford's hands in 1887, it had been in print for twelve years and had sold many thousands of copies.

It is still on the market today. Dozen of editions later, it still scolds and reasons with masculine logic, while it comforts with Victorian gentleness, slipping now and then into a Quaker idiom which transcends a Pollyanna sweetness. By turns, Mrs. Smith is down-to-earth and ethereal, psychologically sound and girlishly naive. But she is never deceitful, and a reader shuts the book with the sense of having just climbed down off the lap of a stern but loving parent, wiping away tears and an excess of kisses and feeling much better about everything.

In a word, Mrs. Smith told Frank Sandford that there was most positively a "best," and that it was as available to him as his next breath.

The Christian life was not meant to be dour and arduous, she said. Perfection was not a matter of mastery, but of a joyful letting-go. At rock bottom lay faith in God's loving attention to the details of one's life. Yet this itself, this trust, was not the stressful work people made of it. It was "resting," or rather, "reckoning," on the "exceeding greatness of His power to us," regardless of one's doubts and feelings. Mrs. Smith called this the "active energy" of faith, as an eagle flies, trusting its wings not by thinking about them but by using them.

But that involved obedience. "There is nothing for you to do, except to be . . . an obedient child," she said. "The heights of Christian

perfection can only be reached by each moment faithfully following the
Guide who is to lead you there . . . Obey Him perfectly the moment
you are sure of His will."

How to determine God's will was another matter. She listed common
sense as one of the guides and seemed to trust blithely in the good
instincts of her readers. She urged the "emptying of self," the laying
aside of every burden—health, reputation, houses, children, business,
". . . your temptations, your temperament, your frames and feelings."
These you handed over "into the care and keeping of your God" and
left there.

But there was a great difference between surrendering one's business
to God and not showing up for work. One signed in each morning
without calling up sick. This was no job for the frail of spirit. Toil
and suffering might very well attend each day. It was those who rose
above the daily boredom and pain of life, relinquished their own wills
and acted in obedience who would find themselves empowered. "If the
Divine Master only had a band of workers such as this, there is no
limit to what He might do with them," she wrote.

The Higher Life struck many Christians as suspiciously narcissistic.
But at its best it carried the potential to free individuals from self-
absorption. Surely that was Mrs. Smith's intended emphasis. "Look away
from thine own weakness," you can hear her saying to Wendell. Then
as he lifted his head to bluster, "Only when self is brought under!" she
would catch him under the chin with a gentle blow: "A religion of
bondage always exalts itself, my dear . . . MY efforts, MY wrestlings
. . . A religion of liberty leaves self with nothing to glory in."

Yet she was keenly aware of the hidden traps in ideas like full
surrender and unquestioning obedience, giving three pages of the book
to the dangers of "special revelations"—inner impressions or "voices"—
versions of the old antinomianism. As time went by she was shocked
at the distortions and aberrations of faith she observed around her and
collected stories of such in a trunk, unwilling to publish them lest she
offend innocent people.

What intrigued Frank was not the notion of perfection, or even
"special revelations." Not yet. Rather he was thrilled by Mrs. Smith's
emphasis on action, on a life that acts on faith, that obeys by doing.
That one concept changed everything for him. It gave him the right to
be the kind of person he was by impulse. Closing the book, he made
a vow, "like a drunkard signs a pledge," as he put it, never to doubt
God, but to obey immediately, as soon as His leading was clear. With

such an ultimatum in place, he was ready to consider other risks. In the course of the next four years he took leap after leap, until he found himself head-on with supernatural forces.

The quest began that July of 1887 at Dwight L. Moody's "College of Colleges," held on the campus of his academy at Northfield, Massachusetts, a green-lawned estate high over the Connecticut River. Here Frank joined over 400 people, 266 of them students, representing 84 colleges in the United States, Canada, and England—Harvard, Yale, Princeton, Cambridge—at the second annual meeting of the Student Volunteer Movement.

It was a consortium of young gentlemen, on the whole more patrician and urbane than Frank himself. They were, as certain New England men had been described by Thoreau, "fellows of education and spirit . . . chaps whose aunts you knew, good stock through and through, sound to the core." Many, from backgrounds of material wealth, were choosing lives of sacrifice and uncertainty. In so doing, they preserved a particular American ideal, a kind of alter-ego of the nation's new affluent personality.

In the morning they arose to the clang of the school bell, then spent the hours until noon in Bible study under the care of teachers whose names were known from Chicago to Boston. In the afternoon they donned their bathing suits or athletic clothes (or perhaps just removed their ties and collars) and gave themselves to "sport"—lawn tennis, baseball, swimming and boating, playing (as Mr. Moody put it) "as if their lives depended on it." Each afternoon Frank caught to the pitching of Amos Alonzo Stagg, a short, stocky undergraduate from Yale, who astonished Frank by pitching "a rise of six inches." In the evening they gathered in the school auditorium to sing and pray and listen to at least two speakers, taking an hour each, on the subject of foreign missions. Mr. Moody presided at every meeting and was everywhere on campus, a tough, outspoken patriarch with a paunch.

However historians may disagree about Moody's importance, or lack of it, to American culture, he was absolutely essential to the changing Protestant world, a giant weaver of safety ropes on the evangelical ship. He was the modern American businessman, informal yet gruffly dignified. Without the later theatrics of Billy Sunday or emphasis on hell-fire ("Terror has never won a man yet," he was known to say), he "lessened the population of hell by thousands." Unordained, operating outside the institutional church (yet working with and for all churches), the man was able to unify within himself the disparate moods of the postwar revivalist spirit.

It was not surprising that he should take his place at the front of a compelling new interest in foreign missions which had grown up out of the colleges of England and America. The excitement of the Northfield conference centered on a piece of paper now covered with over two thousand names of young men and women who had, in the course of a year, signed a proclamation: "We are willing and desirous, God permitting, to become foreign missionaries."

Frank watched that paper as it circulated the grounds, with students clustered about it as if it were magnetic. Feeling its fierce tug he fought it with almost physical resistance. Though the motto of the Student Volunteer Movement, "The evangelization of the world in this generation," captured his imagination mightily, he refused to add his name, knowing it would be a lie. He was not "willing and desirous." As he confessed later, his ambitions still lay in "making a mark on the world." He meant a mark within the Christian ministry, but he wanted to make it where it would be seen, not in Africa or some other remote land.

Northfield formed a crossroads for more than missionary recruitment. Moody, on his revival campaigns in England in the 1870s, had come within the ambit of leaders at Keswick, a center for Higher Life teaching in the Lake District of Cumberland. Soon Keswick lecturers were imported across the water to Northfield. The Smiths were not among them, but their work had left a clear stamp.

By nature a person tuned to action rather than deep thought, Moody measured the role of holiness teaching by the same standard he used for all else—results. "Get full of the Holy Ghost!" he would charge, with typical inelegance. It was the first advice he gave to the college students gathered around him, but with one stipulation. If winning others to Christ was not the fruit of a sanctified life, then holiness meant nothing.

For Frank, Moody's approach cleared the way for another look at holiness ideas. Here was the same emphasis on action, on decisiveness, that he found so appealing. In the early fall he visited two more conferences and opened himself up in ways he had never imagined he could.

Since the middle of the century, when summer resorts began to be fashionable, Maine's Old Orchard Beach had been called "a mecca for half the world." Mammoth white hotels had been built above the long stretch of shore, their multifarious windows facing out over the breakers and the grey sand. Under tall pines half a mile in from the ocean, Methodists owned a large campground with a natural amphitheatre, which they rented to various groups. So popular was this spot that the Boston and Maine Railroad set up a depot called Campground Station and certain "regulars" purchased small plots of adjacent land to put up cottages. Frank's sister Maria owned one of these.

When Frank arrived as a guest later that summer, a camp meeting was in progress, preaching sanctification. He did not like the "sound of the talk," he said later, but in listening without bias he began to see that it could be a "reasonable thing" for God to "separate a man from sin" if He needed a job done in "first class shape." Setting aside "a great deal of ministerial pride," he knelt in the straw at the altar and "came away a changed man"—if not sinless and full of the Holy Ghost, at least more teachable.

One or two days later the Rev. Albert B. Simpson of New York City arrived at the campground with a group of followers for the purpose of organizing the Christian and Missionary Alliance. Simpson's work was already mature, with crowded meetings in the heart of the city, a rescue mission, a training school in the Bible, a home for "fallen women," and an orphanage. Nondenominational and ecumenical, like the work of Moody, Simpson's ministry was equally dedicated to foreign missions and to holiness, as well as to divine healing.

Healing was not a popular subject among evangelicals. Classed in people's minds with the new Christian Science, with mesmerism, animal magnetism, Roman Catholic shrines, electric phenomena, water cures, diet reform, spiritualism, and a thousand and one panaceas, it represented extremism of the worst sort. Frank, like a great many other Yankee pietists, ruled out healing as a present-day miracle. A year earlier his sister Maria, to his chagrin, had declared herself healed at Old Orchard from what the family knew had been a life-long problem with crippling back pain. A widow with five children, she had come home from this healing to do a huge washing, the first her son Alvin had seen her do by herself for years. Nevertheless, Frank had "proved to her conclusively" in an argument that there was "no such thing as healing by faith." He had maintained that position, though Maria remained well and without pain.

A. B. Simpson was a more refined and educated man than Moody. A Presbyterian, he had withdrawn from the denomination when healing turned out to be unacceptable to his parishioners at the 13th Street Church in New York City. He had been healed himself, he claimed, of what doctors had diagnosed as chronic heart trouble. The process of healing, as Simpson preached it, was no more a miracle than the regeneration of a soul: the Savior had carried sickness as well as sin to the cross. His practical-minded Presbyterians saw that as "extravagant mysticism." Hadn't Mary Baker Eddy also said, "Christ came to redeem men not just from sin but from sickness and death"? Simpson did not deny the reality of death, but he made the point that every Christian had a "right to" the same "energy which enabled [Christ] to rise . . . from the tomb." Those who accepted Christ in this "fulness" were not merely healed, but were offered "a fountain of life" for every need.

After listening thoughtfully to Simpson at Old Orchard, Frank concluded that whether or not he understood it, and whether or not he ever healed anyone himself, he must at least "preach that part of the Bible."

It was the sort of cautious yet conciliatory statement Moody might make. Actually, Simpson had entered a tropical forest a bit too steamy for Moody's full comfort. Other evangelical leaders, such as R. A. Torrey, a nationally respected Bible teacher, and A. J. Gordon of Boston, a Higher Life advocate with a varied work like Simpson's, hesitated to place a predominant emphasis on the subject of healing, though they too longed for the restored vitality of the first-century church. Moody and Gordon were making every effort to revive the existing denominations. Simpson, in more of a "come-outer" spirit, had chosen to cut his own trail, and Frank, in spite of his careful Moody-like attitude, was finding in Simpson's more radical approach something that tugged at his own sensibilities.

In fact, he attached himself to this small conference as if he had just discovered long-lost relatives. Among those present was a young woman named Helen Kinney, who had come with her parents. Helen's father, Charles Kinney, a cotton broker on Wall Street, often assisted Simpson at public meetings. The Kinneys were conspicuously wealthy, owners of an estate on the Hudson River and a ranch in Texas. Yet Helen, in her early twenties, carried no rich-girl airs. She had given up a career in art to attend Simpson's Missionary Training College in Nyack, New York.

A soft-spoken and determined girl, with a "peculiarly loving and gentle spirit," as someone said, she was already an experienced street missionary among the newsboys and bootblacks of New York City. Frank had never met anyone like Helen, but if she found him attractive at all, he took a distant back seat to her ambitious hopes. For a Victorian young lady, raised in genteel circumstances, her plans were radical indeed. After asking God to send her to the "hardest place in the world" (reported an issue of the school magazine), she had ordered a special waterproof trunk, "adapted to going up the Congo River." Africa was the goal of her life.

Throughout the winter Frank spent as much time as possible in New York, not seeing Helen specifically, but present at Simpson's various meetings, where she was apt to be. Then, whether or not she had anything to do with it, in the summer of 1888, back at Northfield, he at last signed the Student Volunteer Movement pledge. As if that was not enough, he wrote his name and the date on the bottom of the chair he was sitting on, and bought the chair. He was still not "called" to a foreign land, but the barriers to willingness were down.

Later that summer he settled it for good. Staring across the untamed power of Niagara Falls, he wrote in the back of his Bible:

> O God, help me to do my part in keeping a poor lost world from the terrible rapids of sin. . . . To this end I solemnly consecrate my every voluntary thought, word and deed . . . this world for Christ during my lifetime.

It made sense that this third promise in writing should occur at Niagara Falls. He was there at a prophecy conference. Along with thousands of other American and English students of Scripture, he had become engrossed in the turbulent secrets of the apocalyptic books of the Bible—Daniel, Ezekiel, Revelation. This, a recently revived obsession with the end of the world, was the rope that essentially completed the evangelical network. Intertwined with the Higher Life movement, with missions and healing, each adding strength and tension to the other, for Frank it would turn out to be the most entangling cord of all, with the longest tether. It would take him as far as he needed to go.

Most of the details involved will serve us better further on, except to explain the widespread nature of the craze. It was electrifying, with "great witchery," as one critic warned. Yet with all the wild tangents it fostered, the yearning was genuine—to solve the anguish and ills of the world by the triumphant bodily return of Christ. It was like waiting for the release of a beloved Prince from long self-imposed exile.

Both the exile and the release functioned as part of a master design. That, above all, was the point. The world was not whirling in a mindless spin: God had a plan for the ages, ultimate redemption for His corrupted and travailing creation. It was not just a spiritual plan, without time or space; it was part of earthly history as evangelicals understood it—or rather, it *was* history, the real history of the world, with the future determined and predicted in Scripture, however cryptically.

The question at stake was less *whether* Christ would return than *when*. That and the dozens of satellite questions had been swelling attendance at prophecy conferences, particularly at Niagara Falls, with important evangelical leaders as teachers. Most of those involved were not looking for the exact moment of Christ's return. Jesus Himself had said no one would know the "day or the hour." Rather, they were digging out the order of the world's final events, attempting to bring into harmony bits of the puzzle which had always refused to interlock. The obsession had begun to produce a massive number of publications—books, magazines, tracts, hymns, wall plaques ("Perhaps Today!"), poetry and polemic, heady timetables and charts, and an intricate cross-referencing of Scripture.

A certain logic was part of the appeal. If the Bible was the creation of one Mind, reliable and "inerrant" (a term just coming into popular use), then its prophetic allusions were not accidents. All those pieces were intended to snugly connect. Anyone, any Spirit-led detective of Scripture under the lamp at the kitchen table, might come upon the key that had never been found, the Rosetta Stone of Biblical prophecy, and the whole panorama would fall into place. In the shadow of a threatening rationalism, it was more important than ever to find this key, since it would help to prove the authority and dependability of Scripture.

Just now Frank Sandford was only a beginner in such sleuthing. For the next two years at Topsham, his life was no different from that of many small-town clergymen. He was eager to do his part in winning the world, but he had not bought a trunk for the Congo, he had not healed anyone, he would certainly have hesitated to call himself sinless, and in spite of his fascination with the subject, he did not sit up at night waiting for the return of Christ. He did his work day by day with zest and was recognized as a bright young light in the Freewill denomination.

He was contented—in fact, exuberantly happy. It was not until 1890, after his move to a church in Great Falls, New Hampshire, that the old heart restlessness began to stir itself again.

The Free Baptists at Great Falls, a self-satisfied congregation in an affluent mill town, enjoyed the reputation of being a "hard field." Frank faced the job much as he would a tough roadside school. He was dumfounded, therefore, at what happened soon after he arrived.

He began by meeting the church on its own ground. The building was just now being expensively redecorated. He had no objection to drinking "skim milk," he told the hiring committee, but if *they* were drinking "cream," he wanted cream. He negotiated successfuly for a salary of $1,500 annually (more than even a long-tenured pastor might expect), a brownstone house, his own horse, and a new buggy. He knew he would earn every bit of it, and just now he needed extra funds to share in the support of his mother and his brother Charles. At age thirty-one, Charles had been alarming the family with unexplainable behavior. Dazed and sleepless, he had begun to walk the neighborhood at night and was no longer able to tend what remained of the farm.

One evening soon after Frank's arrival at Great Falls, on his way to lead a mid-week prayer meeting, he was almost paralyzed with dread at the prospect. Though he managed to meet his obligations and return home, during the next few days the depression deepened. He was reluctant to leave his house and was reduced to tears at the thought of standing in the pulpit.

He may not have known that the malady was common among overworked clergy. He did know that it was common for a person suffering from "nervous collapse" or "brain fever" to be confined by doctors to weeks in bed in a shade-drawn room. His distress at the possibility of such helpless "doctoring" was surely complicated by his brother's baffling condition. That has never been stated, nor any hint given that Frank associated the problem with the move to New Hampshire. At Topsham he had been an unfettered spirit, still a student, really, a boy. Great Falls was pouring him quickly into a mold—settled adult, parish minister, *our man,* the rising Freewill Baptist star.

Shut away in his rooms that week, breaking out into a sweat at the idea of slipping beyond his front door, he chastised himself for lack of faith in God's power to deliver him from this weakness, this foolish attack of "nerves." With a wrench of determination, he pulled out a banner he had used at Topsham and hung it on the Great Falls pulpit the following Sunday. It said, SEE JESUS ONLY! ONE HUNDRED SOULS FOR HIM THIS YEAR. The strange spell subsided and his life resumed its course of unflagging intensity.

At the end of nine months he and another young pastor, Thomas

Hobbs Stacy (who had played ball with Frank at Bates), were invited by the denomination to travel around the world. The Great Falls church not only agreed to Frank's trip but underwrote part of the cost, releasing him for more than they dreamed. In a very real sense he would never come back.

The two men crossed the country by train to San Francisco, boarded a steamer to Japan, then proceeded on to China, India, Egypt, and Palestine. They left on Frank's twenty-eighth birthday, October 2, 1890, and were gone until the following March.

After many days of violent nausea, while the beautiful Pacific became "a great salt fact . . . a wilderness of woe," they entered the port of Yokohama on the tail of a typhoon. Somewhat weak and pale, the two men arrived at their quarters, the Women's Union Missionary Society Home. There they "found" Miss Helen Kinney, who was visiting from Mishima, where she was teaching temporarily at a girls' school sponsored by Simpson's organization. To Frank's pleasure, Helen joined the party the next day on a tour of Tokyo.

Frank wrote home in superlatives. Exquisite! Beautiful! He was describing the city, not Helen, but there she was, her small form lovelier than ever in a Japanese kimono, with the same aura of composure that had captured him when they first met. He had not seen her in a while. She seemed more grown-up, her modesty less demure. She talked more freely, in that same soft, almost whispering manner that required all of your attention, her mouth, which turned down when relaxed, lifting brightly at the corners in a little smile as she spoke. Yet she held herself politely aloof throughout the day, and Frank continued on to China a "badly mashed" young man.

With that mixture of sweetness and uncertainty churning in his emotions, he was especially vulnerable to what he encountered in China and India. He was shocked and sickened by the sheer mass of humanity, the hunger and disease, the smell of slime and putrefaction in the streets, the self-maimed beggars. For one month the two men traveled by bullock cart to the interior mission stations of India. Frank had been told that there were an estimated 260 million souls in India. Now that weighty figure broke upon him with horror. The slogan he had embraced—"This world for Christ in my generation"—rang as so much foolish rhetoric. Though the purpose of the Student Volunteer Movement was simply to *present* the Gospel to "every creature," even that was impossible by contemporary methods. He had sworn his life to a job that simply could not be done.

In January (now 1891) the men sailed to Alexandria, and then started for Palestine on a Russian steamer, the *Tchihatchoff.* One night as they moved along the Mediterranean coast, the ship was forced off course in a storm. "Twenty minutes of 5 A.M.," Frank wrote in his journal. "We have just struck on the rocks of Jaffa; but it is well with my soul." He fully expected to die, a distinct possibility. The ship foundered not far from shore, but the breakers were treacherous. Water filled the hold and cascaded into the saloon. For more than an hour he and Stacey listened to the frightened cries of passengers, forced from darkened cabins to the tilting decks.

Help came at daylight, led by Sulieman Girby, chief boatman for Cook's Travel Agency, who swam out to the ship repeatedly, carrying a line and pulling a life boat behind him. When two men died in the rescue attempt, Girby, an Arab under Turkish rule, refused to go on until his brothers were released from a Turkish jail to help him and then given permanent amnesty. The brothers arrived, and the rescue continued until the last handful of the survivors was floated in on a plank.

In the days that followed, while they waited for another ship to continue the journey, Frank made it a point to establish a friendship with Girby, whose heroism he would talk about the rest of his life.

With their belongings lost, he and Stacey dressed for comic relief in cast-off clothing found in missionary barrels from America. In these they toured parts of Palestine on horseback. They looked no stranger than many of the other pilgrims in the Holy Land. The Middle East under Turkish oppression was not considered a safe place for Westerners to wander, but undaunted by the threat of thieves, packs of wild dogs, and bad water, Frank felt more and more of a "passion . . . to know every nook and corner of the land."

At prophecy conferences he had been taught that God had not yet finished with the history of Israel, and that Israel's future was the future of the world. Certain Scripture seemed to indicate that the return of Christ could not occur until two conditions had been met. One was the spread of the Gospel throughout the world and the other the restoration of Palestine to Israel. European Jews had begun to establish scattered settlements by now, some of them to escape Russian pogroms, but emigration was slow and filled with hazards. Observing this and remembering his discouraging visit to the mission stations of Asia, the only hope Frank saw now for either fulfillment was supernatural power. Since God had chosen to work through human agents, how could such a work be done except by a totally obedient and courageous army of disciples? The words of Hannah Whitall Smith rang in his mind: "If the Divine Master only had a band of workers such as this, there would be no limit to what He might do with them. . . . May God raise such an army speedily!"

By early April, Frank and Stacey were back in America, bearded and dressed in their strange assortment of clothing. Frank carried an old sea bag and a French bandbox tied together with cord. But contained in that vagabond luggage was the whole wide world—*his* own world now, he understood, as "joint-heir with Christ"—and the responsibility more than ever his to "take back from the Kingdom of darkness every square foot of the globe."

Before reaching home, Frank had written to Helen Kinney and asked her to marry him. Borrowing from the exalted language of the Book of Revelation, he said; "I believe our union will mean the Marriage of the Lamb and His bride." He was not referring to himself as the Lamb and meant only that as a team they might help to bring about God's plan for the ages. The words smacked of arrogance to Helen. She tore the letter in half and wrote back that she considered the suggestion blasphemy. What was more, to give up her calling as an Alliance missionary and become the wife of a denominational pastor was a step down the "devotional ladder," akin to backsliding. Her own hint of arrogance aside, she may have been the first person to say no to Frank in a long time.

He could not give her up. After all, defeat in any circumstance was not a condition he accepted. Correspondence between them continued. A wider world was calling and he was certain Helen was part of it. Back at Great Falls he felt closed in, like a "hireling." The congregation was growing, yet its vision remained limited, he thought. His efforts to work with the other churches in town were discouraged, and some of his parishioners were not pleased to welcome the derelicts and poor he brought in off the streets. A sermon on adultery affronted members of the congregation and he was warned with true Victorian fastidiousness never to speak of such matters in the pulpit. He yearned to leave, yet where would he go?

In August of that same year, 1891, he had two peculiar experiences, one following close on the other, both convincing him that he must break into freedom.

Visiting Old Orchard campground once more, he met a Bowdoinham friend, Carrie Kendall. Carrie, who was forty-two, had been a teacher in the south and had returned north in run-down health. In a moment of desperation as they talked, she confessed to Frank that she had been harassed for months by religious doubts.

Wanting to help, but not knowing what to say, Frank asked awkwardly, "Do you want me to pray for you, Carrie?" When she consented, he did what he spoke of later as "a very strange thing." He placed his hands on her head and said out loud: "I command everything contrary to Jesus of Nazareth to leave this body!"

Instantly the room was filled with confusion, as what seemed to him to be a "clump of demons" swirled about and vanished. It was over in a second, and Carrie stood up, exclaiming, "Why, all those doubts have gone!" Frank was astonished and shaken. Without thought or plan, he had obeyed the prophecy of Jesus in Mark 16:17, "In my name shall they cast out demons."

The laying on of hands, an ancient Judaic and Christian practice, was certainly not new to him. He had seen it employed at Alliance meetings, though only for the purpose of physical healing. He could not name one occasion when he had witnessed anyone else's effort to deal with demons, not Moody, or even Simpson.

To this point, concern about a devil had been a relatively impersonal matter to him, as it appears to have been in general to the Free Baptist churches. Certainly Satan was taken seriously. He was the author of evil, the underlying cause of sin and misery in the world. Talk of evil spirits was not unfamiliar. Yet few would say they had encountered the devil in any deliberate and obvious way. Mainstream evangelicals tended to be as wary of such a possibility as they were of supernatural healing.

So Frank had not been spoiling for a fight with the arch-enemy. Now the little skirmish at Old Orchard turned his universe inside out. It introduced an undeniable dichotomy. It was a miracle for Carrie's doubts to be banished so suddenly, a demonstration of God's reality. But those doubts had also *come* from somewhere. That source was also real, palpable, a fact. It had received a blow, but not a crippling one. It—he—would be back, ready for retribution. The "Prince of Darkness" had become an adversary of chilling proportions.

Early the next morning, as Frank walked under the tall pines to the first meeting of the day at the Old Orchard tabernacle, he heard in the stillness what seemed to be a whisper. It was one word: "Armageddon." At the same instant the word appeared to slant down visually out of the sky, above the top of a nearby tree. Then it was gone. If he stopped dead in his path, he was not aware of it. Whatever had happened, the unnatural aspects of it seemed merely part of the natural—the wind high in the canopy of pines, the streaks of morning sun, the crunch of the needles under his feet. It took a moment for the truth to register. He had seen a vision. He had heard God speak—"one strange, dread word." Under the spell of another new certainty he continued on to the meeting.

For Frank and the many evangelicals who had been caught up in the excitement of deciphering Biblical prophecy, Armageddon was no abstract symbol of cosmic struggle between good and evil. It was a literal place and a literal future event. The place was the hill of Megiddo in Palestine's Plain of Esdraelon, where many ancient battles had been fought. This area was to be the scene of a cataclysm beyond the reach of human imagination—the conclusive battle of history, when Christ returned as a conquering warrior to destroy the army of the anti-Christ, representing all the ungodly political forces of the world. Frank was convinced that the anti-Christ was already astir in the world, gathering his army.

Prophecy buffs parted company on the question of whether Christ would return *before* the beginning of the Millennium, the thousand years of peace, or *after* it had taken place—that is, after the world had found its way to perfection, with America in the driver's seat. Many still looked for that distant fulfillment, seeing the New Land as the place where the Millennium would finally occur. *Pre*millenarians, however, had always believed the reign of peace could not take place on earth without the ruling presence of Christ.

In the discouraging decade after the Civil War, as a growing number of people found it no longer possible to connect God with American advancement, interest began to move away from the optimistic post-millennial view. The signs of the End were growing unavoidably apparent. "In the last days, perilous times shall come," the Apostle Paul had written. For "men shall be lovers of pleasure more than lovers of God," lawless, arrogant, violent—while the church itself would grow cold and ineffectual.

Evangelicals had long been stressing the importance of a "remnant" of believers, the true Church, raised up out of the apostate institutional church. Since he had left Palestine, Frank had not been able to forget the idea of that band of powerful and obedient Christians, which he saw as a remnant of the remnant. Now, at this moment of "great spiritual illumination," as he later called the experience at Old Orchard, he saw the fulfillment of End Time prophecy dependant upon that group of select, purified Christians in yet another way. Its "signs, wonders and mighty deeds" were to be used "in separating the human race into two great divisions, one under the leadership of Christ and the other under the leadership of the antichrist." God's most important work was not to be done by the Free Baptists, nor by Moody's contingency, nor by Simpson's Christian Alliance, nor any other church or organization yet established. For none of these was going quite far enough in believing and obeying the Bible. Individual members of those groups would surely be part of the new Band. But those who were not would belong to the forces of the anti-Christ. There was no other alternative.

In the spring of 1892 Helen came home from Japan. Things had changed. Frank had won, after all. In the course of correspondence they had become engaged. She was giving up her work in Japan, but not her love for Africa. In fact, she agreed to the marriage only because she felt certain that someday God would lead them there.

That struggle was part of the bundle of tensions Helen assumed in deciding to marry Frank, or marry anyone perhaps. Years before she had talked of becoming "one with Christ," speaking of Him as her "Bridegroom." As a Protestant, such a taking of the veil would not rule out carnal marriage for her, but it did mean she expected God to keep her separated for a special work. From now on her calling would be shaped by her husband's.

Simpson himself agreed to officiate at the July wedding, to be held at the Kinney estate on the Hudson. Contrary to Helen's own chosen style of life, the affair was huge and elegant, not very different from many other expensive nuptials of the day, except that the entire wedding party spent the morning in prayer. While they were on their knees, Mrs. Kinney felt a strong premonition that the couple faced a life of suffering, and apparently felt no restraint in revealing her thoughts.

After a honeymoon on Martha's Vineyard and Five Islands, where they led six people to Christ, Helen and Frank went back to the Great Falls parsonage. Neither doubted that they would soon be moving on, though they had no idea what they were to do or how they were to live when that time came.

One day Frank asked Helen, "What would you think if we should never take another pastorate, never pass another collection plate, never accept any pledged support, but go out and preach the Gospel without charge as the Master did. It might bring us to rags, or to living in a cave."

Her instant reply was, "I think it would be lovely!" And why not? She had wanted "the hardest place on earth" and had long ago proven that she had no fear of deprivation. Spurning dependence on her family, while in Japan she had refused to write for funds, even in desperate straits. When her father urged her to "let her father know" if she had any needs, she had answered firmly, "I'll let my Heavenly Father know."

In October, attending an Alliance convention at Simpson's 44th Street Tabernacle in New York, the Sandfords stood on the platform together and announced their intention to leave behind not only Great Falls and denominational ties, but the care and protection of A. B. Simpson. Helen was two months pregnant.

Finally, in mid-December, to Frank's complete joy, God whispered the word "Go!" On January 1, 1893, preaching with that word as his text, he resigned from the Great Falls pulpit and from the Free Baptist ministry.

The entire nation was soon to be shaken by another major financial panic. A new silver inflation, instituted the year before, was distressing business leaders, and the amount of paper money in circulation was increasing far beyond the gold in the treasury. By all reasonable estimates the country was heading into a long period of joblessness and want.

It made no difference to Frank. He removed his savings from the bank, a considerable amount for the time, money he had earned as a "hireling" of the denomination, and sent it to a missionary in Africa. When he discovered there were still two cents left in the account, he wrote a check for that amount too and scribbled across it, "Hallelujah!" Money had become a tremendously complicated issue in the country—frightening, alluring, entrapping, and necessary. Frank Sandford gave his all away.

From one point of view he had simply joined an army of new unemployed across the country. But from his own perspective he had arrived at last at the best of all possibilities—absolute abandonment to the purposes of God and dependence on God alone for the most basic amenities of life, whatever hardship that might entail.

6

Tongues of Fire
1893–1895

In January of 1893, when Frank and Helen "cut themselves loose," they fell into the arms of the Kinneys. The four of them headed for Honey Grove, Texas, to the Kinneys' ranch, where they stayed until the following spring. So Frank's first stage in "total abandonment to the providences of God" sat in the lap of luxury.

The contradiction is not as sharp as it might appear. Since it was considered inappropriate to be in the public eye during the later stages of pregnancy, it made sense for Helen's "confinement" to be as warm and comfortable as possible. In April the family moved back to the Kinney estate on the Hudson. "My husband is tenderly and lovingly leading and protecting me," wrote Helen to her mother-in-law. It was a brave statement. The medical prognosis for the baby was becoming less and less cheerful, and Helen's own welfare was in question.

As a broker on Wall Street, Charles Kinney rode the train back and forth between one kind of anxiety at home and another in the city. Commercial concerns were folding by the thousands. Banks were failing and railroads falling into receivership at a breathtaking rate. Strikes, plots, anarchy, and acts of desperation filled the newspapers.

Frank cared little for the financial tensions of the nation. He was lost in concern for Helen's safety, and more, worried that either of them might be diverted by trouble from following out God's purposes. By now he was sure that the new work was to begin back home in Maine, but how or when was still a mystery. So far "Go!" had meant only waiting.

In spite of his confidence he was finding himself vulnerable to doubt.

I have never found him quoted to say that he ever questioned the new adventure, but a search for assurance, for some incontestable seal of approval, had clearly begun. If Helen should die, or become enough of an invalid to make a broad ministry difficult, would that be God holding him back from a miscalculated calling, or simply an obstacle to be hurdled by undeterred obedience? He needed the kind of authorization that would carry him through the most threatening eventuality.

In the afternoon hours while Helen rested, he paced under an ancient oak on the banks of the Hudson and grappled with the idea of apostleship. It was a subject of great interest among Higher Life Christians. If early church power could be restored, that suggested the possibility of contemporary apostles, with no less authority than a Peter or a Paul. A purifying movement obviously demanded the leadership of such a person, and "full of impetuosity," as Frank later said, he was making application for the job.

But to his consternation, while reading I Corinthians he noticed that the "signs, wonders and mighty deeds" of the early apostles had been wrought in "all patience." With an "involuntary groan" he saw "that mighty mountain" towering before him. He had yielded his conceit and vanity, his ambition and professional pride. He had given up material possessions and made a vow to obey. But patience was a quality he emphatically lacked, the absence of it perhaps his worst defect. So "the conference ended." He was not ready for apostleship.

In June Helen delivered a baby that had died *in utero.* They named her Patience. Out of danger but needing rest, Helen folded away the new baby clothes and urged Frank to head back to New England alone. That he did, "with a glad bound." He spent the night of July Fourth in Topsham, and the next day took the train to Bowdoinham and the home of his sister, Maria Lancaster.

He had already determined to preach that very night after supper at the old Lancaster Schoolhouse, two miles out of the village. The structure was no larger than a farmhouse kitchen, but like other rural schoolhouses, it served as the public building of the neighborhood.

A total of seven people gathered that evening, most of them Frank's relatives. He preached a sermon on "Expectancy," declaring abruptly to the handful of bemused listeners that, starting immediately, he would hold meetings in the area, in schools and homes and, if necessary, out-of-doors. Whatever the case, he told them matter-of-factly, they must expect a revival, because one was on the way.

Oh, but . . . , they hastened to say, driven to caution by his certainty, haying season had just commenced. Had he forgotten what haying season was like? No one could come to meetings for a good two months, not while they were rushing to beat the weather, or dragging themselves home at sunset sticky with sweat and the dust of the fields.

He remembered the haying season very well indeed, Frank answered (as if anyone could forget it), and he admitted that by any natural standard he had come at exactly the wrong time. He'd have come sooner if God had let him; he'd have come later if God had so ordered. But if those seven people thought he was going to turn around and slink off back to New York because it was haying season, then they did not know him at all.

By any natural standard he had come to the wrong place as well. Talk about "expecting." He expected no honor in his own country; he expected his youth to be despised in a community where age was revered and he was still just a boy to many who knew him. He also expected suspicion. Was he after all a failure as a pastor, come back now to sponge off his old neighbors? He addressed that question before it was asked by announcing his intention to take no offerings. In fact, he told this tiny congregation, never again in his life would he pass a collection plate.

But the question of why he had come still hung in the air. Many Christian workers would not have considered Bowdoinham a mission field at all. For almost fifty years the cities had been the focus of reform. One out of every three Americans now lived in urban areas and that number regularly increased with the flow of immigrants. Crowding had brought its inevitable company of ills, unsafe housing, poor schools, bad air, crime. The hill towns of Maine, though they might have lost half their population since the Civil War, to say nothing of their prosperity and honor, still wore a romantic aura of goodness. These had been the nurturing places of American religion; surely their children were churched, innocent, full of memorized Scripture.

Frank knew the "barnyard idyll" was a myth. In his estimation, among country people there were "no stiffer-necked sinners on the globe," a judgment less condescending than popular sentiments about the quaint and fading Yankee. There were five active churches in Bowdoinham alone. Yet in the back corners of the forty-six square miles of the township scores of people lived too far away to get to those churches without a devoted effort. There were too many children to get ready, not enough best clothes to go around, the roads were too bad, or the horses too slow.

"Oh, they never go to meetings over there. You'll never get them out," Frank was told, as he outlined his plans to move from section to section. Never mind, he answered, it was exactly to these that he had been led, to the neglected fragments of humanity out in the "highways and hedges."

As his relatives had augured, there was no revival during the haying season. Frank set up weekly meetings in six or seven district schools, which meant one every night for himself. Attendance was very poor. Services involved no more than the singing of a few familiar hymns, which he led without instrument or books, his own voice filling the little buildings, and then a shy testimony or two from the gathering before he preached. Wherever he went he hung across the blackboard a large flag he had designed himself, white letters spelling THE TRUTH on a deep blue background.

In August Helen joined him and the work expanded to include other towns. Now there were two to lead meetings, and there were also two to seek shelter and food. "Seek" is the wrong word; they never asked. From day to day they were seldom sure where they would spend the night.

In the six months between August and January both of them were snagged by the humiliation this entailed. Though they prayed that no one would give them anything "from sentimentality or sympathy," there were times when, penniless, dependent on the hospitality of people who themselves had not much to give, they felt like "the very off-scouring of the earth." They had not predicted hearing children hushed at the table when they asked for seconds at supper. No one knew better than Frank the status of the idler and the beggar in such a community. Itinerant preachers were too much like the new population of tramps who moved from farm to farm asking for a hayloft and the leavings of a meal. As an added confusion, word had spread that Mrs. Sandford came from a well-to-do family, which increased Helen's self-consciousness. What was wholly familiar to her husband was new to her—the wash basin on the back step, the community towel, the dark, spidery backhouse. She was absorbing all this without the slightest sign of consternation (it was surely easier than Africa would be), but Frank understood the adjustment.

My wife was dying to the natural, and I was dying to see her die. . . . I was dying to college, ecclesiastical, and every other kind of pride, and she was dying to see me die, so that neither of us could speak of our feelings to the other. We simply walked those blue clay hills in silence . . . . To have hired a room and been independent would have enabled me to preserve both pride and reputation—but never to lose them.

The two could not have been as unwelcome as they feared. They were gracious, entertaining guests. Frank still had the knack of saying what was on his mind and getting away with it. Once on a rare occasion in which he found himself in a fine house being offered the best guestroom, he startled his hostess by teasing, "Why, you treat me better than you do Jesus!"

That way of "coming right out with things" made him seem trustworthy. His earlier parishioners had known he was not a distinguished preacher (nor ever would be, perhaps—lacking Simpson's polished refinement or Moody's gruff authority), but you could count on him to be forthright, without fancy language or ecclesiastical airs. It was an important quality to hill people, the virtue they looked for most in "reverends" and politicians. In preaching or personal contact Frank's blue gaze was steady; he never avoided your eyes or dropped his own.

But the attendance at meetings remained scanty, mostly women and children. In September several other workers, including returned missionaries, joined Helen and Frank to help. They also were "unable to touch the people." During that bleak month it became apparent to them all that they needed to get away and rethink their purposes.

Frank had noticed in a newspaper that this year the Jewish Feast of the Ingathering (or Tabernacles) was to be celebrated between September 25 and October 2, his birthday. Delighted by the coincidence, he chose that week for a retreat. A total of twenty people participated, including his mother and two of his sisters, as well as the Kinneys and the new workers. They met at Great Falls and spent their days at Burgett Park, three miles out of town.

The week did not go well at all. Everyone sensed the need for organization and agreed on a rather cumbersome name for themselves: The World's Evangelization Crusade on Apostolic Principles. Frank, wary of "human machinery," felt reluctant to go further than that. At last he cautiously wrote up a constitution which he thought detoured those dangers and presented it for adoption. In this one-page document, their by-laws were to be the Scriptures, the Lord Jesus Christ was to be their "Head," and their "Director" the Holy Ghost.

The group ignited into disagreement. More than half of them considered the wording ludicrous. One man, their "strongest worker" in Frank's estimation, stomped off in anger, calling him mad. The constitution finally stood, signed by twelve persons. But Frank felt betrayed by what he saw as "traitorism in the ranks."

However, back in Bowdoinham once more, things suddenly changed. Renewing the circuit of meetings, the Sandfords and one helper, a woman missionary from India, began at the Raymond School, down near Center's Point, close to Merrymeeting Bay. This particular neighborhood had a bad name in the town. According to one Bowdoinham resident, a double-barreled shotgun was required to travel through it safely. Drunken brawls were regular events and "outsiders" were unwelcome, particularly preachers.

Meetings began as usual, the attendance largely women. Then one night when Frank had finished preaching, a man with a cast on his leg seated at the back of the room stood up with a loud clatter and began hobbling between the desks to the front. Reaching Frank, he held out his hand and declared, "This is the kind of religion I want."

Every soul present knew how this man's leg had been broken—in a savage fight. He knew they knew, that they knew all about him. The next night the school building was packed out. Chairs were brought in from nearby houses and planks laid across the aisles for seating. Those who could not find a place inside positioned themselves at the windows, lamplight flickering on their faces. It was a "strikingly peculiar audience," as Frank described them. Men, young and old, stood at the back along the walls, arms folded, cheeks bulging with tobacco, spitting juice on the floor.

If their intentions were dishonorable (to "carry out the teacher"?) they never enacted them. In the middle of the sermon one of them gruffly interrupted and asked for prayer. He was, he announced to all before him, "the wildest man in Maine," and he had been "living in sin for half a century."

From that point until late in December one conversion followed another, with people calling for prayer at any time throughout the meetings. Again and again these were men between the ages of twenty and sixty, considered under any circumstances the hardest category to reach.

Frank, like Moody, had never preached "an old ladies' religion," and now, above all, he avoided the stigma of a feminized Christianity, which to him meant a wishy-washy God, too soft on sin, the growing error of mainstream denominations. If any parties present, he told his school-house listeners, thought what he meant by conversion was some vague religious feeling, some squashy notions about being forgiven and then going off to do as they pleased, they might as well leave right now. What *he* was talking about was not easy. "Anything short of the genuine will never pass muster with God," he said. It would be hard every day for the rest of a "man's life." Anyone who came up front to ask for prayer had better mean it, because the first thing he would ask them to do would be the hardest they had ever done in their lives—which was to get down on their knees, right in front of their neighbors and family, those who knew their worst secrets. He would expect public confessions, no hiding, no sham, no hedging. Restitution for past sins must follow.

"It won't make any difference what you tell us here; if there's a lie in your heart God can see it. If you've done a wrong, you must make it right." If a man had so much as stolen a pick from an ice house, he must carry that pick back and admit to being "a poor miserable thief. You've got to call things by the right name."

So at the very same moment when a convert accepted the challenge to manliness, he was stripped of it. It was important in Frank's eyes for these "great, strapping" creatures to be broken by God. He himself, a person often undone by the intensity of his own emotions, had learned not to be ashamed of tears.

"How he did preach!" said a convert. "I never heard the like before. Night after night he slew them. I liked him, for he waded into the old-cold and lukewarm ones, and told them . . . just the way they were living . . . hit the mark every time."

In a matter of weeks the entire town changed. Even the skeptics could hardly deny that something honest and open was moving through the community. The revival continued until Christmas time, with a smoky wood fire roaring in the school stove. Then as suddenly as it had begun, it was over. Winter closed in and froze shut not only the back roads, but the hearts of the people. Attendance at meetings ceased abruptly, and so did the conversions.

In the snowy months that followed Frank became the object of scorn and gossip. To critical observers he was just another unemployed man. Even the Apostle Paul had made tents. Few understood Frank's assertion that for him to take even a temporary mill job or accept lucrative preaching offers in the cities would be disobeying God. His brother Charles was now being treated periodically at the Augusta Insane Asylum (as it was called) and Frank, when he ought to be contributing to Charles's care, was eating off the family. His relatives were embarrassed, he knew, and townspeople were murmuring that he'd "run off the track."

He blamed himself for this confusing hiatus. If God was being dishonored in his life, then something was obviously lacking. With all the steps of committal he had taken, he was still not certain he had experienced the "baptism of the Holy Spirit," and if he had not, that could explain his present inadequacy. The idea of Spirit baptism had become so important in the evangelical framework that books and tracts on the subject were now flooding the religious market. Any leader worth a pinch of salt, even in the mainline congregations, advocated the power of the Spirit as essential to a successful life and ministry.

At the same time the majority of leaders remained careful not to suggest that the infilling of the Spirit would be attended by a special feeling, or any overt manifestation. Frank knew this, but he also knew of many who claimed a striking emotional experience, including his own wife. In the second year of her course of study at Simpson's school, the entire institution had been "visited" with a baptism of the Spirit, according to the school paper. Helen "lay upon the floor for several hours in a half unconscious state," went the report, "knowing that the hand of the Lord was upon her in blessing." It was not an unusual story. D. L. Moody, too, at the beginning of his ministry, had been overcome by such joy that he begged God to "withhold His hand."

Morning after morning throughout the winter, Frank and Helen and several friends rose before dawn, hitched up sleighs and drove to an abandoned church in Richmond, where they lit a fire and knelt on the floor to pray. For hours the group "consecrated and reconsecrated" themselves, until they "wearied of the exercise." Yet nothing happened. For Frank this was very serious. Now he had been denied both the seal of apostleship and the infilling of the Holy Spirit.

At the end of six weeks the morning sorties were given up. Meanwhile, the Sandfords were still homeless and without income. Helen once told a friend that she had put twenty-two patches into Frank's best coat. That at least struck them funny. They were in what they called their "shabby period." Frank's "stiff hat" sported a hole in the back of it. One day on the local train, "alive with pride," he removed the hat and held it in his lap. But only for a moment. "Young man," he said to himself, "you had better wear that hat until you can enjoy the hole in the back from this side, as well as the man on the seat behind you from his side." He put the hat on again and wore it until he "really enjoyed it," and then God "provided a new one."

Many people were in a shabby period. Strikes and the marches of the unemployed had increased throughout the early winter months of 1894. Later that spring, "Coxey's Army" of 1,200 marched into Washington, D.C., from all over the country. Hill people watched the national strife like spectators in a grandstand, safe from the melee but with their money on the game. That summer the great Pullman strike seemed to gather into itself all the fear-riddled issues of the year.

In early August Frank and Helen retreated to Old Orchard one more time (it would be their last), where they listened to the instruction of a man named Stephen Merritt, a Methodist layman, an undertaker from New York City. Merritt was known in holiness circles around the world for his teaching on the Holy Spirit. His approach to faith was rational and unemotional. Hadn't Jesus said that God would give the Holy Spirit to those who asked? One should "rest" in the fact of that promise and not demand proof of fulfillment.

"AUGUST 2nd, SETTLED FOREVER," Frank wrote in his Bible. Following Merritt's lead, "without the slightest feeling or emotion" he made another pact with God: "I do now yield my spirit to the Person of the Holy Spirit; will be led, guided and controlled by Him henceforth. . . ."

There was nothing to mark a change, except a "still, small voice" of reassurance. "The Guest told me that he was in all the experiences of life, making them all work together. . . . He said I need have no responsibility whatever, but simply respond to His movings." It was one more reinforcement of the trust and obedience he had learned from Hannah Whitall Smith, the wings of the eagle put to use without question. The expectation of "signs and wonders" had not been relinquished; that would come in time.

Whatever Frank meant, or thought he meant, by "controlled" and "no responsibility," words stiff with the old holiness problems he had once despised, from this moment receiving the Holy Spirit by faith became a point of distinction in the Sandford ministry.

With the dreadful 1894 winter at an end, the Crusaders were ready to expand. There were 250 closed churches in the coastal hill regions of Maine, and Frank estimated 300,000 "unevangelized and uncared for souls." They intended to reach them all. The Kinneys provided a tent roomy enough for over a hundred people, with a pump organ and chairs, and a farmer in nearby Durham donated the use of his pine grove, high on a hill above the Androscoggin. There the tent was pitched, visible on both sides of the river, almost aglow at night as lamplight filtered through its white canvas. Crowds arrived with an air of festivity, and meetings went on and on, often until midnight.

Plenty of people came for the circus, hoping to witness dramatics— such as the night a woman suddenly burst down the aisle crying aloud, and her husband shook his fist at the Crusaders, yelling, "I'll make ye smart for this!" That combination of comedy and risk was galvanizing. But if people came for a show, at least they came. John Douglas was one of these.

He was a rugged, handsome man in his thirties, an ambivalent Quaker—something of a community scamp. He had married young and divorced, a circumstance that had not enhanced his reputation. Douglas attended meetings "to pass away the time and chew tobacco." He had already "started" as a Christian six times in his life, and had no intention of doing it again. He had seen too many "men and women go weeping to the altar, declare that God had forgiven their sins, tell how happy they were, and inside six months be back where they were before." But one night, when as a joke he feigned conversion and walked down the tent aisle to the altar, he was overcome by a sense of God's presence and the joke became reality. This time he "meant business."

In the weeks that followed John made everything he owned available to the Crusaders—his house and barn, located conveniently close to the tent site, his horses, wagons, tools. That fall he took it upon himself to establish a fund for a "Gospel boat" to evangelize the islands and coastal towns of Casco Bay.

By September 25, when Frank pitched two tents on the Methodist Church lawn in Lisbon Falls for what was now an annual convention, a total of twenty workers participated, and financial contributions (still unsolicited) were plentiful. The local Methodists backed the work firmly and the tents stayed up until cold weather set in.

Back at the Texas ranch that winter Frank wrote the first issue of a monthly magazine, its title an extension of the already cumbersome: TONGUES OF FIRE FROM THE WORLD'S EVANGELIZATION CRUSADE ON APOSTOLIC PRINCIPLES. Copies were sent free of charge to every address available to the Sandfords. Frank wrote as he preached, in an energetic rush of prose, with a bent toward superlatives and large type. "THIS PAPER STANDS FOR THE WORD OF GOD IN ITS ENTIRETY AND THAT WITHOUT ADULTER-ATION," read the lead editorial in January 1895. "The word 'crusade' (war of the cross) indicates an aggressive spirit . . . and determination to seek FIRST the Kingdom of God at any cost. This is a Calvary movement . . . a movement designed to be always on the field or scouring the country for the enemy." Frank's early articles were largely autobiographical, describing his recent spiritual discoveries and intro-ducing the distinctive ministry of the Crusaders to the world.

The April issue of the magazine carried an invitation.

WANTED
One hundred Holy Ghost leaders for one hundred gospel tents . . . . Salary, Matthew 6:33

One hundred singers who can sing the gospel with the Spirit and understanding. Same salary as the leaders.

One hundred men with consecrated hearts and level heads to care for these tents. Same salary as the singers.

At A. J. Gordon's Missionary Training School in Boston a young senior named Charles Holland saw the ad and responded with an application. Frank wrote back: "If you are willing to live in a barn, sleep in a cave, or rot in a dungeon, come along, and I will give you my heart and my hand."

When the school term was over at the end of May, Holland and another Gordon student, Ralph Gleason, found their way to Durham and John Douglas's barn, where they introduced themselves to Frank. The sizing up on either side was instantly positive—the two students trim and smart under their bowlers, and Frank in his farm clothes, wearing a cocky red fez he had picked up in Egypt.

Holland and Gleason were soon sent to conduct meetings at Bowie Hill, several miles away, and then to Great Chebeague Island in Casco Bay. They were an excellent team, Gleason as preacher, narrow-faced and studious looking, and Holland, with calm brown eyes and an affable manner, as song leader.

In the course of a month a flock of young men and women aged fifteen to twenty-five were participating in the work. Several acres of

John Douglas's woods were cleared of undergrowth, providing a large pine grove for outdoor camp meetings. A road was cut, a well dug, and a platform set up. The tents were freed (not a hundred, only four) to move inland and northward.

It was now that Frank began to make enemies. For a long time he had been hearing in his mind the words in Matthew 9: "New wine, new wine skins." While he shared creeds and goals with many denominations, he was seeing more and more ways in which they all stopped short of total obedience to Scripture. He had already offended the local Methodists and Freewill Baptists by his scorching reproofs, while at the same time—as they readily pointed out—he was bleeding off some of their best members.

Meanwhile the Quakers of Durham had welcomed and endorsed him, finding common ground in his emphasis on inner light. Until now he had respected their long-held position that the sacraments, including water baptism, were unnecessary as signs of inward grace. But while preaching to them one day he was suddenly convinced that he had no right to spare them what he saw as Biblical truth. If they refused to be immersed, he told them emphatically, they were disobeying God's Word.

As a result thirty active members of the Friends Society requested baptism, including the leading elder. The remaining Quakers, deeply antagonized, expelled those people from membership. Distressed, Frank protested that he was not trying to break up the Quaker Meeting, nor any church, that he did not, in fact, believe in churches at all, "except a universal Church." The experience renewed his earlier conviction: those who wished to work with the Crusaders must forsake their old affiliations, "come out from among them and be separate."

Charles Mann, editor of the *Lisbon Enterprise,* a tiny weekly published just across the river, had been watching Sandford with skepticism and had already "set him down as a humbug." Mann, in full control of every word in his little paper, used the Quaker incident to make his own kind of hay, and launched into a vicious campaign against the Crusaders, calling Frank an "autocrat" and a "czar."

With such ill will abroad in the area, Frank had no intention of making Durham a permanent location for his work, even though his next project demanded headquarters. On October 2, his thirty-third birthday, he announced that a Bible School would open the very next day.

The idea had been on his mind for months. The summer's work, involving so many young people who were filled with zeal but lacked training, convinced him he must begin immediately. He "knew of no school he would recommend unreservedly," and this meant the prototypes, A. B. Simpson's school in New York, A. J. Gordon's in Boston, and the Bible school in Chicago named for D. L. Moody.

Actually all of these institutions were slipping into a strange role. Along with their founders, popular preachers or Bible teachers, they were becoming alternatives for traditional ecclesiastical organization. Christians disenchanted by their denominations were turning their loyalties toward the new schools, which with growing adjunct services (printing presses, public lectures, correspondence courses, and summer conferences) offered a type of leadership and instruction that was missing in many churches. But to Frank the Bible schools in existence were already capitulating to distracting academic demands, and none taught the "whole Bible."

It fazed him not in the least that his announcement turned up only one enrollee, Ralph Gleason's brother Willard. Ralph had by now gone back to finish at Gordon's School in Boston. Willard, who was eighteen, had spent an unsatisfactory summer in YMCA work at Lubec, Maine, and had come to hear Sandford at Ralph's beckoning.

While Helen was visiting in Texas for a few weeks, Frank was staying with his sister Annie Brown in Brunswick, and it was there that Willard met him the next morning. Sitting unceremoniously on the floor of the attic, they opened the school by praying, in effect, for a school.

The Gleason brothers were related to Ralph Waldo Emerson. That meant very little to Frank, even as irony. He may very well have wished that another of the young people had chosen to be his first student rather than this one. Willard, a slight, thin-faced boy with close-set eyes, shy and self-deprecating in his manner, certainly lacked in public presence.

Over the winter of 1895 ten enrolled—four men, including Charles Holland, and six women, living separately and meeting for classes whenever they could. Most the students had either been working for the Crusaders or had attended their meetings. They came from surrounding towns, with two from Great Chebeague Island—Rose Emmons, a cheerful, pretty school teacher, and Edmund Doughty, a young farmer and coastal sailor. Mary Guptil and her sister Adnah joined the school from the town of Cornish, Roswell Harper from the town of Wales, and Maud Peacock, a sickly but indomitable girl (actually in the first stages of consumption) from nearby Litchfield. All were between the ages of eighteen and twenty-two, except Margaret Main, a strong-minded fifteen-year-old who joined somewhat later.

Most of these young people had been raised in church-going families and had made earlier Christian commitments. Though already baptized in their own churches, all were re-baptized by Frank, washing out the authority of previous denominational experience. All, under his guidance, "received the Holy Spirit."

Sometime during this winter the school acquired a name. It was another mouthful: The Holy Ghost and Us Bible School. No playfulness was intended, though newspapers would find fun in it later. Frank found the words in the book of Acts and used them to signify the school's emphasis on the instruction of the Holy Spirit.

This was not a conventional school. It offered no courses or "subjects," no faculty except Frank, no grading, and no textbooks other than the Bible. The object was to know the contents of the Book which as the only complete and authentic revelation provided all the instruction necessary to life, and to obey it, to practice it together moment by moment.

What it could possibly mean to "obey the whole Bible" under any circumstances was overlayered with considerations, but not to this optimistic group. It was the apocalyptic books they turned to first, which opened for them "as if by magic." The students were profoundly moved. "There was a hush in the house for days," Willard Gleason remembered later. "We did not want to talk aloud, and went about our work quietly." Christ's return seemed "so near, right at the door."

Meanwhile practical realities lost none of their import. By Christmas the school was boarding at the home of a Litchfield farmer. Tuition was free but the weekly dollar for food loomed over everyone's head. No one worked for wages; like Helen and Frank they had entered a life of trust. All participated regularly in meetings in churches and schoolhouses, but no offerings were taken. Stories of small daily miracles collected, as gifts arrived just in time, and needs were filled precisely in answer to prayer—a coat, a blanket, a postage stamp. Friends and subscribers to *Tongues of Fire* sent frequent contributions of money and supplies, such variant surprises as a kitchen clock and an express package of finnan haddie.

By the end of February Sandford could tell his *Tongues of Fire* readers that the young people who comprised the school were indeed "overcomers." These "bashful timid boys and girls knowing but little of the Scriptures have been transformed . . . into MEN AND WOMEN IN GOD."

"If the Divine Master only had a band of such workers as this, there is no limit to what He might do with them," Hannah Whitall Smith had written. "Truly, one such would 'chase a thousand, and two would put ten thousands to flight,' and nothing would be impossible to them." Recently, Frank had become engrossed himself in the Old Testament story of the youthful David's small renegade army, which had stood up bravely to the trained hosts of King Saul. Enchanted by that abandoned rag-tag heroism, Frank had written a hymn. Those who follow David's Son (meaning Jesus), so went the words, might also find themselves an "outcast band," yet accomplishing feats of greatness. The chorus paraphrased his favorite verse from Song of Solomon.

> Fair as the moon, clear as the sun,
> And terrible in war,
> An army with its banners flung,
> Victorious evermore.

Biblical language of armed conflict had long been accepted as symbolic of the most pacifistic goals, in spite of wars in which God had been given sides, in spite of the American war still so vivid in memory, larding daily conversation with its metaphors—in spite, you could say, of Julia Ward Howe's "The Battle Hymn of the Republic." There was not the faintest thought in Frank's mind of training his students in martial skills. Nevertheless, he was preparing the school for Armageddon, a battle of catastrophic concreteness, to be "fulfilled to the letter," when blood would flow "even unto the horses' bridles." So behind the poetry of war, with its useful expression of unquestioning obedience, hung a reality of unthinkable dimensions. "There's a sound of going in the air," the school sang,

> That is more than the whispering Zephyr's sigh;
> There's a sound in the tops of the Mulberry trees
> That tells us the host of the Lord are nigh.

The seeds of the future were sowing themselves deeply in this first little school: personal Spirit-endowed revelation, the sense of being separated for God's ultimate purposes, and obedience at any price. Everything Frank had incorporated into his life since that first Northfield conference seven years before was tied together now in this small package of dedicated young humanity. None of them would graduate. No graduation was planned. In the years just ahead some would leave and some would die, but most would remain as permanent members of David's band.

Christian and Missionary Alliance at Old Orchard, 1887. Helen Kinney stands fourth left, her parents far left. Sandford stands rear, second left. A. B. Simpson, front, third right. Courtesy Albert B. Simpson Historical Library.

The wreck of the steamer *Tchihatchoff,* Jaffa, 1890

Right: Sulieman Girby, the heroic boatman.

Frank Sandford as young pastor.

Helen Kinney, missionary to Japan, 1890.

The Sandfords as country evangelists.
Lewiston Journal sketch.

7

Arise and Build
1896–1897

Early in 1896 The Holy Ghost and Us Bible School began a race against time that would characterize everything it did for a long time to come. Soon after the New Year Frank told his students that the Holy Spirit had been repeating to him the words "Let us arise and build." He felt sure this meant a physical structure, but he had no idea where it was meant to go up.

Late in February he and John Douglas explored the snowy hills of John's farm for possible sites, and as the two men prayed, stretched out on their faces on the cold ground, Frank heard the answer: "In the mountain of the height of Israel." The words were a fragment from Ezekiel.

One of the highest points in Durham was a sandy hill on John's property. More than a hundred years back the town had been a logging camp, and very likely this hill had been depleted of pines, which had been cut for masts and hauled to shipbuilding yards at Bath and Freeport. Gales had since blown away the topsoil and drifted the underlying sand, which in places was now ten feet deep, half-burying an apple orchard. The whole eighty-five acres might have been carted over from the barren wastes of Palestine.

Actually, the hill was questionable as a building site, since no one knew exactly what lay beneath the sand. But the view was fine of the winding Androscoggin in one direction and the White Mountains in another. The location was practical as well, with the city of Portland thirty miles to the southwest by the Maine Central railroad, the depot just across the river at Lisbon Falls, where one also could catch the electric cars to Lewiston.

John Douglas offered the school a vacant old farmhouse near the foot of the hill as living quarters until the new building could be erected. The students moved immediately, undaunted by a late winter blizzard. With each of them bringing their own beds and desks, the baggage was mountainous. Once it had been loaded on the double-horse sled, the women were bundled in to ride, while the men walked all seventeen miles in the storm. The party arrived wet and exhausted but in great spirits, named the tumbledown house Hephzibah (meaning "my delight is in her"), lit a fire, ate supper, and divided up the rooms. Within the next few days they were settled, and Helen joined them from Texas. On the outside of the gable Frank nailed a large sign, "The Upper Room," while the students added other signs in gilt letters on either side of the front door: "Come in. Father loves you." ("Father" meant God; the students called Frank "Mr. Sandford.") Guests were received with a cordial welcome, though food and firewood were in short supply, there were no extra dishes or chairs, and the damper on the stove had to be propped open with a stick.

One afternoon at the end of March, a newspaperman named Holman Day arrived from Lewiston, driving an excellent horse. Taking the sign at its word, he admitted himself, and was met by Frank, who appeared to Day as "an erect, clear-eyed, tense and enthusiastic young man whose face beamed cheery smiles under his close blond beard." In a moment Day realized where he had seen Sandford before—as captain of the semi-pro team in the summer of '86, when Day had just finished his freshman year at Colby. They had hardly seated themselves before they were talking about baseball.

Frank had never seen Day, but he knew who he was. Everyone did. Here was the *Lewiston Journal's* present star among freelance reporters, a new-style journalist who drew his material directly from the people. At this particular time Day was writing a column called "Catching the Drift," which covered the common citizen's thoughts on the free-silver issue. But he was also becoming known as a regional humorist, especially for his witty sketches of typical Maine characters and his command of Down East dialect.

Day had not come to see Frank about the gold standard. As he explained later in an article in *Leslie's Magazine,* he had been invited by John Douglas's uncle, who—"as wrathful a Quaker as that calm faith would sanction"—wanted a "newspaper reporter to come down . . . and show up the man who has broken up the Durham Quaker meeting," a man who had converted most the local Friends and now had the nerve to move into an old Quaker homestead.

"So I have come," said Day, "to the troubled land of Durham to see what's happening." He was not a religious man himself, he acknowledged to Frank. He had been raised a Congregationalist, and was neither a believer nor a skeptic.

He had come looking for a character, though he didn't say so. Characters were his stock in trade, but this one was not what Day expected. Sandford came across as "cultured and devoted," and if he bore a "touching romanticism" in his enthusiasm, he was convincing and honest as well.

"I have to admit I am scared," Frank told Day, directing his gaze out the window at the strange treeless hill. "God has told me to build a five-story building up there, and—well, here is my entire capital." He turned out his pockets one by one and produced a total of three cents. Even the tools were borrowed, he explained, pointing to an old blue wheelbarrow atilt in the yard. "In the morning we will start to dig for the foundation. I suppose the whole surrounding region will be watching, ready to declare, if we should end up with nothing but a hole in the ground, 'What a fool he has made of himself.' But I am positive that after God has given an order He knows how to furnish the means."

"But how does God speak to you?" Day asked. "What do you hear?"

Frank explained that he was not "hearing voices." He heard words in the "inner consciousness," which was the meaning of Biblical statements like "the Lord spake unto Moses." Actually, God spoke to a great many people, he said. "The trouble with most folks is they won't listen."

Outdoors, Day examined a drawing Frank had made of the proposed structure and tried to envision its towering presence on the miserable hill. Glancing around at the nearby farms, it occurred to him that to the "severely practical minds of the people of Durham, there could be no more unsuitable building plot." There was even something "grotesque" about it, he thought—that "a plan for the evangelization of the world should be controlled from such a modest little town," a place that until now had been "placidly stubbing along the theological highway."

Day apparently expressed these reservations on the spot, and Frank, not surprised, told him with a shrug that he was quite typical—"just like all the doubters of the world" over the ages. "You believe neither God nor His prophet. Well, time will tell. In fact, I here and now constitute you as our chronicler. Come to us from time to time, and see what God will do for those who put absolute reliance in His Word."

The idea suited Day just fine. He agreed to make a running record of the movement, to be a kind of scribe.

"My scribe, but not my Pharisee," said Frank, in true form, shaking his hand as they parted.

The school at Durham was perfect subject matter for the *Lewiston Journal.* The paper's readers had learned to expect detailed and dramatic accounts of local stories, unlike the more issue-centered *Lewiston Daily Sun.* Headlines were tiered in a dozen sizes of type. Runaway horses, wrecks at railroad crossings, barns struck by lightning—if a story carried human interest, it could all but fill the paper. Never mind about the trouble that had begun to erupt in Cuba and South Africa, or even the mounting presidential campaign. The "mysterious" suicide of one Mabel Davis of Bowdoinham, placed directly under an ad for Royal Baking Powder at the top of page one, demanded more attention than Russia's efforts to "coerce" peace between Greece and Turkey. Day had a playground, then, for his coverage of the "Holy Ghosters," as the community had begun to call them.

He began collecting material on the next day. Right after breakfast Frank and five men students headed for the hill with the wheelbarrow and a shovel, walking against a damp, piercing wind. The foundation, forty by sixty feet, had been marked off earlier, and the rectangle lay before them, smaller than Noah's Ark and about as ludicrous. Frank turned the first shovelful of wet sand. Frost still hardened the ground a good nine inches down, while the upper surface had thawed to standing water. In this the group splashed about as they spelled each other with the digging. Suddenly someone spotted a coin in the mud, a pre-Civil War penny. Now they owned a total of four cents among them, one an artifact.

The work began again the next morning, and this time curious farmers climbed up to see what was going on, or so said Day in his continuing report. While Sandford explained, the men eyed the ground with doubt and embarrassment.

"How long do you calculate the job will take?" one of them finally asked.

"Oh, that isn't a matter for us to decide," Sandford replied. God would send the money and the lumber "as it suits His convenience," he told them. "All I am doing now is obeying the orders to dig."

Though neighbors may have wondered why God had not waited a

month for better conditions, several returned to help, and as the month of April passed, the nine feet of digging went more quickly. Under the sand, to their delight, they found packed gravel, over 14,000 cubic feet of it. Road repairs (the working off of local taxes) had begun in Durham and neighbors were happy to haul away the gravel for filling pot holes— and who could question the timing of that? Under the gravel was pure clay, a fine foundation.

The strange event on the hilltop was by far the most exciting thing going on for miles around. When horses and oxen were needed they were readily lent. Glancing out the windows of Hephzibah one day in June, Sandford's eyes filled with tears at the sight on the hill, "alive with men and horses."

The school was pressed to the limit by work. At night men students nursed sore backs and blistered hands as they returned to their studies. Keeping the house, cooking, tending to the appetites of young men barely out of their teens, were in themselves steady jobs for Helen and the women students. Frank remained chief writer for *Tongues of Fire* and was compiling a song book as well.

That spring he and John Douglas, as elated as two boys, purchased a forty-foot sloop. Douglas, who had raised the funds from relatives and friends, had dickered the price to far below its original $2,800. In June the boat was launched and took off for the 365 islands of Casco Bay, with Douglas as skipper and two of the students as sailors. Under an awning over the deck as many as seventy-five people could be seated for services.

Holman Day's detailed coverage of these enterprises was published in the *Journal* on June 20 and reprinted in papers throughout the country, all the way from the *Boston Post* to the *San Francisco Examiner*. On July 6 his report of the school's holiday convention on the Fourth shared major space with the Chicago Democratic Convention, where Maine's leading Democrat, Arthur Sewall, had been chosen as running mate of William Jennings Bryan.

The convention in Durham fostered fully as much enthusiasm as the one in Chicago, according to Day. Early on the dark morning families from miles around rolled in their wagons toward what was now known as "Beulah Hill." There they merged with old friends from New Hampshire and new ones who had come by train from as far away as Texas. In the grove, while parade music drifted from the other side of the river, three students, including Charles Holland, were ordained to the ministry of the movement. After a picnic the crowd gathered at the excavation atop the hill and cheered as a marble cornerstone was lowered into place.

Holman Day, with his staid church background, was stirred by the warmth and skill of the singing and intrigued that Sandford should simply talk for half an hour, "without text or notes." Day quoted him at length in the paper but failed to include one comment regarding two men spoken of in Revelation, who were to appear just before the return of Christ—men "endorsed by God," said Sandford, "with such marvelous miracle power as had never yet been manifested on this globe!" The Bible School at Durham intended to "stand by and if need be die" with those two prophets, who were to be murdered by the anti-Christ in the streets of Jerusalem. Perhaps this was all too esoteric for a journalist to get down in his scribbled notes, or if he did, he cut it, unable to fathom its import.

Actually, Day seemed to have little real sense of what the Crusaders were about. The tone of his coverage, while never disparaging, was airy and light, a thin curtain between himself and the serious intentions of the movement. He loved the debonair quality of the school's faith. When the first bill of the project, $20 for the sawing of sill timbers, arrived to an empty till, within an hour someone handed Frank a check for $30. The problem of finding a mason was solved when one arrived all the way from Georgia, not to work (so he thought) but to be baptized. He stayed to lay brick, free of charge.

In the same manner Frank acquired a badly needed secretary. Day's syndicated story in June had swelled the school's already heavy correspondence. Night after night, heads aching, the Sandfords had been working to keep abreast of it, answering every letter in longhand. Caroline Sutherland, Charles Holland's fiancee, secretary to a Boston executive, arrived at Durham on the Fourth of July with her mother to be present at Charles's ordination. She had planned to go directly back to her job, but Frank, watching her walk into the tent, "seemed to see a great derrick swing around, grapple a granite boulder, rise, swing back again, and finally deposit it in its place on the wall."

Caroline nowhere near resembled a block of granite. But the imagery had come to mind naturally, since everyone had been wishing for a derrick to build the granite foundation walls on the hill. Sandford felt sure enough of his revelation to approach Caroline after the service. He asked her to stay, that very day, and immediately take over the clerical duties.

Whether or not to Sandford's surprise (but certainly to Charles's), she consented; her mother returned to Boston with the message to the employer—Caroline would never be back. She and Charles were married in September.

With an annual convention planned for just five weeks away on October 2, Frank announced to the school that God had told him the chapel must be finished and dedicated on that date, his birthday. There could be no finished room without a building around it. With only one carpenter willing to commit himself to such a deadline (a man whose name was Arthur Pray, actually), the young people began a regular schedule of almost twenty-four hours of work, the women joining the men in tasks that were brand new to both.

Hardly a day closed without a breathtaking deadline. If a dollar a week for room and board had seemed like a thousand, that was now mere kindergarten in the school of trust. According to Frank Murray, Sandford had begun early to insist in public, "I am not going to run after money. Money is going to run after me." Part of this bargain with himself and God was to pay for every purchase in cash as soon as he received the bill, and to ask his contributors outright for nothing—though by now both "asking" and "outright" had grown somewhat ambiguous. He had decided it was now permissable to list needs in *Tongues of Fire,* but prayer must be the only direct means by which to call for help. So window frames, lumber, and nails became the objects of an ongoing spiritual battle.

One day three bills arrived at once, totaling $201, and there was no money in sight. Holman Day carried the story in great detail, letting Frank tell it:

> I had always preached boldly, "Owe no man anything," and here suddenly were great towering mountains looking down on me, and saying, "Now we will crush you." And I believe when the secret comes out, I believe you will find that someone in this country somewhere, has a confession to make . . . . It is a hideous and awful thing when God bids us to do a thing, to hesitate about doing it, even twenty-four hours.

If Day quoted him accurately, it is fair to say that Frank did not predict how self-dramatizing those words would appear in print, or how self-contradictory. The man who would not pass a collection plate or ask for financial support was publicly acknowledging his dependence on—not God—but undependable human support. As it turned out, the money did come in and was paid out the next day (before the newspaper story was printed), and a gentleman confessed to having procrastinated in giving the exact amount required.

By September the structure had taken shape, two stories, then a third in a mansard roof, and above that the two stories of the front turret. Rose Emmons's father, stopping by for a visit, was astonished to see his daughter and Maude Peacock (the consumptive) up on the roof in their ankle-length dresses, laying the last course of shingles.

Then just days before the October 2 dedication of the chapel, the coffers were empty again.

"We lacked boards for the floor," Sandford explained to Holman Day. "Brother Rossie Harper [a student] said, Shall I go and get some boards? No, I said, I have got no money." The next morning he "walked around with folded arms dying," imagining people coming "from near and far for the dedication and finding no floor. I could hear people saying, 'He has just made a fool of himself, gone and shown off, advertising a dedication, and he hasn't even got a floor.'

" 'Well,' I said, 'Halleluia! Lord, if you didn't tell me this building was going to be dedicated October 2nd, I ought to be whipped. Go ahead and put it on me all I deserve. . . . But if I did get your voice, Lord, you manage it.' "

At noon Helen handed Frank $10 that had just come in the mail. They needed $17 more. "I don't know how it got started," Frank continued, "but there came in $1, then 50 cents, and I said, Rossie, get the horse and go and get one load anyway. While he was getting the horse, along came some more," and suddenly there was enough.

"Well, we got a double horse team; they went for the boards, and almost before we knew it the lumber was landed here, and all paid for. Then we worked at night until eleven o'clock. It would have done your heart good to have seen the hammers fly. This floor came together as if by magic."

On the day of dedication, as guests arrived at the front of the building, students were sweeping shavings out the back door. The plaster was still wet on the walls, but the room was filled with banners and mottos— a colorful display that was met with shouts of appreciation. Over the platform hung a huge duplicate of a chart displayed at Northfield in 1887, showing the proportion of Christians to the as-yet "unreached" of the world.

After the convention, as several more of the twenty-seven rooms were finished, students moved from Hephzibah into the centrally heated new building. A boiler had been acquired, totally necessary if the plaster was to cure properly (to say nothing of heat for human bodies). A windmill pumped water from a spring-fed well for indoor plumbing and a dining area was set up in the kitchen, big enough to feed the forty or so residents. By architectural standards of the time it was a very plain house and not especially attractive. It confronted the road below, a towering, muscular building with a thick neck. Yet Holman Day was impressed. "It requires not my assurance," he wrote, "to indicate that the structure complete will be one of the showiest places of Androscoggin County."

At midnight on the eve of 1897, Frank climbed to the turret and raised a twenty-five-foot white pennant to the top of the flagpole. The next morning travelers on the road below could clearly read the word VICTORY billowing in the wind. That day students fastened a permanent sign over the main door—THE TRUTH—in tall gilt letters.

The building was already full. Almost every day brought new applicants. Sandford had to "literally scare them away," he told the *Journal*. He had "no use for common, everyday, 19th century Christians," anyone "not willing to die for God." He wanted "first quality only," those anxious to get "out into the deep." Freeloaders and whiners were distinctly unwelcome.

The Sandfords had barely moved into the new apartment on the lower floor when John Sandford was born, a healthy baby boy. Thrilled, Frank called him a "prophet," attributing to his son words applied to John the Baptist:" . . . filled with the Holy Ghost even from his mother's womb." The extravagant announcement, whatever it meant, simply characterized the style of life on Beulah Hill. Everything up there, it seemed to the skeptical neighbors down below, crackled into flame like Moses' burning bush. As important as the new boiler hauled from the Lisbon Falls depot by a "dozen toiling oxen" was the barrel of apples from Aroostook that filled the dining room with "the perfume of heaven." Visiting the "Temple" that February, Day "found the cook down in the rudely finished kitchen, reading his Bible while the pea-soup simmered," singing hymns as he stirred, while "girls who came into the kitchen talked solely of brother this and brother that" and "of the victory won here and there."

Whatever anyone else thought, to the students this was the Higher Life in motion, or as it was now more apt to be put on the hilltop, life along "higher (or deeper) lines." Sandford's schooling took place not only in the classroom, but in thoughts, conversation, decisions, motivations—for, as he told the students often, upon such exactness and minuteness "might rest the fate of Kingdoms."

Caroline Holland wrote up a typical bit of this daily adventure for one issue of *Tongues of Fire*. The weekly laundry for fifty people presented a constant problem. When it became too much for the students to handle, it was sent out to a Christian "washer woman," until the day came when they had no money on hand to pay her. As the student in charge of the laundry prayed, wrote Caroline, she felt God was telling her that the wash might be sent in faith and the money would come on time. She was packing the clothes in the barrels when Mr. Sandford came into the room.

"Are you sure it is to go?" he asked her.

"Yes Sir," she said, "I think so."

"But are you *sure*?" he asked. "You know we can't go into debt. You will be responsible for the bill."

"I believe it is His will for it to go."

"But that is not it," said Mr. Sandford, sternly. "It is your responsibility to KNOW before you take such a step . . . ."

Troubled, the student bowed her head in her hands, asking for assurance. As the horses and sled drove up to the door, she "declared God had given her permission." Then, added Caroline, as the woman answered Mr. Sandford's repeated question "with a firm 'Yes Sir,' he showed her a check which he had a few moments before received which much more than covered the amount."

To the young woman involved, this was far from trickery; it was another lesson from the Holy Spirit in "adjusting" to what it meant to "live in the supernatural," with the miraculous a familiar event. In fact, if the miraculous happened *not* to occur, it behooved a person to find out why, for it might be a sign of something wrong in one's own heart. The idea was to be in a constant state of readiness for the "Holy Spirit's latest," as Sandford often put it. This meant no settling into ruts of any kind. It meant being ready to do any job, especially those you were least adept at—the jobs you had never imagined yourself doing. It meant being open to last-minute changes in the daily schedule. Every day began with a pattern. Students awoke to the roosters on neighboring farms and spent one or two hours in private devotions. After breakfast and kitchen chores, the morning Hour of Prayer was held at 9:00 (the ancient Jewish hour of sacrifice), then classes. After lunch all dispersed into various responsibilities—to household or office duties, or across the crunchy sand to Hephzibah, which now housed the print shop, or to preparation for outside meetings. But that agenda could be interrupted at any time in a call to prayer in the chapel for some special request, or to prayer anywhere, kneeling in any corner. God's work could not be crammed into a human schedule, and fussy ideas about order were not appropriate.

Formal classes also provided a sense of drama that winter, as the school studied the Old Testament patriarchs and prophets. It was not enough to know the history of Moses and Joshua. Their lives must be incorporated—re-lived in a sense. Students prayed to be given the qualities of these Biblical characters as Sandford unveiled them.

"I never saw such a man as you," a woman told him. "When we study about Enoch, you're Enoch; . . . when we study about Abraham, you're Abraham, or Moses or David, or Daniel, or any of the prophets. I never saw anything like it."

That statement was made by Eliza Leger. She and her husband had arrived from Lynn, Massachusetts, late in the fall. Moses Leger, a printer by trade, moved his entire press by a railroad freight car to Lisbon Falls, then by wagon into Hephzibah, where he took over the publication of *Tongues of Fire.* Eliza Leger, an aunt to the Gleason boys, had established a role for herself in the Boston area as a Higher Life evangelist. A dynamic person with snapping eyes, her personality had been compared with that of the prohibitionist Carrie Nation.

The Legers, though later they would find it necessary to rip themselves away, formed part of a core of mature students who joined the school during that fall and winter, their ages ranging from the early thirties to one gentleman in his mid-sixties.

Most typical was Elnora Emerson, a straight, dignified woman—a "lady"—who taught at the Perkins School for the Blind in Boston. Elnora was a sister of Eliza Leger (and an aunt to Willard and Ralph Gleason). She also had been seeking "something better" than she had yet experienced as a Christian, but the expansive reports of the Gleasons had made her nervous about Sandford. Urged to attend a tent convention the previous August, she had "asked the Lord to save me from fanaticism but see that I accepted truth."

Roused for pre-breakfast Bible studies at the convention, Elnora had listened with caution as Sandford gave a series of talks on the Holy Spirit. She had never heard anything like it, yet she had to admit that everything he said was "right in my Bible." In the course of the week, attending meeting after meeting, she "would get something new and slip out and go for a walk by the river," holding her huge hat in the breeze, then go back and "get some more." She returned to Boston, knowing she would soon come back to Durham as a student.

Almon Whittaker, an Aroostook County farmer in his late thirties, volunteered to oversee the school's gardening for a season while he attended classes, bringing his family, his horse, household goods, and farming implements. Whittaker described himself as a "rough, profane man" who had run off to the West at age twenty to lead a "wild, reckless life amid the Spaniards and cowboys of New Mexico." Back in Maine a decade later, he and his wife were converted and for a year held a successful schoolhouse ministry in the north country before hearing of Sandford's work. Noisy and hardworking, with a head of coarse, curly hair and the bowlegged stance of a cowboy, Whittaker was a man Sandford welcomed with delight.

Austin Perry, Whittaker's opposite in looks and personality, slope-shouldered, bespectacled and proper, had resigned as superintendent of a higher lines school in Kansas to join the Durham school. A man smaller than his wife, a hearty woman who looked capable of toting him off under one arm, Perry possessed a keen sense of business and enormous tact, both of which would be called for in quantity in the future.

The influx of young people to the Holy Ghost and Us School had not been hard to explain. They still thought of themselves as trainees, needing a teacher. Frank challenged them with a model of integrity and youthful exuberance that they had seen nowhere else in religious work. A. B. Simpson, learning that a young acquaintance had decided to attend Sandford's school instead of his own in Nyack, New York, remarked (with probable sincerity), "Oh, yes. I see you have his light on your face."

Older, more seasoned candidates were less apt to be drawn by such a personality. In fact, they were inclined to be suspicious. Too many strange religious leaders had peppered the land over the years, too much "wild fire." People who talked about hearing God speak actual words were best avoided. Except that in Sandford's case the words he heard came directly from the Bible (even the word "Go" was at the heart of a hundred Scriptural commands), and even the most cautious evangelicals, heirs of both antinomianism and the Enlightenment emphasis on individual discernment, believed God "spoke" to them through Scripture. It was customary to find personal messages in specific verses, often unmoored from their original context. As long as words could be found "in the Bible" they were safely applicable to contemporary circumstances, regardless of when they were written or why. In spite of this practice, a certain boldness in Sandford's ownership of the Bible raised the eyebrows of seasoned evangelicals.

Then why did they come? William Hiss, in his history of the movement, offers the familiar theory of "push" from the outside and "pull" from the inside. Like the larger evangelical world from which they came, individuals were being pushed to explore radical alternatives by desperate circumstances: immorality in government, confusion in the economy, and above all, the failure of the evangelical status quo. It was the same thwarting of ideals that Wendell White all but embodied, and the same ones that had sharpened Frank Sandford's concept of his own calling. The answer for many was to look for the most incorruptible liaison possible.

Frank Sandford was promising exactly that. But more important than his crusade, says Hiss, was the pull of Sandford himself. He "offered a sense of spiritual safety, of being on the right track with God," undeterred by the critical voices of church and society. More, it was an inside track, an authoritative one. Frank was, says Hiss, like "a prophet and a holy man," one through whom they could look to see the Person who was central to their lives, the risen Christ, the source of the most noble qualities they could imagine. While the sense of Christ's presence, the awareness of His love, the thrill of His call, came and went, glowed and dimmed for most Christians, it seemed to be a consistent part of Frank's daily existence, and he expressed it with a naturalness and enthusiasm that were enviable qualities among committed evangelicals.

My guess is that part of what they saw was the tough/tender combination that had caught the attention of the ruffians at the Raymond schoolhouse. The same boldness that raised suspicion also drew people to Sandford's side. It was the old quality of his boyhood, walking into life face on, brave and vulnerable, exposing himself fully to the risks of whatever lay in wait. He had a habit of standing in an athletic posture, his legs slightly apart, his arms down and forward of his body a little, as if ready to receive the ball. In the same manner he seemed to be looking straight into the frontiers of spiritual truth. He spoke often of "reckless faith," making it seem a kind of gallantry. Either God meant what He said, or He did not. If He did, then nothing else mattered; there was nothing to do except to be "real" with Him—live in the reality of His love and promises, giving Him your "all."

Frank often referred to the Apostle Paul's words as he faced the certainty of arrest in Jerusalem: "But none of these things move me, neither count I my life dear unto myself." Any cowardice was intolerable, and the easiest cowardice of all was the most despicable—to compromise in the face of public opinion.

"If you go on with God, you will be out of joint with all people. . . . You will be amazed. First you will be out of joint with the world, then out of joint with the professed Christian world, then out of joint with consecrated people, and then sanctified people, and then people that believe in Divine Healing, and then the Holy Ghost people you know, and THEN you will find a few other people who have gone on alone with God. 'Lord, I will take it by the wholesale,' is a good recipe for death to the natural in all flesh. . . . Can you say, 'Let it cost what it will, give me Immoveable Christianity. I am going on with God.' "

It was this paradigm which made the defection of John Douglas all the more disturbing. The last reference to John occurs in the April 1897 issue of *Tongues of Fire*. On March 31, one year from the dreary morning when they had turned the first shovelful of wet sand, Frank involved the students in an elaborate ritual of praise. First they marched to the basement of the building, where over the boiler hung the motto "God is Faithful," and over a new "engine," to be used as a source of power for the printing press, the words "Glory to God." In the midst of prayers of thanksgiving John Douglas turned on the power and as the engine roared everyone shouted the Lord's Prayer in unison. Then, to the beat of a martial hymn, the students filed up the stairs to the upper room on the seventh floor of the turret. As they waited there at the top, still singing, the old blue wheelbarrow was carried up and set down in the center of the room. Around its three sides had been painted the text, "Who hath despised the day of small things?" Each person had picked up a stone from the grounds and inscribed it with a favorite verse of Scripture. These were deposited in the wheelbarrow as a "heap of witnesses," as Jacob had done in the book of Genesis. From this point, Sandford told the school, the wheelbarrow was to be a "sermon to spectators. *Anyone unwilling to be the fool with the wheelbarrow will never be a victor in the turret,*" he said (the italics his, in *Tongues of Fire*). There around the stones they ate an evening picnic, as Jacob had done, while the electric lights of the Poland Spring house winked at them twenty miles to the west.

A few days following that festive occasion John Douglas was gone, though he continued to live on his farm at the bottom of the hill. He disappeared from the school's literature as totally as if he had stopped existing. According to a joke the students loved, even the school cat, with the temerity to chase a stray dog, knew enough to brake cold on the Douglas property line.

John's departure played into the hands of local critics, particularly Charles Mann of the *Lisbon Enterprise*. "The world may never know just what passed between John and Mr. Sandford in the dark hours of the night in a . . . secluded spot," gossiped the *Enterprise*. "It is needless to say that John got his eyes opened, and Mr. Sandford found that he was caught in his little game."

The issue was apparently ownership of the boat, for John took the boat with him, claiming that hundreds of dollars of his family's money was tied up in its purchase. He took the boat but not the hilltop. It was not legally his, but owned by an aunt, who had already deeded it to Sandford for $10 and the stipulation that it should never be resold to a Roman Catholic.

The fracas over John's defection hurt. Contributions slowed. A new deadline had been set to complete the still-unfinished rooms of the building, add a veranda and two more stories to the turret. The May *Tongues of Fire* complained that Satan had distinctly planned a campaign to deter that progress. "He has used godless editors and reporters to write up the most sensational and glaringly false statements concerning this work, statements that he knew would be copied far and near, thus poisoning the minds of the people all over the country against God's movement."

Regardless of his sense of humor, Frank had not yet learned that those who take themselves too seriously are the best candidates for someone else's wit. His editorial continued on to say that instead of defending personal interests in writing, "We simply called the Bible School together . . . and called upon God Almighty to defeat His enemies," praying for a "corresponding miracle" for "every lie that the devil can get up." The answers, he wrote, arrived in hundreds of dollars, the specific amounts of which he listed, as "Satan's bitterest attacks recoil upon his own head."

It was not a wise disclosure, whatever its motive. Frank's claims regarding money had always smelled a little sour to some of the local

Yankees, those who had learned the hard way to "pay out slowly and count the change twice." Once, back in the early tent days when someone handed him a note saying there was a wealthy man in the audience, he had cried, "This is how much I care about wealth in the audience!" and kicked his foot clear through the packing box he was using as a pulpit. Some of those who liked that gesture didn't quite believe it and lately he had been underscoring their doubts. More and more he was drawing attention to the subject of money, and not always prudently. In the January *Tongues of Fire* (1897) he had written that on the previous "June third" God had given him an ocean liner for the purpose of transporting missionaries. It was a "settled fact in the eye of faith," he said. "I was as certain of it then and am certain of it today, as I shall be when I write up another editorial, stating it is about to start on its first trip." The *Lisbon Enterprise* took glee in pointing out that the man who had been promised a steamship had not been able to get his songbooks printed. "WAITING UNTIL GOD FURNISHES THE FILTHY LUCRE" was the headline. "The wail goes up for money at every turn," wrote Charles Mann. The school's inhabitants couldn't "complete a sentence without an appeal."

Even Holman Day allowed an edge of mockery in his coverage, noting that as Sandford talked one day about being ready to die for God, "right here anytime," he was "then seated in a plushmounted chair in a room furnished as elegantly as many drawing rooms." (The room was "Ebenezer," in the front turret.) As Day "intimated" to Sandford, "he had nice comfortable quarters in which to die."

The remark stung. Carpeting and good furniture had been secured for the new building, it was true. Sandford was particularly anxious that the students who had worked so hard and faithfully and had proven that they were willing to be poor, to own nothing, should be provided with pleasant rooms, attractive wallpaper, good beds. In praying for this he had even used the word "lavishly," to Caroline Holland's confusion. Sent to Lewiston at one point to purchase carpets, she dreaded the errand. But as she departed she found a group of students waiting for her at the door singing, "In Jesus' Name we'll pay the bills." Later Caroline explained that she had had to learn that she must get "big enough in God to buy expensive things" and was thankful for a leader who knew God's mind in such matters. It was one thing to be willing to live in a cave if God required that; it was another to learn to enjoy a little luxury with peace of mind, if God should provide it.

To the thoughtful witness, Frank Sandford seemed to be simply joining the swell of the new materialism, no longer bucking the tide. It was exactly the kind of inconsistency his critics were watching for. By now the country was moving out of its economic crisis. New discoveries of gold were justifying measures which would lead to the passing of the Gold Standard Act in 1900. McKinley had taken office, and things had quieted under the roof of his steady conservatism. Strikes continued, but the Populists and Socialists had received several telling punches and tramps had all but disappeared from the landscape. Even the plight of the farmer was improving, it seemed. Seven-eighths of America's wealth was controlled by one-eighth of the population, but consumerism generally was on an unprecedented rise.

In fairness to Frank, money, always a touchy issue in the history of the church, had become even more confounding to evangelicals. Though the holiness revivals had championed the poor and condemned greed, clear principles for evaluating capitalism had not emerged. Individuals found their own resolutions, some equating God's favor with poverty and some with wealth.

Dwight Moody and other evangelical leaders had only recently begun to denounce monopolies, heeding William J. Bryan's crusades against "big business." Sandford himself had not meant to articulate a broad social statement by his earlier choice to be penniless. By eschewing human wages for himself, he was protecting his independence as a servant of God, but he had not taken a vow of poverty or renounced materialism, and there was nothing to keep God from meeting the daily needs of His children in a "lavish manner." To the public that appeared as a blatant rationalization.

If Holman Day was beginning to agree with others that Sandford was a "greater blower," it did not show in how he covered the next July Fourth celebration. Easily a thousand attended, sleeping in the tents and at farm houses and eating the free food the school provided. One woman counted "two hundred teams" passing her house in an hour, and party after party was met at the Lisbon Falls depot by a gold-and-white four-seated "gospel carriage," pulled by two white horses (Grace and Glory) in white harness, a gift from a converted horse dealer in Lynn, Massachusetts. (Painted in gold on both sides of the wagon were the words "The Everlasting Gospel," on the back "Take the Kingdom," and on the inside the one word "Israel.")

At 1:00 P.M. on July 4, 1897, exactly a year "to the minute" from the cornerstone dedication, Sandford, standing with students on top of the turret (now forty feet higher), threw the "Victory" pennant to the breeze while the crowd down on the ground burst into song.

> "On to victory, on to victory!"
> Cries our great Commander!
> "On!"
> We move at His command,
> To evangelize each land
> In loyalty, loyalty, yes, loyalty
> to "The Truth."

The building glowed in gold and white. By far and away the most startling new feature, a shining crown, eleven feet in diameter, seemed to float on wire supports above the turret. The jewelry of students, including Helen's wedding gift from Frank, a Tiffany watch on a chain, had been sold to cover the cost of the gold leaf. Gold and white were God's colors, it had been decided, since in Revelation "the white and gold seem to comprise the attire of those standing in closest relationship with God."

Of particular significance were the words which had been carved and gilded across the front of the white pulpit in the chapel—"Til SHILOH come." The meanings of "Shiloh" were multiple. The word itself meant "rest" or "peace." Historically, the city of Shiloh had been a sanctuary or "safe-place" for the Ark of the Covenant and the launching site of Israel's army under Joshua, as it went out to conquer Palestine. Some Jews thought the word indicated Messiah; Christians saw it as a reference to the first coming of Christ. One morning God whispered the word to Sandford as he awoke, and another meaning came to him with poignancy. The word first appears in the Old Testament at the end of Genesis: "The sceptre shall not depart from Judah, nor a lawgiver from between his feet, until Shiloh come: and unto him shall the gathering of the people be." Since Judah symbolized Christ, Shiloh must be the forerunner of His coming.

Sandford's original intention was to name only the building Shiloh. But it was a word that moved with pleasant ease through the lips, far more smoothly than *The Holy Ghost and Us* or *The World's Evangelization Crusade,* and it soon became the name of the movement, the one that stuck.

In the afternoon of the dedication, while the warm crowd filled the chapel and pressed onto the veranda to listen through the windows, Sandford spoke for three hours on "David and His Mighty Men." In the evening Willard Gleason, the first student, was ordained. He was now just twenty years old, and a very different person from the saturnine boy who sat on the floor of a Brunswick attic with Frank less than two years earlier. He had developed into a "strong-hearted warrior."

It was Willard who rounded out the year with a gesture of bold trust. He had been drawing increasingly large crowds to a tent that had been set up in Auburn, Lewiston's twin city. Charged with disturbing the peace and ordered to move the tent, he did—to another corner— in the process swelling the nightly attendance. In September, on his own, Willard purchased a piece of land, contracted for a building, and on Thanksgiving Day, with Sandford's help, raised pledges for the required $1,900. By Christmas the superstructure of the "Auburn Temple" was already in place.

At midnight, as the year turned to 1898, the women students began a vigil in two-hour shifts in the new room just under the crown. So began a relay of prayer day after day around the clock which would continue unbroken for the next twenty-two years.

Wendell White, on his way home from Brunswick Village in the milk wagon, had been reading Holman Day's accounts of the Durham school with watchfulness. "Careful watchfulness," he would have said. At Brunswick after his deliveries each morning he frequently dropped in on a prosperous and devout young businessman named Albert Field, who at that sleepy hour was already opening his jewelry store. The two were keeping each other up to date on Sandford's affairs. Field confessed wistfully to an interest in becoming a student himself at the school, though for a man with a business and a family it looked hardly possible. To Wendell, with growing children to feed and a farm to tend and not a moment of spare time, such an idea must have seemed absolutely laughable. But at some point he began to entertain it—let it rest in his mind for more than a fraction of a second—and perhaps it was now.

8
Remove the Covering
1898

In Shiloh's common memory, the Black Winter of 1902 has always
been referred to as the time when large-scale adversity first visited
the hilltop. But even at the opening of 1898, when all looked well,
trouble had begun to show its face in quick, white glances. Yet if Shiloh
saw those signs, it was not surprised. Trouble was what it expected.
Crisis, after all, was at the heart of its purpose. It was in training for
trouble of supernatural size. Triumph was all that mattered.

By 1898 this had already become the shaping principle of Shiloh's
story—not what happened, not reality itself, but Shiloh's interpretation
of reality, the concept of its own identity. More than anything else the
accelerating motion of that view would speed the hilltop toward the
devastating events not far ahead.

The year 1898 began in high spirits, at a wonderfully bewildering
clip. Early in January Sandford and Willard Gleason traveled by train
three hundred miles north to the village of Spragues Mills in Aroostook
County, where a small following had been begging Shiloh to come.
Northern Maine was not unlike a remote western frontier. For a fortnight,
as the two men presided in a crowded room over the general store, an
angry mob stomped up and down the stairs and hooted and jeered in
the streets below. When converts gathered in a fierce northeast storm
for baptism in the millpond, they found the same crowd waiting and
the hole they had cut in the ice the day before filled with a small
mountain of ice, brush, and debris. Workers and converts patiently
chopped out the hole once more and held a song-filled baptism to a
background of shouts and laughter.

That night a meeting of prayer around the wood stove in the store lasted until 3:00 A.M. Here, about as deep into the north country as he could go and still remain in civilization, Sandford heard God whisper, "Boston next," and then the date, "February fifth." When the families hurried away to milk their cows, the Shiloh party, with three new students, were bundled off in a double-box sled to the railroad station. Dropping Willard off at Lewiston, Sandford returned to Shiloh to report the latest mandate to a full chapel. Without hesitation the students "opened their batteries and stormed the city by way of heaven." When they rose from their knees an hour later, Willard was sitting quietly on the platform.

"Gleason, what are you here for?" Frank asked.

"I don't know," he answered, laconically, to a burst of laughter from the students.

He had simply felt an urge to put in an appearance and had hopped on the trolley to Lisbon Falls. In a matter of days he and Frank were off again, racing over the snow in a cutter, runners squealing, to catch the last train out to Boston. Neither had more than a few dollars and no idea where they would sleep when they got there, or—for that matter—exactly what was to be accomplished. But God had already arranged for their board and room. On the train they bumped into Charles Cummings, a young evangelist who had once worked with the Crusaders and whose parents operated a fine rooming house at 545 Massachusetts Avenue.

Frank would rather have faced a dozen mobs in Aroostook County than tackle Boston. He had frequented New York City and traveled around the world, but Boston was still a place of special awe to him, as it was to hill people generally. No longer the country's center of classical culture, it was still the Hub of the universe for the rural population of New England—though lately that meant the hub of all that was bad about urban living, circumstances brought about, many Protestants maintained, by the Irish Roman Catholic takeover, synonymous with "rum-power," as much a threat as Darwinism and other enemies of Christian civilization.

Actually the city was full of religion, with every shade of difference represented. The "drawing room" lecture, long a fad, involved demonstrations of mind-healing, hypnotism, and telepathy. Spiritism was no less popular, with its "manifestations"—table elevations and messages from the dead. Behind all this ferment, insisted those who held out for the "simple Gospel," lay Transcendentalism and the "old Emersonian pass of the hand." Mary Baker Eddy's Christian Science—her "gnosticism," as evangelical leader A. J. Gordon once termed it—was nothing short of "the elusive opinions of the Concord philosopher come to the surface again, muddy, defiled, yet recognizable." But to many evangelicals, Bishop Phillips Brooks's Episcopalian gentility held as much error as did Christian Science and Romanism and all the peculiar fads. Evangelicalism itself was heavily represented, in large, well-attended fortresses—prestigious Park Street Church, Tremont Temple, and A. J. Gordon's Clarendon Street Baptist, to name a few. On the edge of these a growing segment of higher lines seekers had been waiting for the coming of someone exactly like Frank Sandford.

To Frank and Willard, the city, its streets slushy with brown February snow, seemed full of "the very powers of darkness." The rush and clatter of the electrics, the grinding of scores of carriage wheels on paving stones, the cries of hawkers (lying in wait to bilk you) made Lewiston seem like a Sunday on the farm. The phrase "The Battle with the Giants" kept passing through Sandford's mind as they made their way to 545 Massachusetts Avenue, which sat in an oasis of fine homes.

Inside the five-story brownstone, an elaborate cut-glass chandelier hung from the high ceiling, lighting commodious double parlors full of grand old furniture. Mr. and Mrs. Cummings, a devout middle-aged couple, immediately gave Sandford those first-floor rooms to use in whatever way he wished. When Helen, Elnora Emerson, and Mary Guptil joined the men, they spent two days in fasting and prayer for the city, while the entire school back in Maine did the same.

On Sunday, February 13, the parlors were filled with people from the wide Boston environs, as Sandford began an eight-day convention, confident that he "had scaled the ramparts of this modern Babylon." According to one suburban newspaper, he began by declaring that the city should expect a "perfect cyclone of miracles . . . greater works than even took place in Galilee."

On the last Saturday of the convention, the Charles River (brown like the dirty snow) was the scene of a Sandford baptism, and that evening "one hundred of the choicest saints of Boston and the surrounding region, partook of the Lord's Supper, the service closing but a few moments before midnight." On Sunday the service lasted until six o'clock the following morning. The "banner of the Living God" was "successfully planted" in Boston, the "wisdom of men" made foolish. So claimed Frank in *Tongues of Fire*. Boston as a whole seemed unaware of this impact. Two of its leading newspapers failed to mention either Shiloh or Sandford from February 5 to the end of the month.

So from a wider point of view it could be said that nothing much happened in Boston, except that two days into the convention the battleship *Maine* blew up in Havana Harbor, killing 260 Americans aboard. The country responded with a burst of patriotism as emotional as it had been at the onset of the Civil War. More cautious voices were lost in the cry for retaliation. Against this clamorous background, Sandford's military metaphors rang with validity, particularly in his own ears. He was enormously excited. The possibility of war was the beginning of something intensely personal and cosmically sweeping, though it would be several months before he was able to see it whole.

For now he felt that God was directing him to make Boston the future center for "apostolic religion," but he needed a permanent building to do so. The Cummings couple, touched deeply by his ministry, offered him the entire house, closing it as a boarding place (except for those tenants who embraced the "whole Truth") though they had no idea how they would tend to their own livelihood. Sandford accepted, named the building "Elim" (oasis), and agreed to assume the mortgage. It was meant as a temporary measure. A mortgage was tantamount to a debt, something he had sworn Shiloh would never fall prey to, and Elim was too small. What he really wanted was a temple capable of seating ten thousand people, and he believed God would soon provide it. With the new work in the charge of Willard Gleason, Eliza Leger, and Mary Guptil (the two women students he presently trusted the most), he and Helen rode back to Shiloh to tell the school that "the church all of gold is shaking herself from the dust of human tradition and putting on her beautiful garments."

With Gleason's temple at Auburn nearing completion, attention now turned toward two other buildings in the planning, a "hospital" and a children's building, perhaps an orphanage. An architect had been hired to design these two houses and work was to commence that spring under a professional contractor. The cornerstone for the children's building had already been laid five hundred feet south of Shiloh proper, and in mid-March a flint cornerstone shipped from Moosehead Lake was lowered into place for the hospital, on the bluff overlooking the river.

But by now Sandford had received two more messages. One, which he revealed in May, struck the students with alarm. It was "Jerusalem Next." Sandford himself was at first uncertain as to whether he had heard "the voice of Satan or God." For one thing, the words, like

"Boston Next," did not come out of Scripture, a risky departure from the traditional expectation that God spoke through the Bible. There were other difficulties, as well. Apart from crossing the ocean while America was at war with Spain, the trip could consume enough time and money to undermine the progress of the two new buildings. But after days of consultation and prayer it was finally conceded that "the pillar of . . . fire plainly moved in the direction of that city which is to be 'above our chief joy.' "

What the students were not told was that Sandford had heard another message from God earlier in April, one he would not announce to them until months later, this one a paraphrase of Isaiah 25:7: "Remove the covering cast over the face of the earth." While he himself was puzzled by that mandate, he sensed that "Jerusalem Next" was part of it.

Leaving general administration of the school in Charles Holland's hands, with Austin Perry as bookkeeper and Helen a strong figure in the background ("as brave as the day we said good-bye to salary"), and calling on *Tongues of Fire* readers to not "fail your Creator" in providing the funds needed for the progress of the buildings in his absence ("let us make as brave a battle as Commodore Dewey did at Manila the other day"), he departed for Jerusalem in the middle of May.

As students crowded out onto the veranda to wish him goodbye, he told them: "If this is Mr. Sandford's school it might as well go down; if it is the school of the Holy Ghost it will go on in my absence as usual." Then kissing Helen and eighteen-month-old John, he murmured, "I have no wife and baby," and climbed into the Gospel wagon.

Willard Gleason climbed into that wagon too, with exactly $7.40 in his pocket. Indomitable, he had been certain for weeks that God wanted him to go to Jerusalem, perhaps to stay indefinitely, and so Frank had booked passage for him, without the faintest idea of how that would be financed. Between the two of them they owned no more than $77.

If Sandford felt disconcerted at Willard's assertiveness, he was glad enough for the company. Seated on the train from Brunswick to Boston, the two men carried on a running banter, Frank asking Willard repeatedly if he had his fare yet and Willard coolly replying, "Why no, I supposed you had it." When they boarded the Cunard Liner just days later, they had two one-way tickets to Liverpool. The money was very likely donated by a Boston follower, though the means was not made known.

Once in Liverpool the two men were embraced by a cluster of Higher Life people who were about to hold a four-day convention "on full salvation lines." Sandford was instantly invited to speak. He made a hit, drawing a crowd. By mid-June a new branch of the movement had been established in England and enough money raised to send the Americans the rest of the way to Palestine.

Many nationalities had now established communities in Jerusalem, particularly Germany and England. The Jewish population had increased by many thousand since Sandford's visit in 1891, and Zionism, though not accepted universally, was a formally recognized term, thanks to the work of Theodor Herzl and the recent World Zionist Congress in Switzerland. With the American colony as their base and a home in Bethany where they were welcomed by two Christian women (whose names, in truth, were Mary and Martha), Sandford and Willard toured the environs for two weeks. Finally, after a day and an evening of fasting and prayer in Jerusalem, Sandford was convinced that he must get into writing a subject he had been finding more and more significant throughout the past year, and which—he now understood—clarified most wonderfully why God had brought him all the way to Jerusalem. In the cool hours between midnight and the next noon he and Gleason dashed off 9,000 words in longhand.

The paper began with a direct statement of its purpose—to "explain who God's ancient people Israel really are." Israel, Sandford pointed out first, did not mean the Jews, the present-day Jews of the House of Judah, who had "forfeited God's blessing by crucifying the Messiah." Rather, Israel meant the Ten Tribes, the Lost Tribes, who had been carried into captivity by Assyria in the year 721 B.C., never to be heard from again, who were still very much in existence somewhere in the world and with whom God must yet keep His everlasting covenant.

Summarizing the promises of God to the early Patriarchs, Sandford concluded that the nation of Israel, as foretold in Scripture, could be identified now, in the present day, by four characteristics. One, it must be vast and powerful among nations; two, it must be "princely in character"; three, it must be peculiarly blessed; and four, it must be actually two nations, though "one blood," just as Joseph, in the book of Genesis, had become two tribes, Ephraim and Manasseh.

Only two modern nations on the entire globe fit that description— the United States of America and Great Britain. The evidence was undeniable. The long search was ended. "THE LOST IS FOUND!" wrote Sandford, penning great capitals on the page. England and America were the blood descendants of the Old Testament Hebrews. They *were Israel,* genetically, as well as spiritually.

What Sandford failed to acknowledge in his 9,000 words was that these conclusions were not a product of his own study. The search for the Lost Tribes had fascinated historians and Bible scholars for many centuries, and the possibility that they had wandered or been carried to western Europe, to Germany and Denmark, and thence to the British Isles as the Jutes, had long been entertained. Lately skeptics of Biblical authority had been using the riddle of the tribes as evidence of God's failure to keep His promises—or rather as evidence that the promises were a figment of human minds in the first place. In an effort to respond to that challenge with "scientifically" researched answers, certain Bible defenders had initiated extensive studies. One of these, C. A. L. Totten, a professor of military science at Yale, had been publishing exhaustively on the subject since 1891.

Classing himself with Robert Ingersoll and other free-thinkers, Totten had originally intended to use the Bible as evidence against itself. Instead, the Scriptures convinced him of their own veracity, and in a matter of a few years he produced dozens of books and pamphlets tying together a system of history, astronomy, and Biblical chronology.

Totten was not taken seriously by the larger segment of evangelicals (though they were glad enough to have him on their side) or by historical authorities. His theories proposed a tricky and convincing logic, wearing the face of scholarship, while actually grounded in presuppositions. Yet the basis for his ideas grew out of the old American identity of itself as the millennial nation, a dream right now gaining a new rush of popularity.

For a long time England and America had been helping themselves to the symbolism of Israel. Even one as unorthodox as Herman Melville had written: "We Americans are . . . the Israel of our time; we bear the ark of the liberties of the world." That analogy had often slipped over the line into the distinct sense of *being* the peculiar people, God's favorites in the world. Hadn't the Anglo-Saxon "race" proved its superiority and spiritual discernment again and again, in the German Reformation, in England's stubborn preservation of the Gospel against the threat of the Papacy, in the courage and intelligence of the American Puritans? The "grandeur" of Anglo-Israel truth would save the world for civilization, thought Totten. The recent imperialism of England and America was justified as "the sacred history and . . . chronology of the chosen people."

It was simply Manifest Destiny in one of its more sublime forms, and Frank Sandford was officially adopting it at the very moment America was becoming an empire. His night of frenzied writing occurred on July

22, 1898. On May 1, two weeks before Frank sailed to England, Commander Dewey had destroyed the entire Spanish fleet of vessels in Manila Bay. On July 1, as Frank journeyed toward Jerusalem, Roosevelt's Rough Riders dashed up San Juan Hill in Cuba. On July 17, Santiago fell. A few days earlier, the islands of Hawaii had been annexed, and in another week yet ahead, United States troops would invade Puerto Rico.

Back in America the *noblesse oblige* of Western ideals was being exalted by statesmen and churchmen in just about every combination of lofty language they could produce. Though a large number of Americans were opposing expansionism, by far the prevailing view echoed that of Protestant leader Josiah Strong, who had been asserting for years that the "Anglo-Saxon is accumulating irresistible power with which to press the die of his civilization upon the world."

Even those who deplored war were able to rationalize the takeover of the Phillipines and Puerto Rico as God's will, a "cannon" which had "torn holes in the walls of barbarism and heathenism." No one expressed this more bluntly than President McKinley, who on his knees realized that "there was nothing left for us to do but to take them all and to educate the Filipinos and uplift and . . . Christianize them, and by God's grace to do the very best we could by them. . . ."

There was an inherent disparity in all this that many evangelicals found disturbing. If American culture and government had proved to be corruptible in the past, and if the prophetic role of the church had been dissipated by the acceptance of civil religion earlier in the century, what would it mean now for the "cross to follow the flag"? In spite of the seeming inconsistency, it was much easier to separate from an apostate church than from an apostate country. The latter, in fact, was unthinkable to many, and so the questions went on being rationalized.

No one was more patriotic than Frank Sandford, and no one more hated loose ends. In understanding God's plan for the history of the world, he needed a resolution to the contradiction implied in being true both to secular America and to the Bible. Totten's proposition of an Anglo-American Israel gave him the missing piece. This contemporary Israel, like its Old Testament ancestor, was rebellious, idolatrous, stiff-necked, but still the "peculiar people," still destined to be saved. God must still use Israel as a "rod for the nations," as His "battle-ax" to "break in pieces the nations." It would be "carnal Israel," physical Israel, the Anglo-Saxon, as represented by England and America, who would "overthrow" the ungodly kingdoms of the world and help bring the Jew (Judah) back to the Holy Land, where all twelve tribes would be properly reunited.

Now God's April words, "Remove the covering," made astounding sense. The covering was the "carnal mist," the earthly perceptions that made it impossible for humanity to comprehend spiritual truth, and it was from Jerusalem that the covering would be removed. Jesus had commanded that the Gospel be preached first in Jerusalem and then in the uttermost part of the earth. He had meant exactly what He said: Jerusalem was to be the headquarters for the evangelization of the world. The prophet Hosea had written, "Then shall the children of Judah and the children of Israel be gathered together [all twelve tribes, that is], and appoint themselves one head." God was going to restore the Kingdom to Israel, and in this majestic plan for global history, Shiloh, the spiritual remnant of Anglo-Israel, was to lead the way. Shiloh was the crucial link to everything.

This, Sandford saw, was why he had always felt so at home in the Old Testament, so drawn to the glory of its rituals and images, why he so often thought of God as Jehovah, why they had been ordered to build in "the mountain at the height of Israel," the empty sand hill that would one day blossom like a rose. He was more than ever sure that the Shiloh of the Old Testament alluded "in plain language" to the Shiloh of Durham, Maine, U.S.A. Why not? If the movement had been "commissioned of God to evangelize the world," it was "worthy of being in the Scriptures." Shiloh, a little school tucked away in the farm country of the New England hills, had been part of God's plan from the beginning.

What a difference that made. It colored the whole world, colored history, and the meaning of the Bible itself. Nothing would ever be the same again.

The writing completed, Sandford left Gleason in Jerusalem to pray and headed home, stopping in Liverpool so that nine new students might join him on the trip. They were greeted at Shiloh on August 13, one day after the signing of the armistice between Spain and the United States.

To the new enrollment at the Bible school in October, Sandford made the standard of commitment unmistakable. He was feeling the burden of leadership tremendously, for every person must keep pace or the mission was lost. To stick it out at Shiloh, he warned the students (in a talk later published in *Tongues of Fire*), they must be ready to slash every natural tie—turn their backs on their families, if families should oppose obedience to God. More than ever, Shiloh students must recognize that this was the training ground of a spiritual army and they must be prepared for the "utter and unquestioning obedience of the battlefield."

Their prayers, should they prove faithful, would be "active forces in history," Sandford told them, "a more effective protection for the nation than the armies and the navies. Think of administering affairs in China, governing Russia . . . ; the man that is true on this hilltop is going to be made ruler of the Gentiles, or over the whole globe to that extent that God can trust him." The days of drudgery were all preparation for those responsibilities.

However, there was a threatening downside to this prospect. They could expect appalling consequences if they "murmured or complained," as had the followers of Moses.

"He wants you to be so true to God that there will not be the slightest pity or mercy shown to the man, woman or child in this place who is not absolutely true to God. He wants you to be so true that you will take God's part against yourself . . . against the whole Bible School, wherever there is sin. He wants you to be so real—so absolutely uncompromising in your antagonism to sin—just as real as if you were to take a sword and drive it through the bowels of your son, your wife. . . . as real as if you were to slay your father, your mother, your brother, your sister, or even yourself. . . . You are actually to *hate,* WITH A PERFECT HATRED, your father, mother, brother, sister, child, and even your own life, in so far as these are not in conformity with the word of God."

The school was dreadfully crowded that fall, in spite of the fact that some of the earlier students were now "on the Front" in various parts of Maine and New Hampshire, in Boston, in Chicago, and as far away as the state of Washington, where centers of interest were growing. The building had been designed for thirty people. Three times that many occupied it now, and new students were appearing nearly every day from various parts of the United States and Canada. To make matters more complex, married students with small children had begun to enroll. Sandford began to talk about adding on to Shiloh Proper. What he had in mind was a huge U-shaped dormitory, including an immense kitchen and dining room, and a variety of classrooms.

He announced in early October that he had gotten the message to "Commence tomorrow" on that project. There were apparently no questions this time about the origin of the words. Orders for materials went out immediately, though progress had only begun on the hospital and children's building and the funds needed for their completion had not yet come in. The Extension, as the addition was to be called, would cost in the vicinity of $50,000. The venture seemed foolhardy only by natural standards. Like a seal of God's approval, a baby girl, Esther, was born to Helen and Frank in December.

On the last morning of the year, during nine o'clock prayer, Willard Gleason slipped into the room and dropped to his knees behind the pulpit. Sandford, also on his knees, looked over and said, "Well, Brother Gleason, I suppose the people would be glad to hear from you." He was greeted by a roomful of shouts. Browner, thinner, a bit weary-eyed, he had been gone since May, had traveled 13,000 miles on four continents, had battled fever and hunger, had discovered that going to Jerusalem was "not all poetry," and would go back again in a minute—expected to do so, in fact. In his pocket was half of that original $7.40.

Even Sandford's sharpest critics were quiet at the end of this year, feeling perhaps, as Holman Day often did, a little dazed. One evening in the previous August as Day had driven his horse and rig down from the hilltop, lightning flashed "all around the black horizon . . . blue flame, torches of violet light." From the barren height of Beulah, as he described it, "the scene was weird." Turning his eyes up toward the Shiloh tower, he saw a cheerful steady "stream of mellow radiance" coming from its windows and felt comforted "that up on this bleak sand-hill in Durham there is an honest soul at prayer day and night."

Shiloh Proper, 1897, with the white chariot.

Shiloh Proper, 1898. Two Gospel tents in the foreground.

Lisbon Falls, turn of the century. Courtesy Charles Plummer.

Interior chapel, Shiloh Proper, 1897. *Lewiston Journal* sketch.

Bible School on steps of Shiloh Proper, 1898. Sandford stands at the far right, Charles Holland far left. Seated front: Ralph Gleason second left, Almon Whittaker center, George Higgons third right, Willard Gleason, second right. The Fergusons and the Perrys stand center, top row.

9
Found Perfect
1899

"As a Lion" was the motto Sandford gave his students as the new year began. Last year the movement was like a lion's whelp; this year it had matured to "rugged, lordly" strength. As they studied Israel's military victories in Deuteronomy he drew an analogy to America's victory over Spain, God's work on behalf of Anglo-Israel. But as spiritual Israel, Shiloh's real strength sprang from Christ the Lion of Judah, who would hurl "into the sea every mountain opposing His progress." If the school would take down its "little, miserable bars of half-faith," God would "take care of the enemies for 1899."

The first skirmish took place almost immediately. Roswell Harper, one of the first young students, became gravely ill with typhoid fever and was carried down to the old farmhouse for isolation and care. Prayer and anointing did no good, and his condition quickly worsened.

Alarmed that God should so turn His back, Sandford begged for insight. Given James 5:16, he hurried to the chapel where the students were praying and read the verse aloud: "Confess your faults one to another and pray for one another, that ye may be healed." The response overwhelmed him. One student after another stood up and admitted in tears to faults more profound than Sandford had suspected.

It was not that the students had been sneaking off to the pine grove for clandestine trysts. Sexual indulgence was an unthinkable sin, and overt flirtations considered bad taste, as they were in general society. Sandford had always been concerned that male-female interaction be above reproach on the hilltop, knowing the risks these close quarters presented to sincere and fresh-faced young people. Relationships might be congenial, but social outlets were restrained—no dancing or playful games—and if some students were falling in love (as some were), they conveyed this to one another most discreetly, with careful smiles and shy notes. One observer claimed that there was an "utmost unconsciousness of sex" at Shiloh, that such a thing could not live in the school's "rare atmosphere of reality." More accurately, a strong undercurrent of sexuality did prevail in Shiloh's special circumstances of soulful intimacy—spiritual bundling, it might be called, with innermost emotions shared side-by-side but not touching—but those who found themselves stimulated unduly by such feelings quickly subordinated them. Outwardly at least sexual impropriety was seldom a problem.

But residents on the hilltop were discovering what had always been sin's most alarming characteristic: you got rid of the old to make room for the new. Just when they had at last cleaned the house, swept out through the front door all the old trash, the Prince of Deception burst through the back, wearing the guise of their best intentions. What they were learning was that certain sins were possible only for those who lived on a high spiritual plane. They might even be called "holy sins," not recognizable to the ordinary Christian, and of no importance whatsoever in the eyes of society.

Now something as simple as vanity took on a complexity similar to narcissism in the world outside, while at the same moment it scorned the world's trappings and foppery. How tight to lace a corset was not an issue; there were no corsets at Shiloh—no feather boas or frizzy bangs. As for men, in the world they might occupy their minds with how they carried themselves, how they held their heads or swung their walking sticks. At Shiloh another far more insidious vanity threatened— pride in creating an aura of spirituality, which could indeed come down to personal appearance, to cultivating a certain sweetness about the mouth or smoothness in the brow, to modesty even in the knotting of a scarf or the cut of moustaches. Holiness had a "look."

Willfulness meant nothing so simple as breaking the house rules, but rather resistance to God's leading. Laziness meant cheating at bearing a burden in prayer, letting the mind wander. Fear was any pulling back that might inhibit Spirit-directed action, and doubt was giving in to the sneaky thief called reason. Covetousness in ordinary circumstances might be easily defined—desiring someone else's overcoat or wife. But to be filled with envy because God had answered someone else's prayers and not your own, or had given someone else the privilege of leading a particular soul to Christ, even conferring that honor on someone less earnest than yourself, this was far harder to scout out and identify, simply because it was integrated with the highest spiritual standards of the school—and complicated even more by the fact that it was often difficult to distinguish between Mr. Sandford's approval and God's. To compete for either was unthinkable, and to confess such an offense before the whole company took far more courage and humility than it would to confess to a drunken binge in the back alleys of Boston.

"Spiritual ambition is an awful thing when it is not in the sway and control of the Holy Ghost," Sandford told the school. "It is horrible, it is awful, and you must put your foot on the neck of such a thought when it comes into your mind, as you would a snake." This was what it meant to live without the slightest compromise. If they were to participate in a movement which bore in its daily life ultimate responsibility for the world, they must depend on the Holy Spirit to throw a spotlight on any deviation from exact righteousness. Their sins had become global in their significance.

When the period of confession was over and the chapel had fallen into a silence, broken only by a song wavering gently across the prostrate forms, Frank returned to Rossie, lying deep in his fever at the farmhouse, and prayed again for his healing. This time Rossie responded, and in a few days he was out of bed.

Healing itself was hardly new at Shiloh. Since the occasion ten years earlier when Sandford had casually accepted it as a part of Scripture not to be ignored, he had grown more certain about its necessity in a God-directed ministry. Healings had been occurring in Shiloh meetings with mild notice since 1894. Now scarcely an issue of *Tongues of Fire* lacked a healing story, performed either by physical contact at various meetings (anointing the patient and "laying on hands") or by prayer with the sick one at a distance. At least once the magazine published a list of ailments that had been cured over a period of time: pneumonia, cancer, galloping consumption, diphtheria, asthma, bad humor (referring to body fluids), catarrh, rheumatism, "sick headache," sprained wrist, blindness, measles, la grippe, "severe contusion," dropsy, heart trouble, "chronic fever," typhoid, broken eardrum, dislocated shoulder, twisted neck, scrofula bunches, mental derangement, broken bones (set and mended) and "utter exhaustion."

The same curious and touching terminology appeared in other publications, such as Mary Baker Eddy's *Journal,* and was used to describe the multitude of disorders paraded across daily newspapers in ads for patent medicines. As many as a score of these ads would be sprinkled throughout a single edition of the *Lewiston Journal,* directed toward "exhausted women," "depleted men," and "puny children." The products healed everything from fits to gonorrhea, chilblains to blood-poisoning, always in double-quick time. The "Great South American Kidney Cure" did its job in six hours. Peruna would eliminate "catarrh from a woman's pelvic organs," and Dr. Miles' Nervine restored "shattered nervous systems."

Nomenclature aside, the suffering was real, as the hawkers of patent cures knew well, and many who sought Shiloh's help were women harassed by a collection of miseries recognized as common to female hypochondriacs. They varied from the lady with "bad stomach trouble" who was "convicted" (conscience-smitten) about the use of tea and pork and became "perfectly well" on abstention, to a mill-worker in Lowell, Massachusetts, who had suffered from "cancer" for eight years, felt that a rat was gnawing at her insides, and battled a "spirit of hatred and revenge" in her heart. In each case the story indicates more than relief from physical pain. The mill-worker wrote back to Shiloh: "All this was crushing me to death when you came. . . . I did not know [God] cared for me like that. . . . Such a cleansing God gave me, soul and body." Only eighty-nine pounds at the time of her encounter with Shiloh evangelists, this patient quickly gained weight and enjoyed a "deep, untroubled peace."

Edythe MacIntyre, a girl in her late teens from Medford, Massachusetts, suffered from hallucinations and nightmares, the result of a once "congested brain." Any excitement caused intense pain and nose bleeds. "Insects" crawled all over her, and "serpents" waited in the corners of rooms to spring at her. Her head ached constantly and she could not see without thick spectacles. Ready to take her own life, she went to Shiloh workers in Boston for consultation and prayer, was quickly relieved of every complaint, and in a few weeks found she no longer needed the glasses. She remained well and became a strong Shiloh worker.

Against this tangle of obsessions and questionable diagnoses, certain other stories stood out. Some were published by local newspapers, including one report by a "well-known Brunswick gentleman," no friend to Sandfordism, but impressed, nevertheless, by the case of a three-year-old girl. The child had been determined permanently sightless by medical authorities at Bowdoin College, yet woke up from a nap suddenly able to see on the day prayer was offered for her ten miles away at "Holy Ghost Hill" in Durham. Whatever the cause of the girl's blindness in the first place, enough community members witnessed the incident to make the account a sobering one.

Even more convincing was the story of Mrs. Emma Whittemore, a wealthy friend of the poor who had founded the nationally acclaimed Door of Hope, a home for destitute women and girls on East 61st Street in New York City. While a guest speaker at Shiloh, Mrs. Whittemore described her earlier healing (under A. B. Simpson's ministry) of a spinal cord deformity. She confessed with some embarrassment that she had never been able to trust God to heal an equally troublesome malformation in her eyes, and that she found it impossible to function without strong and complex spectacles. No sooner had the words left her mouth, there at the podium in the Shiloh chapel, than it seemed to her God whispered, "Now . . . now is the time." Raising her hand to her head, she announced to the audience, "The time has come for me to remove them and I take them off in His name."

She turned and placed the glasses in Sandford's hand. Immediately the students rose from their seats and clustered around the woman to pray. Before leaving for the depot a short while later, Mrs. Whittemore was seeing as well without her glasses as she had with them on. At the depot she read a notice on the side of the train aloud to a companion and later sent Shiloh her first piece of correspondence written without the aid of spectacles.

It ought to be said that if any of the women or men helped by Sandford and his workers had at one time found their identity in physical frailty, part of the healing process seems to have been a change of mind. That, perhaps above all, the Shilohites were doing for them—giving them a sense of good health as appropriate, even essential to godliness and to proper manhood and womanhood. Healing was not a separate event but part of the transformed outlook, and self-pity must be banished along with the ailment.

But Sandford's view on healing had been taking a narrow turn. Even A. B. Simpson, thought to be on the fanatical fringes of the evangelical network, carefully allowed a possible role for medical science. Frank was going a step beyond that, prompted by his determination to obey every Scriptural directive with exactness. "God's eternal Word says, 'Is any sick? Let him call for the elders.' [James 5:14] The preachers of the land are saying, 'Call for the physicians' and are giving God's Word the lie."

Possibly he had been heeding a publication which had been arriving at Shiloh from John Alexander Dowie of the International Divine Healing

Association in Chicago. Dowie angrily condemned medical doctors and pharmacies, insisting that Satan caused all illness and disease, as if the world of microbes was a kingdom that could be controlled by a will, and lately Sandford had been saying the same thing. In contrast, the larger evangelical community often talked about sickness as "the ultimate fruit of sin," in the words of one spokesman, "the penalty of violating God's laws," a notion not entirely in conflict with the perceptions of the medical profession of the day.

Everything considered, if you were sick, you had better find out why, beyond the physical cause. God might *permit* illness as a way to discipline and instruct, but those who lived in absolute trust lived in victory over Satan's onslaughts. In another year Sandford would say that the Shiloh hospital stood for "perfection through the power of the Holy Ghost" (which meant "the utter annihilation of sin") and for "health throughout every organ of the body." That rhetoric aside, he would have scorned tackling the problem of evil in philosophical wrangling. The concrete evidence was what counted. Hadn't he with his own eyes seen people delivered from mental and physical torture when he had met Satan head-on? Just as the disciples had been directed to "lay hands on the sick, and they shall recover," they had also been told they would be given the power to cast out devils. Any Christian who hedged on that, Sandford said, was "untrue to the compassion of Christ for a suffering humanity." The *Lisbon Enterprise,* quoting this material, added puckishly, "The Ghosts hold that to cure the afflicted it is necessary to get at his Satanic majesty in the solar plexis."

Holman Day was also finding it hard to swallow this particular Shiloh tenet. Seated with Frank in Ebenezer, the comfortable study in Jerusalem Turret, he recorded a conversation on the subject.

"You people laugh when I talk about casting out demons," Sandford said, "but I tell you there are just as many demons in people as there were when Christ was on earth. Lots of people are sent to insane asylums . . . who are not crazy, but only possessed."

Then he turned to Day and said: "I shouldn't wonder if *you* had a devil."

If he said it half in jest, Day failed to indicate that. He wrote, "I had—a devil of a desire to smile, but I didn't." In a different context Day might gladly have confessed to a demon or two, but in this setting he merely gazed across the room with his best man-of-the-world expression, eyelids at half-mast. His article closed with the following paragraph:

The people living near the Bible School say that a few weeks ago the scholars cast a devil out of a man and it got into the building. They prayed and sang and shouted for half a day before they could succeed in driving the devil from the building. The devil finally departed and the school rested easy that night, and since then they have been careful where they cast their devils.

Whatever anyone thought was happening that day, one fact was undeniable—the neighborhood in Durham was finding the noise generated on the hilltop unnerving, probably in part because of an unfounded notion that prayer was supposed to be quiet. To be accurate, while Shiloh never thought it necessary to tiptoe into the presence of God, it also did a lot of quiet praying, sometimes sitting in silence for long periods at a time. Yet over the last year a style of prayer had developed which astounded the uninitiated. Rumor had it that even across the river on the Pejebscot-Topsham Road teamsters would stop their horses and listen to the distant shouts.

It was called a "Charge." The military nomenclature was no accident. A charge was a skirmish with a real enemy—Satan himself—with prayer the weapon. "God has made me able to use a sword and spear just as really as warriors on any battlefield," claimed one student. Intercessory prayer—nothing new in Christian circles—combined petition, argument, and demand, very like the style of a determined child pleading a cause before a parent. No spiritual posturing was involved in this kind of encounter—no rolled-up eyes or folded hands. It was a wrestling match. Shiloh called it "prevailing prayer" and took it very seriously. Charges were an extension of prevailing prayer. One *Lewiston Journal* reporter listened with awe to the "burning eloquence" of a "weak woman" and "prayers from unlettered men that fairly set the heart to quivering."

A visiting listener had two alternatives, to be drawn in by such power or make light of it. One critic, visiting on a Thursday when Shiloh regularly prayed six hours straight for the sick, a day which happened to be one of the hottest in the season, sat under the front steps, the only cool place in the vicinity (there were still no trees) and listened with a fascination that grew to nervousness. The meeting "rapidly increased in fervor and intensity, until there seemed to be "a hundred people talking at once." When a woman's screams rode over the babel, the gentleman began measuring with his eye the distance to the foot of the hill, wondering if he could "get there first" in the event of an attack.

Demon-casting, particularly, involved warfare with sinister physical aspects. Willard Gleason, holding the fort at Elim in Boston, discovered this one afternoon when a tortured gentleman visited him for prayer, confessing to frequent "murderous thoughts," even the impulse to take the lives of his children. Willard's prayer, rather than calming the man, seemed to incite him more. He "felt an uncontrollable impulse to do something wild," he announced. Alarmed at his manner, Willard commanded the demon to come out of him. At that, the man fell convulsively to the floor and, rolling and twisting, propelled himself from one side of the room to the other with uncanny speed. Suddenly on his feet, he caught up a rocking chair and heaved it to the opposite wall. For forty-five minutes, as Willard struggled with him, the man turned the room into a shambles.

At one point the demon spoke. Charged by Willard to depart, he asked, quite reasonably, "In your name?"

"No!" shouted Willard. "In the name of Jesus Christ of Nazareth!"

"Perhaps so, perhaps so," said the demon, in a "hesitating doubtful tone," then added, as if in further thought, "Pretty quick!"

Finally, said Willard, he felt the demon's power "weaken and give way." The man broke down and confessed to a life of "disobedience." In a while he received the Holy Ghost and went home "to have a quiet time with God," feeling much better about himself—for it was not he who had entertained those abominable thoughts, nor he who had smashed the furniture in that frightening rage. He felt sure of that, he said, because throughout the whole melee the demon kept saying, in a cool evaluation of Gleason, "He don't use the name of Jesus enough!"

Shiloh people found nothing absurd in this, not even those with impeccable grammar, and the scene Willard described in a letter to the school had no human psychological explanation. It was one more victory over "principalities and powers." If the account struck anyone as crude and clownish, that was just another way for profound evil to show its face. Like the Rossie Harper incident, it reinforced the reality of both God and the Enemy. There was the Lion of Judah, and there was that other lion, the one that "roareth about," as the Apostle Peter had warned, "seeking whom he may devour." That beast would do everything he could to destroy the movement that had been established to bring about his own final defeat.

In view of Shiloh's position on medical care, the idea of a hospital on the grounds aroused great public curiosity. What was it for? A place where the "oppressed" might "get away from the unbelief which surrounds them and have an atmosphere in which to wait for God's deliverance," wrote Helen Sandford in *Tongues of Fire.*

But Frank himself seemed to have ambivalent feelings about the hospital. He had deliberately put off completing it because he felt unready for the burden of a house full of sick people and the scorn that was sure to bring from untrusting neighbors. Digging had begun for the foundation of the Extension, and across the stretch of blowing sand the granite walls of the children's building were rising rapidly into view. Beyond it the brick shell of the hospital stood bright and promising, but with its doors and windows boarded against the weather, like a giant baby animal, eyes still shut.

Early in February, while Sandford was in Chicago, where he had gone to teach new followers, he was haunted by the thought of the empty brick shell. A sense of haste had been bearing in upon him more and more with the echo of his vow, "in my generation." Now the order "Complete it!" rang in his mind, and while praying with friends there in the middle of the country, he suddenly exclaimed out loud: "Oh God, I solemnly promise before men and angels that the building will be finished on March 17th!"

Back at Shiloh the checking account totaled out at $65. As much as $8,000 (over and above expenses for the other two buildings) would be needed for the interior of the hospital—the plaster, plumbing, elevator, and furnishings. Students once again took a deep breath and assumed the impossible.

A month of continuous haste, confusion, and high spirits followed. As many as sixty carpenters, painters, and steam fitters stumbled over each other inside the building. Charles Holland, his brown eyes calm in the midst of the worst upheaval, supervised the workers while Frank dashed about to various locations, using stable teams and electric cars, making arrangements and paying bills as fast as they came in.

Donations of all kinds arrived daily, even an express package containing $500 in small change and paper cash, and another box filled with someone's family silver, yet day after day there was only just enough. The head carpenter, though a Shiloh sympathizer, found the dependence on daily contributions too hazardous and habitually modified his plans with *if*—*if* the lumber comes on time, *if* the money comes in for the

doors—until the students teased him mercilessly and "removed" the *if*
"in the name of Jesus."

No sooner had the carpenter begun to catch on than it appeared his
doubts might be justified. One day things "looked very black," in
Sandford's account of it. He started out " 'not knowing whither I
went,' " returned late that night in a blinding snowstorm, surprised
everyone in the morning with the news that every penny had been met,
then "leaped into the team and sped away to Lewiston to finish out
the orders for furnishings . . . amounting to about 1600." He arrived
home late at night once more and the next day, faced with another bill,
was off again, in three hours sending back a jubilant note.

> Dear Shiloh: It is hard to beat
> God Almighty. Enclosed find check
> to cover today's bills. Halleluia!
> O, how I appreciate Shiloh's true-
> hearted warriors. Be of good courage.
> God cannot fail us and we cannot fail
> Him. That settles it.
>
> Yours in the saddle, and putting spurs
> to the charger. F.W. Sandford.

What he did on those forays "out" is not revealed, but the money
was not found lying in the street, and chances are it did not "run after
him," as he had once said it would. He raised it, of course, through
friends and supporters, though he insisted now, as always, that he had
no wealthy backers and that the Holy Spirit simply led him to those
whose hearts had already been touched to give to God's work.

March storms blustered in to hinder the exterior work. Prayer "held
a threatening storm when the bulletins said it would rain," read a
student's report in *Tongues of Fire,* "and then God sent a snow storm
which saved us driving the costly furniture over the frozen [and rutted
roads] the following morning, enabling us to haul it easily without
scarring, on the sleds." Materials coming by rail—pipes, radiators—lost
or delayed along the way, added another hazard, and the warriors "seized
the freight trains, side tracks and railroad officials by the coat collar."

The structure was to be dedicated, free of debt, at three o'clock on
the afternoon of March 17. With a crowd packing the chapel, contributions flowed in. But at 2:30 they were still $2,000 short. Holman
Day told the story with his usual flourishing headlines:

THIRTY SECONDS TO SPARE.
But the Heavenly Promise
Was Kept on New York Standard Time.

When the Rev. F.W. Sandford dedicated the Auburn church, the Heavenly Director came within two minutes of breaking his word, but yesterday that record was brushed aside, and today the mark stands at thirty seconds. You may think that is figuring pretty close, but you will remember that Mr. Sandford and the Lord have a thoroughly businesslike understanding, and that down in Durham they talk about these things in an everyday manner. To them, God is . . . one of the family, one who can be consulted at any time and with whom it is advisable to argue all matters at any moment.

Emptying his pockets on the altar, Frank said: "I can always dedicate a building better with my pockets empty."

"Praise the Lord!" shouted the audience.

"I have a check for a thousand," said the preacher.

"Praise the Lord."

"I have another for five hundred."

Then they sang the doxology, and the preacher exhorted them to follow his example and empty their pockets, telling them that a person never began to have anything till he had given away his last cent. The bills rustled onto the table and the silver clinked merrily. . . . Every few seconds there would be a donation of fifty or seventy-five dollars.

Jewelry and watches were donated and given a value, and in the last minute, while the audience waited in a hush, a pledge in writing was presented for the final amount.

And once more they sang the Doxology, and sang it with a force which would lead no one to suspect that they had been holding steady services for six hours and were singing on empty stomachs.

After it was over, Mr. Sandford wiped the perspiration from his brow. "Wonderful, wasn't it?" he asked. "It was the closest shave I ever had. I wasn't afraid that the Lord would break his word but I was afraid that I was going to be afraid."

I asked him where the note came from that appeared so providentially in those last thirty seconds, but he didn't care to discuss the subject.

"We never give any names." he said.

The building, named Bethesda ("House of Mercy"), was a fine one, three stories of red brick topped by a blue slate mansard roof and a glassed-in monitor, reachable by the elevator. The rooms and wards, outfitted with Brussels carpets and excellent beds and mattresses, were furnished down to the last bedpan.

Doctors would be permitted at Bethesda for diagnoses and consultation, but no medications would be provided, not so much as a headache powder or a laxative. Care would be free. Bethesda would not be "a resort for cranks," Sandford warned. Cranks would find it "the hottest place" they had ever been. Nor was it a house where cripples could come and "camp." They must "either get healed or go home."

But this was not the climax of the building project. At the end of March Sandford told the Bible School he had heard three messages: "a hundred men," "June 20," and "Consummation August 18." Decoding this together, they decided God meant them to dedicate the gigantic Extension on August 18, that He wanted it half done by June 20, and that it would take a hundred workers. With hardly a week's rest, the school began its biggest Drive of all.

Half of the building, including the massive David's Tower, was finished on schedule by June 20. Pulling up the dusty driveway not long after, Holman Day was startled to find the hilltop in dead silence and the customary air of hearty cheer replaced by melancholy. The work force had all been laid off.

"For the last three weeks, we truly have not had enough money to buy grain for the horses," Frank told him. He admitted with tears in his eyes to being "blue," but not discouraged. "God is mysterious with me many times. But I ask to be taken into His confidence only so far as he is willing that I should be."

Sending the students away, Sandford wrestled the old blue wheelbarrow down from the front turret, and donning his red fez, began digging by himself for the foundation of the second half of the Extension.

How far he got is not important. In a matter of days the Holy Spirit said, "Order the lumber sawed." So Sandford paid a visit to the Lawrence Brothers, owners of a large saw mill in South Gardiner, told them he needed 250,000 board feet cut from the Aroostook stock, and that it would mean sawing for Shiloh day and night for the next two weeks. He would pay them $12 a thousand board feet, as he had been doing, and though quite honestly he had no funds at the present, and no idea where the money would come from, he would guarantee them immediate payment on receiving each bill.

"I can get $16.00 for 'every stick' I send to Boston, and you expect me to turn the whole operation over to you for $12.00 a thousand?" asked Charles Lawrence.

"Yessir," said Frank.

When the students were recalled, they arrived as lumber by the carload pulled into the Lisbon Falls station and was dragged to Shiloh by teams of six horses. Now friends were invited for a "working vacation" on the hill, bringing their tools. Crews worked in shifts day and night without a break Reporters, some from faraway cities, crunched about on the sand between the buildings, doing their best to get interviews.

The Lawrence Brothers were duly paid, and on the afternoon of August 18 (now called Armageddon Day, honoring the occasion of Sandford's vision at Old Orchard) the building was ready for dedication. William Hiss describes it as a "hybrid of a Maine resort hotel and a vision of the New Jerusalem." Connected to Shiloh Proper by forty-foot-high wrought-iron gates, the building measured forty feet wide by six hundred feet long, enclosing a courtyard. The three stories of Shiloh Proper in the front were paralleled by five stories at the back, to accommodate the slope of the ground. "David's Tower" at the rear center soared eight stories high, while the two turrets at the front corners, named "Ephraim" and "Manasseh" (England and America), were five stories each. Twelve glassed-in monitors around the roof symbolized each tribe of Israel.

Inside were suites planned for five hundred students, a large central kitchen and dining room at the rear, various shops and work rooms in the ground-floor tunnel, and a large upper-floor auditorium called the Armory, decorated by wooden facsimiles of shields and bucklers.

By now Durham was getting used to building drives and celebrations. But this occasion beat them all. Wagons by the score parked on the grassy plain below the hill, where as many horses grazed, and the hill itself became a waving mass of humanity. It did seem like a resort, with guests strolling the lower veranda, matrons in flowered hats fanning themselves in rockers, and children in sailor garb playing in the sand. As always, tables of food, set up in the grove, fed the crowd free of charge—a generosity that Holman Day said amazed the "worldly" as much as any other miracle at Shiloh. Day found Sandford serene and refreshed, though he had been up all night and had been preaching lengthy sermons every day of the convention on the subject of Armageddon. The building was not to be dedicated that afternoon until every penny to pay for it had come in, but even so, Frank said to Day, "I feel so entirely easy and unconcerned that I am going to get into my team and ride over to the Falls and have my hair cut."

Day followed him a little later, and found Frank still in the chair, convulsed with silent laughter under the sheet, while the barber chattered on, unaware of his customer's identity. "Well, that Sandford may be a crank on religion, and he does some curious things, but I tell you, mister, he's nobody's dam fool."

At three o'clock the bell rang and Frank, shaved, trimmed, and immaculate, stood before the crowd for one more race against time.

The next day the *New York Times* chose to make it a front-page story: "Strange Scenes at Shiloh. Large Amounts of Money Received from Mysterious Sources." An early afternoon telegram had promised half of the $20,000 needed. Placing on a marble-topped table a single penny donated by an elderly woman who had come on foot all the way from the depot, Sandford asked God to increase it—to "work wonders with it in His own way." By dusk the second half of the $20,000 expenditure had been paid with cash and jewelry, and silver spoons. As they were brought forward, valuables were appraised for their value by Albert Field, Wendell White's Brunswick friend, who had now sold his jewelry business and moved his family to Shiloh.

At sunset another elderly woman walked forward with a bankbook that more than covered the $64 yet due, and Sandford shouted: "Praise God! The mountain has been rolled into the sea!"

Four flags shot up their poles. The "Victory" flag waved from atop Jerusalem turret, the Stars and Stripes from Manasseh turret, the royal war standard of St. George from Ephraim (the British commercial flag would not do), and from David's Tower a banner representing Israel: sewn against a background of deep blue, a large white star signified Christ, twelve smaller stars the twelve tribes, and a sprinkling of smaller ones the scattered Gentiles who were yet to be saved. The stars had been cut from Helen Sandford's white silk wedding dress.

As the flags were raised, the crowd stood in silence, looking upward. Then led by the bright notes of a cornet, a choir of students, perched on an open platform under the golden crown, burst into the refrain of "We Will Crown Him." While the crowd slowly began to disperse, the cornet played on alone, its sound following departing visitors far down the road to the Lisbon Falls depot.

It was the kind of success story any good American could love. Now only the children's building waited completion.

10

Waking the Dead
1899

Olive Mills, at age forty-five, was one of Shiloh's more seasoned students. A former teacher for the New England Evangelistic Association, which sent missionaries into difficult unchurched areas, she had been trained in hardship long before joining Shiloh. Frank often referred to her fondly as a prophetess. She was particularly loved at the school—a tiny, frail-looking woman, less than five feet tall, with large dark eyes and a demonstrative, open-hearted nature.

Along with everyone else she had worked hard on the Extension, so was not surprised, about a week prior to the deadline, to feel quite overcome by weariness. She had not expected to maintain the vigor of the younger workers; in fact, she supposed she was coming down with a cold. Not until a few days later, when a deep and unusual ache settled into the back of her neck, did she feel concern. It was a symptom she recognized from a bout years before with cerebro-spinal meningitis.

The pain increased quickly, becoming almost more than she could bear. On the evening of August 18, as activities came to a close, Sandford was called to pray for her. Though he had planned to leave immediately for England, he decided to postpone the trip until she showed improvement.

Yet Olive remained sick. No cleaning-out time—no period of confession—was called to address her affliction. Her illness seemed qualitatively different from Rossie Harper's. It was as if the attacks of Satan had entered a new stage, one more sinister than anything yet encountered. Meningitis was deadly. Patients seldom recovered from it, regardless of the treatment. Sure enough, one night Sandford was roused from sleep and told that Olive was dead.

He quickly awakened two other ministers, one of them Ralph Gleason. The three climbed the stairs to Olive's room and, entering, found it full of "the sense of death." The woman lay lifeless. Her lower jaw had dropped. Her eyes were set—glassy and staring. She had ceased to breathe and showed no trace of a pulse.

Kneeling by the bed with his hands on her head, Sandford poured out prayer for her life. Nothing changed. In desperation the three men raised their voices together. Still Olive remained mordant. By all perceivable signs she was truly gone. At last, unable to give her up, Frank grasped her head and summoned her in a shout: "Olive Mills! Come back! In the name of Jesus of Nazareth, come back!"

Instantly, behind him, Ralph Gleason grabbed his own head, called out, "The blood! The blood of Christ!" and fell to the floor in a faint. Whirling around, Sandford roared at the demon to depart. Ralph sprang to his feet, unharmed, and at the same time Olive Mills opened her eyes. In a few hours she was up and dressed. Two days after the adventure, Sandford told Holman Day that things so wonderful had been happening at Shiloh that he could not yet speak of them to the world.

It was a peculiar time to make such a statement, as it turned out. Day had appeared unexpectedly that morning during chapel, carrying a copy of charges brought against Frank by a Rev. and Mrs. Appleby of Salem, Massachusetts. Shiloh had been entirely unaware of this, though the Applebys had been busy for a week contacting the newspapers. Only the day before the *New York Times* had carried a front page story, misspelling Frank's name.

HOLY GHOST CAMP OUTRAGE
Weak Woman Says She Was Beaten by Sanford's Men

The item went on to say it was "probable" that "Sanford" and Willard Gleason would be arrested in a matter of days. Mrs. Sarah Appleby, wife of a Methodist clergyman, who had come to Shiloh to the convention the week before, claimed that she had been "brutally attacked," thrown out of the "Temple of Truth," and her "trunk containing all her wearing apparel thrown from a third-story window."

As Mrs. Appleby explained it, she had been humiliated in the chapel because she knelt at a chair instead of lying with her face on the floor during prayer, and that later when she left to go to her room (at Bethesda, where some visitors were housed), Willard Gleason followed her and with a "murderous look" on his face, struck her on the back with his Bible and shouted, "Get out of here, you devil!" When she tried to go, claimed Mrs. Appleby, "Mr. Sanford arrived on the scene, and, grabbing me around the waist, he dragged me to the stairway and threatened to throw me down stairs." Then, as she attempted to pack her things, "three big men" stood over her and called her "vile names." She had been "constantly growing weaker" since arriving home, because an old spinal injury, from which she had recovered "only eleven years ago," had been renewed. Mr. Appleby had "engaged counsel" and planned to see the governor.

Sandford's version of the incident to the *Journal* (printed next to the story of Admiral Dewey's "million dollar welcome back from the Fillipines") asserted that Mrs. Appleby had grossly exaggerated the event. He was not at all amazed, he told Day, that people went away to tell stories. Shiloh discipline was demanding, and it was "slow work, searching into a man's heart and leading him to adjust himself to God entirely. Many there are who do not come through the ordeal." He admitted that it "is only human nature to cry out against the man who shows you that you are wrong," but reasoning and arguing did no good at Shiloh. "It is obey the rules and tactics in the Great War Book or get out, and cease to be a stumbling block to those who are resolved to follow and obey."

Fearing accusations of charlatanry, he said not a word to Day about Olive Mills, though he made it a point to observe that someday somebody would die at Shiloh, and when it happened the public would ride it for all it was worth. To date, there had been no deaths on the hilltop, other than Helen's mother, who had died of a stroke during a visit.

Nothing came of the Appleby affair, but its threat still hung in the air a week later when someone on the sidewalk of Lisbon Falls handed Frank an ad for a publication just off the *Lisbon Enterprise* press. SANDFORDISM EXPOSED, read the title page, A WARNING AND PROTEST, by Rev. C. S. Weiss, "Who was on the inside, and others who are conversant with the evil of this Modern Abomination." The cover promised to relate "some of the delusions" by which Sandfordism "has grown—Showing the temporal and eternal injury it does its victims—Describing the strange fanaticism of its Author and Head, and GIVING THE SECRET OF HIS POWER."

C. S. Weiss, a young Methodist clergyman, had lived at Shiloh during part of August, working as a volunteer on the Extension. He had not been on the hilltop many days before concluding that Shiloh was the "outcome of a diseased mind" and that its students were being filled with "abominable folly and nonsense." When he made the mistake of voicing his opinions too openly, he was, as he put it, "called into the private office of the owner of the plantation and informed gently that they could survive in my absence." He had already begun a written record of his observations. Leaving, he took his treatise directly to Charles Mann at the *Enterprise*. Mann, glad enough to print it, included a publisher's preface with a photo of himself and filled the back of the book with reprints of his own articles about Shiloh.

Weiss's evaluation of Shiloh was not a weighty one, but it carried the clout of someone who had been a participant, and it voiced what many outsiders had been suspecting all along. Sandford's big "secret" was fear. By the "most awful anathemas, maledictions and threatenings," wrote Weiss, Sandford actually frightened those under his influence "to give their last cent." Weiss did not believe Sandford's motive was to "amass great wealth." Rather, he was a man "so deluded by his own notions of spiritual authority AS TO BE CLEARLY INSANE."

A person was not permitted to think for himself at Shiloh, Weiss continued. Sandford's suppression of "reasonings" forbade objectivity on the part of the "poor, ignorant, narrow-minded class" who followed him, some of whom had not enough money left to buy a toothbrush— and, noted Weiss, "many of the girls were much in need of toothbrushes when I was there."

Nor was Sandford the miracle worker he claimed to be. Huge, elaborate buildings he might erect, but he was not able to solve the problem of the water supply. In the last days God might indeed bring the 144,000 to Shiloh from the ends of the earth, but "the water is very apt to fail, as it did during the last convention."

Finally, Weiss took rather undue pride in managing to get back the $7.00 he had donated at his arrival. Ordinarily, he said with glee, Sandford would never return a cent of what had been given him, but "if you strike him under the 'Emersonian Environments' you may get your money again, if it is not much more than Seven Dollars."

Sandford had already dismissed Weiss as an arrogant trimmer, but like the Appleby case, which drew national attention, Weiss's fulminations reflected the hostility gathering in the world outside the hill. Bad press catches on quickly. In spite of that, thrilled by Olive's restoration, Frank felt jubilant. He left for England at last at the end of August, with no idea that even worse difficulties waited on the other side of the water.

The previous June, three women had been chosen to go to Liverpool to continue the work begun there the year before—two original students, Mary Guptil and Margaret Main, and the evangelist from Lynn, Massachusetts, Eliza Leger. Mary was now in her mid-twenties, Margaret eighteen, and Eliza in her late thirties, slightly older than Frank himself. The three had not found things easy in Liverpool in these ten months. Frank had brought back to Shiloh a year before the most enthusiastic respondents, and the women had found it necessary to start from scratch with their teaching. Their letters had reported great difficulty in rallying Christians who stood for the "whole Bible"—to find them at all—and wherever they spoke, "the truth caused a division."

They had taken their lodgings in a boarding house in Charlton-cum-Hardy owned by relatives of a Shiloh student. The ladies who ran the place were famed for their hospitality. The house welcomed returned missionaries and others who needed temporary homes. It was, in fact, a decidedly ecumenical mix, and while the three Shiloh evangelists at first held themselves somewhat apart, Eliza Leger felt drawn to the warm and open ambience. Margaret, too, made friendships. Mary Guptil, by nature more reserved, sensed in the liaison a dangerous compromise for a movement that as "new wine" had been called to "new bottles," and wrote Sandford of her confusion. It was Mary's letters that had drawn him to England in the first place.

Arriving, he found himself nose to nose with the question of separation, always a sticky problem for "come-outer" religious groups with a purifying mission. How much "fellowship" was it possible to enjoy with any Christians, however genuine, who had not been called to the keen air of the Shiloh movement? When did such mixing begin to lower the standards and cloud the vision? It was one thing to *minister* to other Christians and another to enter relationships which implied a spiritual union.

The risk seemed monumental to Sandford. When Eliza Leger begged him to come to their residence and meet the people she had learned to love, he refused, and instead asked the three women to move from Charlton-cum-Hardy to Liverpool. Mary and Margaret began to pack without question. Eliza turned him down icily, offended at his unwillingness to trust her enough to at least come and "see." A slender woman with a lift of the chin that suggested breeding and self-confidence, she had learned in her years as an evangelist how to convey a point. She had lost confidence in her leader's judgment, and she made that painfully clear.

Considered on the most obvious level, the moment came down to a request and a refusal. He had asked her to move. Eliza, a free agent, had said no. She had a right to that privilege. She had the right to cut herself off from him entirely, if she wished. But it must have occurred to Sandford that if she did so, she would not just disappear. She would find her way back to America and Durham and her husband. Her word was valued at the school. What would she say when she returned? Even if she remained silent, what would it suggest for her to return alone? Sandford could absorb the insult to himself, but to what extent ought he to protect Shiloh from the damage that might result, both in America and here in Liverpool?

Yet apart from that, another dimension to the matter filled him with panic. If Eliza was right—if she had valid reason to doubt his authority as the instrument for conveying God's will, if she instead of him was realizing God's mind in a matter that seemed unquestionably plain to Frank—then everything was in jeopardy. The possibility that he had been wrong again and again hung like a thunderhead about to open its destruction on the entire movement.

To make matters worse, right at this time letters from home brought devastating information. An alarmingly large block of students, some of the most devout and loyal, had left the school, disillusioned by a huge debt which had been disclosed and for which there were no funds. Apparently, in spite of the claims that the $20,000 bill for work on the Extension had been covered, something had gone wrong with the first half of that amount, the portion that had been guaranteed by the mysterious telegram on August 18. Certain workmen had not yet been paid a total of over $15,000, though they had been due for payment immediately. An attachment on the hilltop property by two contractors had been served by a sheriff shortly after Sandford left for Liverpool.

The awful news increased the darkness of his own questions about the dimensions of his leadership. In the depths of that quandary Sandford felt "stripped and bare, hated by the world," as he wrote to Shiloh afterwards, "the laughing stock of hell." He became physically ill. An eight-day convention in Liverpool had been planned. In spite of his fever and weakness he was determined to preach. "Out of the very blackness of hell . . . I rose from that lounge . . . and hurled the truth for about seven hours," he continued in his letter. He fasted and prayed all the next day. "God has been doing the rest," he wrote, "driving all hell in glorious onslaught."

What happened in the course of the next week is evasively subtle. Frank himself later considered it a period of terrible extremity, a watershed of ultimate significance. A watershed it was, most certainly, but one that could be seen two ways. Two possibilities edged so closely together that we can think of them as a double camera image of the same subject, with figures and scenery overlapping—one, but not one.

The questions at stake for Sandford were these: Should he, or should he not, as the spokesman of God's purposes, expect to be obeyed, instantly and without question? And ought he to expect loyalty and trust, even in the face of evidence that seemed to cast doubt on his reliability?

If the answers turned out to be negative, what would happen to Shiloh? Others in his shoes might have been able to envision a future for the movement that exactly fulfilled its original purpose, the evangelization of the world and the restoration of God's Kingdom on earth, without the necessity of unquestioning obedience to a single human being. Sandford saw that as disaster. Though he had been training warriors who could be Gideons in their own right, though he believed that the Holy Spirit could empower the humblest and most ordinary in his following, if the perceptions of the movement and his personal role were mistaken, if he had *not* been chosen for that role of leadership, there would be no Shiloh, for there would be no God-given authority. It was the old dilemma of the antinomian.

On the night of September 24, in crowded Selbourne Hall in Liverpool, Sandford stood to preach in "billows of anguish," fearing that God himself had turned away his face. His text was Psalm 118:27, "Bind the sacrifice with cords, even to the horns of the altar." As he spoke he suddenly saw himself as a lamb—one as helpless as the hundreds whose feet he had helped to bind back on the farm in Bowdoinham— tied to the altar, "an inert mass utterly unable to extricate myself from the answer to my own prayers. . . ." That lamb was bound "to entire conformity to the will of God, the Word of God, and the providences of God." His vow to obey at any cost had been drawn to the fullest demonstration. It was settled; there was no escape, no release, no running away, even though he knew with a dreadful stab of certainty that what he had suspected all along was true—his martyrdom was to be the consequence. His will and God's were in absolute unity and he himself was nothing, his future destiny of no personal importance.

But there were two ways to be nothing, and therein lies the double image, the two outlines only a hair apart. Another person than Frank Sandford might understand the "letting go" as a breakthrough into a fine broad plain, a great release, the willingness to be unimportant in the scheme of things by customary standards, *without* specific authority, *without* autonomy or control, willing to be led to another model for the work, and to trust the Almighty to fulfill His own purposes through other people and other means.

But this was not the nothingness Frank saw. "I knew it was done," he said in his description of the experience. "I knew my prayer had prevailed and that it was utterly impossible for the devil to keep that prayer from being answered." At that moment God said, "Dance!" Behind the altar Frank "sobbed and shook" with the "most wonderful joy" he had ever felt. He had been affirmed and confirmed for all time as the agent of God's ultimate purposes. He who had now burned behind him all possible bridges to self-indulgence and was willing to go all the way to hell if that was where God led him—could and must require the same abandonment of others. The swamp of uncertainty was gone forever. From this point on he must assume that when he was "in the spirit" his words and decisions were synonymous with God's. The lines of the double image separate, or rather one disappears from the screen entirely and forever. From now on "nothing" meant "everything."

No one has ever explained what happened to the gathered body of people Sandford had been addressing in the hall, but that night he and Eliza talked until almost dawn, and "finally agreed that while as a man [as a human, that is] he did not deserve any special confidence, she could have confidence in the Holy Spirit to control him." In other words, if she trusted God, she could trust Him to do His work in her leader. The basis of their confidence, hers and Sandford's, was the shed blood of Jesus that made them "perfect in every good work to do His will." They followed the truce by cooperating in a month of meetings in Scotland.

Two significant questions appear not to have been asked. Was Sandford expected to have confidence in Eliza when *she* was in the Spirit? If so, what if her leadings differed from his? If Eliza entertained those questions, she yielded to an odd logic in finding their answer: She must indeed be "controlled" by the Spirit just as much as Sandford, but the evidence of that would be her recognition of his special role as God's agent. Therefore, though he would, as always, carefully consider her insights, ultimately she must accept his authority. She conceded, and both of them thought this was the end of the matter. It was not.

Sandford returned to Shiloh alone in November. On the day of his arrival he chose three others to hurry back to England, including Olive

Mills. Olive, who had recognized her leader's authority even in death, was no Eliza. She was carrying lighted kerosene lamps in the hall of Shiloh Proper, hanging them in their places for the night, when Sandford found her and called her aside for prayer. Laying his hands on her head and naming her a "light-bearer," he told her she must pack quickly. She agreed without a second's hesitation.

Sandford had always loved aggressive people, but what a relief Olive's instant acquiescence must have been just now. In fact, he had already been shown the magnitude her obedient spirit bore to his own future, and he would soon make that public.

Sandford's ecstasy lingered on for the remainder of the year. It seemed to him that his "spirit stood on eternity-swept heights," the past, present, and future laid out before him. He was conscious of a fellowship "with Moses, Elijah and Melchisedek, and such men as had known God face-to-face." The commission to "Remove the covering cast over the face of the earth" lost its formidable onus and appeared to him "as no more than when a father asks his son for some trivial service."

By Christmas nearly all of the students who had departed in disgust had returned. The debt which had been the focus of their defection had been accounted for, the failure laid at the feet of those who had made pledges and failed to keep their promises.

The year ended with a ten-day convention. It was not the turn of the century, not for another year. The world in general had decided that after much debate. It mattered very little at Shiloh, where significant beginnings and endings had become a regular event. Though the students had been sent forth as lions twelve months earlier, now they should expect to be "lambs among wolves," Sandford told them.

He made the announcement with his usual sense of drama, illustrating it with three large oil paintings, still incomplete. George Ferguson and his wife had joined Shiloh in the previous summer when a portion of the Chicago followers moved east. In their late thirties, the Fergusons had studied art abroad and taught in the Midwest. The paintings they were executing at Sandford's request were of a lone sheep on a mountainside, a flock with their eyes lifted to the shepherd, and one (titled *The Basis of Our Confidence*) of a slain lamb on a stone altar.

The secret Sandford had learned in the last year, he told the students, was that it was far better to be a lamb than a lion: "The strongest character is the one who can suffer the most." They must not "strike back." They were to "expect snarls, cuffs, kicks, hatred." Real religion had always been hated, he said, "and you are just as liable to be killed if you are true to God as ever a Christian was." Their ability to suffer was "the exact measure of their power."

There was nothing passive about this power. "Go, I send you forth as lambs," he said at midnight, and as the words left his mouth he realized with his old boyish delight that this was the same "Go" he had heard and preached on seven years earlier in Great Falls, New Hampshire. Within days, seventy students were sent out in pairs, as Jesus had sent the disciples, to take the whole state of Maine.

The Durham Medicine Man on his way to Shiloh one dark night.

From *Lisbon Enterprise*

Courtyard of Extension, 1899. Hollands and Sandfords and the flag of the Twelve Tribes.

Crowd gathered at 1899 convention. Sandford stands right.

Frank Sandford and the wheelbarrow, 1899.

Interior chapel, Shiloh Proper, after 1899. Chart on the wall is similar to one at Northfield 1887.

Shiloh Proper with Gates of Praise.

Duplicate of Northfield chart of proportionate population, circa 1886. The white squares indicate Protestant Christians. From *Prophetic Studies of the International Prophetic Conference* (Chicago, November, 1886).

11

The White Horse
1900

The winter of 1900 was a fierce one. Local newspapers gave themselves over to winter storm gossip—the knots of gale winds, the depths of drifts, the number of moose and deer swept off the Boston and Maine tracks, frostbitten hands and feet, sleigh and sled accidents. In January an early thaw flooded the ice fields on the rivers, which quickly froze again in a sleek surface. "Razooing" became the craze, racing on horse-drawn runners across a mile of that clear ice, "every kind of hitch out," reported the *Journal,* "from the pung of the job-team owner to the pacing sleighs of the high-bloods, going like all possessed." In February the blizzards piled in, one "howler" after another. The northern part of the state was snowbound for weeks.

At Shiloh, seventy unabashed students braved the elements in every direction, wherever they felt God was leading them, mostly on foot, if not to prearranged meetings then to wherever they found an audience of one or more listeners. Stories of God's provision and deliverance (from almost certain death by freezing, in several cases) were posted back to Shiloh and read aloud around the stove in the chapel.

Sandford insisted that the women be given money and their whereabouts monitored, but two of them exerted independence and slipped off unnoticed. By accepting rides and hospitality as they were offered, they managed to elude the two men Shiloh sent after them. A gentleman in a sleigh discovered them struggling through deep drifts, their long skirts crusted with snow, headed for a railroad station eight miles away.

"What, going to walk?" he asked, astounded.

"God will help us along if that is His plan," they replied.

"What's the matter with me helping you?" he asked. "Get in here and we'll see what can be done."

He was told about Christ all the way to the station, where he bought them tickets and waited with them three more hours for the delayed train. By the time the story was told back at Shiloh, the presumption of the young women had transformed itself into Spirit-led boldness.

While the students were gone, Sandford wrote a book. Working day and night in Ebenezer, with three trusted women as assistants, he put his autobiography together with ease. In two months it was being printed in *Tongues of Fire,* and soon after appeared in book form as *Seven Years with God.* It was actually a public declaration. The seven years had begun in 1893 on the banks of the Hudson with Frank's "impetuous" quest for apostleship and the power to perform "signs, wonders and mighty deeds." At that time, he wrote, God had rejected him for lack of patience. It was as if the Holy Spirit had said, " 'Young man, when you can endure anything that comes and enjoy your suffering, when you can have your will crossed at every point and turn . . . , then we will talk to you about signs, wonders and mighty deeds.' " God had said "no more" about the matter "until these seven years had nearly passed."

Shortly after "the horror of that awful blackness" in Liverpool, when Frank had "bound himself to the altar" and "entire conformity to God's will," a letter had arrived from Olive Mills in America, "giving the particulars concerning her restoration to life."

She had known she was dying, she said. She was aware even of her jaw dropping, of losing her powers. Afraid for only a moment, she found herself filled with a sense of peace, and the dark valley she appeared to be in became a "passage way with light at the farther end." Her spirit raced for the light, but was stopped at the opening by the word PREACH in large letters. She "faltered," she said, but the scent of heaven was real, like the "fragrance of grapes." It was then that she heard "the voice of the man of God as he gave the command," and though she did not want to return to her body, which seemed to be no more than a "dirty, cast-off garment," she did so—because she had learned "to obey that voice."

It was then, Sandford wrote, that "the meaning of these seven years rolled out" before him. "I saw that the long years of suffering had introduced 'all patience' into my soul, power to suffer so supernatural, that of my own free will I had chosen to bind myself to that which I well knew would finally result in a martyr's death." The indisputable sign of God's approval, sought seven years before, had been given. The "mighty miracle" of Olive's resurrection "was His seal of my apostleship."

The credit for it all, Sandford concluded in a note of rapture, must go to the Holy Spirit. "My Companion,—Ah! the glory is absolutely His."

More immediately practical matters were being administered as well this winter. On the advice of an attorney, Sandford turned over all financial business to "seven men of honest report," Charles Holland and Austin Perry among them. It was past time for such a measure. When Shiloh talked money now, it was always big money, at least by the standards of the day and place. Charles Holland estimated a need of $75,000 to wrap up the children's building and complete the interior of the Extension. Annual expenses just to eat and produce the magazine were requiring roughly $20,000.

By now the town of Durham had seen fit to levy a tax on the residential part of the hilltop structures, though the property was described on the books of the Androscoggin County registry of deeds as belonging to "God Almighty," with Frank W. Sandford as "steward." Shiloh had added considerably to the taxable polls and some of its members had become residents in the town. Durham was concerned about two possibilities: a Shiloh-controlled town meeting, and—in the event of bankruptcy—scores of unemployed living on town charity.

Those anxieties might have grown to downright alarm if enough of Durham's residents had taken seriously Sandford's vision of world-sweeping evangelization, with Shiloh as the educational center for that endeavor. Boston was now being called the general American headquarters, Liverpool the headquarters for all Anglo-Israel (where "today Queen Victoria is sitting upon the throne of the Prince of the House of David"), while Jerusalem was soon to be "the outpost, the sentry box where we shall await the coming of the Lord."

Groups of followers were springing up in Canada and other American states faster than Shiloh could supply them with workers. For several years interest had been stirring in faraway Tacoma, Washington. Early in the spring of 1900, the Rev. Nathan Harding Harriman, leader of the Ecclesia Mission in that city, invited Shiloh to hold a convention on the Pacific coast. At the end of April, God said "Go West," and Sandford, accompanied by six workers crossed the country with unbounded optimism, headed for the kind of trouble that never goes away.

Nathan Harriman was an excellent example of higher lines holiness leadership. A graduate of both Harvard College and Bangor Theological

Seminary, an articulate and courtly gentleman, he had served as an army chaplain and as pastor of several large churches, Baptist and Congregational. When he insisted on preaching the "deeper truths" (healing, sanctification, separation from denominations) to his church in Tacoma, the congregation dismissed him. He left, taking forty people with him, opened the Ecclesia Mission, and ever since had been looking for ways to expand the ministry. More than anything else he wanted a training school for his followers. He felt a "premonition," he had written Sandford, that Shiloh was to be used of God to help in reaching that goal.

After a stop in Winnipeg, which sent twelve new students back to Shiloh immediately, the Maine party reached Tacoma, where the meetings began, with Sandford as the main speaker. In a matter of days, houses were put up for sale, job resignations were tendered, and personal goods crated, as Harriman and his family and two dozen other people committed themselves to Shiloh.

Among these was Harriman's seventeen-year-old son Joseph, who had made a wrenching independent decision. A principal of a small grade school at Fern Hill, a suburb of Tacoma, Joseph had expected to enroll at Harvard in the fall. In his own words, he had already started "on the dangerous road to cynicism" when Frank arrived. Throughout his teens he had been exposed to a "great number" of speakers and teachers at his father's Mission, "all claiming to be Spirit-led, and no two teaching the same thing." He had found it sickening. Sandford was different. Listening to him preach on the first night of the convention, Joseph had felt he was "the first utterly genuine man" he had ever heard. "Something in me made me know that I could safely follow that man." After an intense discussion with Sandford which lasted until dawn, Joseph gave the Holy Spirit control over his life. Even before his father had made up his mind to join Shiloh, Joseph was fully committed, his Harvard plans cancelled forever.

Joseph and his father were much alike. Nathan Harriman wore an air of personal sureness, which Joseph emulated. The boy carried it with a simplicity which won him the trust of people older than himself. Nathan, at age fifty, had never lost a slight edge of arrogance—evident in a military set to his shoulders and a precise manner of speech—which made Frank uncomfortable and wary. Yet in spite of that portent, he found himself drawn to the man exactly because of his aggressive qualities. Here was someone who knew how to assume responsibility and could share the mountainous burden of leadership. To date, no one of the present ministers fell into that category, though most had been there from the beginning. Charles Holland, though utterly dependable, was wanting in directness and force. Willard Gleason tended to be too impulsive, his brother Ralph too cerebral and stiff. Almon Whittaker, the hearty "cowboy" from Aroostook County, lacked refinement, Austin Perry lacked fire. All of these were beloved, their peculiar talents indispensible. But Frank saw in Nathan Harriman an instinct for creative leadership and spiritual discernment not evident in the others.

Early in June the two men rented a private railroad car (with $1,000 raised in twenty-four hours) and headed back east with thirty-six people, ever after referred to as the "Tacoma Party." This meant Harriman, his wife Martha and five of his seven children, most of the Ecclesia Mission congregation, and an odd collection of others—a converted prostitute, the chief matron of the Chicago police (also recently converted), and Mary Strauch, an eighteen-year-old heiress to a substantial fortune, whose story preceded the travelers all the way back to Maine.

According to the *Seattle Post Intelligencer,* Harriman and Sandford forced Miss Strauch onto the train against her wishes, while her mother went into a "swoon." More accurately, Sandford had talked with the mother earlier and the woman had given permission for the girl to go, but then changed her mind the last minute. Appearing at the depot in Tacoma with a hypnotist and "two strong men," the mother tried to "persuade" her daughter to stay. When Mary refused, they tried to drag her away. She broke loose and ran to the Shiloh train car, where members of the Tacoma Party surrounded her and brandished their umbrellas as the "strong men" tried to climb aboard. A policeman called by Mrs. Strauch remained aloof when he learned that Mary was not a minor, and as the train pulled out, the girl was safely on her way to Maine.

At Topeka, Kansas, the party was joined by another small holiness group, and then by another at Kansas City, Missouri, where Eddie Doughty, one of Shiloh's first students, had been working with a teenaged brother and sister, Victor and Emma Barton, to nurture a core of higher lines Christians. These were swelled by twelve more from Manitoba, Canada. Altogether the party numbered seventy-two people. Filling the railroad car, they sang and prayed their way on the long journey east with such fervency that "conductors and porters removed their hats."

But Sandford and Nathan Harriman had already gotten off on the wrong foot. At the farewell meeting in Tacoma, Harriman had made a statement that seemed disturbingly audacious. "Not only has God given me to Shiloh," he said, "but God has given Shiloh to me." All he meant, he explained later, when Frank took issue with the comment, was that God "had furnished us with a training school for our workers." In Chicago, during a layover between trains, they had their first real "quarrel." The word is Harriman's, used in his later description of events. The dispute apparently had something to do with the logistics of managing a cumbersome crowd en route. Quite naturally the Ecclesia Mission people looked to Harriman for directions, and undoubtedly he still considered himself in a position to give them.

By the time they arrived at Boston, after two weeks of travel, the men had begun to enjoy each other's company. At Shiloh an elaborate welcome waited. As the long string of wagons pulled up the hill, a trumpet rang out under the crown and a choir burst into song, while all the verandas fluttered with white handkerchiefs.

Harriman was thrilled with the place. As soon as he arrived, that "strange sense of ownership increased." He was moved at the sight of more than two hundred students—"the grandest, happiest, most resolute and most triumphant company of young people on the face of the earth." But he felt grief that circumstances had prevented the completion of the children's building and the interior of the Extension, a delay especially embarrassing since Sandford had thought the rooms of the Extension would be plastered by the previous October and his critics were not letting him forget it. ("God has been making and breaking promises since 1894," said the *Enterprise.*)

Harriman was equally distressed at the unsightly state of the grounds. The great desert of sand waited to be landscaped, while the driveway up the hill was a hazard of muddy ruts. At the end of June, as the school gathered in the pine grove to pray for the completion of the Extension suites, Harriman was startled by an inner command: "Promise Him that they shall be finished by Christmas." Apparently he was not as accustomed as Frank to hearing such messages, and it "staggered" him. But the "spirit whispered courage," and before he was hardly aware of what he was doing, he was making the promise out loud in front of everyone.

If Frank was "staggered" also at this further presumption on Harriman's part, he covered it nobly. Or God did, for after several more minutes in prayer, Frank himself heard a message, the word "Majesty." Probably no one noticed that Harriman had gotten a full nine-word sentence from God, while Frank got his usual cryptic one-worder. Anyway, it certainly did not matter to Frank. The wonderful word arose from Ezekiel 7:20, "As for the beauty of his ornament, he set it in majesty." Frank preached on it in chapel the next day and put

Harriman in charge of the most encompassing of all "drives," to finish the Extension and landscape the estate—to set the hilltop in majesty. All this was to be done while Frank himself spent a month back in Winnipeg.

Harriman began by a campaign to raise the needed money through *Tongues of Fire,* which he was also editing for the summer. He was a more polished writer than Sandford, though the *Enterprise* insisted that "Shiloh's New Leader Talks Like the Old One," noting that the Rev. Mr. Harriman was hearing those "Peculiar Voices." Throughout the summer the community worked furiously on the buildings and grounds under Harriman's direction. The master design called for lawns and groves of trees, walkways, gates, and flower beds in the soft white sand, and a street ("The street that is called Straight" after the one mentioned in the Book of Acts). There a series of ten-room cottages were being planned to house the leading ministers, the first of these, for Charles Holland and his family, already begun. In the Extension new rooms were to be framed and Jerusalem Turret remodeled, with the crown raised twenty feet up on seven pillars and set on a dome.

With hand and horse labor the driveway up from the public road below was graded into two arms which circled back to meet behind the Extension. One day a woman student praying in the turret looked out and saw in the terraced configuration a huge bow. Instantly she thought of "God's quiver," which was Shiloh, and the "trained warriors . . . His arrows." Someone else, in response, thought of Revelation 6:2, describing the first horseman of the Apocalypse: "And I saw, and behold a white horse: and he that sat on him had a bow, and a crown was given unto him: and he went forth conquering and to conquer." From that day at Shiloh the magical bow became a symbol of the school's worldwide mission, though prophecy buffs had long considered the white steed and its rider a symbol of the false prophet, a religious leader who would appear in the Last Days prompted by the anti-Christ.

By the time Sandford returned at the end of August, the work on the hilltop was half done. Nathan Harriman was proving himself an effective manager in Frank's absence, and the Tacoma Party had brought a badly needed surge of physical and spiritual energy to the hill. But the matter of allegiance was more than ever confused. Confronted, Harriman insisted that he was not deliberately encroaching on the boundaries of Sandford's leadership. On the contrary, he believed in God-appointed authority, believed in Sandford's, and thought holiness work in history had often suffered because of too much personal freedom. He had written as much for *Tongues of Fire.*

To complicate matters, in the midst of this dispute Harriman's thirteen-year-old son Paul got into trouble, serious enough to warrant Sandford's attention. The boy was "brought to trial and confessed it," in Harriman's words, who gave no more details about what had happened. (Somebody's son started a fire in the Extension, and it may have been Paul.) What annoyed Harriman was the part Sandford assumed, taking "complete control of the investigation" rather than simply turning it over to the parents. Harriman was told by Sandford that he had failed in ruling his family properly and was therefore "unfit" for leadership. He was "disfellowshipped" for twenty-five hours, isolated from the community until he repented. Humiliated and angered, Harriman's first thought was to leave on the spot. He was shocked to find himself trapped. He had no money and was responsible for a wife and five children, who would, of course, go with him. That is, all but the two older ones, Joseph and Flora, who were by now devoted Shiloh students and would not want to leave. He might, indeed, be risking an unthinkable family split.

He and Sandford were soon reconciled once more, but the money had dried up and work on the buildings and grounds came to another sudden halt. Almost immediately typhoid invaded the community again, bringing the death of a small girl, and quickly spreading to others. An epidemic seemed to be certain. A doctor was called for diagnosis, as state public health laws required, and the afflicted (about twenty-five) were bedded down at Bethesda. Only one case was determined to be typhoid, and there were no further deaths.

The press and public reacted with relief and reasonable sympathy. But to Sandford another onslaught of sickness, whatever its consequences, meant that something was badly amiss. On September 24, one year from the date when he had been "bound to the altar" in England, he walked three miles to a hill which overlooked Shiloh and there, with the complex spread out below him "like a castle," wept for hours as he thought of "the awful hatred of the world, thought of the fearful misrepresentation—all manner of evil poured upon this hilltop and poured upon my head." Finally, half-asleep with exhaustion, he looked up to see a thorn tree and cut a branch, realizing that he was getting "all my master got—a crown of thorns."

He knew what was wrong, and he had already decided what to do about it. The personality of Nathan Harriman was only part of far more pervasive difficulties. Higher lines Christians on the whole were not passive sheep, and as a rule they were not expected to be. The holiness movement had been pointedly Protestant in its emphasis on an individual's direct line to God. Sandford had always believed that unity would be the natural consequence in a group of individuals led by the Spirit. It was the basis of the Constitution he had written six years before for the Crusaders. But Eliza Leger's strong will had brought to light the danger in allowing a variety of personal leadings, if unity was to be preserved. And Eliza was only one among many. Nathan Harriman was only one among many. The sudden influx of the contingency from the West, a large collection of strong wills, was forcing the issue once and for all. The cherished antinomian principle of personal authority that had meant so much in Sandford's own growing sense of identity was now his biggest problem.

Something else was at issue, also new at Shiloh. Women in holiness circles had always assumed a large portion of the out-front leadership, however "masculine" that might seem, believing that the gifts of the Spirit in the End Times transcended the Apostle Paul's instruction that women should play a silent part. In accordance with that, Frank had expected women in the movement to express themselves as much as men. He had never treated them as inferior, or more fragile for that matter; they had not been spared the rigors of Shiloh life, or burdened with the dubious honor of being emotionally superior. Probably women at Shiloh had been moving more freely and creatively than most would have been able to do in secular society. But that was about to change.

Since yielding in her argument with Sandford in England, Eliza had been writing a series of articles on the standing of women in the church and the home. On the thrust of these, she and Sandford had published a tract. In summary, it declared that woman, created as a "helpmeet" for man, should stay in "her appointed place" as a subordinate, or run the danger of assisting Eve "in wrecking the world." Because woman is "more open to spiritual influences good and bad," more amenable to the "supernatural" (as their involvement in Christian Science and spiritualism proved), "the devil finds her an unsuspecting instrument for his evil designs." Weak people are always a danger to the strong, therefore woman in the home must yield in obedience to man as a safeguard provided by God, and in the church "keep silence."

There was certainly nothing original about these ideas. They might have been copied verbatim from dozens of published works available in both the church and secular society. Sandford edited the tract and wrote a portion himself, focusing on what he knew was at the heart of the question for a woman at Shiloh, the necessity of putting Christ first in her life, with obedience to Him superseding her obedience to man. But, said Sandford, a woman is not obeying God's direction unless she first acknowledges His already revealed will (in Scripture) regarding her relationship to man. Christ was *not* being put first when a woman asserted her will and "thus became a silly Eve playing into the hands of the devil," whose purpose was to "bring down the headship of man in his own family." A willful woman presents "to the world a monstrosity, a two-headed person in charge," or worse, "a woman the head of a man," which meant "God's order reversed, angels astonished, the church shamed, hell rejoicing."

As the fall convention began on September 25, Frank announced an official chain of authority at Shiloh, level to level—from God the Father to God the Son to the "prophet" whom God had chosen to order the affairs of this age. The ordained ministers were directly subordinate to that prophet, with other workers subordinate to the ministers. Families provided a parallel system, with women and children in obedience to the husband and father. "Obedient children, obedient wife, then the thing passes on to the husband."

Just days before this announcement, Sandford explained, he had seen the "whole plan of God's church swing out in all its beauty."

> I saw that as the woman took her place, obedient at every point and turn to her husband, and as the woman and man took their places obedient to men of God, and as the men of God took their places, obedient to my Lord, that my Lord took the whole company of us and stepped in behind His Father, obedient at every point.

This company was completely "safe" because it was obedient, "each carrying out the orders of the one next above, and the whole company with God to the front was facing the devil, and it was a battle no longer between this man or this woman and the powers of darkness, but it was a battle between the Almighty and Satan."

Disobedience, then, at the lowest level, was actually disobedience to God the Father, with all the ramifications that could entail. What had begun with Eliza Leger in England had now become incorporated as a system of management.

Nathan Harriman called it an "exquisite order," in a series of rapturous articles about Shiloh which seem absolutely quixotic in the light of his ongoing argument with Sandford. At the very time of Harriman's writing they were only weeks from their "fourth quarrel" over matters of authority. Yet, Harriman insisted, he found order everywhere at Shiloh, even in the "wildest charges [of prayer] in the most intense meetings." There was "perfect order, perfect protection, perfect safety, on the Shiloh hilltop," for "the Word of God, the Spirit of God, and the Providence of God, determine everything. When these speak, no thinking, theorizing, reasoning, imagining, or guessing are tolerated. . . . It is exactness; it is reality." Exact obedience brought liberty. The "humblest member" was "just as much respected and honored as Mr. Sandford." In the submission to authority there was "no servility."

Of course the final decisions rested with God's appointed leader, but one need not be anxious that the prophet might mislead the people, Harriman went on, for Mr. Sandford spends days in prayer and fasting to get "God's latest thought," and when in doubt "consults the whole school, takes light from the simplest, and will not hurry." He did not explain how that would be guaranteed.

Harriman's son Joseph was at least giving a nod to the inherent problems. Long after Nathan Harriman could no longer find feasible the "exactness" he now claimed to admire, Joseph would write, "I expected to find authority at Shiloh. Before I ever knew Mr. S. at all, through my knowledge of how other movements had failed, I had come to know that God's authority must be the basis for success in any Scriptural church." Joseph, reflecting the popular Protestant position on Roman Catholicism, saw "Popery" as a "most clever imitation of God's true order in the Church," with "its iniquitous example" throwing all Christendom into fear of anything that sounded like it." He hailed with delight "the news that God had found a man [Sandford] ready to give orders in His name." Satan had gotten people to "be afraid to bow to anything that is not in close keeping with the democratic, worldly spirit of America! . . . The Church and the world join hands when Christians fear the word 'authority.' "

No one was using the word "infallible" at Shiloh, but neither was anyone suggesting that democratic representative governance and its New Testament model might be a more appropriate system of order for a movement whose purpose was to "obey the whole Bible." Sandford himself was not blind to these tensions. The hierarchy of the chain of authority must operate as if it *were* a democratic system, and there was only one way this could be true.

Short of physical coercion, as Sandford knew, authority is not vested in a leader because a leader says it is. You can yell "Obey!" forever and it will mean little unless obedience is granted in a spirit of freedom. Even God, as the Freewill Baptists and other evangelicals had long averred, wanted obedience only from those who willed it in their hearts, motivated by the "law of liberty." Sandford honestly believed that if individual members of Shiloh were each properly adjusted to the mind of God, got in tune with the Holy Spirit's leading in every corner of their lives, there would be no barrier to accepting the chain of authority. All would see with one eye, see exactly what God had given Sandford to see, and vote "yes" at the deepest level of their beings.

With the convention over and doors shut to the public, he set about cleaning house once more. A year before, at the completion of Bethesda, he had preached to the school on the Song of Solomon, the mysterious and passionate collection of poetry in the middle of the Old Testament. Sandford had loved the book for a long time and had often quoted it but had seldom taught from it, fearing the students might misunderstand the specific language of physical love. Remarkably, but perhaps inevitably, the one book in the Bible which exalts female sexual charm, was becoming the vehicle for curtailing the power of women at Shiloh.

Though some Biblical scholars thought that this scrap of ancient Hebrew literature might once have been used as erotic entertainment at wedding festivals, for centuries the book had been read by Christians as an allegory of the love between Christ and His bride, the Church. Sandford saw in it a mirror of the spiritual beauty of the perfected believer, a beauty so great that God would say, as he had to *him* at the completion of Bethesda, "Turn thine eyes away from me, for they have overcome me."

God would not be satisfied, Sandford said, until He had a bride of that purity for His Son, and to bring it about, He "is going to grind to powder every last thing about us that does not please Him, and after He has ground our very bones up, He will proceed to work them over into some other form that will satisfy Him better." It meant nothing less than the death of the self, "going to your own funeral day by day," but with the abandoned Song of Solomon in your heart.

This was the spirit of the "Fair, Clear, and Terrible" purge which began that November of 1900. Two of those who participated were my grandfather, Wendell White, and my grandmother, Elvira Bartlett.

Elvira had enrolled as a student in February of 1899, directly after the Cleaning-out time precipitated by Rossie Harper's illness. It would be hard to overestimate the importance of Shiloh at this moment in her life. She thought of it afterwards as the salvation of her sanity as well as her soul, the restoration of a self she had lost sight of long ago. For the last decade she had felt no ownership of the person she had been forced to become, somber and nervous, with money—or the lack of it— always on her mind, always looking for more work, for anything that would carve another thin layer off her long indebtedness.

Few people understood, even people at Shiloh, the high wave of faith that had brought her to the hilltop, for it meant leaving Merlyn and Leander behind, obeying God in a manner that seemed to go against nature. Yet in her eyes it was an act of total trust, first that God would provide the funds necessary for her children's care at her sister's home, and then that He would reunite them in circumstances more wonderful than she could have devised herself with all the cash in the world. Already, in the eighteen months Elvira had been at Durham, the miraculous had happened. This past May, just at the time when it seemed her daughter would be taken from her forever, God had brought Merlyn to the hilltop.

Not many months after Elvira's enrollment at Shiloh, the White family, Wendell and Annie and the children, moved from the Growstown farm to Lewiston, to the house provided by Annie's father. It was in this fall of 1900 that Wendell began attending classes at Shiloh, taking the electric cars to Lisbon Falls each Monday morning and staying throughout the week, and it was on a Friday night in this November, that Arnold overheard his parents in conversation in the Lewiston kitchen.

Wendell, other than expressing his fear that he would not make it through the purge, never explained any more than that in Arnold's presence. The words "fair, clear, and terrible" were from Sandford's favorite verse of Scripture, in the sixth chapter of Song of Solomon: "Who is she that looketh forth as the morning, fair as the moon, clear as the sun and terrible as an army with banners?" The event was intricately planned. To make the experience as concrete as possible, Sandford printed tickets with the words, "The bearer 'looketh forth' from the Upper Room, 'Fair, Clear and Terrible.' " The ticket admitted a person to the Armory, the large auditorium above the eastern wing of the Extension, for a special service of celebration. To obtain a ticket, one must pass a grueling examination of the inner and outer life.

"Those tickets meant more to us than anything material would ever have meant," remembered one woman. "Mr. Sandford showed us that nothing but the absolute transformation of our natures into Christ's divine nature would be acceptable. . . . 'Fair' meant no blemish . . . beautiful from the heart. . . . 'Clear' meant without guile . . ., transparent in every word and act," and "Terrible" was what a child of God became to Satan when "transformed by the power of Christ within. We were told that a Church like this would mean the whole world redeemed back from the devil's power."

The examination began at the top, with the ordained ministers, followed by the students, with those tested and passed becoming the examiners and chastisers. The first Cleaning-out had come about spontaneously. The Fair, Clear, and Terrible purge was carefully planned, and incorporated not just confession, but long day and night sessions of open and unrelenting criticism of each other. One's capacity to accept that scouring in a contrite and cooperative spirit, without resentment or defensiveness, was the first step in passing the grade.

Sandford lived in Jerusalem turret for most of the time involved, praying almost constantly, believing that the entire movement hung on the cleansing force of the intense process. It was he who gave out the tickets to the Armory one by one as individuals were brought before him for a final scrutiny by "the seven eyes of God." Those not yet examined at this final level gathered in intercession for each other, and those who passed prayed for those not yet "come through." The finished product of this refining fire must be a company of people "adjusted"— tight, dependable links in the new chain of authority. It was a spiritual matter, after all, as it was presented, not a political one—not a case of obedience to man, but obedience to God.

Wendell White, so sure he would not make the grade, may have been worried about his temperament, the old uncontrolled fits of anger which still filled him with shame. Or perhaps he questioned ultimate human authority, or maybe he felt uneasy about the meaning being squeezed from the Song of Solomon. He had no trouble saying so, if that was the case. Expressing his opinion was a personal habit.

Whatever was at issue, a two-inch scrap of browned newspaper from a column in the *Lisbon Enterprise* tells the story. Nathan Harriman, as a minister who had passed the test (in itself significant), was present at Wendell's final examination by Sandford and apparently was later interviewed by the *Lisbon Enterprise*—either that, or the *Enterprise* got its information in the usual way, by overheard gossip. According to Harriman, says the news item, Frank Sandford prayed for Wendell with his hand on his head, and then announced that Wendell's "skull had been scraped clean and his mental machinery was in good working order."

To Sandford, Wendell's sins were not of his heart but of his head— his penchant for "reasoning," his inner wrangling, the "but . . . but . . . but." Somebody, and perhaps it was Sandford himself, put a finger on a flaw in Wendell's personality—the arrogance that required him to be right, to be in intellectual control, a White family trait. From Sandford's point of view, living in the power of the Holy Spirit had nothing to do with your brain. He despised theory. You could sit around arguing about things (as Wendell had obviously done) for years and accomplish absolutely nothing. Your life changed when you acted in faith.

Wendell may have accepted this insight about himself. His family would certainly have agreed that he needed to be willing to be wrong, or at least sometimes without final answers. Maybe, as Hannah Whitall Smith would have said, he needed to "Let go and let God." But if he did, exactly what did he let go of? How far did he let the hurdle of faith take him? I can only guess at that from what happened next in the life of the Whites.

By November of 1900, as the Fair, Clear, and Terrible purge took place, Annie and Wendell had been wracked for six months with anxiety for the baby, Avis, who had suddenly stopped using her arms. As she had been ill briefly with a fever, a doctor had diagnosed the problem as infantile paralysis, and began a series of treatments with hot packs and massage. The baby, now fifteen months old, had recovered the use of her left arm and hand, but not her right, though the treatments continued in hope that some good would result. Late in the fall of 1900, with the Shiloh purge at an end, visits to the doctor suddenly ceased and Avis's recovery was committed to prayer alone.

Quite apart from whether or not the doctor's methods would have been finally effective, apart from making a judgment at all, we ought not to overlook the tremendous investment involved here for Annie and Wendell. It was a radical and irreversible step at the point when the risk was the greatest. That was the key to it all. They were choosing faith over reason as the method of living their lives and they were proving that they meant it. Faith at Shiloh allowed no room for both prayer and the self-protective hedge of human means and methods. It was all or nothing. More was at stake than the healing of a child's limb. It was almost as if they had offered part of their daughter's anatomy as the surety of a larger promise, the lives of their family.

We must conclude that with his "skull scraped clean" Wendell passed the Fair, Clear, and Terrible exam. Elvira Bartlett did not—not because she was rebellious or proud or resisted her place in the chain of authority, but because she was financially in debt, a fact that had come to light under scrutiny. Her flight to Shiloh a year earlier, though she thought of it as an act of faith, appeared to Shiloh's ministers more like a self-indulgent vacation from care. She was expelled until she had paid off her bills. Hurt but not angry, she removed herself from the hill immediately and began work as a live-in housekeeper at various homes in neighboring towns.

But what was she to do with her daughter? Merlyn had been at Shiloh since the previous spring and was willing to stay. Somehow Elvira arranged for her to live under the aegis of other families—first the artists from Chicago, the Fergusons, and then the Shaws, a farm family from New Gloucester with teenaged twins. It was a temporary plan until (Elvira hoped) God provided a better arrangement for herself and her children.

Actually Merlyn had already established her own niche at Shiloh by recovering from tuberculosis. Not long before, Mr. Sandford had been asked to pray for her healing. Looking into her face, he had clasped her hands and laughed and said, "I do not believe this child is a consumptive!" Merlyn did not believe it herself, now that she knew she was supposed to be one. While the adults were scrutinizing their innermost thoughts, she and her friends were sliding down "Pine Needle Hill" in the grove and skipping stones at "Good Shepherd Beach." Classes in math, spelling, Bible, poetry, and music were held for the dozen or so children in the "Living Waters Room" at the old farmhouse, taught by Joseph Harriman and Ernest Tupper, a recent Colby graduate, and one or two women who had been schoolmarms in the world.

So, with her mother gone, Merlyn was still in limbo, still waiting for the reunion of her family. Yet there was no time to feel like an orphan. Here were all the parents anyone could want—the light-hearted Fergusons, the ample, affectionate Shaws—all the fathers, Mr. Sandford himself (who still called her "Leah the tender-eyed"), and the "H-Men," Holland, Higgins, and Harriman. Joseph Harriman especially, with his softly lidded blue eyes and gentle manner, resembled her own father remarkably. She was here without a family, but as everybody's sister and child.

When the Fair, Clear, and Terrible test was over and the wash out on the line, almost all of the students found themselves reinstated, many who later pointed to the experience as a supreme spiritual turning point. The weeks of tension ended in celebration, with the wedding of Ralph Gleason and Christine Marple in the Armory. Sandford himself was enormously relieved. Shiloh had been "set in order." He had heard God whisper, "An eternal excellency." But though money once again streamed in from donors and the work on the Extension suites resumed, Nathan Harriman's promise to "finish" them by Christmas was not kept, and in fact, they were never completed.

As the year 1900 drew to a close Sandford began a series of sermons later published under the title, *The Art of War of the Christian Soldier; The Last Study of the Century Given by F.W. Sandford to the Bible School at Shiloh.* It was his most militant statement yet, a battle-by-battle comparison of Joshua's Palestinian conquest and the campaign that lay ahead.

Following a wonderful, mad, ten-day Christmas, when 20,000 presents were exchanged before a bank of greens in the chapel, Shiloh turned itself out to finish the "Maine Campaign" begun the year before, an army which traveled any way it could go. Two boys, aged seventeen, "shot" by song off the terraced bow, walked 300 miles to Aroostook County. Men and women stopped at farms, railroad yards, ice houses, factories, and logging camps, saying "This is mine," with true American zest. By human logic, if they had heeded the experiences of the year before and gone in good weather, they might have covered more land with less energy, but that was not Shiloh's way. Back at the hilltop those in the field were supported by special prayer in not just one turret, but two, for now the men had begun a permanent twenty-four-hour prayer relay in David's Tower.

Wendell White, one of the missionaries, operated out of his own home, which had been turned over temporarily as headquarters for the Lewiston-Auburn area. The family crowded itself onto the first floor, with Wendell's and Annie's brass bedstead in the parlor, while Nathan Harriman and several of the students lived in the upstairs bedrooms.

At the close of the campaign, the Whites moved abruptly back to the Growstown farm. Wendell was no longer a student. There is nothing in the records to explain the decision, or anything to suggest that Wendell had lost faith in affairs at the hilltop. Perhaps it was just the same old answer—when you don't know what to do next, you farm. So Wendell was milking his cows once more and making deliveries in Brunswick when Shiloh positioned itself in the shadows of the world's theater.

12
The Art of War
1901

The prophets of optimism and doom at the beginning of the twentieth century in 1901 agreed on one thing—whatever happened it would be faster. At Shiloh life took on such speed some students thought they could not keep rank. "Every day was something way beyond what we had received the day before," remembered one. They would no sooner absorb one revelation than another would call them to higher ground. Even Holman Day, now a desk editor at the *Lewiston Sun,* made no effort to keep straight the frenzy of activity.

At times, Sandford confessed to the students, he forgot he was still in the present, and seemed "to be living in the millennial age." He had begun to concentrate on the Great Tribulation, the future period of seven years on earth filled with unprecedented war, famine, and plague. Premillennialists, right now at the turn of the century, were in dispute over whether or not those dreadful seven years would fall before or after Jesus returned. In the last two decades a particular system of interpreting prophecy—of understanding the whole Bible, in fact—had been approved by a large segment of the evangelical community. Known as Dispensationalism, its formula seemed to provide the Rosetta Stone, the key to the prophetic visions that had been sought for so long. Its most controversial innovation was the introduction of two Second Advents.

Students of Scripture had always been puzzled by what seemed to be contradictory descriptions of Christ's return, one a secret, silent occasion and the other dazzlingly public—with a shout and the sound of a trumpet. Dispensationalists decided this meant He would actually return

155

to earth twice, the first time in a "Secret Rapture," a split second when true believers, the Remnant of the Church, would be "caught up to meet Him in the air." That event would occur before the Tribulation began and would not be witnessed by the rest of the world, which would experience it as the sudden unexplainable disappearance of millions of people—along with the unimaginable circumstances such a phenomenon would provoke. The absence from the world of the redeeming presence of true Christians would increase the horrors of the Tribulation, at the end of which Jesus would come yet again. This time "every eye would see him," an awesome conquering warrior bringing the raptured saints as a militia, winning the world war at the battle of Armageddon and saving Israel from extinction.

In the years in which Frank Sandford had been formulating his own ideas about the End Times, the prophecy movement that had inspired him was being splintered by arguments over the timing and even the probability of the Rapture. Now Sandford was deciding on the basis of his own Rosetta Stone, which was Shiloh itself, that at least some of the believers were to endure the Tribulation, and more, that the new terrible time had already begun. As Mary Guptil explained in an article for Shiloh's paper, "The 'acceptable year of the Lord' is now giving place to 'the day of the vengeance of our God.' " From this point people would turn to God out of terror, as the seals of Revelation were broken and the horses of the Apocalypse thundered onto the scene.

World and national affairs now were getting regular press notice in Shiloh's literature. In a brand-new periodical, *The Everlasting Gospel* (which replaced *Tongues of Fire*), each issue opened with a selection of news items called "The Daily Trend of World Wide Events in the Light of the Holy Scripture." The Boxer Rebellion in China, war in South Africa, the death of Queen Victoria, the assassination of President McKinley—all were part of the scenario of the final times.

No effort was made to analyze trends in culture or commerce, or to evaluate decisions on state or national levels. J. P. Morgan's wealth foreshadowed not the expanding gap between the rich and the poor, or the increasing American infatuation with money, but the work of the Beast (like the False Prophet, a puppet of the anti-Christ, this one with political power), who "shall declare a boycott on every human being on the face of the globe who shall not receive his mysterious mark."

Voices prominent in the outside world got no hearing at Shiloh. Eugene Debs, Henry Adams, Edith Wharton, George Santayana, William or Henry James, Mark Twain might as well not have existed. Theodore

Roosevelt did. Sandford liked Roosevelt, another fearless individual unafraid to speak his mind.

Rumblings of war earned space in nearly every issue of *The Everlasting Gospel*. With Victoria's restraining hand gone, the "Great European War" was close at hand, "the Tribulation struggle for supremacy between England and Russia in Palestine." The land of Gog and Magog mentioned in Ezekiel, a mighty army from the "north parts," was Russia, which would attack the restored Kingdom of Israel (Anglo-Israel) in Palestine and lay siege to Jerusalem. Measures to prevent it were useless, as were any efforts at peace. Sandford called a national organization's call to prayer for peace "utter ignorance." Social reformers, as well, he said, were wasting their time applying bandages to small cuts, while global disasters were about to crash over the heads of all humanity.

Sandford was not alone in his evaluation of reform. Many premillenial Christians had lost interest in improving society, while those who still looked for the Kingdom of God in a Christianized, civilized world were taking over as the leaders in social change. To them the Kingdom was here and now, an earthly condition, and Jesus Christ less a metaphysical agent of salvation than a human example of justice and goodness. This portion of the American church, growing in influence among middle-class Protestants, was being defined as the "Social Gospel."

This was the liberal (or progressive) half of the metaphorical ship that had "divided" in the middle of the nineteenth century. The conservative evangelical half, meanwhile, after splitting many times again, seemed to be forming two segments of permanence. A wide concern was stirring, especially among educators, for the "fundamentals" of the faith, for tidier articulations of creed and the inerrancy of Scripture. Others cared more about individual experience than correctly worded theology. Very soon the labels would go on unmistakeably: the fundamentalists and the pentecostalists. The center of their differences would be the demonstration of the Holy Spirit in the personal life, and right now in 1901 the lines were being drawn in what had not yet been a serious issue—the viability of speaking in tongues, or ecstatic language.

In fact, a student at Shiloh, Charles Parham, who had come with the Tacoma Party, had recently broken fellowship with Sandford over this very issue and had gone back to the Midwest to found his own school, where speaking in tongues soon began to be practiced. Sandford, who believed the phenomenon of tongues was simply the gift of dialects sometimes given to missionaries in foreign lands, repudiated Parham for gross error.

But actually, Shiloh had no real interest in any movement except Shiloh. It saw itself as separate and "out ahead" of all others. The future and the present both were the Tribulation, and the Tribulation was expected to focus in the Holy Land. That was where Shiloh now turned its eyes. It was past time to establish headquarters in Jerusalem.

Sandford had originally thought that only he and Helen would go, and possibly Mary Guptil, one of his most reliable students. But at the end of the convention, after forty hours of waiting on God, "without food or sleep," a party of twelve was selected. The choices were made meticulously, for the group must, in its purity, represent the *New* Jerusalem. They were to open the doors into the Holy City—to *be* the doors, the twelve gates to the spiritual city within the earthly one, each gate representing a tribe of Israel. Through these would pour the 144,000 redeemed Israelites of the restored Kingdom (including Jews), and then the great multitude of redeemed souls from the Gentile nations.

The "Jerusalem Twelve," as they would be called, were Frank and Helen Sandford, Nathan Harriman and his son Joseph, Almon Whittaker, Elnora Emerson—and six of the original students, Margaret Main, Edward Doughty, Mary and Adnah Guptil, and Willard Gleason and his new wife Rose Emmons. It had been decided that John Sandford, now age four, would also go, while Esther, a toddler, and Marguerite, the Sandfords' third child, still an infant, would temporarily remain at Shiloh under the care of their nurses. No other spouses or family members were included. The possibility of a long separation was particularly difficult for Almon Whittaker, who was leaving behind three young children and a pregnant wife. Of the Twelve, four would not see America again for nine years, one would die in Jerusalem, one would return blind and another close to death with tuberculosis, and one would defect from the movement, with far-reaching consequences.

Before their departure, the entire school was photographed on the arrow of grass in front of the main building. Sandford stood at the point, nervous and weighted with responsibility, feeling "that somehow the main battle would be ability to keep, as the American says, 'a stiff upper lip.' The whole movement will go down in terror if the leader is terrified. But when the leader is triumphant in his faith, full of courage, without the slightest idea of being whipped, 'more than conqueror' when the other side is sure they have got him down, always on top when he is underneath, *never, never dragging his flag,*—a company of people learn to gather with supreme delight around such a man, and God can use that man to keep them steady until the work is done."

On June 19 the Jerusalem Party sailed out of Boston Harbor. They arrived in England at the end of the month. Immediately the Twelve yielded to an intense period of purging which lasted ten days, as the standard of the New Jerusalem was applied. The full dimensions of what occurred would not be public knowledge until later, but it was rigorous enough to give pause to Sandford himself. In a letter back to Shiloh he said he had "never known a fiercer conflict for the absolute unity of this party. . . . I find that having 'all things in common' includes weakness, ignorance and shame, as well as knowledge, power and glory." For a while things looked close to breaking apart in the "mighty crash," as "the arrow . . . hit its mark."

"Oh, it was just purging!" exclaimed Margaret Main, later. "It was a small group and he could fire at close range."

Margaret's remarks were adulatory, but two years later Nathan Harriman described two confrontations which had to have occurred in those impassioned sessions. The account that follows is in Harriman's words, and the details never corroborated openly by anyone else. He did not provide names, but the first woman mentioned is almost certainly Helen; the second, as evidence will bear out in time, was Mary Guptil.

Once in England, with the whole Jerusalem party present . . . I saw him rise from his seat in sudden rage at something _____ had said, walk quickly behind her chair and give her a sharp slap in the face. When in his embarrassment he stammered, "Well, it is the first time that I ever did it, isn't it _____ ?", she replied, "No, it isn't, you struck me once before," and proceeded to tell him when and where. . . . He had great mortification over this, but [explained] that God had allowed him to be humbled for _____'s sake, who was rebellious. . . . The poor woman accepted the verdict and went away to fast and pray to get the "stuff out of her." I think it was this time that she remained nine days alone in the attic. . . .

The case of Miss _____ is that of an unusually bright, keen, conscientious and consecrated young woman, one of the early pupils of the Bible school and deservedly popular with her teacher and all the pupils. In a time of pressure when the "prophet" was disciplining one of his ministers, this young lady presumed to take exception to something he [Sandford] had said. . . .

I will give the details as they were reported to me, for I was not present. I saw the results, however . . . and I have no doubt that I will give the particulars substantially correct. So great was the anger of the "Holy Ghost" at the spectacle of one of his principal pupils daring to oppose him at such a time, that he was beside himself. He turned to her with such wrath that she sank under his words.

He told her that her sin was too great for forgiveness; that her soul was doomed; . . . that she need not think to pray—that God would not hear her; that He would not even let the "prophet" pray for her. What language he used I can only guess at from hearing him in similar situations.

After a time . . . another young lady [Adnah, Mary's sister] takes the place of this lost soul. . . . goes down into hell for her; there makes confession for her awful sin, which the first one could not do; and then the tormentor prays them both out of hell, as it was reported to me.

Nathan Harriman himself, it appears, was the major target. He may have been the "minister" Mary was defending and may have been absent at the above occasion because he was taking his own turn "in the attic," having been "cast off," demoted as a minister and ordered to fast fourteen days because of his "reasoning head." He emerged from the process bearing a new name—Saul—after the jealous king who tried to murder David. The label carried startling echoes, even on a symbolic level. No one thought Harriman intended Sandford physical harm, or that he intended to commit suicide, as Saul had done. But in Sandford's eyes the peril was even more alarming. Harriman was in danger of ruining his own relationship with God (worse than suicide) by his spirit of rebellion—and more, of ruining the work of Shiloh.

King Saul had been possessed of an "evil spirit." Apparently Harriman was accused of falling under the same kind of power, as he explained it. The possibility of demon possession was a constant threat to them all. Those who reasoned, whose logic questioned authority, were "snared." A snared person was so influenced by demons that, "think clearly as he may, judge as soberly as he will, he cannot get anything correct," until "there is only one way out, the person has to submit" or is "sent away in disgrace."

For example, Harriman continued, something might come up in which "the man" is declared to be in the wrong. He does not see it so, and loses his temper. He holds out and will not be "reduced." Then he is told, "You certainly have a demon." Everything changes. "A man who up until this time was ready to fight for his rights, suddenly finds that he has no rights"—or responsibility, for the blame "is suddenly transferred to another . . . a demon is to blame." As frightening as this is, "it is better than believing he is wrong when he does not see it," and he yields to the verdict. The quarrel is over.

In a position now of needing help from those he once resisted, "the man" is ordered to fast for seven days. At the end of that time he is exhausted and ready to "accept almost anything" the prophet suggests. They kneel, there is thundering, stamping, and the pounding of fists. "Then the man is told that the demon had departed and he is delivered." It was through this convoluted process, we are meant to infer, that Harriman himself relented once more.

When it was all over the party was unified and "mightily strengthened," as Sandford wrote back to Shiloh. But this time the wounds of cleansing went far deeper than he knew.

The delay in Liverpool was intended to be only long enough to prepare for the rest of the journey. It turned out differently. During the previous year the two Shiloh women working at Liverpool (one of them Olive Mills) had been slowly gathering converts, though no more than a dozen or so to date. While preaching to this group, Sandford began to hold lively public meetings which grew quickly in size.

One warm night, at the close of a service, a crowd gathered in the street outside, listening to his great voice through the open windows as he prayed a "mighty prayer for England" in which he "broke her national pride, and then turned against her national enemies in the very power of the Almighty."

He had been thinking about the word "rock" on the way across the Atlantic. Now, in "the heat of the giant prayer," he felt as "like a very god," and as though he "could hurl back, single handed, in the name of my God, every Gentile nation that dared so attack Israel." When he was finished it seemed as though "personal responsibility" for England had passed from his own shoulders to the " 'Man of War,' the Lord of Hosts."

The new revelation meant a postponement of the trip to the Holy Land, while he established a Bible School in England on the model of Shiloh, a school which in the perilous times ahead was to be "the secret of the safety of the British Empire." The dozen or so students selected were of Irish, Scottish, and Welsh blood, as well as English. But other converts, not chosen as students, not ready to be "100-fold warriors," begged to be somehow included in the organization.

The problem was solved in a most natural way. The students, giving up their livelihoods and "forsaking all," moved in with the Shiloh evangelists in rented rooms. The other converts remained in their own homes and continued in their occupations, supporting the students financially, while the students in turn ministered to the spiritual needs of their supporters.

Such an arrangement was hardly new church history, and the same thing had been going on at Shiloh for years in an unstructured manner. But watching the small-scale model in Liverpool work so well, Frank knew he must not wait to bring the truth home with a new application. He was off again. Leaving the work in England in the hands of ten of the "Twelve," he headed back to America with Nathan Harriman (thinking it best, perhaps, to keep that man by his side). The others waited in Liverpool.

Since 1899 Shiloh had often referred to itself as "The Church of the Living God," yet without ecclesiastical organization. Now Sandford preached for eight days on the church as a three-level concept—with 100-fold, 60-fold, and 30-fold members. He had always been disturbed because Shiloh had consistently turned away those who felt as yet unready for total involvement. Now anyone willing to make at least a thirty percent commitment of time and assets could be considered for membership. The *Enterprise* saw it as just another way to squeeze money out of those "who would not give their all."

The new church was to follow four ordinances: baptism, healing, the Lord's Supper, and worship. Saturday had already been determined as the true Sabbath, "restored" by Sandford earlier that year. Both communion and worship, which had always been open to the public at Shiloh, would now be closed to all but baptized members, and baptism represented much more than inner cleansing. On October first, Sandford led the entire school down the hill to the Androscoggin and immersed 218 of them in a "restored and authoritative baptism," regardless of whether they had been baptized before, even by himself. For the rest of the month he dashed throughout New England, explaining the concept of the new church and the new baptism.

> God is here, and the representative of God is here that has power and authority from God to remit your sins. . . . I declare that every one of your sins will be remitted today if you are baptized. Beware how you hear it! If you accept it, you accept the "counsel of God." If you reject it, you reject "the counsel of God."

Soon new "churches" reported in from around the country. Some were very small, one with only one member. Most of these had already separated themselves from other churches and had been meeting in their homes. To those who suggested smugly that what Sandford was doing had a most familiar echo, that what he was forming was what he himself had once called "the old dead snake of denominationalism," he had an airy answer. This was *not* a denomination. He was making it possible for "true, higher-life Christians" to leave "denominational apostasy" and "get under the authority and order of the appointed man of God." He was doing exactly what the early New Lights had done in the hills over a century before.

Charles Holland and George Higgins were also given authority to baptize and in another month over seven hundred had been immersed. The *Lisbon Enterprise* quoted someone who proposed "that an endless chain be arranged on which pulleys could slide and the victims could be placed on these pulleys and pass down and through the water."

Something about outdoor baptisms had always aroused public curiosity. The widespread nature of Sandford's latest drama was bound to get the attention of newspapers, particularly as cold weather approached. In mid-November, when Shiloh evangelists moved in to Brooklyn, New York, the *New York Times* launched into a series of sensational reports, with such headlines as "Girl Dragged Screaming to the Icy Bay and Immersed." The baptisms occurred at the beach in Bay Ridge, where Sandford stood in the shallow water at low tide and plunged the converts under when waves rolled in from the channel. On the day seven-year-old Dorothy Barton was immersed, dressed only in a cambric slip and white stockings, a strong wind blew from the northeast and the temperature was just above freezing. An angry *Times* editorial claimed that "The Apostle of the Durham Sand Dunes" was "half-drowning helpless children, imbecile old men, and weak-minded women" and was an "entirely fit subject for incarceration in a mad house." Sandford's malady might have "several names—megolamania, folie degrandeur, and the like—but it is always the same thing."

If Frank saw that editorial, it was of no importance to him. God was moving ahead with impeccable timing.

The promised return of the Old Testament prophet Elijah had been a subject of intense and frequent discussion at the school over the years. A giant of a figure in Biblical literature, Elijah represented qualities a lot like those attributed to an American Western hero. Rough yet vulnerable, formidable but loving, he came and went, a wilderness dweller, appearing when needed and disappearing without explanation, each time calling apostate Israel back to active faith in the God of Moses.

But Elijah was too important to disappear forever. To Jews his return became an expectation coupled with the coming of the Messiah. John the Baptist, for one, similar to Elijah in his fearless criticism of contemporary power, was said to go about in "the spirit and power" of Elijah, and Jesus, of course, was a candidate for such speculation. Both denied they were Elijah. Yet Jesus also said, "Elijah truly shall first come, and restore all things."

Sandford had been making connections between Shiloh and Elijah for a long time. Now he was preaching that the new church should be called an "Elijah church," since it heralded the Second Coming of Christ. In fact, he said one day, "everything hinges on the personality of that man Elijah."

On the morning of November 23, while it was still dark on Shiloh hilltop, a student named Olaf Peterson was taking his turn at prayer in David's turret. Happening to glance out over the huge courtyard in the square of the Extension, he saw the figure of Frank Sandford pacing back and forth across the lighted window of Jerusalem Turret. Without the least idea of what might cause such restlessness, Peterson continued in prayer, until just at daybreak, as a wintry sun reached over the trees, he was "conscious of myriads of angels about the Hilltop."

Sandford had been up all night, waiting on God in Jerusalem turret. He knew that the theme of the coming Thanksgiving convention was to be "The Kingdom," but the full meaning of that had not yet been made clear to him. At 4:00 A.M., God spoke:

> [He] said something to me, and when God speaks, I know what His voice means. Like a thunderbolt three words were spoken, and they went down into the depths of my soul. These were the three words,

> "ELIJAH IS HERE!"

> I hardly knew what to make of it at first. I listened, and waited, and walked the floor, and at last, just before I left the room, he said,

> "TESTIFY!"

At nine o'clock that morning in Shiloh chapel Sandford related the experience to the school, and later that day, at the Temple in Auburn, he "testified" publicly.

The experience of the Second Elijah would parallel that of the first, Sandford said. He would be ascertained as a "public enemy" and would be "bitterly persecuted"; nevertheless he would be a "terror" to evil doers, and in his presence all false religion would be "annihilated." According to Malachi, the final book of the Old Testament, Elijah would bring families back into their proper order and lead Israel to "heart religion." More, Sandford emphasized, Elijah was to be one of the two "witnesses" who were to be murdered by the anti-Christ in Jerusalem during the Tribulation.

"I have a feeling of ease," he said to the Auburn company, "though at the very moment this declaration is given out I am well aware that all the batteries of hell are going to open up."

God had given him the words, "Lurid lightning." But the lightning would flash from both sides. Though he expected to be himself, he said, "just as natural and at home in the battle as I am at home with my little children," he also expected to "thunder when God wants me to thunder."

Things were to be different now. As Frank Sandford, ordinary Christian, under the law of love, or ordinary citizen, under the law of the state, he had not owned the right to call down God's vengeance on enemies. As Elijah, he did.

"I warn every lying pen," Frank told reporters. "I warn every lying editor, that I will bring swift and awful witness against them for all the lies they have written about this man of God for the last eight years. Now I promise every such man that before long he will meet the God of judgment."

It did not improve the press's reaction that the healer Alexander Dowie had recently announced in Chicago that he himself was the Second Elijah, and that Dowie had been fighting sensationalized law suits arising out of the deaths of several "unhealed" persons. Asked what he thought of Dowie's claim, Frank answered coolly: "All I know is that God said to me, 'Elijah is here' and I presume He knew what He was talking about."

Those evangelicals who had been engrossed in the same lines of prophetic study, whether or not they were waiting for Elijah, understood the potential locked in Sandford's announcement. Someone heard A. B. Simpson make the remark that "Frank Sandford will never be satisfied until he is extra-plenipotentiary with the Almighty Himself."

The reaction inside Shiloh was divided. Many were not surprised at all—not nearly as surprised as Sandford said he himself was. They had believed for a long time that their leader was Elijah II. Most of those for whom the idea was new found ways to absorb it.

"The great things we have always read about are upon us, we must keep up or be left behind," said a woman in Shiloh chapel. She had taken a leap, she said, "which brought her in line with the latest truth." Listening to her, another woman bridged by faith "that which had seemed such a chasm, and I knew I was in line with Elijah."

Others, appalled at the new development and the inflammatory tone of its proclamation, quietly took themselves away.

"If I am a false prophet, then I am going to have all the false people," responded Sandford, to the criticism. "If I am the true prophet, all the true people will come to me."

Whether or not he knew it, many "true people" fell between the cracks, those who earnestly wanted to accept the new revelation, but could not yet make the leap of faith. Expecting Elijah in an animal skin was one thing; to acknowledge his presence in a business suit was another. It was as if they had suddenly found a brand-new verse in the Bible, a new claim or promise they had never seen before and hardly knew what to do with. In fact, to many Shiloh members, Sandford almost embodied the inerrancy of Scripture. Certainly he wore the magical authoritative aura associated with the Bible, and that alone confused this rangy group, whose doubts would surface later, no matter how they tried to suppress them.

On Thanksgiving Day, five days after the Elijah announcement, ninety-eight people were baptized through thick ice in the Androscoggin. An item in the Lewiston papers the previous Monday had told of another baptism in Auburn, not Shiloh-related, which authorities had attempted to stop. Though each member of the County Board of Health was polled for advice, "none of them knew what the law was or dared to do anything." The baptism came to a halt anyway when the evangelist involved became too badly chilled himself to continue. Yet Sandford stuck it out for ninety-eight dippings—a very long time for one man to stand in icy water, regardless of how well protected he might be by suitable gear.

Not so hardy was a sixty-five-year-old widow from Auburn, who went home from her baptism in Durham to die of pneumonia. Frank was gone by the time the newspapers had milked that story, on his way back to England, and he was on his way to Jerusalem before the hilltop was invaded once again by illness.

On February 10, 1902, the Secretary of the State Board of Health, Dr. A. G. Young, received word that smallpox had been detected at Shiloh. He quickly verified five cases, already isolated in Bethesda by Dr. Ida Miller, who had diagnosed them herself. Dr. Young urged vaccination for all hilltop residents, expressing his confidence to Dr. Miller that there would be no prolonged need for a quarantine if Shiloh followed his directions "to the letter"—which Shiloh did, "carefully and efficiently," says the report—all but the vaccination. In the course of the next three weeks ten more cases developed. It was May before the hill was released entirely from quarantine.

Scattered epidemics of smallpox were still a common event in the country. Vaccination, long known to be effective, was still not mandatory in all states, and not in Maine. Shiloh was hardly unique in its opposition. In Boston, where smallpox had been rampant since November, vaccination had been called "an infringement of personal rights" by protesting groups.

Most of the hilltop's fifteen cases were "supernaturally light," though one young man was convinced that if he had "doubted God a particle" he would have died. His entire body was covered with sores. He counted seventy on one hand. But he was well enough to count and he did not die. This was not the Black Winter. That was still seven months ahead.

Shiloh's representation of the white horse of the Apocalypse.

13

A Splendid Heroism
1902

The population at Shiloh under quarantine those months was the smallest it had been in a long time. A quarter of the hilltop had sailed away to England early in December. It was a last-minute decision. Sandford, on his way to Boston Harbor with Nathan Harriman, was in Brunswick changing trains before he realized that God wanted a "large party" to go with him, and hastily telephoned back to the hilltop.

In "a joyous fury of activity" thirty-nine students packed their trunks and rushed to the Lisbon Falls station. It was storming badly as they left and when the train got to Portland it was blocked by snow on the tracks, a serious delay since the steamer was scheduled to leave that night. Prayer claimed "a genuine Elijah miracle," and soon four extra locomotives pulled and pushed the train to Boston.

As might be expected, no one in this "large party" had any money. The funds for passage were raised at Elim in a tremendous battle of prayer, the last dollar "in" from the Boston faithful just minutes before sailing time. Then, in a thrilling confusion of boat whistles and shouts, they were on their way.

Sandford had wired ahead to Whittaker to lease living quarters for the English school and all the American workers, and Whittaker succeeded beyond anyone's imagination. Once at Liverpool, the travelers were escorted to Highfield House, a magnificent forty-room mansion in the suburb of Knotty Ash. Entering the gates, an entourage of carriages full of marveling Shilohites paraded up a tree-lined drive a third of a mile long, with lawns and gardens spreading out on both sides. Designed in English Victorian style, the spacious grounds included a conservatory, tomato house, swan pond, kennel, sheep house, dairy, and laundry. Inside the white marble entrance hall, the arriving party smelled hot chocolate, and sure enough, in the midst of all that elegance they were offered— not high tea—but cocoa and homemade doughnuts. At dinner time Whittaker topped off the party with an "Elijah feast" of a whole fatted calf.

Frank renamed the house "Pas-dammin" (the place in the Old Testament where David slew Goliath), and on Christmas Day two score British members were baptized in the swan pond. Austin Perry was given charge of the work in Great Britain, while workers scattered throughout Scotland, Wales, and Ireland. The watchword for the year 1902 was "Occupy."

Now the Twelve were told once more to prepare for Jerusalem. The months of waiting had been hard. Sandford was moved by the traces of suffering he saw in their faces. Conditions had been crowded and uncomfortable prior to Pas-dammin, with not enough heat or food. Mary Guptil had been seriously ill and was still not well, and Edward Doughty had been tormented by spiritual problems he could not discuss.

British newspapers were full of exciting news about Zionist activity in Palestine, but since an epidemic of bubonic plague was ravaging the Middle East, too high a risk for westerners just out of a sunless English winter, Sandford decided the trip should be undertaken in stages. They would go first to Egypt, where the disease was under control, and where he intended to open African headquarters. After "shaking flat the financial mountains," at the end of January the Twelve began a two-week journey from Birkenhead to Port Said on a small British ship.

Nathan Harriman did not go. The unresolved conflicts had resurfaced. Little John Sandford, on the verge of his sixth birthday, was named the last of the Twelve in Harriman's place.

"Oh, dear ones," wrote Sandford to the faithful in Maine, "Daybreak is at last appearing over the hilltop of the Eastern Hemisphere." They were moving fast toward another climax, "and lo, the horizon lights up before our very eyes."

But Margaret Main, dreaming twice of shipwreck before they embarked, expressed in her journal the persistent nervousness they all felt as they faced the trip. "We are like a company of hothouse plants," she wrote, "being thrust into lands where the devil has full control." In the Bay of Biscay, the second day out, they were caught in a ferocious storm, bad enough to make Joseph Harriman, seasick in his bunk, ask himself wryly if the restoration of the Holy Land was "worth it if it means this."

Four days later they arose on a bright morning to find Gibraltar on their left, and the continent of Africa on their right. Sandford hurried to his cabin to awaken Helen, so that she might see—fourteen years after the purchase of that special trunk for the Congo—the land she had once been so certain she would serve. Early in February, at Port Said, the group shot off a telegram to Maine: "Hallelujah! Shiloh, Take Africa!" That night, through prayer, "the history of Africa was permanently changed."

Very soon they were safely in Alexandria, at a beautiful frescoed mansion. God had whispered, "Wide open," and the owner reduced the rent by more than half. But this was just a sojourn on the way to Jerusalem. Early in May, after another party of five from Liverpool had been brought to Egypt to take over as Shiloh's first permanent missionaries to the Dark Continent, the Twelve entered the Mediterranean once more. At Jaffa, Suleiman Girby, the Arab who had rescued Sandford from shipwreck twelve years before in 1890, pulled them to shore in his own boat, and "fairly intoxicated with joy," Shiloh entered the Holy Land at last.

Little John kissed Girby warmly in greeting, because he had saved his "papa." Girby, who had been awarded medals from five countries for his bravery, was now a wealthy businessman with a large house on the beach. Sandford had stayed in touch with him over the years and often referred to him as an example of true manliness, his "marvelous natural strength, heroism and unselfishness" reminding him of Christ.

Yet in Shiloh's portrait of the future, Girby (and all Muslims who rejected Christ as explicit and exclusive Savior) would soon be the subject of God's final wrath. Sandford never made any effort to resolve that conflict, at least not in public, and it was probably not on his mind just now as the Twelve accepted Girby's sumptuous hospitality. The paradox was heightened further when deep into the night Sandford was roused by the whispered word "Gabriel" and a "sense of angelic hosts" surrounding the house. For two hours he and Whittaker breathed out "praises to Jehovah," convinced that "an angelic escort" had come to meet them, as it once had the patriarch Jacob (renamed Israel).

Angel or not, Israelite or doomed Mohammedan, it was Suleiman Girby who gave them their breakfast the next day and sent them off to the Holy City in a carriage drawn by three horses. At sunset, the awe-stricken twelve entered Jerusalem's great Jaffa gate, on what they believed to be the most significant errand in contemporary history.

But one still had to eat and sleep, so quarters were quickly found on Ethiopia Street, furniture and supplies collected, and housekeeping begun in the "Homeland." After several visits to Bethlehem and Calvary, the group traveled to the Jordan River, and John, wearing his white sailor suit, was baptized by his father.

John, a pensive, good-natured child, inserted a welcome lightheartedness into the group. Pint-sized among eleven adults, he seemed like "the ark of God being carried by the Israelites to the Sacred City," his father said. In whatever degree of humor that statement was made, John's role did appear to be growing in importance, in the eyes of the adults and, inevitably, in his own. But just now he was simply a little boy who seemed to be saying goodbye with baffling frequency.

For his father had raced off again. Leaving the Jerusalem headquarters in Willard Gleason's charge, Sandford headed back to America by himself, stopping briefly at Alexandria and Liverpool. The coronation of Edward VII was at hand, and all England was abuzz with preparation. At Pasdammin, Sandford preached on the royalty of the restored Kingdom from two o'clock on one afternoon until 3:00 the next morning—though he said later he had not intended to talk more than ten minutes. At that thirteen-hour service, God was crowned King of the Jews, and then recrowned as King of every nation represented in the ancestry of the gathered people (all Anglo-Saxons, as it turned out, all representatives of Anglo-Israel). Sandford closed the session declaring a "Coronation March"—a two-week vacation for workers, during which they might do exactly as they pleased, even to "picking the flowers in the hothouse or selling the silverware."

He was in a relaxed, jovial mood as he traveled home to America for the summer conventions in Durham. Somewhere in the middle of the Atlantic, he "took by faith" the ocean liner God had promised six years ago, then quietly completed his coronation rites by crowning God "monarch of the sea . . . Sovereign of the shipping world, of captains and officers and seamen on many waters."

Frank Sandford was home for just one intense month. In that time he preached day after day in a series of July conventions, baptized another ninety-seven people, married eight couples in a combined ceremony, served communion to six hundred in an outdoor service, ordained a dozen new ministers, and took a group of Shiloh boys on an outing to a local park.

The crowd on the hilltop was larded on the Fourth with the curious who had come to see Elijah. "It is God that you want," Sandford told them bluntly. If they would "get God" and forget everything else he said, they would go home rich. But he followed that with another specious disclosure. God had shown him that he was from the Tribe of Judah, the same tribe which had produced David and Jesus. He frequently returned to the subject of royalty, drawing analogies between himself and King David. In his last sermon he announced that God had said to him, "Prepare a throne," and "Occupy till I come."

In the middle of the month he buried his mother. Mary Jane Sandford, who was seventy-eight, had been an invalid in her daughter Maria's home for the last five years. A stroke victim, she had not communicated rationally with anyone for much of that time. Frank attended the funeral with six of his brothers and sisters, his first reunion with the family in a long time. Only the youngest sister, Annie, had joined Shiloh; most of the others lived at a distance, and Charles was still a patient at the State Hospital in Augusta.

It must have been a painful and uncomfortable time for them all. Frank had been aware for years of his family's bemused and often hostile reaction to his activities. Now there he was, Elijah among them as they gathered at the grave, yet in their eyes (and his, inevitably in spite of everything) just the baby brother who had once tagged around behind them on the Bowdoinham farm.

At the end of the month he was tired and said so. He felt as if he "had no strength left," and yet he must admonish them once more, warn them of disaster ahead for those who rejected his message. It would be a fearful day when the Son of God came and asked, " 'What did you do with my Forerunner?' "

Then he set his mind to the expedient business of wrapping things up on both sides of the water. He had decided it was imperative to present God with a "perfect Kingdom" before the end of the year, which meant that every last detail on the buildings must be completed. It added up to an onerous schedule before Christmas, to be carried out in his absence.

And who was to do it? By now most of his dependable leaders were overseas or at posts in North America, and he intended to bring a dozen more workers back to England, including Charles Holland, who had been the administrator on the hill for six years. To take over in this vacuum Sandford appointed three men: Ralph Gleason, George Higgins (an itinerate rural evangelist who had joined Shiloh four years earlier), and a newly ordained minister, Joseph Sutherland. All three were to find it a dubious honor before the end of the year.

To supplement the depleted work force on the buildings, members of the new churches were invited to spend the summer on the hill in the same kind of working vacation that had succeeded so well before. Just before leaving, Sandford rallied all the youngsters in residence and led them in a noisy parade seven times around the children's building, as Joshua had led his Israelite invaders around Jericho. The crusade belonged to them now, Sandford told the children. They were to be part of the work and prayer force that would bring down the walls of delay and incompletion. Then, like Elijah, he disappeared once more.

On arrival at Liverpool, he went abruptly into seclusion, shut up in his room at Pas-dammin. He remained there for more than two weeks, while perplexed students tiptoed in the hall outside. Some thought he was ill, or grieving over the loss of his mother, or lonely for Helen, whom he had left in Jerusalem and had not seen for months. Later he would only say that it was the "most awful fight of his life," and that he knew "Satan was giving him his personal attention."

Even his critics might have been sympathetic if he had confessed to being simply tired of people—of leading, cajoling, challenging, comforting, of being always the one who was "up." He had been riding high for months and would not allow himself to come down. "I want this company to come up with me," he had cried in America, "up, *up,* UP where God is." A plunge in mood was quite natural, like the struggle with depression years ago in Great Falls, New Hampshire, when he wept at the thought of leaving his house.

This occasion, like that one, must have frightened him. He had always been an emotional person, with extreme hills and valleys that sometimes startled him in their intensity. He had heard enough accusations of megalomania and insanity for the question to arise in his own mind. He knew the classic symptoms of old-fashioned madness as well as anyone—voices, grandiose notions, feelings of persecution. He knew how things could look to the world and dreaded the label of religious crackpot. He had responded rather transparently to such innuendo with his own intemperate accusations. "Many are the ministers that have gone to the insane asylum who have declared that I and some of my workers are insane!" he had once exclaimed.

Whatever else was wrong just now, certainly he was alone, and more alone than ever before. By declaring himself Elijah, he had become a superlative of the self-made man, and as such he was now different from all other human beings in the world, however much he determined to be natural.

Sandford had other reasons to be depressed as well. Word had come from Jerusalem that Mary Guptil's physical condition had grown worse, and that Eddy Doughty was gone. A loyal student since 1895, the Elijah announcement had been more than Doughty's faith could encompass. After wrestling with his doubts for eight months, he had cut himself off from the Twelve and had taken a room somewhere in Jerusalem.

Then there was still Nathan Harriman, the displaced member of the Twelve, who had been waiting in England, his future undecided. While Sandford was in seclusion these two weeks, Harriman was in isolation as well, sorting out his own reservations. If he could bring himself to the point of accepting Sandford's authority without resentment (without jealousy, he had been told), his role as a member of the Twelve was still open to him.

Sandford was in a bind. Unity was more essential than ever, and accurate timing absolutely crucial. The Feast of the Tabernacles would take place in Jerusalem at the end of September. Since the holiday marked the "ingathering" of faithful Jews from all over the world, it was imperative that all of the original Twelve, the gates through which Israel would return, be present, or God's purposes could not be carried out successfully. It was now the end of August. If both he and Harriman were to go, they must be reconciled immediately.

With that pressure as an added incentive, the two men made up once more. Every time they had a quarrel, said Harriman many months later, "every doubt I had ever had would come up, and then I would put them down and go on and try to believe things were going on, and succeeded in believing that I believed them."

It was September 11 before they were ready to go, too late to take the customary and most direct route, via Alexandria, since the plague had now closed that port to all ships. Sandford asked God to send them "like an arrow straight to its mark" and he meant it literally. An agent at Thomas Cook and Sons suggested going by land to Palestine either by way of Egypt or Constantinople. Out of the question, replied Sandford. Neither would be "straight" from London. The mystified agent, studying train and boat schedules, could see no other "straight" way. But he was in for a Shiloh surprise. Almost as they talked, a new sailing route was opened directly from Trieste at the head of the Adriatic to Jaffa. If a two-dimensional map could be trusted, the line as the crow flies between London and Jaffa shot as straight as any could be.

In a scene which harked back to the days when Frank would hitch up old Kate and dash for the depot in Bowdoinham, he and Harriman departed on a 1,500-mile rail trip, with uncertain connections to make in every country through which they passed and no assurance that they would arrive in time to book passage at Trieste. With a bit of jogging off the straight line—Paris, Basel, Lucerne, and Milan—they made it, boarded the *Bucovina,* and sailed blissfully across the Mediterranean, arriving in Jerusalem on September 21, three days before the Jewish festivities were to begin.

But as they stepped onto Palestinian land, the words "imminent peril" hissed in Frank's head. It was not unusual for western visitors to feel frightened in this country. Even under ordinary circumstances Turkish authorities required tourists to hire armed guards as a measure of protection against outlaws and political factions, and now, with thousands of pilgrims pouring into the city from all over the world, soldiers seemed to be everywhere, their weapons on display. But Sandford drew his uneasiness from the conviction that he and those in his charge had been targeted by more sinister forces. Satan would do everything in his power to undermine the movement at this most delicate time. Only intense prayer alleviated the shadow of danger and set the Twelve free to enjoy the thrill of the occasion.

The first task was to bring back Eddy Doughty—body, heart, and mind. Sandford sought him out, and to everyone's relief, the young man returned, vowing never to "rebel" again. A wire was zipped off to America: "Original party united. Alleluia."

The Twelve observed the Feast with their own concentrated agenda, including a night of prayer. Then at twilight on each of the days of the Feast they shared the Lord's Supper on the flat roof of the house at 17 Ethiopia Street. On the horizon they could see the Hill of Calvary, and from the narrow streets below the joyous festivities rose up to them as Jews in colorful robes greeted each other in a clamor of dialects. One night, yielding to impulse, Sandford stood at the edge of the roof and roared into the din of the city, "Behold your God!" The words came from the fortieth chapter of Isaiah, ". . . say to the cities of

Judah, Behold your God!" But to those who heard Frank's voice, it must have been like one more indecipherable cry in a strange language. No one in the streets had the faintest notion what momentous events were taking place on a housetop just above them.

Days earlier, sailing through the beautiful Greek Islands, Sandford had heard the words, "Renew the Kingdom." On October 2, his fortieth birthday and the last day of the celebration, he awoke early in the morning to a whispered word, "Beloved." The word had been more than an endearment to him for a long time; it was the Hebrew meaning of the name David. Excited, he dressed and climbed the stairs to the roof, where pacing back and forth in the dawn light, he received a "birthday message." It came in two parts. "I give to Jerusalem one that bringeth good tidings," followed quickly by "I have found David."

The first message was a fragment from Isaiah, recorded originally in the future tense ("I *will* give to Jerusalem"); the second was from the 89th Psalm: "I have exalted one chosen out of the people. I have found David my servant." Both passages had always been thought to herald the coming Messiah, but today Sandford heard them like ancient telegrams, sent out three thousand years ago and just now being delivered.

The Jewish-Christian world had been keeping one eye out for Elijah for a long time, but King David was not expected. True, long after David had lived and died, the prophet Ezekiel heard God say, "And I will set up one shepherd over them, and he shall feed them, even my servant David. . . ." But once again, Jews universally had accepted this as an allusion to Messiah. To the writers of the Gospels, Jesus, with lineage through Mary, was the Son of David, who would return to reign over both the Kingdom of the old covenant, the old promise, and the Kingdom of the new. Within that scheme of things what could it mean to Frank Sandford to be "found" as David? He knew, because he had been thinking about it for a long time. It was not that he was claiming the throne, or not permanently. But he believed that the Kingdom (old and new) was being restored to authenticity *now*. Jesus had told his disciples to "Occupy till I come." God had given the Twelve the watchword "Occupy" for 1902. "Prepare a throne," God had said. All put together, it meant unmistakeably to "hold the position," occupy the throne, as if Jesus Christ had said, in so many words, "Save my seat till I come back."

But it signified something beyond that. The words in Ezekiel, Sandford would soon explain to the Twelve, "refer to a man of God so spiritual . . . that seeking David . . . is equivalent to seeking Jehovah."

For almost ten years he had been drawn magnetically to David, the fair King of Judah, to his abandoned courage, his reckless jubilation, a "man after God's own heart." Even more than Elijah, David manifested the qualities Frank loved best in a man, a "splendid heroism" proven in the crisis, a prince, a king, a single worthy person who rose above the masses, representing strength, beauty, and benevolence.

A kingdom with David recrowned as king was not exactly the American Republicanism in which Frank had been raised. But David, in spite of his royalty, had presented himself as God's *servant* after all, the earthly ruler of a theocracy. Like Frank Sandford, he was just a farm boy, with ruddy cheeks and handsome eyes and a true aim. "I took you from the sheepcote and from following the sheep, to be ruler over my people," God had said to David, and Frank had written in *The Art of War,* "God is able to take a man out of the sheepfold or off the dunghill and set him among princes." He himself knew what the sheepfold meant. Hadn't he carried the scent of it on his clothes for all the days of his young life? David had moved from the pasture to guerrilla warfare, as head of the rag-tag army whose main source of strength was in the heart. Frank knew all about that as well. The parallels had grown and lengthened with the years.

"And now that God has given me to this land," he added in his journal, "now that I am henceforth identified with Palestine; now that my future headquarters is in this City; now that the future tense is changed to the present. . . . The Kingdom of our Father David, Rent and Shattered for Nearly Thirty Centuries, is today renewed!" The Church of the Living God, once the World's Evangelization Crusade on Apostolic Principles and the Holy Ghost and Us Bible School was immediately renamed—simply—the Kingdom. The movement had arrived at the heart of the history and the most important hope of every Christian and every Jew.

Of all the meaning packed into this moment, this strange non-event in the eyes of the world, there is one possible implication Sandford himself might not have been able to acknowledge. As a young man he had seen in the careers of baseball and politics a nod to his own ambition and ego that had no place in the life of a Christian. Yet as an American male, personal confidence and ambition were desirable, and as David those were possible. If, like any bright boy in the nineteenth century, Frank had ever contemplated the presidency of the United States, that goal seemed anemic now. He had incorporated into his private vision the maximum of power inherent in the tradition of the western world, and it was happening to a New England farm boy, one who had, in the most real sense he understood it, "climbed to the top."

Yet, wrote nineteen-year-old Joseph Harriman, also keeping a journal,

> No display, no robes of office, nothing to satisfy the world and feed the imagination with proofs of the greatness of our calling, and yet a work given the greatest commission ever conferred, with a leader called closer to God in authority than any human being who ever walked this earth. . . . A deep strong consciousness underlies all we have been doing today . . . , a new epoch has commenced, the time of completeness . . . ; we have been compelled to see that the greatest thing we could do was to be simple and natural.

There was no semblance of a coronation. To mark the occasion the group was photographed that day on the roof—fourteen of them, including John and an infant recently born to Willard and Rose Gleason. In that picture, taken under what must have been a beastly sun, the women and John all wear white, with straw hats on their heads. The men are dressed formally also, in frock coats and vests and pith helmets. Five of the men stand in the back row: Willard Gleason, Joseph Harriman, Nathan Harriman (turned sideways in the group, not quite facing the camera), Almon Whittaker and Sandford (both with head and body in direct confrontation with the black box). Helen Sandford and Mary Guptil stand between the two Harrimans, Helen with her deferential smile, and Mary very straight and unsmiling, her chin high over the white ruff and bow at her neck. She is dying.

So is Edward Doughty, who has come from his sickbed for the picture. Too weak to stand, he sits in a chair next to the small, white-clothed communion table with its pitcher of grape juice, a single glass, and plate of broken bread. He is buttoned up tight in a heavy coat. A visored cap is pulled down over his eyes, a cap similar to one he might have worn on a fishing boat in Casco Bay before enrolling as a student at Shiloh. With a full black moustache, he looks older than his twenty-nine years. Across his chest and down to his knees spreads a new banner—a white star and scepter on a purple velvet field. Eddy's head rests on the back of the chair; to his right are seated the other women and John, on the floor of the roof, and directly behind him with a hand on his chair stands Sandford.

After the picture was taken, Doughty went back to bed. While he lay ill during the next several days, the Twelve studied the meaning of the Kingdom. Sometime during that week Sandford made his triad complete. Melchizedek, the king-priest in Genesis, was thought also to be a genealogical branch of David—designating the ancestry of Messiah. In this complicated overlapping of symbols, Sandford, the forerunner of Christ, assumed the qualities of prophet, priest, and king.

Meanwhile, Edward Doughty grew progressively worse, sinking into delirium. No doctor was consulted, not even for diagnosis. Seven days after the David announcement, Doughty died of what the group now supposed was typhoid fever. Since no one else was sick, they assumed he had been contaminated by food or water while living away from the Shiloh house in his period of rebellion. He had been ambulatory for days after the onset of the fever, feeling somber and tired but not ill, until September 29, two days into the Feast of Tabernacles, when he could not leave his bed. Twice after that Sandford had prayed for him and declared him healed, according to Nathan Harriman's account. The first time Doughty had gotten up for dinner; the second time he had climbed to the roof for the photograph.

The loss of the young man struck a hard blow. He had been with the movement from the very beginning, one of those who had dug through the hard clay for the foundation of the first building. But it would be a mistake to spend time mourning. Satan had won a skirmish. It would not do to let him think his volley had done any more than to cause them a moment of reeling before they resumed their course. Doughty was given a tiny paragraph without the use of his name in a terse report Sandford sent home for a coming issue of *The Everlasting Gospel*. "We laid one to rest on Mt. Zion. During my absence he had rejected the writer as the Prophet of the Restoration and departed from our Company. Upon my return, however, he had seen his error. A little later God took him." He was buried in the English cemetery in Jerusalem, since there was no room in the American.

Nathan Harriman, who had been at Doughty's bed when he died and had watched to see "a perfect physical giant" reduced to "a skeleton," struggled with his own reactions. By law, doctors were called in after the death to issue a burial certificate. Harriman, one of those quizzed for information, was dismayed at the horror of the medical officials when they learned that Doughty had been taken up and made to move around at the height of his illness. The mortality rate from typhoid was known to be directly connected to the care received, with death nearly always not from the fever itself, but from complications, very often ulceration in the intestines. Unnecessary movement could cause internal hemorrhaging.

But whatever Nathan Harriman thought, he was not yet ready to reveal his growing convictions. If he was disgusted by the contents of a message from Sandford to Doughty's mother, a widow on Great Chebeague Island, explaining that "her boy had died gloriously," he kept it to himself.

A few days later the three Sandfords, with Mary Guptil and Almon Whittaker, left Jerusalem for America, intending to get back for the completion and dedication of the children's building at Christmas. They stopped at Liverpool to pick up thirteen returning workers, and to leave off Whittaker.

Almon Whittaker had now been separated from his wife and children for a year and a half, and had not yet seen the new baby, born soon after he left. If it had been his original intention to go home to them in America at this time, he did not. Sandford might not have directly ordered any of his workers to go or to stay in whatever circumstances, but he certainly would have advised Whittaker to go home as a "warrior and a conqueror" and not as a defeated soldier, unable to endure the suffering of separation. To be emotionally free for sacrificial service meant losing the fear of sacrifice. Recent life for Sandford himself had been an ongoing rehearsal of distancing, giving natural ties secondary importance. "I have no wife and baby," he had said years ago as he embarked for Jerusalem.

Whittaker, in the throes of the same schooling, was planting a tree that would bear bitter fruit years ahead. He stayed at Liverpool. The others sailed for America across a grey November sea, where another kind of harvest waited to be gathered.

Frank Sandford as Shepherd, after 1902.

On the rooftop at Jerusalem, Oct. 1902. L. to r., standing: Willard Gleason, Joseph Harriman, Helen Sandford, Mary Guptil, Nathan Harriman, Almon Whittaker, Frank Sandford.   Seated, l. to r.: Rose Gleason, Margaret Main, Adnah Guptil, John Sandford, Elnora Emerson, Edward Doughty.

The Extension as seen from Bethesda.

School on the bow and arrow, 1901, before the departure of the Jerusalem Party. Sandford stands at the tip of the arrow.

14

At the Strait Gate
1902

My father's family moved to Shiloh on October 3, 1902, the day following Frank Sandford's birthday message in Jerusalem. They knew nothing about that, of course, and if they had they might not have gone. After the former tentative connections, the decision to go was a sudden one, but still temporary, so they thought. To all appearances the return to the Growstown farm from Lewiston had been intended as permanent. They had even begun to attend the Free Baptist Church down the road, a measure that suggests deliberate independence from Shiloh.

Yet *The Everlasting Gospel* arrived regularly in the mail, and there was considerable talk in the house about Mr. Sandford, the children observed, especially whenever their father's brother and sister, George and Louella, came to visit. Their presence had always meant a zesty, drawn-out discussion about religion, anyway. Lou would hang her Salvation Army bonnet in the front hall and lie down on the kitchen couch, sick with what she called "woman trouble," but she was well enough to argue vehemently. Words like "eternal security" and "full salvation" shot around the room, while she plunked her fingers down on this or that Bible verse, and Wendell pulled out his commentaries and concordances to prove a fine point.

As for Shiloh, it was Arnold's impression that Louella was in favor of Sandford, but that Uncle George was now distinctly not. He did not like the sound of "all that Elijah stuff," Uncle George said. Wendell seemed to argue with them both.

Off and on students from the hilltop were invited to the White farm for brief vacations, and the discussions continued, in the kitchen, in the fields, in the barn. A new language was added to these conferences, words with thrilling overtones, Arnold thought—the "arch enemy," "the wrath of Jehovah," "applying the blood." Yet these allusions never seemed threatening. There was even a happiness and a hope about them, in the way they were spoken. In the evenings, as everyone worked together in the barn, cleaning the stanchions and bedding down the cows, those words, pitched by the students from the shadows beyond the lantern, seemed as harmless as clumps of clean hay.

True to her nature, Annie White seldom took part in the dialogue, though she listened with interest. One morning two young Shiloh men were holding forth in the kitchen as Annie prepared the noon dinner. Wendell was making milk deliveries in Brunswick, but all four children were present and a great deal was going on at once. Annie had just removed a cake from the oven, shoving back in an identical pan filled with suet scraps to be tried out for fat. When smoke poured from the stove, in her distraction Annie thought the cake was burning. Grabbing a holder, she snatched the suet tin. The hot grease spilled over her hand.

She immediately plunged her hand into a pail of cold water standing in the sink. But when the two students hurried to her side, she let them lift her hand from the water and hold it between their own, as they raised their voices to God on her behalf. The children, who had never seen their "stoical mother" cry, watched as tears ran down her face while the hand was shaken and pressed in the vehemence of the prayer.

The burn healed slowly and naturally many days after the students had gone back to Shiloh. Nothing more was made of the incident, even as little was said about Avis's arm, which still hung limp and useless at her side while she grew normally in every other way. At age three she had still not been healed. Yet the possibility that she would be had become tacitly accepted by the whole family.

In these ways, as Arnold saw it, Shiloh was very much part of their lives while it was actually happening at a distance. It proposed no decisions, certainly not for him. His own eyes were turned elsewhere. He and his sister Enid were growing up. In the worst of the haying season they were trusted to drive the dairy wagon alone to Brunswick to make the deliveries, pouring milk into the waiting containers on the back stoops and leaving off butter and eggs. Both looked forward to entering Brunswick High School in the fall. As young as they were—

he twelve and she thirteen—they had been tested and determined ready, thanks to their own fierce intramural competition and the tutoring of the Growstown country schoolmarm. Arnold had already decided he would go to college and study medicine.

He and Enid had always measured their growth by the work they were given to do, and Enid, a little older, a little taller, as strong as any boy her age ("when she grabbed your wrist, you might as well be manacled") had usually gotten the best of the honors. It was she who got to milk the best cows and to handle the horse. So when, in the middle of August, Arnold learned that boys were being recruited to finish lathing the interior of Olivet, the children's building over at Shiloh, he volunteered his time for two weeks. He had no idea what the children's building was for or why it was needed at a school for adults, but men's work in the company of other boys appealed to him, and Enid was not invited.

He traveled there alone, his first venture away from home by himself, taking the train to Lisbon Falls and the morning mail wagon to Durham (as Merlyn Bartlett had come three years before). Arnold had seen the place by now, visiting with his parents at last summer's convention, when he had heard Mr. Sandford speak for the first time. Today the grounds were filled with bewildering movement, men and women everywhere, carrying pails of loam or driving teams of horses pulling dump carts and scrapers. Piles of lumber lay here and there, along with cement troughs and ladders. Shouts carried over the sand and hammers rang in multiple echoes. The wind itself never seemed to stop.

In the front office of Shiloh Proper, where he shyly reported, several men sat in conference at a table. He recognized one of them as Mr. George Higgins, the minister in charge of Shiloh while Mr. Sandford was away in Jerusalem. Arnold knew Mr. Higgins at sight, because his father had once pointed him out. He had been tarred and feathered in Aroostook County a few years back for preaching Shiloh principles, so the story went. A good-looking man with a stern face (or perhaps a brave one), he seemed only kind now, he and the other men at the table. Someone said, "That's Wendell's boy," and someone else said "Halleluia," which seemed to Arnold vaguely like a compliment. He was instructed to go directly to Olivet and report to the "foreman of the lathing gang." So, with his shiny new lathing hatchet in his hand, he followed the sound of the hammers across the blowing sand to the square, granite building off to the southeast. To his left, as he proceeded, the monitor and blue slate roof of the brick hospital rose above the

dunes and pines, and to his right the hill dropped quite steeply, down
to the River Road and the old farms that raggedly edged it. Somewhere
a cow bellowed and from somewhere else another answered.

Once at Olivet (five hundred paces, Arnold counted), he crossed the
deep porch and climbed the unfinished staircase to the second floor.
There, in a large sunny room filled with noise and dust, a half-dozen
boys with hatchets and hammers shouted and laughed above their own
racket. Foreman there was none, it appeared, until a boy slightly older
and taller than himself, a robust-looking lad with large brown eyes and
tanned skin, walked over to greet him.

"I'm Leander," the boy said, in a voice that had already changed.

"I'm Arnold White."

"Have you acknowledged the Lord?"

"What?"

"Have you acknowledge the *Lord?*"

For a moment Arnold merely stared, fixing in his mind for life that
one brief moment—Leander with his bright face and rich coloring, and
he himself before him, feeling small for his age and wishing very much
that his voice were deeper.

"Had I acknowledged the Lord?" wrote Arnold, in memory of the
occasion. "Actually, I did not know what he meant and I doubt if he
did either. I knew that tasks undertaken at Shiloh were preceded by
prayer, but the rite was seldom designated by a term as erudite as this.
I realized that how one stood in the eyes of God was the all-important
thing, and that there were superiors who could make that judgment.
Leander was, at the moment, a superior. I took a chance and mumbled,
'Yes.' "

Up on the stepladders Leander gave instructions in the art of nailing
the horizontal wooden laths to the joists, spaced just right to receive
the first layer of the lime-and-hair plaster, to be applied by the next
crew. In a few days Mr. Parillo, the man in charge of the plastering,
would exclaim with a shake of his head: "The Holy Ghost is holding
up that ceiling! Praise God! Praise God!"

Other than meals, when the entire community gathered in the immense
dining room at the back of the Extension, the world of the lathing gang
was the small one of Olivet. Most of the boys, like Arnold and Leander,
had come only because of the work. They slept dormitory-style in a
finished basement room in Olivet, under the supervision of Mr. Tupper,
a cheerful, round-faced young man from Colby. At the end of the long
hot days, they dashed for the river to swim off the sticky dust of their

work, and sometimes early in the evenings a few of the men students joined them on the athletic field below the grove for a game of ball before dark.

As for strange praying, Arnold heard none. Singing he heard in plenty, a great choir, carried by the wind all the way across the sand from the chapel in Shiloh Proper, lively martial tunes that some of the other boys already knew. "Storm the forts of darkness! Bring them down, down, down!" There were others set to old Civil War tunes, such as "Marching Through Georgia" and "Tenting Tonight," and one that made Arnold's heart beat faster:

> Give me a place in the world's great fight,
> The fight for the good and the true,
> A place where the wrong outrivals the right
> And there's a soldier's work to do.

He went back to the farm in a glow, feeling part of something important, glad to be home, anxious to get to high school, and amazed and excited to learn that the entire family would be moving to Shiloh early in October to stay for three months. At Mr. Sandford's request by telegram, a new deadline had been set for the completion of Olivet, and all Siloh supporters who could possibly do so were being asked to live on the property until Christmas and donate their time in this last big drive.

Wendell and the children were eager to go, but Annie was quieter than usual, Arnold observed, as she began to pack. She liked dependable routine, and once more the family schedule was to be disrupted, the children extracted from school, and the dairy rented to a neighbor. That may have been all that was bothering Annie—the restless jumping about, knowing that in three months it would happen all over again.

In spite of that they carried a great deal with them. They drove away from the farm looking like gypsies, their baggage wagon piled high with furniture and bedding and trunks of clothing and necessities— dishes, soapstones, lamps, chamber pots, and wash bowls—the two younger children perched on top while Arnold and Enid rode their bikes. It was a bright, promising day, with an Indian Summer heat drying the damp morning air in the shadows of the stone walls. The ten-mile trip, up hills and down, took all of three hours. That was how they went, feeling no rush, sparing the horse all they could and enjoying the trip, riding lazily into the next eighteen years of their lives.

Shiloh in the fall of 1902 was an enigma to the White children, both stimulating and perplexing, an anomaly in which the boundaries of their family life merged into the boundless, unmapped territory of the surrounding community. Their new home was at the back of the Extension, a second-floor suite over the communal kitchen. The quarters duplicated the other suites in the building, one main spacious room with a bay window and a row of five small bedrooms. It was a finished apartment, clean and filled with the good smells of new lumber, though the staircase lacked risers and a railing, and the hallway remained unplastered. Over a hundred extra people had come to supplement the work force, all 30-fold and 60-fold families. Inside as well as out one was aware of a constant sense of population, footsteps overhead, voices in the halls. The large windows of the main room looked out over the rear grounds to the pine grove and across the river to the tracks of the Boston and Maine, but the windows of the bedrooms opened into a central airshaft. Sounds traveled through this ventilations system, a cozy hubbub of conversation, laughter, and crying babies.

Each day began with the same routine, but by mid-morning the schedule was up for grabs. A hand-bell awoke them at 6:30, rung around the verandas. While the aroma of baking bread and cornmeal mush drifted up from the kitchen below, there was leisure time for family worship, something the Whites had never done at home. At 8:00 the verandas and halls began to hum with the tread of feet as residents headed for the dining room, where families shared tables and serving bowls—except on Saturdays, when cocoa and hot gingerbread were delivered to the suites.

Breakfast was followed by a daily hour of prayer and singing in the chapel. Children aged fifteen and under stayed for only the early portion of this, then were ushered out to their own classes. There was no secular schooling, since those who had been teaching the previous handful of Shiloh children were occupied in labor on the buildings. Now, the more than fifty temporary scholars met each morning in two large groups in unused rooms of the Extension. Arnold and Enid belonged to the older class, as did Leander Bartlett and his sister Merlyn (a thin, dreamy-eyed girl whom Arnold caught looking at him on several occasions—or perhaps she was staring into space.) Their proctor was Mr. Tupper, who supervised them in something like a daily Sunday school, an hour that moved quickly as he taught them the lives of Old Testament heroes, adding contemporary details with his pleasant, deadpan humor.

When that class ended, so did any consistent organization to the day.

The older children headed for Olivet as a rule, to work there in whatever way they were needed. Adults fasted until dinner at 4:00 P.M., but at noon children were served a thick slice of homemade bread and molasses, with milk for the little ones. Arnold and Enid drank water, feeling comfortably righteous in the sacrifice.

The afternoon, too, might be spent in work, but Arnold found himself with hours of time on his hands for free play and, in spite of the wonderful variety of friends, with not enough to do. Exploring the premises was always an option, racing down to one of the barns where the Shiloh horses were kept, or out to the pine grove where long swings carried you on a thrilling ride over the deep hill. You could pick fragrant, wormy apples from the ancient orchard (the lower branches in easy reach because of the sand dunes), or play at the Mouth of the Brook, a stream that fed into the river. Enid and Arnold often sailed off on their bikes down the River Road, but were careful not to go together. Boys and girls, they had been told, were not to be seen with each other unchaperoned, not even brothers and sisters, to "avoid the appearance of evil." Usually Arnold went with Herbert Jenkins, a friend he had made in August. Herbert and his sister Maud, members of Shiloh's one Negro family, were living under the care of other parents while their own worked as evangelists in New York City.

Parenting tended to be an across-the-board affair in any account. In principle any person older than yourself was a superior and must be obeyed. New rules sprang up out of the air, their reasons not always clear. But it was absolutely essential to obey, instantly, without stalling, the way soldiers must obey in battle. Arnold, who had learned long ago to comply with adult standards and still keep a sense of freedom, took this in stride. He was beginning to catch on to the fact that everything mattered at Shiloh. It mattered how you acted, how you talked, even how you thought and looked. Every person was an important unit of behavior.

He liked that, though it carried taxing expectations. He liked being included in the great push to get things finished. If anything puzzled him, it was that the work week involved only four days, when they must accomplish so much before Christmas. Very little was done on Thursdays, the day of prayer for the sick of the world, and both Saturday and Sunday were sabbaths. Saturday was the true Sabbath, a family day of rest, with no active play, and Sunday was the day of worship. At home on the farm there had not been even one day of rest a week, for the cows must be milked in any event, and Wendell and Annie had

never been strict about keeping Sunday special. As for church, there
was church at Shiloh every morning.

Yet to Arnold's surprise, church was never tiresome. On weekdays
the older children's class was allowed to sit together in the balcony for
the half hour they attended, looking down into the light-filled room
under the white tongue-in-groove ceiling. Three large pictures hung on
the walls—a grey battleship *Maine* plowing the seas over a map of the
state, an eight-foot-wide oil painting of sheep on a hillside, and behind
the platform a long chart of the world's population, divided by religions.
Arnold memorized the incomprehensible numbers and wondered who
had done the counting: 856 million heathen, 170 million Mohammedans,
8 million Jews, 190 million Roman Catholics, 116 million Protestants.
The heathen were represented by the bottom two-thirds of the chart,
in black squares, a square for each one million lost souls. One white
square, all by itself in that encompassing blackness, stood for the million
who had been converted to Christ in the last century.

There were certain rewards in arriving early for chapel. While the
piano, and sometimes a horn, played a lively tune, the room filled quickly,
women adjusting white handkerchieves on their heads (a sign that they
were "under protection," the children had been told), men removing
their hats—those just in from early work in the gardens revealing a
two-toned forehead, white above the rim of the hat, sunburned below.
Blustery Mr. Kent huffed in off the front steps, a perfect "John Bull"
with his thick grey beard and bald pate. He had "played cricket with
Edward, Prince of Wales," he once told the boys. Up in the balcony
they laughed at him secretly. Chairs scraped on the floor as people knelt
to pray before seating themselves. Someone would distribute the white
hymnals; someone else would wind the oak clock and adjust its hands.
All brought their own Bibles, books which looked oddly small and soft
in the big, gnarled hands of some of the men. Mr. Anderson, who ran
Shiloh's sawmill, was known to put his calloused palms flat down on
a hot stove to warm them. Yet he leafed through the thin pages of his
Bible with delicacy.

There were few formalities at these meetings. Mr. Higgins and other
ministers sat in white chairs on the platform (there was an empty gold
chair for the Holy Spirit) and took turns leading, which meant announcing
hymns and Scripture and perhaps reading a letter from Mr. or Mrs.
Sandford. Birthdays were recognized and prayers requested for this and
that, or people told of being healed of colds or rheumatism. It was like
a huge conversation which included God, since it was interspersed with

prayer. Anyone could pray, but no one ever prayed alone. The pray-*er* was always in danger of being drowned out by the vocal support of others, and sometimes several voices would rise together in a rapid-fire volley so clamorous you had to open your eyes, thinking there was something to see as well as hear. There often was. Fists hit the air, knees and chairs bumped the floor. The women always prayed last, and sometimes, before the children were beckoned out to their classes, several women would rise to their feet, waving handkerchieves and singing whichever song won over, while little Sister Purdy danced up and down the length of the balcony behind the chairs, her hair and headgear flopping and her hands clapping.

In their schoolroom later the children could still hear the faint sounds of these "Charges." The class was urged to pray that God would make them strong warriors who could resist the forays of the devil and the anti-Christ. If they were loyal and true, they might be chosen some day to be part of Christ's great army at the battle of Armageddon. Arnold found this undisturbing, hearing it from a good-natured teacher in the company of friends, but secretly he hoped nothing would happen until he and Herbert Jenkins had finished building a raft at the Mouth of the Brook.

Meanwhile the artists, Mr. and Mrs. Ferguson, were working on a six-foot-square painting depicting the children of Shiloh with their arms raised to a crowned, robed Jesus returning in the clouds. All of them were included in this, posing several at a time or one by one, watching with fascination as the scene grew on the canvas, girls with braids down their backs and boys in knee pants and high shoes. Even Avis was in it, holding up two good arms to the sky. The painting was to hang in the chapel at Olivet when the building was completed.

Arnold's sister Doris found the painting a comfort. She had been told in her class that the sun would darken and the moon turn to blood before Jesus returned, but the picture presented no such threat. In that, He was coming on a normal, sunny day. Avis, little more than a toddler, was too young to catch the overtones that worried Doris. What she dreaded was the clanging of the brass bell, calling her mother away to meetings in the chapel. Then, left in the care of her siblings, or at times by herself in the suite, she waited a chain of small eternities for Annie to return. Standing now and then in the hall outside the chapel door, she was baffled by what she heard, as people shouted and sometimes wept. Words of hymns met her ears in a confusion of meaning. It was a long time before she knew that "fill with fullness divine" was not "fill with full nasty vine."

The bell was disorienting to all of the children. Anything could be interrupted by it, as adults were called to prayer—almost always for money, breathtaking amounts of it that seemed to evaporate as soon as it was provided. No sooner had thousands of dollars come in answer to prayer than another emergency arose, for lumber and hardware, and for expenses overseas, where many people depended on Shiloh's prayers for their rent and their food.

One morning early in November as Arnold walked by the kitchen on his way out doors, he overheard a conversation. Men from John Cartland's dairy farm, who had brought the milk as usual, were being told by the young woman in charge of the kitchen to take it back. "There is no money to pay for it," she told them. The dairy men offered to leave it anyway, to be paid for later; it would go sour, otherwise, they said, and Shiloh should have the good of it. But the woman was adamant. They were never permitted to buy on credit.

That day there was no milk, not even for the small children, a shocking state of affairs to Arnold, who had never imagined the absence of milk, though family fare at home had been buttermilk, or the pale skimmed milk Annie had kept in a crock in the cellar where the children could help themselves.

In a day or two milk was restored, at least for babies and the sick. But soon the children noticed a paring down of portions. Slices of bread were cut thinner, and people were asked to pray for the barrel of flour a day it took to make enough bread. Wendell, on his return from the farm each week, had been stopping at a store to pick up snacks for the suite—stale Boston brown bread or a clump of dates—and Mr. Shaw, the buyer for the Shiloh storeroom, had persuaded a Lisbon Falls grocer to give him the cooky crumbs and peanuts from the bottoms of barrels as a treat for the children. Now these snacks substituted as lunch, for the children's noontime bread and molasses was stopped.

Shiloh meals had not been sumptuous so far, but they had been adequate and often very good. Dinners were familiar fare—creamed codfish, hash and applesauce, baked beans on Sunday night (slow-baked by hot rocks in the ovens), and on Thursday night pea soup which soaked all day during the six hours of prayer for the sick. But now every dinner consisted of fall produce from the gardens, sometimes only one vegetable at a time, carrots, potatoes, or turnips. No one complained. At this very time the Fergusons had begun to paint a ten-foot-long mural on one wall of the dining room, a splendid sunny harvest of vegetables under the words, WHETHER YE EAT OR DRINK OR WHATSOEVER YE DO, DO ALL TO THE GLORY OF GOD.

Whatever their content, the two meals a day were served in exactly the same manner. Tables were set with ironed cloths and napkins. Everyone stood until a blessing had been asked and after eating no one was excused until someone had "returned thanks," at length, as if they had just been served a banquet. It did not pay to eat fast. Arnold learned—a hard lesson, since fast eating was a family trait. There was nothing to do but sit when you were done and wish for more. Coffee and tea were taboo, even for adults.

Still, these communal mealtimes, with their orchestra of voices and clinking dishes, were always sociable. So it came to Arnold with an unexpected twinge one day that he missed the farmhouse kitchen. The familiar hub of private family life was gone. This was not something he dwelled on, or even mentioned. He knew that any hint of dissatisfaction would be most unacceptable to his parents, who had never under any circumstances countenanced self-pity. No one talked about food in a nostalgic way, though many prayed for it. "We must trust God for br-raid," said a lady from Scotland, with a gentle smile. People were turning in every penny to the office—all spare coins, postal cards, and stamps. Veiled stories were exchanged of pressure put upon various persons who had resources they were not sharing, and prayers often carried unveiled protests against those who were "robbing God." Here and there in the dining room, faces were suddenly missing, as certain families who had come to help in the drive "deserted."

Others were sick in bed. In fact, more people seemed to be sick than well. A bad strain of "La Grippe," with its attendant stomach cramps and dysentery, was making its speedy rounds from suite to suite. Annie became a full-time nurse, as many of the women did, going from family to family with soup, cleaning up rooms, and doing extra wash.

To make things more difficult, temperatures were dropping to winter levels, and there was no money for coal. The dining room and most of the suites were unheated. In fact, radiators had not yet been installed in the White family quarters or many of the suites. Bethesda, which was heated with steam and for which the coal supply was reserved, was already overcrowded with the ill. The smaller children's classes were moved to the bakery, which held the warmth of its early morning fires in the big brick ovens. Wendell brought a round wick kerosene heater from the farm and kept it lit mornings and evenings in the main room of the suite, now divided in half by blankets hung as curtains so a family from a colder area of the Extension could camp on the other side.

Though the original plan had been to provide one full bathroom for every four suites, the only facilities actually operating in the Extension were clear to the front of the building, in Shiloh Proper. To these toilets people carried their chamber pots, discreetly covered, each morning. Daytimes, two large outhouses in the pines, a men's and women's, bore the traffic, referred to as "down over the hill," six holes each with hinged covers. It was a provision wholly familiar to the Whites and other farm families, and the places were kept meticulously clean, whitewashed, and regularly limed. The problem was their inadequacy. In ordinary circumstances they were busy enough, especially after a long chapel service. Now half the population, it seemed, had what Wendell called "Dame Trots." What would have been taken in stride by a family of average number without indoor plumbing became a problem of monumental size.

Arnold did his best not to arrive first at that place in the morning, as it was the first-comers who melted with body heat the frost accumulated during the night. On the other hand, if you were late you shivered as you stood in wait outside. Once inside, numbed fingers struggled with buttons. Feeling sorry for himself one morning, Arnold remembered that even now he ought to be conscious of the love of God. Nothing was supposed to separate him from that. It occurred to him with some comfort that the Apostle Paul had lived in a better climate when he wrote those words.

Ernest Tupper and others who led the children's classes guided them in "getting right with God" so they might be delivered from illness. This required protracted periods of kneeling while they explored their inner lives and prepared themselves both for confession and for insight into each other's shortcomings, which it was their duty to present. "Introvertish examination of ourselves and watchfulness over others didn't feel right," notes Arnold, "but we made ourselves conform."

The more they did it, the more they found to confess. One must be honest, willing, kind, industrious, and unselfish. Then there were the "secret sins," the hardest to disclose. Enid got up in meeting one day to "deny the flesh life," admitting she thought she was pretty and "liked to look in the mirror." She was "against that pride" now and no longer had "any fellowship with it," she said, in a perfect imitation of Shiloh vernacular. She was indeed pretty, Arnold remembered, switching her brown braid with determination as she talked. She was praised by Mr. Tupper for her "brave cleansing of spirit."

In the long periods on the hard floor Arnold began to use a large soft Bible as a buffer for his bony knees, until Bessie Parillo, a daughter of the mason, took him aside with a gleam in her eye to say she thought he was "treading on the Word of God." He complied with meekness, as he had been instructed to do. But his own efforts as a vigilante failed. One day, red-faced, scraping up all his will-power to be a "tattler," he reported to Mr. Ferguson that his son Paul had been "wrestling" with another boy in the out-of-bounds area of the unfinished Extension. Ferguson scolded Arnold sharply for "rat-hunting" and told him to tend to his own sins. Though embarrassed beyond words, Arnold was able to absorb this minor flaw in the system. He was doing as he was told, and it must be working, since he had not gotten ill.

Protracted illness, he observed, carried a burden of shame. Something was wrong with people whose bodies resisted healing. Several persons with odd maladies lived at Shiloh that fall. One was Mr. Flynn, a tired-looking young man who had come to Shiloh to be healed of epilepsy, or perhaps it was demon possession. The White children had seen him in seizure once in the dining room, and wondered why he did not break every bone in his body, catapulting himself from his chair, twisting his head and pounding the floor with his heels. Ministers rushed to his side to pray, while families tried to go on with their meal as if nothing were the matter.

One night the Whites were startled from sleep by a crash somewhere up in the airshaft, as if a very large person had fallen out of bed. Strange new noises followed—thrashings and choked cries. The hall thundered with running feet as men's voices began to shout, three or four at once, in a rush of language. "The blood! The blood! By the power of the blood I order you out! Down you go! Down, down in the mighty name of Jesus! I bind you! I chain you! I smite and blast you!"

Avis began to wail in fright. Annie, in her nightgown, her hair in a braid down her back, hurried to the children's bedrooms with a lamp to assure them nothing dangerous was happening. It was just Mr. Flynn having a spell. After what seemed a long while, things grew silent in the room overhead.

A few days later Mr. Flynn left the hilltop for good, still unhealed.

By the middle of November Arnold was more than ready to go home. Sickness had cut the work force drastically and the money for materials was gone. Days went by with no lathing or painting to do in Olivet.

The weather was grey and damp and daylight closed down quickly in the afternoons. Outdoor play was unpleasant. Children cast about the gloomy halls with nothing to do. There was whispered talk that a boy had run away, and then another. The brass bell gathered adults into the chapel day and evening, with meetings that ran far into the night.

Then on a particular day in the week before Thanksgiving, the mood changed. Word spread quickly that Mr. Sandford and his family, who had been on their way home for a month, were due to arrive any time, bringing a large party of new students from England. The news was absolutely energizing, as if a long train had reached the top of a grade and had begun the descent with a new burst of speed. "Things will be different now, you'll see," people were saying. Some of those who had been ill were suddenly up and about, preparing for the occasion. Children were rehearsed for a role in the grand welcome. It was like the return of a king from a prolonged and distant battle.

Early one evening the Gospel Carriage went to meet the travelers at the Lisbon Falls station. An hour later it pulled up the hill to a Shiloh ablaze with lights—lamps in every window and lanterns hanging from the flagpoles. The band began to play through the windows of the front turret, while down at the foot of the driveway Arnold joined two rows of boys with lanterns who escorted the vehicle up the hill, each with something memorized to tell Mr. Sandford about the progress on Olivet.

Shiloh viewed from a distance. Far right, Bethesda. Center, Olivet. John Douglas's barn left foreground, with Holland Cottage behind it. Hephzibah farmhouse sits exact center. Courtesy Androscoggin Historical Society.

Olivet

Bethesda

Some of Shiloh's children.

15
Day of Vengeance
1902–1903

The exact chronology of events in the early part of the Black
Winter is hard to assess. Everything appears to have happened
at once, and perhaps it did. To sort that out, we must begin with
Frank Sandford's expectations. He crossed the Atlantic to America riding
the tips of the waves, exhilarated by the certainty that a crucial point
had been reached in Shiloh's agenda. In a matter of months he had
accomplished the work of years. The Restoration of the Kingdom had
been authenticated in Jerusalem. The Holy Land awaited the return of
Israel and the House of Judah. He was more than ever convinced that
the events he had been talking about were breaking upon the world.
Over forty missionaries were actively at work in Europe and Africa,
and at the centers in North America scores more were ready to go to
the uttermost parts of the world at a moment's notice, the stone in
Daniel's prophecy which would grow to a mountain and fill the whole
earth. He was coming home in November of 1902 to share the revelation
of "David Truth" and all it implied for the future unity and power of
the Kingdom.

Instead he came back to a nightmare—a hilltop overrun with some
three hundred people who seemed to have fallen half-dead in their tracks.
It was like discovering three hundred versions of Olive Mills on their
deathbeds, and it was up to him, as it always seemed to be, to bring
them back to life. The work he had hoped to see completed was far
from finished. Dozens of suites in the Extension still lacked floors. Olivet
had come a standstill, and an estimated $8,000 was required for its
completion.

Sandford's reaction, after the first shattering disappointment, was to call home all the 100-fold members throughout the country and Canada for a forty-day working convention which would start immediately, merging with the Thanksgiving convention. As the telegrams went out, a kitchen crew swung into the preparation of the holiday dinner, to be served to as many guests as the dining room could hold. The prospect astonished the hungry families in residence, but somehow the money materialized, as it always did when Mr. Sandford was present. Dependable reinforcements began to arrive for the forty-day Drive, the Thanksgiving convention brought in hundreds of dollars, and the work on Olivet resumed.

It was only now, in early December, after the guests had departed, that Sandford began to assess the actual breadth of the problem. It came down to the familiar specter of mixed spiritual levels. Many of the dozens of 30- and 60-fold members who had moved in temporarily for the Olivet Drive had little comprehension of requirements for life on the hill. In fact, some of these very people had already been rejected in the past as unsuitable for 100-fold membership. Since July, when they first began to arrive, their numbers had created a context of carnality—grumbling and self-pity—which had corrupted the entire community. Sandford himself had invited these people, and Shiloh needed them, but he had expected the Bible school and the ministers to bring the visitors up to Shiloh's high standard. Instead, everyone had dropped to the "lower lines," a compromise that ran diametrically counter to God's purposes for the hill. As a flagrant manifestation of this laxity, three teenaged boys had run away, all of them sons of ministers.

Inevitably, in these circumstances, sharing the sublime news of the David revelation was akin to casting pearls before swine. Many of the less committed members, Sandford now understood, had never made a "right adjustment of heart" to Elijah. The new truth seemed to fall on ears of stone.

It appears that George Higgins was disciplined first. As minister in general charge, Sandford held him responsible for the pedestrian spirit on the premises. Higgins was banished to Hephzibah and forbidden to see or speak to anyone but the members of his own family. Praying for him, Sandford was engulfed in an ominous sense of God's judgment. The words "Prepare to meet thy God" repeated in his head. Higgins was to be severely punished by God, "if not killed," Sandford said in a letter to the workers overseas. "I have been holding my breath," he wrote. If the man should die, "a dozen hells would not be any too bad for him." It seemed that "public justice would demand the full penalty of God's wrath."

Two weeks later another message, "Set him free," released Higgins from condemnation. By this time it was clear that everyone on the hilltop—every adult and every child—had fallen under judgment, a landslide of wrath and retribution that nothing could stop, that even Sandford himself was powerless to control. "The white searchlight of eternity" had been turned on them all.

In the first week of December, before the last of the workers had managed to make their way back to Maine, bad weather set in. Blizzards with forty-mile-an-hour winds buried the northeast, making travel all but impossible. Gales and storms continued throughout the week while temperatures dropped lower than most adults could remember. The *Lewiston Sun,* which the Whites received by post each day, reported frozen rivers and channels and accidents at sea as coastal craft iced up and bore down upon rocky ledges. Yet the workers straggled in to the Lisbon Falls depot almost daily, filling the hilltop's quarters to capacity just as a coal-mining strike in Pennsylvania shut down stoves and furnaces throughout New England and banished any new hope of heat in the Extension.

Herbert and Maud Jenkins had been waiting anxiously for news of their parents and younger brother, on their way from New York, with the last lap of their journey to be taken by sea from Boston to Bath. They arrived safely on the tenth of the month. Two days later Herbert told the Whites that his mother and brother Theodore were in bed with bad colds. That was the last Arnold saw of his friend for many weeks. On December 10 Dr. Ida Miller brought Sandford the news that there were two cases of smallpox in the Extension—Susie Jenkins and her son Theodore—and that a large and undetermined number of people had been exposed. Within another week a quarantine was imposed, and four hundred souls on every level of spirituality found themselves trapped together on the hill, forbidden to leave by the laws of the State of Maine.

Though the state required notification to the Board of Health in cases of infectious disease and Shiloh sometimes called outside doctors for diagnoses to facilitate nursing care, that was still the extent of Shiloh's dependence on help from the medical community. Several licensed nurses worked at Bethesda. These and others who had survived the epidemic earlier in the spring were put to work, monitoring every suspicious incidence of illness. The Holland Cottage became a pest-house, with the red flag of contagion hanging from one of its windows.

"The most frightening thing we children saw," Arnold recalled, "was a sheet-covered victim on a stretcher, being edged down the stairs in the Extension, on the way to the Holland Cottage." The Jenkins's quarters were scrubbed down with carbolic acid. The halls reeked of disinfectant. Outgoing mail from the post office at the foot of the hill began to be fumigated before pick-up. Deliveries were left outside the service entrances by nervous tradespeople.

On January 4 Susie Jenkins and her three-year-old son Theodore both died. That day five new cases were reported, including Mr. Jenkins.

Everything that happened at Shiloh for the rest of the winter must be viewed against the backdrop of isolation. No one in the surrounding world knew what was going on behind the walls of the quarantine, and Shiloh members were forbidden to discuss hilltop affairs in correspondence with outside relatives and friends. Shut up together for months with no way to escape, feeding on each other's perceptions, the people on the Durham hill faced the possibility of physical extinction, of being actually wiped out. This was no ordinary epidemic.

Early in the quarantine Sandford and the ministers entered a fast, seeking special power to heal the sick and stay the infection. Throughout the school prayer began for deliverance, but very soon it was determined that prayer was useless, and that in the case of certain individuals it was actually "against the will of God." There was no way to hold back the inevitable. Those who had sinned were no longer "under protection." In these days when God was "going to cut down men like grass," not only the unsaved of the world were to be the subject of His anger but those of His people who failed "to do His will as fast as He makes it known."

The words were Ralph Gleason's. As a minister in charge, he was one of those under particular judgment. So was Joseph Sutherland, whom Sandford had left as overseer of the progress on the buildings. Joseph, a middle-aged man who had lost his wife to illness some years before, had come to Shiloh to begin a new life and had been married for the second time in the multiple ceremony the previous summer. Sutherland's son was one of those who had run away. Finding his way to his mother's relatives in Lynn, Massachusetts, the boy had refused to come back. His desertion may have had more to do with the new marriage than conditions at Shiloh, but Sandford saw it only as a case of parental weakness and Joseph was denounced before the assembly in chapel.

The weather, keeping everyone indoors on many days, contributed to what followed. Fierce winds held temperatures far below zero. Great rumbles rose from the frozen river as water churned under the ice at the "starting up" of the mills. On the hill, where the wind was seldom still even in mild seasons, a walk across the grounds from building to building was exhausting. Drafts swept through the halls of the Extension from the unheated sections. One day water spilled at the swinging doors between dining room and kitchen froze on the floor. Mumps and whooping cough, adding confusion to the huge nursing responsibility, made their way from family to family. Every cold, every initial fever, was potentially smallpox.

The children who lived through the Black Winter had trouble later putting a finger on the exact time when they themselves became the focus of the terror, except that it began with the talk of those three "bigger boys" who had run away weeks before. The idea of running away from home, under any conditions, aroused scary emotions. For the child of a minister to do so was even more scandalous—all Shiloh children knew that, for the ministers were just below Mr. Sandford in the chain of authority, and under Elijah's leadership, they had been told, the "hearts of children would be turned to the fathers." That truth had now entered a whole new level of danger: if a child misbehaved, it was as if the parents had directly disobeyed God, and God might punish the parents by punishing or even killing the child.

"We were frightened to the point of spinal chills by the talk of leaders about the danger, unless we each lived close to God and made sure all faults were confessed 'one to another,' " recalled Arnold. There were no grey areas. You were on God's side or Satan's. Periods of confession intensified under Mr. Tupper's guidance, to protect them from the "plague," as the first-born of the children of Israel had been protected at the first Passover. Doris, told in the class of younger children to "strive to enter in at the strait gate," found those words a frightening mystery. "Strive as in an agony," her teacher had said. In tears, Doris went to Enid and begged her to explain. What did that mean, and what was the "strait gate"?

At age ten she had caught full-face the wind of abstraction that was buffeting Shiloh's adults. A set of rules for behavior she could readily understand and obey. But obviously one could do everything right (or at least nothing wrong) and still fall short of the standard. It was the inner landscape, your feelings, that needed monitoring most, and how on earth could you tell when your *feelings* were right?

Enid gave her the best comfort she could but was at a loss to shed light that was meaningful, and Doris went away in great anxiety. If she could not evaluate her own behavior, how could she confess to her failure? And that, she saw clearly, put her in danger of being struck down by sickness.

One of the parents from Tacoma, Washington, Estella Sheller, was appalled at the "rat-hunting" encouraged among the children. Combing through each other's lives looking for sin, they were influenced by what adults saw or "felt" in them. "If there was sin or rebellion in them, they were punished by severe whipping or fasting, or both, as the case required. Apparently Frank condoned the beatings which began at this time. Mrs. Sheller heard him say that whipping was the "schoolmaster to bring them to Christ."

Crowded together at Shiloh under a blanket of widespread disapproval, all were schoolmasters and all were helpless students in a system of control that was spinning away beyond any control at all. The beatings went on as if no one knew how to stop. Day and night the airshafts carried the cries of youngsters being "chastened." The general rule, observed Estella Sheller, was that a child must be whipped "until there was no doubt in the mind of anyone that he was conquered." She was made sick, she said, by the screams of one small boy whipped by his father night after night, often as late as 1:00 A.M., waking everyone in that section of the Extension, until someone finally "stopped it." Stories circulated of several older boys whipped by their fathers in the woods, one with a horsewhip.

Wendell and Annie, like Estella Sheller, belonged to a cluster of parents disgusted at this escalation of discipline, though they hardly knew how to deal with it. Their suite was invaded by the cries of two boys who belonged to the family on the other side of the blanket curtain. They were spanked so often Doris could not imagine what they had done to be so naughty. Across the shaft a woman "spanked her children every morning," according to Arnold, "because they wet the bed." The pattern of sounds astonished him. Though the children always cried at first, soon there would be silence—all but the whacks of the slipper (or whatever was being used) on a bottom. He stood it as long as he could, then in spite of his earlier failed mission to George Ferguson, screwed up his courage once more and knocked on the woman's door, interrupting a spanking. He explained politely that he did not think it was God's will for her spank so long and so often. "She was a dour person. But she took it meekly, standing in the hall outside her suite." The spankings did not stop.

Meanwhile cases of smallpox continued to break out, slowly, new ones occurring just as it appeared the danger was past. At some point soon after the deaths of the two Jenkinses, Joseph Sutherland and Ralph Gleason volunteered to visit the newly sick for prayer and the laying on of hands. Gleason covered his mouth and nose with a handkerchief dipped in antiseptic, as those who nursed the sick had been doing. Sutherland, with more to prove, used no precautions, acting against Sandford's advice. He entered the quarantine cottage shielded by the Scriptural promise, "They shall take up serpents; and if they drink any deadly thing, it shall not hurt them; they shall lay hands on the sick, and they shall recover."

In the course of that week in the middle of January, Leander Bartlett was one of those visited for prayer by Sutherland and Gleason. Leander was ill in his room in the Extension, his symptoms as yet not diagnosed.

Leander had come to Shiloh for one reason: his mother and sister were there. His mother, welcomed back on the hill to aid in the Drive, had called for him in July. For the first time in ten years the three of them were living together, sharing a suite with another family in the Extension. Yet at this point the Bartletts were actually as homeless as ever, their future still unclear. Elvira and Merlyn both hoped that Leander's temporary visit to Shiloh would develop into a permanent one, and Elvira lived constantly in the expectation that some day she herself would be readmitted more than temporarily to the fold. Leander may have been ambivalent about staying at Shiloh. He thought of Boston as his home, and since July had gone back two or three times to visit his relatives, catch up on eating, and stuff his pockets with bananas and other goodies for Merlyn and his friends.

Of the boys his own age at Shiloh, he was one of the least likely candidates for the privilege of remaining there on his own. At age fourteen, he had not distinguished himself spiritually or in any special way, except in the eyes of those who loved him most. Merlyn remembered him as very different from herself, "smarter," and a terrible tease, full of energy and ideas. Those qualities might get him far in the world, but in themselves would not admit him to a place of honor on the hill. He resembled his mother, with dark eyes and red cheeks—not the preferred Shiloh look, like Merlyn's, with her pale, transparent skin.

The quarters in which he lived with his mother and sister on the first floor of the Extension were small and crowded. Merlyn remembered them as also very cold, since the single layer of flooring in the unfinished room was only a foot from the ground. It was so cold at times she could see her breath freeze on the mirror as she lit the lamp in the morning. Her chores that season included cleaning in Shiloh Proper before breakfast. She had worked out a routine that made it possible to get dressed without freezing. Each night she filled an earthen jug with hot water from the big brass kettle in the kitchen, corked it, and took it to bed with her for warmth. By morning it was cool, but at least not frozen like her washcloth, hanging stiff over the side of the china basin. Using the water from the jug, she washed her face, then grabbed her stockings and underwear and took them back to the warm bed with her, pulling them on under the covers as efficiently as possible (fastening the garters on her BVDs was especially tricky), then climbed out to add her waist and skirt and shoes, leaving every other button undone, along with her shoe laces. Sometimes she got all the way to the Ladies' Reception Room at Shiloh Proper before she addressed these finer details. More often, spying a line of light under the door of a suite she knew was equipped with a stove, she knocked for admission and spent a few minutes in that warmth while she braided her hair. Her favorite places were the quarters of "real families," with diapers strung on limp lines over the stove, and babies waiting to be held and snuggled before she dashed off to scrub down the stairs of Shiloh Proper. It was on these dark frigid mornings that she wept in spite of herself, as her hands ached from the icy water in the pail. That early no one could see her; she would not, for all the heat in the world, have cried in front of another person. Nor when Leander got sick did she cry, not even when he was too weak to get out of bed or when they came to carry him, half-conscious, on a cot to Bethesda.

At this point Merlyn had no idea what was wrong with Leander. No one did. She knew only what everyone else knew, that twenty-four hours before he was taken to Bethesda he had confessed to the worst sin of all. He had planned to run away.

Less than a week after Leander was admitted to Bethesda, Joseph Sutherland, who had been ignoring his own symptoms for many days, was brought to the Holland Cottage severely ill with smallpox. Sandford, attempting to pray for him, heard God say: "Dead. He said he would hearken unto thee, and he hearkened not." Sutherland had acted in spiritual arrogance, entering the smallpox quarters (in Sandford's word) "in the exaltation and presumption of his own strength rather than humble faith in God." He had been told him to cover his face. Sutherland's disobedience was not a just a failure of good judgment; it was a deliberate disregard of his leader's instructions.

That Friday, January 23, was also the last day of an extended fast in which Sutherland and 100-fold members had participated, and that morning the Nineveh Fast was instituted. The Nineveh Fast was modeled after the days of repentance in the city of Nineveh following the preaching of Jonah. By decree of the king it included "the greatest to the least," and "neither man nor beast, herd nor flock" could "feed, nor drink water." At Shiloh it was called for a seventy-two-hour period. As many of the residents understood it, every living being at Shiloh, including infants, animals, and the sick, were to go without food and water for the first thirty-six hours. The significant factor was the restriction of water. With food such a scarce commodity, a partial fast had been in effect anyway for the last two months, with dinners unpredictable and breakfast often no more than a piece of corn bread. Gifts from outside Shiloh members and sometimes near neighbors who sensed conditions often arrived just in time to provide a meal.

Both Avis and Doris were at Bethesda, in a large ward among many other children sick with mumps. Annie was there to care for them. All three participated in the Nineveh Fast. Avis never forgot the look on her mother's face as she tried to explain why she could not give her a drink. If there were parents who succeeded in excluding their children from the thirty-six-hour restraint, they kept their secret well. Estella Sheller, who was pregnant and living then at Bethesda for its "special food," remembered hearing the nursing babies crying in a room over her head like "a flock of little lambs." It was a period of great strain. The whole place seemed to be "on tiptoe," said Mrs. Sheller. Sandford was in David's Tower for the duration, and for some reason everyone spoke softly, "even in whispers, and the children were being constantly hushed."

On Sunday morning, January 25, word went out that Leander had died of diptheria during the night. Joseph Sutherland died later the same day. "God is showing His wrath toward the ministry," wrote Helen Sandford to the workers overseas. The word "wrath" must have looked strange in Helen's hand, for those who knew her would read the words in her soft, understated voice. She was not known for proclamations of wrath. "God has been showing His jealousy for David Truth," she said, "the curse falling on those who deviate from it in the least degree."

"Wonderful and awful days at Shiloh," read Austin Perry's letter to Jerusalem. "The old Jehovah aspect of the work has come again to the front." As for Joseph Sutherland, it was "very sad," said Perry. "God has made it very plain to us that it is His judgment blow, therefore we cannot mourn for him without incurring His displeasure." The Restoration could not be completed, "until God could get a people who were really holy," and to do this He "would think no more of killing anybody who stood in the way of the restoration than he would of killing a mosquito." Nothing was said about Leander in either of these letters.

According to Estella Sheller's story, Sandford had "laid hands" on Sutherland's wife in a chapel meeting, to separate her from her husband just before he died. "She said she knew she was completely separated from him and cried about it, but Mr. Sandford told her that was all right; that she was married to Christ; that he had never liked the match, anyway. From that time she seemed changed, and the day he died she sat on the platform while they told why God had struck down her husband. That he had had spiritual pride; and was seeking popularity; did not rule his house. . . . And above all, had belittled Mr. Sandford."

Sutherland's resistance to David truth, said Mrs. Sheller, had become all too apparent one day in the chapel when a woman who had stood to praise Sandford and declare her allegiance was rebuked by Sutherland. "Let us get our minds on Christ and not on man," he said. The implication was insulting, since it suggested that Sandford himself intended to draw attention away from Christ. Sutherland had not only misconstrued God's purposes but had misjudged the mind and heart of David.

"Just about the time Mr. Sutherland died," wrote Perry, "Mr. Sandford had a wonderful time in the turret. Living waters broke out through the north corner of the room, as truly spiritually as they will sometime literally from beneath the throne of God, of the Lamb, and of the threshold of the temple in David's time."

The fast was broken on Sunday by sips of the "Living Water" (quite real) from the spring at Hephzibah. No one was allowed to eat or drink until they had partaken of that particular water, brought around in a new pail with the words "Cold Water for a Thirsty Soul" painted across it. Doris, licking dried and cracked lips, thought the wait was interminable.

Five had now died, seven were ill at the Holland Cottage, and six-year-old Dorothy Barton lay close to death with diphtheria. During the Nineveh Fast she had helped herself to a crust of bread in the family suite and had been brought before a group of ministers to confess. Could there be any doubt now that this was no game of coincidence?

The children needed no convincing. Two of their number had disobeyed and both had been touched by a lightning bolt of judgment. Almost daily, angry voices from the chapel had been reaching them in the halls or their classrooms. "Another blowing up!" they whispered to themselves, listening in wonder to Mr. Sandford's voice, pouring out words in great rapidity and volume. It was the anger of the Holy Ghost "getting after something," they were told. Now they were certain that it was directed against themselves.

On the morning following the deaths of Leander Bartlett and Joseph Sutherland, as adults met in the chapel, the children were gathered in their own service in the Men's Reception Room, where the high gilt radiators still hissed with steam. As they were led in songs by their teacher, they could hear the familiar inflection of adult voices, rising and falling in prayer in the chapel across the hall.

That gentle fugue of sounds ended abruptly in a crash. A woman screamed, and then another. Crashes and shouts followed in frightening succession. As their teacher disappeared into the hall to see what had happened, the children leapt from their chairs and scrambled through a side window onto the Extension veranda. When the teacher returned he found the majority of his class of twenty shivering outside, many in tears. Doris escaped all the way to her suite to hide. She had caught the shouted words, "Hanging over hell!" She never heard her teacher's quote, "The wicked flee when no man pursueth."

That light estimation of things was not being shared in the chapel. Sandford had evicted the ministers from the platform, kicking and throwing their chairs after them into the dodging congregation. The ministers were demoted, the Bible School closed, students and all others dismissed, ordered to pack their trunks and be off as soon as the quarantine lifted. The only way he could save himself, he said, "save the whole movement from going to pieces," was to sever all connection to them. He left the room, declaring that he would not come back unless God ordered him to do so.

Feeling like Adam and Eve driven from Eden, as one woman described it, the school "dropped to the floor," asking God "to help them take the truth into their hearts, and to send Mr. Sandford back."

If they had been "thrown bodily into the pit," observed Estella Sheller, their sufferings could not have been more real. "He said they had no right to use the blood of Christ as a protection, and for awhile people seemed to be possessed." Some became hysterical and "cried for Mr. Sandford to save them."

In Sandford's own words to Victor Barton, one of the young missionaries in Alexandria, there were twelve, "including every person, almost without exception, that has any responsible position on this hilltop" who would "receive their sentence" the next night.

The most of them I believe to be worthy of damnation. I am sorry to inform you, Brother Barton, that your father is among the number, and that your mother, though under quarantine, is one with him in his guilt; and that little Dorothy [Victor's sister], has been for days at the point of death from diphtheria. God said to me, "Take her up," although I am not sure as to what it means, yet I am hoping that it means He will accept my faith for her in spite of her parents' condition. Well, God is love, as well as justice.

Though another methodical scrutiny began of every person, it seemed to do no good. Early in February Sandford heard the words, "Rebellion. Wrath renewed." Within three days the message of a death was brought from the quarantine cottage, then another on the following day, including an infant. In despair Sandford told God to take one of his own children, if that would somehow stop the plague. Five-year-old Esther immediately fell ill with smallpox.

But it was not Esther who was destined to save the movement. On the night of February 16 Austin Perry wrote again to the churches abroad: "The most wonderful and far-reaching thing that has ever occurred in the history of this work has taken place the last three days here at Shiloh. I am in hopes Mr. Sandford himself will write you the particulars next week."

He did not. Instead, his present secretary, Jean Stevens, unfolded the story to the "dear Ones in Foreign Lands" in language which must have raised the eyebrows of even the most devoted.

It had been "a strange, strange week," wrote Jean Stevens. John Sandford, who had just turned seven on the seventh of the month, had begun to keep a journal on his birthday. On Friday night, the 13th, he climbed to Ebenezer, his father's study in the turret, to get help in writing another page in the journal. So far, said Miss Stevens, every night that week John had been able to record that God had kept him holy during the day.

It was Mr. Sandford's prayer that little John's seventh year should be a Sabbatic year, a year of absolute holiness unto the Lord; and for a week God kept him so that even his father with the seven eyes of God, had not detected a thing that was wrong in him. God had used him in a wonderful way in a lesson in the Bible School held in the turret, and he was certainly a fulfillment of the prophecy, "a little child shall lead them." Well, that night he came up bright and happy and dictated to his father what he wanted written in his journal.

Mr. Gleason, Dr. Miller, Mr. Sandford and myself were in the turret at the time. Mr. Sandford called John's attention to the fact that he had been holy for seven days: and the dear little fellow was so glad, and said after he had finished dictating that he wanted to have a dance before the Lord to celebrate his triumph; and so we all danced before the Lord and little John played on his tamborine."

The "dancing" had apparently been done on occasion by the Twelve in Jerusalem as a form of worship, simulating King David's dance "before the Lord." John asked his father for permission to "go through the house [Shiloh Proper] and ask others to dance." Two hours later Sandford found his son conducting another meeting of adults in one of the rooms of the turret.

As it turned out, John had entered the room and "ordered" the women gathered there to come to his "meeting." He was so "saucy" that Olive Mills refused. Others, a total of five or six, complied. When his father found the meeting in progress and questioned it, John disregarded him, and when his mother entered the scene to take him to bed, he was impertinent.

So now the son of the prophet had disobeyed. Frank had often said that he and Helen would not abide a moment of insubordination from their children. Though strict, they had been viewed as loving parents, not unreasonably rigid. A story Frank had once related of holding a match to John's fingers when he told a lie might not have sat well with everyone, but it made sense that the children of Elijah should be examples of obedience.

Now all the hilltop was watching. God told Mr. Sandford to whip John, continued Jean Stevens in her narrative. But this was to be no ordinary whipping. John must want it. Out of the liberty in his own heart he must be "willing for his father to whip him all that God wanted him whipped," and John must fast, without food or water, until he got "to the place where he really loved the will of God." He must be *glad* to be whipped.

Mr. Sandford did not make it easy for him. He had shown him the rod he would use and told him it made no difference whether God wanted him whipped once or twice or all day, he must be willing to have it done.

With his father up in Jerusalem turret waiting, John prayed and searched his soul in his room down in the family apartment. Water was readily available—a glass of it kept by his bed. The fast, said Jean Stevens, was of John's "own accord," though it was "an awful battle to him." It lasted three days. On each of those days he climbed slowly up to the turret to take his whipping, but each time "his father felt he had not gotten absolute victory, and so sent him back to his room."

Monday night (now February 16th) Mr. Sandford felt it must be settled before midnight, and that it meant victory for the child or ruin. . . . About nine o'clock Mr. Sandford went to John's room and talked with him for the last time. He said afterwards that if the child went to hell he could not have said another word to him, because he seemed to be under the spell of the devil and had no power to do what his heart really wanted to.

Meanwhile, said Miss Stevens, "an awful battle went on in the chapel."

We all felt and knew that if little John did not get through by midnight, we would none of us get through. The salvation of the movement, of the world, hung on the Blood making that little child perfect to go to the turret and take his whipping gladly and willingly.

The "rod" was a small brass curtain rod, which Sandford had shown to the students in the chapel. Helen, who was four months pregnant, was present, and according to several witnesses "came near bolting." She had apparently tried to intervene, without success. The "oppression" in the chapel was "something awful," said Jean Stevens, but word came at last that night, at half-past eleven, that "little John had gotten victory" and gone to the turret, in tears, but quite ready for the will of God.

He was taken to the room where he had held his "meeting," where the students he had "ordered about" were waiting, and had been fasting themselves as sharers of John's guilt. Jean Stevens was there as a witness.

Mr. Sandford explained to the boy that he was going to receive "three whippings, one for the Father, one for the Son, and one for the Holy Ghost." A whipping on his hands or feet should make him think of the spikes through the hands and feet of Jesus; a whipping on his back would represent the scourging Jesus had suffered for him.

> The little fellow took it all in, and was willing to take the three whippings—was perfectly firm in all his answers, and had no desire to back out of it. Then his father told him that because Jesus had been whipped, and Jesus had suffered and died for him, he would not have to be whipped at all.
>
> Oh, how Calvary rolled out before that dear little boy! and before that guilty company! and before the entire church at Shiloh when we were told of it!
>
> Dear Mr. Sandford came down and told us all about it, and also told us that after they got through praying [he and John] John asked for a drink. He had suffered intensely from thirst. His father told him that Jesus was three days in the grave, and that his three days would not be up until nine o'clock next morning; and while he could have the water that night if he wanted it, yet he felt it would be better for him to go clear through. The little fellow said that he wanted to do that, so he was put to bed.

Frank remained in John's room with him throughout the night, at one point calling Dr. Miller to be sure he would get safely through the night. The boy slept only an hour or two, and "asked seventy-five times for water," but each time turned it down when it was brought.

At 9:00 A.M., somewhat pale and dark-eyed, John was finally brought to the chapel and given water from Hephzibah and a cup of gruel before the students, who had also fasted through the breakfast hour. Jean Stevens continued:

> After he had his drink, he said that any one who was thirsty for the water of life might come and drink out of his glass. Everybody in the room went up and drank. John said that everyone that drank that water would drink power to live a holy life.

Then as the adults filed past him, taking their sips, he announced

to them that if anyone wanted *him* to have some more, they could say
as they returned the cup to his hand, "Ho, the water of life!"

"That was quite a test for some people," observed Jean Stevens.
Some, feeling foolish, did not say it at all. Others spoke so softly no
one could hear them, and "some spoke as though they really wanted
little John to get something."

"Ho, the water of life!" must not have seemed much different to
John than "Water for a Thirsty Soul" painted on the side of a pail.
From the start he had only done what was most natural to him, play
out the adult world around him. Some children played house, some
played church; he played Shiloh. No doubt he had been peremptory that
day in the turret as he insisted on leading the women in a meeting,
and no doubt he needed very pointed instruction. Ironically, the fast
changed nothing. He had survived an adult ordeal, but he was still six
years old, still doing what it was essential for him to do as a child,
process the world around him. Standing there on the platform before
that room full of grownups, so small those at the rear could hardly see
the top of his head, he was still playing Shiloh, his voice piping—"If
you want me to have some, say 'Ho!'" Maybe it was Shiloh's purest
moment, and its most bizarre.

John had not only saved Shiloh from the Black Winter. He had saved
the whole movement from failure and the world from unspeakable
disaster. Esther recovered safely, as did Dorothy Barton, and though
two more died before the quarantine was lifted at the end of May, there
were no more new cases. Soon the ministers were restored and the Bible
school students reinstated.

Remarkably, work had gone on in Olivet for much of this time, and
on the fifteenth of March, the birthday of John's dedication to the Lord
seven years before, the children's building was dedicated.

At approximately the same time Nathan Harriman, in Jerusalem
reading Jean Stevens's letter, which had just arrived from America, began
to plan his defection. It was, he said later, the description of those last
moments in the chapel which made him "see that some spirit other
than the Holy Spirit, was running Shiloh." John, in applying his child's
imagination to the intricate adult performance unfolding around him,
set in motion for Shiloh a process of humiliation which would never
end. "Ho, the water of life!" was not a scene Nathan Harriman could
play. By it the entire mosaic was reduced for him to the level of a
child's game. "It was the real beginning of my 'unbelief,'" he would
soon say, "and so of my escape."

16

Persecution
1903

When the quarantine was lifted in the spring of 1903, six deaths had resulted out of a dozen cases of smallpox. The percentage was a heavy one at the time. The severity of the disease had been gradually diminishing in the country as a whole, and throughout Maine that year the death rate was very low. Out of 2,096 cases in the state in 1903, nine deaths were reported, two-thirds of those on the Durham hilltop.

Those who escaped illness at Shiloh surveyed their good fortune with awe. Herbert and Maud Jenkins, who had been isolated at the Holland Cottage with the sick during the entire seige, had not developed so much as a mild fever. Their father survived, with a badly pocked face.

If the hilltop needed another purge, the Black Winter provided it. No one had to contrive this one. It cleared Shiloh like brush burned out of a forest floor. At the end of May families fairly burst out the doors. If records were kept of the numbers they were certainly not made public. Most disappeared quietly. A few, like Estella Sheller, remained angry enough to tell their stories to reporters later.

Familiar refrains repeated themselves in these accounts—that Sandford "ruled by fear," that reasoning and individual thinking were forbidden, that money was "cleaned out" of people by pressure, that the Sandfords lived in plenty while others went hungry, that a movement which claimed to unify families divided them, and that many who had stayed behind were too frightened to leave.

Defections and expulsions, as well as peaceable leave-takings, had been part of Shiloh phenomena for a long time. Going in any manner had never been a simple affair. In the spring of 1903 it began to take on larger significance. The words "quitter," "turncoat," and "traitor" settled in as part of Shiloh vocabulary, while the names of defectors were erased from conversation by even close friends and family members. After the Shellers had removed themselves, their nineteen-year-old daughter Georgia, who had refused to go with them, wrote to her parents to say she could no longer have any "fellowship" with them. "I am following Elijah, and since you have deserted him I cannot and do not have anything more to do with you. I am going to stand true to God; and if you want to be with me you will have to turn about and start toward God. If you don't, the time will come when you will hear Christ say, 'Depart, ye cursed.' "

With the help of an attorney, Moses Leger removed his printing establishment and returned to Massachusetts, minus his wife. They had been in Liverpool together that winter, where life had been brutally austere and somber. Though Eliza continued a loyal member, Moses returned to America on a family errand and never went back. In the basement printing room at the Extension, he packed up his boxes of type in an atmosphere of intense hostility. One man held a bit of paper over a lamp chimney, saying as it caught fire, "This is how you will burn."

Yet even the spectacular defections made only a small dent. By far the majority chose to remain, including the Whites. In August of 1903 Wendell and Annie sold the farm in Growstown and turned the proceeds over to the Shiloh treasury. To all intents and purposes they had become full-fledged members of the movement.

Why now, at this most unlikely moment? Why not get out with the others? No light-shedding data exist to explain it. Back in 1881, while in his sophomore year at Bates, Wendell had written in a school copybook that he considered himself to be an indecisive person. He longed to be "direct and firm," he said. The sale of the Growstown property was decisive, at least, another burning bridge behind him. But it was not the end of decision-making. That process would straggle on for several more years, until the options ran out altogether.

Right now, one other hopeful prospect may have influenced Wendell's choice to stay. Joseph Harriman was being called back from Jerusalem to help design a new school system at Shiloh. There were to be seven schools, from kindergarten through high school, to start immediately, with a college program planned for the near future. Together these comprised the future University of Truth. Wendell was enlisted as a teacher in the high school. For the first time in many years he knew he was needed.

Elvira Bartlett also remained faithful, though once more she was dismissed from the hill. She moved back to Boston that summer, while Merlyn, now going on seventeen, fell again into the cracks of Shiloh's society, without a family but with her own status as a young adult and a prospective member of the high school. By now she was as old as some of the original Bible School students had been.

The Bartlett drama, like that of the Whites, had not yet played its last act, and Merlyn was only just beginning to control a combination of emotions too potent to permit recognition. It was she who had been supposed to die at Shiloh, not Leander, so strong and healthy. Her body dealt with this incongruous fact in its own way, with the introduction of nauseous headaches, which soon became as much a regular and accepted part of her life as the cough had been in the year she first arrived.

Apart from everything else, Shiloh was an exciting place to be that summer. God was showering down blessings in the old accustomed manner. Another coat of white paint soon shone on the Extension, flowers were set out in the beds, and acres of garden planted with vegetables and corn. A new printing press was purchased and a new periodical, *The Glad Tidings of the Kingdom,* left the postoffice each month by the bale. Negotiations had begun for the purchase of a dairy farm so that milk would never again be scarce, and a second brownstone, next door to Elim, was added to the Boston property. John Douglas's boat was at last replaced, by *two* sea-going vessels and a fishing craft. To be sure, none of these was the ocean liner Sandford had been so sure God would give them, but all were delightful to own and useful in Shiloh's plans for a wide Atlantic-coast ministry.

One of the boats, the yacht *Wanderer,* had been built originally for the tobacco merchant Pierre Lorillard at a cost of $55,000. Shiloh bought her for $2,500. The other vessel, purchased to conduct revival meetings throughout Casco Bay, was a thirty-foot awning-covered gasoline launch christened the *Overcomer.* That golden summer of 1903, like convalescents emerging from their darkened rooms, Shiloh's faithful rested and played for trip after trip among the beautiful islands of Maine's bays and coastal rivers. On Barter's Island, where Sandford had once taught school, hundreds turned out for a revival in the old Crusader tents.

All this took place as serenely and confidently as if Satan himself had already been chained for the Millennium, when in fact he was working furiously to bring about Shiloh's own private Tribulation.

At the end of May Elnora Emerson made an entry in her diary: "Saul disappeared during the service." Elnora was one of the remaining seven of the original Twelve in Jerusalem—the service, the Thursday six hours of prayer, observed by Kingdom members in Jerusalem as well as at Shiloh. While the others were on their faces, Nathan Harriman slipped from the room, walked out of the building and through the gate in the garden wall. Before his absence could be registered as more than a trip to the bathroom, he was on his way to the docks. Since March and his secret decision to leave, he had been earning money for passage at the offices of the American consul. No one else in the Jerusalem party had known where he went each day, not even his son Joseph, and Joseph was as mystified as anyone else at his father's disappearance on this Thursday.

Harriman went first to Liverpool, where his wife and their youngest son, Gordon, joined him to sail to America. His daughter Flora, no longer a minor, chose to remain in England. Like Joseph, she was not told that her father's plans involved any more than a return to America, though she must have wondered at the decision, since changes in location were not made without Sandford's knowledge. One of Harriman's reasons for secrecy, as he soon explained publicly, was to protect his daughter Grace, a teenager at Shiloh (the one remaining Harriman at that location) from being "driven insane" by pressure from Sandford before her family arrived to remove her. But secrecy was hopeless, of course. Wires zipped back and forth between Jerusalem, Liverpool, and America, and Grace spent three hours in conference with Sandford before leaving to meet her parents in Boston.

Once she had safely joined him, Harriman wrote Sandford in open declaration of his intentions to do all that was legally in his power to destroy the movement. As an early step he sent a lengthy document to the governor of Maine, "urging him to close Shiloh and disperse the inmates." The governor answered that he could not interfere unless it could be proven that some of the people at Shiloh were detained against their will. At the same time, Harriman sought the help of the North Cumberland Conference of Congregational Churches in Maine. This association, a group with wide influence who undertook to finance part of Harriman's legal expenses, sent a request to Auburn County Attorney William B. Skelton to investigate Shiloh, and then rallied the clergy and businessmen of the Auburn-Lewiston area. After lengthy discussion, that group agreed warily to requesting an investigation, maintaining Sandford had the right "to preach whatever he believes" and that any measures taken be "aimed wholly at those things touching the innocent and helpless."

The Lewiston papers covered that meeting. By now the story had leaked into the journalistic wires and others began to offer their assistance, one of them an agent of Maine's Children's Protective Society.

Scratching out an income from the offerings at various meetings and pulpit supplies, Harriman next began to contact as many of Shiloh's defectors as he could locate, among them Estella Sheller, the Bartons (though not Victor and his sister Emma, who remained faithful in Alexandria), and a family named Swart, all of whom had moved to Auburn and found employment. George Barton, one of the ministers "worthy of damnation" in January, had been in charge of transporting the sick and burying the dead during the epidemic. He had supervised Leander's burial. John Swart, whose two small sons had been ill with the mumps at Bethesda, had volunteered to nurse Leander at night and was with him when he died.

In August, Arthur Grey Staples, editor-in-chief of the *Lewiston Journal,* traveled to Boston to confer with Harriman and to examine a manuscript Harriman wanted him to publish. The editor found the four members of the Harriman family crowded into a one-room basement apartment. Staples was impressed with Harriman as a "tall, earnest Christian man of emotional personality," who paced about the shabby room as though it were a palace." Boston papers had refused the story (although Boston was no friend to Sandford), but Staples agreed to take it, and on September 26 the *Lewiston Journal* gave it a full two-page spread, complete with large pictures of the Shiloh grounds, and Sandford's name again misspelled.

THE INSIDE STORY OF SANFORDISM AND SHILOH.

Rev. N. H. Harriman, Formerly a Co-worker of Mr. Sanford, Comes Out In a Statement Against the Work.

"IT LEADS TO THE UNBALANCING OF HUMAN REASON,"
says he.

The article was introduced with an acknowledgement by the paper that it had published "many columns in the past commendatory of Shiloh," and now still preferred an "open forum," inviting Mr. Sandford and any others to reply.

Then began Harriman's long, impassioned statement.

> I have spent three full years under the tuition and leadership of the Rev. F. W. Sandford; have submitted to all the discipline that he prescribes; have stuck at no humiliation, no labor, no suffering. I have gone to such lengths that no one could go further, and I blush for my manhood as I look back over the history of the unspeakable degradation to which I have submitted for three years.

It was a startling, if self-serving, beginning for an article that gradually found its strength in Harriman's admirable struggle to describe what was almost indescribable, the communal yet individual experience of several hundred people. Some of the Black Winter letters from Shiloh leaders to workers overseas, all of which Harriman had copied, were included verbatim along with a summary of John's fast (but not with the full details of Jean Stevens's letter), and a series of examples of Sandford's coercive methods of raising money.

It was exactly the kind of thing the public had been waiting to hear. Even more compelling was Harriman's attempt to explain the mystery of Shiloh's holding power and the enigma of his own hesitation in breaking away. He did not pretend to understand it, he said, except to call it a kind of hypnotism, something "abnormal" in the atmosphere which alters one's ability to think, until "your very mind seems held in the grip of some foreign power."

> The fact is, the God of the New Testament is crowded out of your consciousness, and His place is filled with a God of law, whose feelings, requirements, will, are identical with those of Sandford. If you could really get through to the God you once knew, you would not fear Him; but you cannot find Him. He has disappeared. In His place is a God of awful holiness, awful exactness, whose "seven eyes" are looking you over and through. . . .

This was not something one could see and understand, said Harriman. "Oh no; if you did, you would have some hope of escape. It is so subtle and so cunningly adjusted that you think that your mind and spirit admit to it fully." One of the first steps in the process of intimidation was that you must "take the eyes of the man of God."

> This is how it works. An emergency arises and you are told that something is wrong with you. You say you do not see it and are answered with the unanswerable statement that your seeing it cannot affect the fact, nor your seeing it. "There is a fly on your head," will perhaps be said. "Now the fly is there just the same whether you can see it or cannot see it." Then is launched on you the question, "Will you take my eyes for it?" When you have said yes and have "swallowed" the principle that lies back of it, viz., to doubt your own perception and accept that of another, reasonable as this may seem, the first coil has been placed about your neck of that silken thread which will gradually, at Shiloh, choke the spiritual life out of you. It is Scriptural to "try the spirits," but Shiloh says no, trust your leaders without question; to question is to break unity.

The final act in any of this was Sandford's rage. "Once he gets angry, woe betide the persons who are the offenders: they will have to repent to the 'fingertips of their beings.' This he brings to pass in the exercise of his apostolic authority by surrendering them to Satan."

It was now that Harriman described the function of alleged demon possession as a means of control, the manipulation he was subject to himself in the purging of the Twelve at Liverpool three years earlier. It was at this time also that Mary Guptil had been the subject of Sandford's wrath and was banished to hell for contradicting him. The outcome of Mary Guptil's story, Harriman said, was her death. She had, in fact, died on August 31, less than a month before the publication of this article.

> From one of the healthiest of young women before this, the victim of this torture emerged a physical wreck. She coughed, and the ministers said she had consumption. Her mind was in a pitiable state. . . . She was seldom free from terror for long at a time. Her inquisitor, apparently made sober by her condition, got a message to reassure her. "A diamond." He told her that her sufferings were imaginary; . . . in all sorts of ways he tried to rouse her.

On arrival in America in November of 1902, at the onset of the

Black Winter, Mary had gone to her home in Cornish, Maine. Following the smallpox epidemic she returned to Shiloh, against the advice of her parents, who had become aware long before, said Mr. Guptil in a letter to Harriman (included in full in the article), of a "power brought to bear on all members, that broke down their individuality and will." Yet Mary insisted her parents were wrong. She was happy.

Harriman concluded his representation on a note so spectacular that it could not have helped his own image as a trustworthy witness. Under the subheading "All Shiloh Threatened with Insanity," he listed a half-dozen cases, all unsubstantiated, of young women who had "gone through" and been "broken" by the Shiloh system of control, and who were now deranged or suicidal and under confinement. His final paragraph designated the movement as an "institution of practically abject slaves" who were thoroughly subdued and terrorized, "their lives one succession of 'tests' and sufferings, ending often in wrecked health, and sometimes in early death or insanity."

Three days later the *Journal* printed Sandford's reply. Though he had no intention, he said, of being drawn into any newspaper controversy, he felt "heartily sorry" for Harriman and was baffled at what had come over him. "I am not seeking personal aggrandizement," Sandford said.

So far as I personally am concerned, I do not desire to be the dominant head of the movement. . . . There is nothing more to say. My people are behind me and are not to be diverted by baseless slanders. The malevolence of our detractors only shows that the devil fears the work that we are doing and will take any means to balk us. But God will not allow Satan to triumph over us.

The timing of Harriman's *Journal* publication was on Shiloh's side. Charles Holland and others who had been in England were just now pulling in to Boston Harbor on the steamship *Mayflower,* along with the Honorable Artillery from London. It docked, obligingly, on October 2, Sandford's birthday, and the last day of the fall convention, held in Boston at the opulent Corinthian Hall. Reporters hovered there too and were rewarded. Sandford, filling the remaining gap in Shiloh's mosaic, disclosed that Holland was the "second witness," one of the two Tribulation evangelists who were to be martyred by the anti-Christ in Jerusalem, where they would lie dead for three days before rising again. It had already been determined that the first of these would be the modern Elijah, who could "shut heaven that it rain not," causing a drought on earth. The second witness, able to turn "rivers to blood," was believed to be a modern-day Moses. Charles Holland had failed often in meeting Sandford's standard of aggressiveness. He was not one by nature to turn anything to blood, but he was often referred to at Shiloh as having the patience of Moses, since he was frequently the subject of Elijah's fire. Whatever the motivation, the pronouncement worked well as a diversionary tactic with the reporters.

But in the long run Sandford's best defense against Harriman was the use of the man's own words. Barely three years before his defection Harriman had written:

> People who come to the hilltop, look those lofty truths in the face, hear the call to fall into line with God's plans, and [then] fail to yield to God, usually go away demonized, and not infrequently wrecked, spiritually, for life. They have a shield offered them for the battle, they refuse it, throw it away, and the fiery darts of the wicked one come thick and fast upon their unprotected souls, and they are cursed.

The unfortunate paragraph was one small part of Harriman's laudatory series, "Shiloh As It Is," written for *The Everlasting Gospel* in 1900. Sandford gave part of this to the *Journal,* prior to publishing it himself in book form.

Harriman must have wondered, in spite of his present determination, if his earlier words had not been prophetic after all. He had lost years of work; he had lost the Ecclesia Mission, swallowed up by Shiloh; most painful of all, he had lost the respect of two of his children— Joseph and Flora, both of whom were horrified at his attack on the movement. And soon he would lose Flora altogether. She was ill now in England, another victim of pulmonary tuberculosis.

Shiloh members were instructed not to defend the movement in public. They began to develop a courteous taciturnity, an old Yankee trait. "We speak evil of no man," became the stock answer to the questions they encountered in almost every contact with the outside world. The words were serene, but it was hard to ignore the harassment—the curious who stopped in the wagons on River Road to stare up at the white complex, or those who dared to knock at the front door and ask to be shown around. "Newspaper fellows" arrived regularly, some having traveled several hundred miles, expecting instant interviews. Papers were having a run on extremist religion during these months, particularly the activities of Alexander Dowie, the other "Elijah," who had begun to hold huge rallies in New York City, hammering away at denominations and doctors and causing near riots.

Early in the New Year, at the urging of Austin Perry and a Lisbon Falls attorney, Henry Coolidge, Sandford took another important business step. Coolidge, who had admired Sandford for several years, urged him to protect himself from the mounting accusations of fraudulence and the growing possibility of legal action by angry defectors. All the properties which had been deeded to God and held in Sandford's name as a trustee were now deeded to the Kingdom, with Frank and Helen, the Hollands, the Perrys, and Ralph Gleason as directors. The Kingdom of David, "lost to Israel of old but 'renewed' by the authority invested in the Restorer," was now incorporated under the laws of the state of Maine.

The arrangements were completed days just before Sandford's arrest.

17

The Charge Is Manslaughter

1904

In January of 1904 Shiloh watched with the rest of the world as Russia and Japan prepared for war. Arnold heard Mr. Sandford utter a prayer into which he seemed to throw all his physical strength, imploring God to "shatter the fleet of Gog and Magog."

The young people had just been taught that Gog and Magog, northern nations mentioned in Ezekiel, referred to Russia, destined to be a leading enemy in the Last Days, and that the conflict in the Far East was directly related to Shiloh, that—as Mr. Sandford explained—"actual war in the east between the nations of the earth would closely accompany actual, spiritual war in the west . . . open persecution against the Kingdom, or real warfare between light and darkness."

The possibility of a state grand jury investigation of Shiloh had been surfacing on the pages of the *Lewiston Journal* for several weeks. In the middle of the month, a score of Shiloh members were called for questioning at the county buildings in Auburn, while the ministers gathered to pray in David's Tower. On Saturday, January 23, shortly after Sandford finished preaching on the text, "In the last days, perilous times shall come," he was arrested by the sheriff of Androscoggin County, who courteously bundled him into a sleigh and took him off to Auburn in a messy storm of hail and sleet.

There in the county courtrooms, enveloped by the smell of stale cigar smoke, Sandford was booked on six counts. The indictments were read by County Attorney William Skelton, once an acquaintance of Frank's at Bates, who also greeted him in a friendly manner. The charges, preferred by the Androscoggin County Humane Society and the Cum-

berland Conference of Congregational Churches, all involved children.
Three counts of cruelty were brought in the case of John Swart's
children, one count of cruelty in the case of John Sandford, and both
cruelty and manslaughter in the case of Leander Bartlett.

Bail was established at $5,000. Since Shiloh's coffers at that time
contained nowhere near that amount, Henry Coolidge and Austin Perry
hurried off to make arrangements while Sandford waited in the sheriff's
office. Other than appearing to be "a trifle pale," observed a reporter
on the scene, "his face wore the same pleasant look and his eyes the
same brightness that so characterizes him."

"Is there anything you would like us to say for you tonight, Mr.
Sandford?" the reporter asked.

"Nothing. . . . However, I want to treat you with courtesy. I have
nothing to say regarding my position."

"Perhaps a statement from you might make some difference in the
minds of the public."

"I do not care to explain myself to the minds of the public."

With bail provided at last by friends of Coolidge, two women
sympathetic to Shiloh but not members, Sandford left the county buildings
in the company of Coolidge and Perry and returned to the slushy streets.
By now news vendors were hawking the six o'clock edition of the
Journal. "The charge is manslaughter!" piped the boys over the late
afternoon noise. "Rev. Mr. Sandford arrested!"

Standing on the corner in the city dusk, Sandford was fascinated at
how distanced he remained from those shouts. "I felt as calmly superior
to it as though those cries had been about another person," he wrote
later. "I really could not detect a single ripple across the placid surface
of my soul's calm—not the slightest difference in my feelings whether
the boy cried about 'Rev. Mr. Sandford' or 'the great fire in Chicago.' "
On the front page of the paper waved under his nose was his own
picture, sandwiched between the stories of shipwreck and fire and a
cartoon of Russian and Japanese soldiers lighting a fuse while Uncle
Sam fiddled. Back at the hilltop, Sandford told an anxious gathering
that he "was never so full of courage, nor of glad expectation for the
extension of the Kingdom."

Of the six charges only two actually came to trial: "Cruelty in the
case of John Sandford," and "Manslaughter in the case of Leander
Bartlett." The trial in John's case was heard first. It began in two
weeks, on Wednesday, February 3, at the Supreme Judicial Court in
Auburn, and it was over in a day. The presiding judge was the Honorable

A. R. Savage, while Sandford was to be defended by his own lawyer, Henry Coolidge, and a state legislator, Henry W. Oakes. All three men were locally known and respected. Several members of the jury had watched Frank play baseball at Bates.

If ever Shiloh needed Holman Day, it was now. But Day was off writing novels and nursing a shaky marriage. Another reporter, with fully as much curiosity if not empathy, took over. "No hearing that ever occurred in Maine has been so vitally interesting to the hearers," he proclaimed. It certainly drew a crowd. On the morning of the trial the corridors outside the courtroom were packed with men and women, some of whom had been waiting to get in for an hour. Rev. C. S. Weiss, the Shiloh critic who in 1899 had published the booklet *Sandfordism Exposed,* hawked his left-over copies at the door. A rumor had been circulating that "reserved seat tickets" were being sold, and as a consequence Sheriff Cummings had received telegrams and telephone calls "from all parts of the state." Anticipating a packed house, he had issued tickets to witnesses to assure their seating, and benches had been sectioned off for "the attorneys and their ladies." Galleries were held for the women, many of whom were from Shiloh.

At stake in the courtroom that day was not the whipping John had faced at the end of his fast, but the fast itself and the dilemma it proposed to the boy. The State was contending that the fast was cruel and gratuitous punishment, in violation of a statute which makes it criminal for "any parent, guardian, or other person, having the care or custody of any child," to "cruelly treat" such child "by abuse, neglect, overwork, or extreme punishment."

If the reporters at hand looked for a good show, they were in for a letdown. After County Attorney Skelton's description of John's fast, which essentially agreed with Shiloh's version of what had happened, the entire session, in contrast to public expectations, turned out to be colorless and unsensational. Testimony was in before the noon dinner recess, with a dozen people on the stand. All of those witnesses were Shiloh people, called by the State, both faithful and deserters, including George Barton and John Swart. Spectators leaning forward to get a good look at the hilltop "inmates" were disappointed. They appeared to be perfectly normal. Their demeanor was gentle, even shy, their voices evaporating into the echoey, high-ceilinged recesses of the room. Jean Stevens ("a thin-featured woman," said the paper), the first witness, answered questions so softly she could hardly be heard at the press table.

The questioning throughout the morning added no new details to what Skelton had given, and denied none, except that all those quizzed, including the defectors, firmly assured the jury that the relations between John and his father were generally excellent, that John was "often in his father's arms," and had never indicated the slightest fear toward him.

Merlyn Bartlett was among the ten witnesses for the defense. The choice was curious. Merlyn was not asked to participate in the upcoming manslaughter trial, as one might expect, and there was absolutely no reason for her to be selected as a witness in John Sandford's case over any one of four hundred others at Shiloh. Confused by the realization that her testimony might injure Mr. Sandford, on the day prior to the trial she had sought him out for advice. There was nothing for her to worry about, he told her. All she had to do was get up there with her angel-like face and tell the truth exactly as she remembered it and that would be positive testimony for Shiloh, regardless of what she said.

So, wearing a borrowed skirt and blouse (none of her own clothes were suitable to wear in public), Merlyn took the stand. "A retiring young lady of small frame and delicate health," said the newspaper, adding nothing about angels or her identity as Leander's sister. Answering the handful of questions with brevity and truth, she gave a piece of potentially damaging evidence which may have swayed the case.

Asked by Henry Coolidge if she had heard Sandford "say anything about John calling for water" during his fast, she replied that she had. She had heard him say that "John called for it seventy-five times." Skelton had already given that number in his opening statements, but none of the other witnesses had mentioned hearing the information from Sandford himself. Merlyn's recollection left no doubt that he had been totally aware of the child's suffering.

Following the recess for noon dinner, the Court announced two surprises, reported the *Journal:* "a sudden suspension of state's evidence" and "the announcement that the defendant had no testimony to offer." These were frustrations as well as surprises, since the crowd had mostly come to see and hear Frank Sandford.

Neither Skelton nor Oakes improved the bill of fare with their statements to the jury, though Skelton resorted to a moment of histrionics: "Water, water, papa, water!" Oakes remembered that President Lincoln had called the American people to fast three times. A fast in itself was not necessarily cruel, said Oakes. Cruel and malicious intent had not been proven at all. Rather, Sandford had acted with his son's best interests in mind, and John "did not suffer injury."

By evening, after deliberating only a few hours, the jury voted Sandford guilty. His attorneys immediately appealed with a list of ten exceptions.

The trial for manslaughter began the next morning in the midst of a blizzard, which did little to discourage the public, stamping in out of the snow with better hope today of something for their trouble. The argument between medical science and faith healing had only recently begun to enter the country's courts. In an unlitigious society, where the medical profession was apt to produce as many failures as the cultist, it was not until mystical healing practices began to be associated with organized religion and pit themselves against the proven advances of medicine that they clashed with the law. In the ten years since Shiloh's early beginnings the treatment of contagious disease particularly had taken giant steps forward. Antitoxins and vaccinations were working. Society was growing more sophisticated in its detection of quackery and less tolerant of the personal right to refuse what was becoming standardized care.

Most of those who crowded the Auburn courtroom knew that Sandford could be sentenced to as much as ten years in prison if determined guilty. So they were baffled to learn that the charges in the case had been built on a vague premise. Judge Savage explained to the jury that "the particular kind of manslaughter" in the indictment was not even mentioned in the statutes of the state of Maine. Rather, the indictment had based its definition of manslaughter on common law, specifying "negligent omission" on the part of Sandford, that "he willingly, knowingly and feloniously did fail, neglect and refuse to furnish" the nourishment and medical attention needed by a person dependent on him for that care. By this means, said the indictment, had Frank Sandford caused the death of Leander Bartlett. It was up to the jury to decide whether or not such "negligent omission" was a fact.

In the course of the next two days of testimony the aspects of that were given many hours of attention. But the public went home unsatisfied once again. As it turned out, something quite different than the failure to provide food and medicine emerged as the hub of the judgment. Under Judge Savage's own guidance, one particular question was introduced which threw the jury into disagreement so intense they could not concur on a verdict, and they declared themselves hung.

The same question would predominate again in another three months. For the case was not thrown out. A retrial was scheduled for May in Farmington, a small city in a different county forty miles to the north, where the defense lawyers hoped to find a more neutral climate.

The Farmington trial almost aped the one in Auburn. Like the first, it lasted two days. The defense lawyers were the same, Judge Savage presided, and William Skelton represented the State. Many of the thirty-five or so witnesses returned, all from Shiloh (as faithful or defectors) except two local doctors. Only the jury was different—and the weather. At Farmington the windows of the dusty courtroom were open, and dozens of girls from the Normal School arrived in pretty spring dresses to fill the galleries.

Sandford, sitting with his attorneys and Austin Perry, remained throughout both sessions as "unmoving as a sphinx," said the papers. Actually, he admitted years later, he "felt like a man skinned alive" as he sat there listening to people "tell lies" about him. As in the cruelty case he did not take the stand at any point in the questioning in either city, nor confer with his lawyers in the courtroom.

State's witnesses again included George Barton and John Swart, and the star, Nathan Harriman. Dr. Ida Miller and Elvira Bartlett were among the twenty-two witnesses brought by the defense. Both sides began by attempting to establish the extent of Sandford's personal responsibility to Leander. The defense, citing the laws of the state that "a parent is in control of his child unless he gives control to someone else," insisted that Elvira Bartlett had understood before her arrival at Shiloh what the living circumstances were to be, and that Leander, as a minor, was directly under her care and control.

On not one single major detail did all Shiloh witnesses agree, other than the facts that there had been much frightening illness at Shiloh in January of 1903, that Leander had sickened and died that month, and that he had been "in rebellion" and planned to run away. Memories collided on the exact time and nature of the fasts and whether or not the sick had fasted along with the well. Even journal entries and marginal notes in Bibles made at the time were in discrepancy.

Nathan Harriman understood fully what the State was after—proof that personal freedom at Shiloh was curtailed, and that Sandford exercised hands-on authority among individual members when it suited his purposes. Harriman was on the stand for over an hour, with much argument sparked between the attorneys over how much of his testimony was permissable, since he frequently plunged beyond the questions in his answers.

"Did Mr. Sandford's authority reach to individual members of families?" Skelton asked him.

"Entirely so," answered Harriman.

"Did he exercise authority and direction in the correction of individual members of families?"

"He saw to it that individual members of families were corrected according to his wishes."

"Did he exercise this to the extent of the training and care of children?"

"Yes sir, his theories had to be carried out in every family."

"Did he exercise authority limiting or in any way controlling the relations of individuals with one another at all?"

"Oh yes. There wasn't anything in the way of relationship that he didn't take cognizance of and direct if he felt like doing it," said Harriman.

Against Mr. Oakes's repeated objections Harriman was permitted to give instances in which Sandford directly intervened in private domestic affairs, such as arranging Ralph Gleason's marriage, once forbidding Caroline Holland to go to the bedside of her sick infant because there was "an unnatural bond" between the mother and the baby (Caroline later firmly denied this), and influencing Almon Whittaker's decision to remain separated from his family.

Continuing under Skelton's questions, Harriman described Shiloh's chain-of-authority in detail, explaining that Sandford was the third in order—"God the Father, God the Son, and Mr. Sandford," and that disobedience to Sandford was "subject to all the penalties of disobedience to God."

Charles Holland, with every opportunity to modify Harriman's statements, showed up poorly under Skelton's scrutiny, stammering and contradicting himself. Pressed to explain whether or not Leander, as a minor, would be considered in rebellion to Sandford rather than to his mother if he ran away, Holland finally acknowledged that it would be to Sandford.

"If Mr. Sandford objected," asked Skelton, "would the mother then have the right to permit the boy to do something against Mr. Sandford's objections and without putting both herself and the boy in rebellion?"

"I think as far as the mother was concerned at least," said Holland.

"What about the boy if he went?"

"If he went he would be considered in rebellion."

Elvira Bartlett, called by the Defense, caused an audible stir in the courtroom as she took the stand. Still young-looking in her forties, with black eyes and a flair to her nostrils that suggested a more patrician heritage than she owned, she appeared proud and unnatural ("heartless" someone later said) to the general public in attendance. No tears were shed, no grief expressed. Elvira had her own reason for that, and she did not intend to make it public. Under questioning by Coolidge, she explained the circumstances of her presence (and her children's) at Shiloh.

"When you came here was this boy under your control?" Coolidge asked her.

"Yes sir," answered Elvira.

"Was any interference in any way made with your control and management of the boy?"

"No sir."

"Mr. Sandford ever suggest it in any way?"

"I seldom ever saw Mr. Sandford except on the platform," said Elvira, "seldom ever saw him to speak to him, and he certainly didn't suggest anything of the kind."

"Before you came to Shiloh, did you know what the rules were?"

"Yes sir."

"Did you know that divine healing was the method employed?"

"I did."

"That you would be treated that way if you were sick?"

"Yes sir."

"And your children?"

"Yes sir."

Under cross-examination by Skelton, Elvira claimed she knew of no time when Sandford's orders were "vetoed" by the people.

"You understood any orders from Mr. Sandford were to be obeyed, or else leave the institution?"

"There weren't any cast-iron rules upon the hilltop."

"You understood they were to be obeyed, or else be regarded in rebellion?"

"As far as right and wrong go, yes."

"Didn't you understand that any orders from Mr. Sandford were to be obeyed?"

"Yes sir, in a way."

Little by little, as the questions continued, Elvira put together Leander's story. Until now most of Shiloh had never heard the details. Sometime in the middle of January during the Black Winter, Leander had developed a sore throat. Though every sign of illness was potentially dangerous, he did not seem very sick—in fact, went outdoors and worked on Olivet—until one day when his weakness and listlessness struck Elvira as unusual and she phoned Bethesda for an examination. Dr. Ida

Miller, responding, found no suspicious symptoms but gave orders that Leander should remain in bed under observation for six days, as designated by the state in the circumstances of quarantine.

That same day Elvira also asked for prayer. Ralph Gleason and Joseph Sutherland responded. As part of the usual procedure Leander was given the chance to confess anything that might stand in the way of healing. It was now, explained Elvira to the court, that the boy, in the presence of the two ministers, "admitted to some things he had done wrong." He and the Sheller boy (the son of Estella Sheller) had been building a hut in the pine grove one day earlier in the month, using left-over scraps of lumber from the Olivet project. Someone in charge, hearing the hammer blows, had ordered them to stop. Angry, the boys secretly made plans to run away as they walked back to the Extension.

"To leave you?" Coolidge asked Elvira.

"Yes, to run away from me," she answered.

To Elvira, it was herself Leander intended to run from, rather than Shiloh. To Leander, it may not have been really running away at all, but running home to Boston, taking his friend with him. Nevertheless, he had been spiteful and was anxious enough about that to confess it. Soon afterwards he began to feel better. The fever dropped. He sat up in bed and ate an egg-on-toast. But twenty-four hours later, too weak to walk and hardly able to speak, he was carried to Bethesda, where he sank quickly into stupor and delirium. The nature of his illness was uncertain, but it was not smallpox. Elvira herself nursed him throughout each day of the next week. Nights he was watched by John Swart.

"Did others to your knowledge pray for him?" asked Coolidge.

"Yes, the whole hilltop was praying for him."

"Did Mr. Sandford pray for him?"

"Not by my personal knowledge. I didn't see him pray."

"Did he come down to Bethesda?"

"No sir."

Frank Wood, a male nurse at Bethesda, explained to the court that one of his duties had been to visit the patients every morning, take their pulses and telephone Ida Miller at the quarantine cottage with his estimation of their condition. Leander, he said, "gradually declined— kept growing weaker and weaker." John Swart, caring for Leander at night, said the boy grew steadily more delirious throughout the week. Asked if he had taken "good care" of him, he answered that he did, according to the directions he had been given. It was his opinion that Leander needed more nourishing food, but that Dr. Miller thought it was "a case of brain fever" and had left orders to give Leander "only milk" and liquid foods.

Frank Wood said that to his knowledge Dr. Miller did not go back to see Leander herself until Friday evening of that week, five days after Leander had been admitted. Swart, when he was questioned, thought she visited once. Ida Miller herself insisted she went back two or three times, but she could not remember exactly when. A tall, dark woman thought of by Shiloh people as "crisp but kindly," Miller faced Skelton's grilling with cool composure.

"There was an interval of about three or four days you didn't go near him at all, wasn't there?"

"I don't remember exactly."

'And you still didn't know what ailed him?"

"No sir. . . . I still didn't know what ailed him."

"Still, you knew he was sick enough to be taken to Bethesda?"

"Yes."

"Strength leaving him?"

"Yes."

"Temperature high?"

"Yes."

"Face flushed?"

"Yes sir."

"Throat in a bad condition?"

"It wasn't until the last part of his illness."

"How many times did you examine it that week?"

"I don't remember."

"There was an interval you didn't see him at all?"

"Yes sir."

"Didn't watch the boy very closely, did you?"

"I have told you all I know about it."

Both attorneys gave a great deal of attention to one moment in Shiloh chapel on the day before Leander died. That day, said witnesses, Mr. Sandford doubled his efforts to impress on them the seriousness of their circumstances and of the extreme danger of rebellion or disloyalty. All but a few of those who were questioned about these statements agreed that Sandford had mentioned Leander by name or implication. But memories differed widely about what he said, and how he said it.

"I don't remember the exact words, but he said he didn't care if he saw his dead body lying before him."

"He stretched his hands out before him and said he wouldn't care, or he would like to see—I don't know which he said now . . . he wouldn't care if he saw his dead corpse before him. . . . He said he couldn't pray for him."

"Well, he didn't say anything like [that], that I heard him say. The thing that comes in my mind was the fact that unless we did pray earnestly, we would have corpses stretched out before us. . . ."

"He said something like this, that it would cause him no surprise if he knew Mr. Bartlett was dead."

"I heard him pray for Leander Bartlett."

As for the all-encompassing Nineveh Fast, begun on the Friday evening before Leander's death, both John Swart and Frank Wood declared under oath that Leander fasted throughout the entire seventy-two-hour period. Elvira insisted he was not included, but she admitted she was not in the room at all on Saturday, the day before his death. Coolidge asked her why not.

"Because we ascertained that he had diphtheria Friday afternoon along toward night quite late. I couldn't give him his food in the usual way, because he wouldn't open his mouth. I asked Mr. Swart to come and help me, and he asked Mr. Wood to come. They put a knife blade between his teeth and swabbed his throat. Then they gave him milk, and from that time, that evening, I came out myself. I was completely tired out and didn't go into the room afterwards."

Leander's throat had been "filled up to a certain extent all day" on Friday, said Frank Wood. That evening Ida Miller returned and discovered the grey rubbery membrane peculiar to diphtheria. By this time Leander was completely unconscious. Wood and Swart once again opened his mouth with the knife blade and Miller removed the membrane.

"And did you at that time think it was diphtheria?" asked Coolidge of Dr. Miller.

"I thought so myself, yes sir."

"Did you take any measures to get other advice about it?"

"Yes sir."

She telephoned Dr. Wilson at Lisbon Falls, Miller said, but was not able to reach him. She heard from him on the following afternoon, Saturday. He said he preferred not to come because of the smallpox quarantine, but since Dr. Miller thought the case to be diphtheria, she "might consider it as such." So she gave directions that no one should enter Leander's room other than his nurses. She could not remember whether or not she had seen Leander again herself on Saturday morning, or talked to John Swart through the door.

So it had been two weeks, concluded Skelton, in cross examination, that Leander had been ill, one week of that time in delirium at Bethesda, before a doctor was called to help in the diagnosis. "And still it was the practice at the place in serious cases where you couldn't tell, to call in outside assistance?"

"They did it sometimes," said Miller.

"But the Bartlett case was an exception?"

"I don't consider it was."

"They did it this time Friday when you found the conditions you have explained?"

"Yes sir."

"And not before that?"

"No sir."

"And you knew he had been very sick up to that time?"

"I knew he was very sick at that time."

"And prior to that time?"

"A few days."

On Saturday morning Wood and Swart forced Leander's mouth open once more and removed the membrane. At ten o'clock that evening the door to his room was sealed with paper and paste as a quarantine measure. Swart was inside, where he remained the rest of the night, on duty for thirty-six hours. Leander died in the early morning.

The trial ended with Skelton's examination of Elvira. Did she know before Leander's death, he asked her, that Mr. Sandford had referred to the boy in chapel as "rebellious, and not right with God?"

"I don't know anything about that from personal experience," Elvira answered, carefully.

"You were not aware while you were in Bethesda, relying on prayer, that there was any question as to Mr. Sandford's being satisfied with his condition?"

"I don't know just what you mean."

"You were not aware, while you were in the hospital, relying on the prayer of faith, that Mr. Sandford had any question as to the sufficiency of Leander's confession?"

"I thought he was perfectly satisfied with the confession."

"You felt he was?"

"Yes sir."

"You are not aware that he still regarded him as rebellious?"

"I don't think he did."

"You were not aware that he did?"

"I know that he did not."

"You didn't know that he did then, did you? Answer that question by yes or no."

"Didn't know that he did?"

"That Mr. Sandford regarded Leander as rebellious that week?"

"I don't think he did regard him as rebellious."

"That is the best of your knowledge?"

"After he had made a confession. That is the best of my knowledge."

"You didn't know Mr. Sandford was saying anything about his not being right with God at that time?"

"At that time?"

"During the week he was in Bethesda?"

"No sir, not to my personal knowledge."

"And you were acting or feeling all the time confident that Mr. Sandford was satisfied with Leander's spiritual condition?"

"I don't know as I thought anything about it, especially."

"Had no occasion to think otherwise, did you?"

"Not from personal knowledge."

"Had no occasion to feel as though he wasn't getting the full benefit of Mr. Sandford's conviction that he was entitled to the prayer of faith and receiving that prayer?"

"You have asked me that question three times, the same thing."

"Yes, Mrs. Bartlett, I see you are able to take care of yourself."

"I can tell the truth."

"Now will you answer the question?"

The question was read but not included in the court records.

"I don't just understand it, the way he read it."

"You are not positive I have asked that same question three times, are you?"

"I don't want to answer it until I understand it perfectly."

In redirect, Coolidge asked, "Mrs. Bartlett, did Mr. Sandford at any time ever indicate to you any ill feeling or anger toward your son?"

The line containing her response was skipped in the court records, but there can be no doubt that it was one word: "No." So Coolidge got the answer he wanted, and Skelton missed the boat by a hair. For all that Elvira's black eyes snapped as she addressed him, she did not tell the whole truth. What she knew as she sat in the stand at both trials, and what Frank Sandford knew as he listened to her, what most of the Shiloh members present in the courtroom knew, was that she and Merlyn had been charged not to grieve for Leander, since his death was an act of God's judgment. Elvira, unable to accept that, had talked about it so much at Shiloh that it became common knowledge and she was reproved. Some weeks later, still mourning Leander's death as a "lost soul," she received a letter in which Sandford assured her that her son was "safe."

At the Auburn trial both Ida Miller and Ralph Gleason, who at the time was acting as chief-of-staff at Bethesda, admitted that no effort had been made to secure the services of a second physician for diagnosis when Dr. Wilson proved unreachable. Wilson himself was not called as a State's witness, but at the Farmington trial two other doctors were, both with mature local practices. The two men agreed that antitoxin serum was the only sure treatment for diphtheria, that its use had been widely accepted for more than eight years, that it was effective in almost 100 percent of cases, especially if administered in the onset of the disease. The use of antitoxin was so successful, they said, that diphtheria was no longer considered a threatening disease. Even in the latter stages of the illness antitoxin could "show a benefit," if the patient could live long enough for it to work—twenty-four hours or more. Though diphtheria might be hard to diagnose in its early stages, the slightest possibility of it warranted a microscopic examination of throat secretions at the state laboratory.

No one picked up on this enlightening piece of information. Ida Miller was not called back to be asked whether or not Shiloh policy would allow such a lab examination in the diagnostic process. But even apart from that, if the jury was able at this point to keep things straight, they might have remembered that as a rule Dr. Miller had been very careful to obey the requirements of the state health laws in cases of possible contagious disease. Yet for one week after Leander had been admitted to Bethesda, no doctor was called for diagnostic help.

Neither within the bounds of Shiloh's own principles nor within the implications of the law did anyone act until it was too late. It appears that at a minimum, four adults—Sandford, Gleason, Ida Miller, and Elvira Bartlett—allowed Leander to die, whether out of passiveness, ignorance, negligence, or a theology which permitted disobedient persons to be expendable and required obedient ones to surrender responsibility. No determined steps were taken to save his life. But Ida Miller was not on trial, nor Elvira, nor anyone but Frank Sandford, and as it turned out, the question of appropriate medical attention was actually a moot one. Guilt or innocence were to be determined on other grounds.

It was not until both sides had rested in the Farmington trial and

Judge Savage had made his final remarks to the jury that all the quizzing about prayer and confession made sense. Savage explained that the major issue raised by the definition of manslaughter in use at this trial centered in the quality of Sandford's authority at Shiloh. The jury, he said, was not to pass judgment on "the worthiness or unworthiness" of Shiloh's religion, only in so far as it related to Sandford's duty to Leander's welfare. The indictment charged that there was a "criminal breach of duty" in Sandford's failure to provide Leander with medical care. But Sandford did not believe in medicine. He believed in the prayer of faith.

"Well, now," said Judge Savage to the jury, "to many of us it may seem surprising that such a doctrine is sustained by the law, but it is." It was upheld by the same common law that could indict for negligence.

The rule the jury was to use in determining guilt or innocence, advised Savage, was one "recognized by our fathers generations and generations ago, and is the law in this State today." When death results from the omission to call a physician, it was not to be viewed as criminal negligence unless "criminal indifference" could be proven.

But it was Sandford's duty to apply the method he *did* believe in, the prayer of faith. If he had failed to "use" prayer as a means of healing for Leander, that might be considered negligence. It was important for the jury to determine what Sandford's attitude toward the boy had been, whether or not he had felt "ill will" toward him or "wanted to make an example of him," or whether, as the defense claimed, "there was not any anger or passion or ill will displayed," but that "it was part of the belief that persons rebellious would suffer . . . ," and that Sandford "was doing all he could" to help the community to "save themselves from sickness and trouble." If he did deny Leander the prayer of faith, the *manner* in which he did so was important in determining his guilt or innocence, for that could be viewed as "criminal indifference." Did Frank Sandford deny Leander Bartlett the benefit of the prayer of faith? That was the pivotal question in both the Auburn and Farmington trials.

Whatever the jury understood, it took less than two hours to come up with the verdict of guilty. The lawyers and Judge Savage were walking to dinner when a messenger caught up with them on the street and brought them back to the courtroom, where the Shiloh people sat waiting patiently, no one running for dinner—no one having eaten since breakfast.

The defense immediately filed exceptions again, and bail was arranged at $2,500. Frank and his attorneys were jolted by the jury's conclusion, as they had found hope in Savage's treatment of the medicine-faith controversy. It was that very element which would arouse the Supreme Judicial Court of Maine in Portland, where the case was finally forwarded. The cruelty case was also moved to the courts in Augusta, and so the proceedings dragged on, with the outcome still in the future.

18

The Call to the Wilderness
1904

It would be natural to suppose that throughout this ordeal Shiloh put itself on hold, retreating to its towers to pray for victory. On the contrary, said the *The Glad Tidings* (another new periodical), "The movement seems to be a healthy, growing, laughing child."

The spring and summer of 1904 were months of further expansion. At the end of March, halfway between the Auburn and Farmington trials, a parade, complete with band music, stretched out across the countryside of Durham. It began on the front veranda of Shiloh Proper, where the twenty band members in new navy blue uniforms, brass instruments under their arms, were anointed along with their conductor, Merwyn Wakeman. As these men played their flashing horns, Frank Sandford anointed a new buggy, a modern one with rubber tires and ball-bearings, drawn by a high-stepping mare from Aroostook county. Then the parade, led by the band, filed across the sand past Olivet, crossed Pinkham Brook to a recently acquired forty-acre pasture, and trudged through the still soggy fields down to old barn next to Hephzibah, where Wendell White prayed "mightily" for a new barn suitable for the increasing livestock. Back again on the hilltop a surprise waited— a new "Gospel Barge," a $1,000 four-seater built in Boston, originally for worldly Bar Harbor parties, and two beautiful matched teams, one brown and one "royal black" (the blacks named David and Jonathon), with shiny harnesses and brasswork. Off again, some folks in the conveyances, some walking the miles of roads rutted with mud to two farms just bought by Kingdom members, one of them equipped with hothouses, and once more to the chapel to consecrate a gleaming new

"Davidic harp" (which Sandford himself intended to play). The band performed at each stop.

As usual, God was transforming Satan's work into a blessing. The legal persecution, the worst of all the crises Shiloh had yet faced, one which Sandford had so clearly not manipulated or manufactured (as critics believed other crises had been) had gotten the attention of the nation and was drawing to Shiloh's side believers tucked away in corners of nearly every state. Not long after the conclusion of the Farmington trial in May, they began to come. Even with the doubling-up of families in farmhouses, there was hardly room for all. Many of the newcomers tented in the grove or built themselves rough cabins, enjoying three long warm-weather conventions.

The "laughing child" must have been a prosperous one too. It appeared to be buying up the entire town of Durham, farm by farm. Over in Lisbon Falls, rumors spread that a harness shop and a shoe factory were soon to be established on the hilltop, and that a large power station was in the works, along with an electric railroad bridge to be installed from Lisbon Falls across the river to Durham for carrying freight.

At last Shiloh was making sense. The surrounding communities eyed the movement with new respect. Here was salvation of a kind ordinary people could understand. Interest in "cooperative capitalism" as an economic solution, a corrective to an unrestrained capitalism, was running high in the country at this time. One of Lewiston's foremost entrepreneurs, the owner of Peck's Department Store, had lately been promoting an elaborate design to reconstruct the entire city around such an idea. "Christian communism" was not an unfamiliar idea, even in evangelical circles, at least in terms of distributing wealth to meet the needs of the poor. In an area where the population had been steadily dropping and where farms regularly failed as a means of livelihood, the Kingdom, Incorporated, suggested the best American capitalist tradition, even if shareholding was replaced by just plain sharing. Without waiting for the final outcome of the trials, the Lisbon Falls Board of Trade appointed a committee to confer with Shiloh leaders.

But they had misjudged Frank Sandford again. He was not the least bit interested in corporate capitalism or in modeling economic solutions for the country. He was not out to set up a utopian community or an "experiment" of any kind. There would be no need—indeed, no opportunity—for anyone to repeat what he was doing. His sole intent was to make the movement self-sufficient during the uncertainties of the

Tribulation—for the present legal entanglement was only the first stage of persecution in a world dominated by the anti-Christ.

Back in January Sandford had written a letter to Wilhelm Marstaller, the patriarch of an extended German family who owned a cotton ranch in Kyle, Texas. Marstaller had expressed an interest in migrating to Shiloh, and Sandford was now urging him to come. He explained that just three days earlier the Kingdom had been incorporated and was in a position to purchase a farm in Marstaller's name. Shiloh was inviting believers who were anxious to remove themselves from "the world" and bring their children to where they might have a "Christian education," people who would live in the region "on some kind of a basis whereby we can control who shall be on land under the Kingdom," wrote Sandford. They were looking for a "class of people" who would "gradually learn the life of walking with God and at the same time the art of self-support."

Marstaller, who knew all about the art of self-support, responded favorably. Three months later, just before the March parade across the town, Sandford heard God's direct message: "Begin to possess a Place in the Wilderness." The actual words, taken from Revelation, referred to a refuge to which a woman, after giving birth to a man-child, would flee from the "beast" who would stalk her during the Tribulation. Some Biblical interpreters thought the woman was Israel and the man-child Christ. Frank believed that the woman was the Church—that is, "the spiritual Kingdom restored to Israel"—and the man-child symbolized "a company of overcomers who are to rule all nations with a rod of iron." The Place in the Wilderness, which God Himself had named Shiloh, this quiet sanctuary in Durham, Maine, was the one spot on earth "to which the people can flee," where "every David-hearted man and woman would be safe in the terrible days to come."

Since the time when the wilderness had been an awesome physical reality, it had symbolized not only the dark recesses of evil, but innocence as well, a stubborn, unpolished naturalness that was particularly American. Those ideas were not articulated in the least at Shiloh, but they reverberated, nevertheless, for many of the adults. In the midst of the world's evil, good was being established, where cows and pigs were herded down the road and woodpiles towered by kitchen doors.

The Marstallers and dozens of other families around the country accepted Sandford's offer. "Not a hoof left behind!" shouted one man joyously as he walked up the long driveway. He had sold his home and livestock and all his possessions, as most did—though some brought their status symbols to donate for Shiloh's use, parlor organs and pianos and blooded horses. Marstaller brought a team of oxen and his ten (soon to be twelve) children, who already knew how to work, and a great deal of money, which he turned over to the Kingdom.

Meanwhile properties throughout Durham were being purchased in the names of individuals sending money in advance. The new corporation, to forestall confusion, stood as agent and buyer. Landowners in Durham were happy to make a dollar on what they had long considered to be white elephants. Wendell, chosen as an assistant in the purchase of farms, was shocked at Sandford's willingness to pay some of the prices asked by shrewd farmers, far above the value of the overworked soil. "Ridiculous!" Wendell would interject scornfully, facing down both Sandford and the sellers.

Altogether twenty-two properties were acquired, 1,470 acres, a total of close to two square miles of Durham land. These farms were to produce all of Shiloh's food, through gardening and livestock. Two ice houses capable of holding 175 tons of ice (cut from the river) were now constructed, planned to preserve the harvest of the *Ripple*, the fishing boat in Casco Bay.

As for the shoe factory, that consisted of Mr. Grant, a man twisted with arthritis, who worked in his home, praying for Africa and China while he stitched leather. He proudly produced as many as 1,300 sturdy ankle-high shoes, some bearing a tag on the tongue: "This Globe for God." His careful skill was duplicated many times over in Shiloh's accumulating artisans—blacksmiths, carpenters, mechanics, coopers, tin smiths (107 heating stoves for the Extension, as well as zinc bathtubs), masons, plumbers, and even a taxidermist. None of what was produced and manufactured was meant to be sold. Not even barter was permitted.

Actually Shiloh had already sold livestock and other possessions and would continue to do so when funds were needed. But the long-range impact of summoning the faithful out of the world was more seriously ironic. Wendell later told his children that the call to the Place in the Wilderness was killing the goose that laid the golden egg, since it meant that many of the church members who had been contributing a percentage of their income to Shiloh now depended on Shiloh for their most basic needs. That was not the original intention. The new owners of the farms, after providing for their own needs, were meant to turn the surplus back into the organization.

But as it turned out, only seven of the twenty-two new properties were actually registered in the names of the buyers. There were few if any contracts between the Kingdom and its members designating agreed terms of ownership or management. Some new owners were baffled, on arriving, to discover that there had been a change; they had suddenly been "promoted" from members on the fringe and were to share "all things in common" as if they were 100-fold members. The "art of self-support" meant the support of all, each supporting the other.

In the course of this Sandford's public reputation for talking people out of their money was established beyond redemption. But for most of the new residents something else was at work. They already knew that any religion worth its salt took you beyond the familiar. That was what getting David truth meant—to transcend mediocrity. To give over personal control of one's financial circumstances was as radical a sacrifice as a person could make, and therefore more of a triumph. To leave behind the farms and businesses they had worked for years to develop (and which perhaps had been generations in the family) went against all the values they had absorbed from American culture and history. They were abandoning the prevalent version of the American Dream for the dream at its most supreme, and the shout "Not a hoof left behind!" represented in a special way an extinction of the past. They were doing the hardest thing God could ask of them; they were becoming fools for Christ's sake in the area where it counted the most—economics—leaving behind their nets, as the disciples had done. Their money would go to evangelize the world, and meanwhile their own needs would be provided and their children would grow up in a holy environment. It was a good bargain after all.

Sandford, no stranger to the Yankee mind, believed that a person's reality with God was demonstrated by how easily a person could let go of money. Once that joyous abandonment had taken over, David's flock would learn what he had experienced often: "You can't get ahead of God! He will always give back more than you give Him."

Of all those who owned Shiloh property George Higgins seemed to be the one most in charge. No more cottages were ever built on "The Street Called Straight," but farther on down, next to Hephzibah, Higgins constructed a ten-room house, visible from the southeast windows of the hilltop buildings. He did this with funds from his father's estate, in spite of brothers who had done all in their power to keep George's share from disappearing down what they saw as Shiloh's bottomless hole. He won that fight, but agreed not to turn the money over to the institution. Instead, he and his wife (who had also come into an inheritance at close to the same time) shared their home generously with

Shiloh people and opened a "store," reselling at wholesale prices items they had purchased with their own funds—fabric, soap, shoestrings, toothbrushes.

In mid-October the Auburn Temple was moved to Shiloh. Many of the Auburn members were now living on the hill and the structure was needed for large winter conventions. The building was dismantled, brought to Durham by train and wagon, put back together and renovated, all in three weeks.

So here was Shiloh in 1904, buttoned up snugly against the outside world, but not against itself. Not only had the goose been sold, but new and multiple tensions had been introduced, wrinkles that would never iron out. Instead of fighting to keep the mix of spiritual levels at arm's length, all levels were being embosomed. The band of pure students still operated at the core. Shiloh Proper was set aside as holy living quarters for a select group of the proven, and pulling a small, trustworthy squadron out of the larger army would go on being Sandford's greatest obsession. But the term 100-fold had grown ambiguous. It was possible to give 100 percent of your time and possessions, but not qualify spiritually or politically. The life of faith meant trusting the leaders and a holy few to make corporate decisions by which everyone was affected and yet in which not many had a say. In time, even the most committed members would have trouble keeping those balls in the air, including Wendell White.

Wendell was already finding himself frustrated by the emotional juggling act involved in being a loyal, unquestioning member of Shiloh while he disapproved of how things were done. It could be said that from this point on, he gave his life to the study of loyalty.

The most shaky moment for Wendell, after the Black Winter, may have been on the day of the triumphant parade that March of 1904. At the end of the festivities a ten-foot scroll called "The Pledge of Loyalty" was presented in chapel for the signatures of everyone present. The articles of faith were spelled out in detail, most of them traditional evangelical doctrine. The final three items read as follows.

I believe not only in the Father—the only Potentate—and in Jesus Christ—the King whose millenial reign is to prepare the globe for the great God—but also in the prophet-prince-priest who is to prepare the Kingdom for the Christ; I believe in the man who as prophet is called in the Bible *"Elijah,"* and as prince is called "David," and as a priest is called . . . *The Branch* [Melchizedek] I believe that F.

W. Sandford of Shiloh, Maine, U.S.A. tells the truth when he makes
proclamation that God said to him, *"Elijah is here. Testify,"* and again
"I have found David," words spoken as applying to himself personally.
I believe in and accept him as such.

If Wendell signed it, he perjured himself. Years later he told his
children that he had never been taken in by Sandford's extreme claims
about himself. Frank Murray, in his biography of Sandford, says that
all of those present signed the pledge. Yet it was only once brought
out again, and as the princely aspect of the modern David began from
this point to give way to the concept of David as shepherd.

All uncertainties aside, I am sure of one thing: Wendell *wanted*
Shiloh to work, and he wanted to help it work. He believed as much
as Sandford that "the night was far spent," and he wanted to be an
active part of the preparation for the end, whatever call to hardness
that might entail for himself or his family. Everything in his life and
heritage seemed to point to this. Shiloh was not just a last resort, the
answer to failed ambition, something he passively fell into, but God's
best purpose for him all along. Its imperfections were, in a way, proof
of that. It was not heaven. It may have proven itself full of human
error and failure, like his own life, but it was the only bright slice of
hope he could see, for the church and the world—and here it was, not
in Indiana or Salt Lake City, but in his own back yard, under his nose,
so close as to be unavoidable, the Kingdom of God as the last primitive
frontier, complete with stumps of trees and frost-heaved stones and
capricious turns of weather.

As for hardship, that was inevitable, After all, the Whites chose to
stay at Shiloh at the close of the Black Winter. They knew how bad
things could get. Hardship was part of the cosmic vision, even (or
especially) if that suffering was a purgative process at their leader's hand.
If Wendell never fully accepted Sandford's metaphysical roles, as God's
appointed man he could still *act* as prophet, priest, and prince, representing
Christ, even in outbursts of anger—and who understood anger better
than Wendell? To all those at Shiloh who realized the function of the
Old Testament prophets, especially the apocalyptic prophets, anger was
morally justified. Sandford's personality was "irrelevant," says William
Hiss, "hardly more important than the cut of his clothes," at least to
the "spiritually attuned members of the Kingdom, assured that their
lives were part of a larger struggle on which all of human history
depended." Their own suffering—and in some cases, humiliation—was

also unimportant. What mattered was the improvement of their souls and that was what Mr. Sandford was after, with standards higher than their own, like a good coach, exacting from them more than they dreamed they could give. They treasured that about him. If His relationship to God was "the promise and potency of Israel," as had been believed of the Old Testament prophets, then it was easy to see his revelations, says Hiss, "as a spiritually glorious detachment from the self and a representative identification with God," and not as extreme egotism. His scathing judgments of others were not sadistic, but an effort to make his own experience theirs. If he seemed pugnacious and bombastic to the outside world, well so did President Theodore Roosevelt, the man now in office, whose challenge to the country to be a "nation of men, not a nation of weaklings" sounded not unsimilar to Mr. Sandford's challenges.

If Sandford's affronts were outrageous—calling a man an agent of the devil or a woman a harlot, "reeking of fornicative desire"—it was not, as Nathan Harriman had told the newspapers, "a refined ingenuity in torture," but was meant to awaken the saints to the danger of spiritual laxity. If he chewed out Charles Holland or slapped Helen in public (for he did, as many had now seen—once on the chapel platform, witnessed by Enid White), it was only to make examples of those who were closest to him. His moments of spontaneous affection and boyish humor were as compelling as his anger.

But signed or not, the Pledge of Loyalty was a serious departure from the evangelical tenets of Wendell's boyhood—particularly in Sandford's role as priest. "Hang on to my coattails," he frequently said, "and I will get you through to God." Human power to damn or save was far afield of either the Puritan Calvinistic trust in predestination, an unbreakable covenant, or its antithesis, the Arminian view of the Methodists, which allowed the possibility of backsliding all the way out of God's grace. No third party, in either case, could come between the soul and God.

There is nothing to suggest that Wendell would have consciously relinquished his own personal priesthood as a believing Protestant or his freedom as an American to another man. If in his basic loyalty to Sandford (for that was true, however much Wendell might snort) he was letting go of the dignity of choice established for him by his "New Light" ancestors, he rationalized it as God's sovereignty in his life. But Wendell would go on equivocating for three more years, until 1907, before the options suddenly shut down.

In the fall of 1904 public attitude toward the hilltop, always capricious, turned again. In the three months of summer local papers had carried brief, rather indifferent stories of Shiloh, compared with the concentrated attention of the spring. The on-going trials, the retrials, were pending and the emotional climate was important. In the middle of October, at this touchy point, dreadful news arrived from Jerusalem.

Things had not been going well overseas for a year. All three posts—England, Egypt, and Jerusalem—had passed through Black Winters of their own, suffering from a lack of funds and at times prolonged hunger. At Pas-dammin, the beautiful estate outside Liverpool, often only one slim meal a day was served, sometimes only hot water, and so little suitable clothing to wear that the workers had to take turns going abroad of the house. Someone told of walking the six-mile round trip to Liverpool each day in bedroom slippers. Under those circumstances not much evangelism had been done.

In August Sandford recalled the Liverpool school almost *en masse.* One hundred fifty workers and converts arrived at Shiloh in time for the August convention, treating Lisbon Falls to hymns of praise as they poured from the train and were carried in wagons across the bridge to Durham. One of these was Almon Whittaker, coming home at last to his family after three years of separation. With nearly all of the Liverpool church and school now in America at the Place in the Wilderness, there was no center for the Kingdom in England at all, "The secret of the safety of the British Empire" removed.

The Jerusalem party, reduced to five people, rattled around in an expensive sixteen-room house, accomplishing little in terms of outside contacts. The work in Egypt, where six missionaries lived at the dockside house in Alexandria, had been often dramatic, but largely disappointing in its long-range results. One after another sincere inquirers turned out to be ne'er-do-wells looking for hospitality or an English lesson, and Islamic anger toward the Shilohites had sometimes been frightening.

Nevertheless the African mission station in Egypt had been an active one. Two of the young men, Victor Barton and Frank Templeton, were energetic in their outreach and unabashed by danger, often bearing witness (most tactfully), to men with revolvers in their belts.

In March 1904 Sandford suddenly closed the mission in Alexandria and sent Barton and Templeton to join the party in Jerusalem. The reason was not made public, though rumors surfaced that the Elijah and David claims had stirred controversy. Puzzled and reluctant, the two men obeyed, throwing themselves into the work in Palestine with the same disregard for danger, learning Arabic and making effective contacts.

In September, in Jerusalem for just six months, both Frank Templeton and Victor Barton died of fever, ten days apart. The story broke without much fanfare on page three of a mid-October *Lewiston Journal,* and it might have passed almost unnoticed by the general public, except that Nathan Harriman, horrified at what he saw as the totally unnecessary deaths of two young men he had known and respected, sent copies of letters from the American consul at Jerusalem to the newspaper, which printed them on page one a month later.

The consul, Selah Merrill, had been thwarted in all of his efforts to assist the sick men. His letters included quotes from the "principal English physician in Jerusalem," who had been called to the Shiloh house at the very last moment and had not been permitted to give medical treatment. The deaths, said the doctor, were caused not only by malarial fever but by "culpable neglect," as Edward Doughty's had been two years before.

The story triggered off a kind of journalistic madness. The paper, forgetting its dignified resolve to keep an "open forum," began to print everything that came its way at a time when Sandford could not answer without contempt of court. It was now, at the end of November, that Jean Stevens's account of John Sandford's fast was published, from a copy of her letter furnished by Nathan Harriman—just two weeks before that case was scheduled for retrial. Then early in December Eliza Leger offered the *Journal* a story of a shockingly fanatical experience at Liverpool during the Black Winter. After being "metaphysically stoned" by her Shiloh colleagues, who had circled her prone body on the floor, shouting and screaming for hours as they accused her of "spiritual lapses," Eliza had been banished to her room for two weeks of fasting. Under the guidance of Almon Whittaker and Charles Holland, she was not "released" until she was willing to die and go to hell if that should be "God's will."

A week later both Moses and Eliza Leger provided the press with further evidence of Sandford's insidious control. It was a letter he had written to Eliza the previous September to persuade her to remain in the Kingdom in spite of her husband's defection. Eliza was at Shiloh, recently returned from England; her husband was in Massachusetts.

Caught in the tangle of her own tract on the proper place of women, Eliza had candidly shared with Sandford her struggle to make the right decision. Should she go obediently to the husband who had left her alone at Shiloh, had all but deserted her, and was now asking her to rejoin him? Or now that he was out from under the Shiloh chain of authority through his defection, was it her responsibility to ignore him and follow the prophet? After emptying herself as much as she thought possible of personal motives, even going to the edge of hell, here she stood between the two most important men of her life.

The marriage may have been on rocky ground for a long time. Eliza outmatched her husband in strength of personality. Seeing Sandford in any romantic light might have been unthinkable for her to acknowledge, yet she surely accepted him as the model of the husband they were to obey. Not many men could compare, either in personal appeal or authority—or in a talent for showing appreciation. There is no reliable basis for assuming that sexual improprieties transpired at Shiloh. If they did they were the best-kept secrets in the world. Most likely, neither Eliza nor Sandford were aware of the Freudian overtones in the letter she offered the public, in which he all but advised her to leave her husband. After expressing his confidence in her ultimate good judgment, he encouraged her to "hold her position" and fight "every form of influence" that could sever her "a hair's breadth from loyalty to the man of God now writing to you."

> You have a constitutional right guaranteed you in the United States, and that is the privilege of serving God according to the dictates of your own conscience. I should exercise my liberty with no uncertain sound.
>
> The act of your husband is so dastardly, so utterly dishonorable . . . so utterly unscriptural that there is not the slightest reason that he should have the slightest consideration.
>
> . . . I somehow feel you belong in the work as a special piece of machinery, and I believe a fearful woe will fall upon whoever attempts to steal you out of the place where God has located you. I would not be the man to attempt that thing for a million dollars a second. I believe that the judgment blow of the Almighty will lay your husband out in death if he plays on that subject too far.
>
> I wish to assure you that you shall have all there is in my heart of faith, of courage, of sympathy, of Christian love, of Christ's own compassion, of boundless confidence, holy enthusiasm, and of world-

wide victory—all is yours. You can count on it through the blackness
and the light; and as far as that is concerned, Sister Leger, I feel as
if Hell were dismayed already as I dictate this letter. . . .

Yours triumphantly, yours on top, yours victorious, yours fighting,
yours more than conqueror, yours with a crown on his head, yours
riding a white charger, yours with a bow in his hand, yours with
sharp arrows, and yours to the end. F. W. Sandford.

P.S. After you have thoroughly digested this I would advise you to
destroy it; for I would not like anybody to read it but yourself.

As Eliza told the press, it was Sandford's reminder of her "consti-
tutional right" that gave her "the courage to dare to hope" that her
freedom could be restored. She joined her husband. How much freedom
she actually stepped into remains a question.

As well as satisfying the public craving for sensation, these stories
were making it clear that the experience of breaking away from Shiloh
was far more radical than the decision to join had been, and as demanding
of public testimony as conversion itself. Once the new "liberty" was
realized, the burden to find some way to help release those left behind—
a kind of reverse proselytizing—was overpowering. "The hypnotic spell
began to break as soon as I dared decide that something was wrong
with this man," wrote Eliza. "I say 'hypnotic,' for I know that is a
part of that dreadful, subtle snare that some have broken away from,
but that holds so many still under its power."

For most discontented Shiloh members it was not as simple as it was
for sixteen-year-old Wallace Daggett, who said to himself one day in
the utmost surprise, "I don't have to be hungry. I can leave and get a
job." But for Daggett the move was not much different than the one
he would have made under most circumstances—to get out on his own
at an age when many boys did. He was not held by a dozen complicating
ties.

It was those multiple holding forces that people outside Shiloh could
not seem to penetrate. Relatives and friends were beginning to use every
means they could think of to release their family members, convinced
they were prisoners of some special power. Only a few were succeeding.
Charles F. Dunlap of Portland brought a suit against his own son at
Shiloh in order to gain guardianship of his young grandson, for whose
life he feared. His much-publicized case produced a rash of other suits,
most of which never came to trial.

In Aroostook County, where citizens had less patience with the slow wheels of justice, a mob of 800 (so said the *New York Times,* which may have added an extra zero) descended on the George Jones family in the town of Blaine when word got out that they intended to sell their farm and give the money to Shiloh. A brother of Jones, not favoring violence, appealed to a judge of probate court to appoint a guardian of the estate, "alleging that the said appellant is so spending and wasting his estate as to expose himself and his family to want and his town to expense." Meanwhile, the mob ordered Jones out of the county. He went, taking his wife and nine children to Shiloh.

The frustration was exhibited further in a series of discussions just before Christmas by the Lisbon Falls Board of Trade, which had not given up on the Kingdom as a commercial enterprise. Prompted by the recent deaths in Jerusalem and by the fear of another epidemic in Shiloh's crowded conditions (which next time might not be contained), this large group of businessmen, attorneys, and doctors locked horns far into one night. The result was a resolution to call for a legislative investigation of Shiloh. In the debate Henry Coolidge, Sandford's attorney, entreated the others to drop the matter until the trials were over.

Deploring the attempts of newspapers to "crush" Sandford at a time when he could not reply, Coolidge called him an "honest" man, not a criminal. "As for the [Shiloh] people themselves, have you ever watched them when they come over here to Lisbon Falls? Have you seen any cigar stubs in their mouths? Have you ever seen them chewing and spitting? Have you ever seen them drinking and reeling down the street? No, if you were to go to Shiloh you would find a religious school where the men and women are decent and honorable and upright."

Coolidge lost this particular out-of-court argument, and so did the Board of Trade. Though in time they were able to institute and investigation, it effected absolutely nothing.

It was now the middle of December and the cruelty case involving John Sandford had just been determined in the Auburn Supreme Judicial Court under a different judge. It had taken much longer than expected, because the court stenographer had died and his shorthand proved indecipherable. Attorneys found it necessary to reargue the case from their own briefs. Exceptions filed by Shiloh's attorneys were disallowed and the verdict of guilty stood. Sandford was fined $100 and costs. It was paid by his attorney, Henry Coolidge.

On January 3, 1905, the Supreme Judicial Court of Maine at Portland handed down a long-awaited decision in the manslaughter case. The conviction of guilt brought by the jury in Farmington in May was reversed. The verdict of the jury, said the Portland judges, was based on opinion, not fact, because a portion of Judge Savage's charge urged the jury to make a decision "not on the . . . findings as to the truth, but upon the belief of the individual member of the jury upon the question of the efficacy of prayer as a means to cure the sick." This made it possible to convict or acquit with the same evidence.

In October 1905 the tired case would be tried all over again in Auburn under a different judge, again with a hung jury, unable to agree on the charge of "culpable indifference." It was well into 1906 before the interminable details of the legal process were finally wrapped up, and Shiloh could consider itself triumphant.

By this time Frank Sandford had taken to the water, far away from courts, juries, reporters, the curiosity of the public, the self-pity of traitors, and (perhaps harder yet to take) the emotional dependency of his followers. For the next half dozen years the ocean itself would become a great moat of safety, while forces and circumstances gathered and regrouped for another encounter with the laws of the land and the sea.

Shiloh from the southwest, after 1905. Higgins Cottage, foreground center. Hephzibah, foreground right, with Olivet behind it.

Village of Freeport, Maine, turn of the century. Courtesy Freeport Historical Society.

The *Coronet*, circa 1898. Courtesy New England Society for the Preservation of Antiquities.

Sandford family aboard the yacht *Wanderer*, 1903. Deborah is the babe-in-arms.

19

Breaking the Power of Hell
1905–1907

"There is an old sailor's maxim that 'they who go down to the sea in *ships* behold the wonders of the deep, but they who go down to the sea in *schooners* see Hell.'" The remark was made by Arthur Curtiss James, one-time owner of the racing yacht *Coronet*. He was referring to the specific dangers in sailing, but his words imported a larger meaning for the future of Shiloh.

On March 9, 1905, Helen gave birth to the Sandfords' fifth child. John was now eight and Esther six. Two other little girls, Marguerite and Deborah, had been born since 1900. The arrival of a boy was a matter of great rejoicing. They named him David. "In honor of the occasion," said Frank to Charles Holland, "take steps to purchase the *Coronet.*"

"Racer To Be Gospel Ship," reported the *New York Times,* in a small page-one item. The *Coronet,* once the flagship of the New York Yacht Club, was famous among the sea-going rich. Designed on the New York pilot model by Captain Christopher Crosby, she had been built in 1885 by C. and R. Poillon of Brooklyn at a cost of $75,000, and refitted at half again that amount for the 1887 race across the Atlantic in which she bested the schooner *Dauntless* (owned by Caldwell and Colt, of Colt Revolver). By the time the *Coronet* caught Frank Sandford's eye, she was a thoroughly experienced craft, the first registered yacht to sail east to west around Cape Horn. While most of the great schooners came to violent ends sooner or later—with an average life of thirteen years, like a good dog—this yacht was already twenty years old when Shiloh acquired her and still beautiful, hardly showing her age.

In 1895, Arthur James used her to carry a group of astronomers to Japan to study the eclipse of the sun. On that particular voyage Mabel Loomis Todd accompanied her husband, Professor David Peck Todd of Amherst College. Mrs. Todd, a musician and writer, known to the literary world as co-editor with Thomas Wentworth Higginson of Emily Dickenson's first published collection of poetry, had recorded her *Coronet* adventure in *Corona and Coronet* in 1898. Enthralled by the lovely boat, Mrs. Todd described her as "white, schooner-rigged, carrying every sort of sail, and as airy as a bird . . . a thing of beauty indescribable" when her "cloud of canvas is spread to a brisk wind."

In landlubber's terms the *Coronet* measured 133 feet long overall, her width 27 feet. Her masts rose as high as the boat was long, with a sail area of over 8,000 square feet, which meant that she appeared as much sail and very little boat. She was capable of over 14 knots, her average in a good run about 8 knots, or close to 300 miles a day, a marvelous speed for a craft of her size and style.

This was a gentleman's possession, every inch top quality, framing and planking of Maine white oak, deck of almost luminous white pine. Steps of marble curved down from a mahogany deckhouse to a pair of swinging doors of leaded stained glass, through which one entered the saloon, a room delightfully comfortable with green plush easy chairs and divans, a piano and bookcases, observed Mrs. Todd, "and an open stove of red tiles shows a glowing bed of coals in chilly weather." Two large staterooms, decorated in rosy velvets and brocades, were furnished with brass bedsteads. Etched mirrors and glass reflected art nouveau grace, including the sensual figure of a most unShiloh-like mermaid. Four other rooms, plus the forecastle, offered easy living space for a total of thirty people.

Frank Sandford bought the *Coronet,* minus the Haviland china and oriental rugs, for $10,000, raising the money in the usual way, by prayer—in this case, forty days and nights of it, with shifts for eating and sleeping. Any sticky questions about unfinished Extension suites or mortgages on the Boston properties evaporated when the boat was brought home like an adopted princess, sailing smoothly into Port Royal— as Sandford was calling the shallow waters of South Freeport, locus of the new Kingdom Yacht Club. Shiloh now owned a fleet of four boats, including the three bought earlier—the fishing boat, the gasoline launch, and the small yacht *Wanderer.*

Something about the *Coronet* had excited the emotions of all her owners. Her previous passengers and crews had spoken of her with affection and honor, as if she were a living being—if not human then certainly with the responses and will of a superb horse. For years to come her beauty and strength, her astonishing adaptability, would symbolize the loftiest and purest of Shiloh's standards. All the heroism and toughness that had been emulated over the years, the drives and charges, the blow-ups and clean-outs, icy baptisms and days of hunger, endless hours of work and prayer, the ability to "stick," all would culminate in the white nobility of the *Coronet*.

As for the Kingdom Yacht Club—an idea, not a building or an organization—more than anything else in the movement's history, it represented the paradox of poverty and wealth hand in hand. For at the very moment Shiloh was taking on the trappings of this most worldly Edwardian era—yachts, brass bands, uniforms, hunting expeditions on tropical islands, trophies, and taxidermy—periods of deprivation began again on the Durham hill.

If a shortage prevailed, Shiloh members knew why. The Place in the Wilderness was sacrificing to "break the power of hell." The yacht would be used to carry missionaries to posts around the world. Kingdom members hardly imagined that soon the boat would supplant the hilltop in importance, but the Place in the Wilderness was already losing its supremacy as the center of adventure. Its luster was gone, as if stained by the events of the past years—an actuality that Sandford himself could not yet acknowledge, though his plans for the *Coronet* were already awesome.

At the moment his appointments with the courts forbid more than swift excursions. His intention to assume personal headquarters in Jerusalem must wait. Nevertheless, a quick trip to Jerusalem was crucial, to carry reinforcements to that post, and he was only waiting for God's orders to go.

Three days into June, at an afternoon meeting in Ebenezer, one of the women timidly handed Sandford a note bearing words she had heard God say: "Start for Jerusalem at the going down of the sun." With a leap of joy, he turned to the west window, saw the sun on its journey downward, exclaimed, "I'm starting for Jerusalem," and hurried to his room to grab a suitcase, already packed. By the time local farmhouses were lighting their lamps for the evening, a parade of wagons loaded with luggage and supplies ground its way toward Freeport. At dawn the crew lifted anchor, flags dipped, and the two brass cannon on deck boomed a farewell salute.

> Out of Port Royal the Coronet sails,
> She's homeward bound, homeward bound. . . .

ran the first lines of a hymn to the occasion written by Joseph Harriman, who with his new wife, Adnah Guptil, was one of the party headed back to Jerusalem. The sailors, Shiloh men who had been training for months under a hired captain on the *Wanderer,* were now in the charge of Captain Benjamin Sellick, a new Shiloh member from Canada, with Austin Perry as navigator. Perry, though not a sailor since his boyhood when he had been tutored in navigation by his father, had agreed to the responsibility out of obedience to Sandford's request.

New faces appeared among the sea-goers, two families from Canada's Maritime Provinces, the McKenzies of Nova Scotia and Gordon Murray of New Brunswick. Lester McKenzie, an experienced sailor in his early twenties with four generations of sea captains behind him, had promised his mother he would never go to sea, and had no idea when he arrived at Shiloh in 1903 that he would be breaking that promise. Jean Dart, his cousin, a young woman who resembled an earlier Helen Sandford in her combination of quiet composure and strength, had completed a year of medical studies in preparation for foreign missions before joining the McKenzies in Durham.

Like Lester McKenzie, Gordon Murray represented a refreshing new specimen of young "Christian manhood" at Shiloh, says William Hiss. Though not as tall as Lester, Gordon was reputed to be "the strongest man in the Kingdom" and was greatly admired by one teenager, Arnold White. Both Murray and McKenzie wore a no-nonsense air and were not inclined toward spiritual gush. In later years Lester liked to tell of the time when Murray sensed an emotional shift in the atmosphere of the company and whispered, "Let's get out of here before somebody starts a prayer meeting."

The *Coronet* arrived in Jaffa early in July, good time for the apprenticing crew. Sandford stayed only long enough to bring encouragement and solace to the handful of Jerusalem workers, a tired four of the original Twelve, who had been waiting over three years for his return. Small, blond Emma Barton embarrassed herself by weeping on his shoulder. She had grieved profoundly over her family's angry departure from Shiloh after the Black Winter and her brother Victor's death. The yacht returned home but returned to Jerusalem in November, this time for a wedding in the Holy City. Emma and Gordon Murray had fallen in love during the *Coronet's* previous visit, and all Shiloh, like a great body of proud parents, was thrilled at the union.

But as if to prove that God's favor had shifted from the hilltop, back at Durham bad news awaited the schooner's return. Caroline Holland, in her early thirties, the lovely bride of the school's first romance, had died giving birth prematurely to her sixth child. Convinced such a thing could not have happened if he had been present, Sandford censured the school for its shabby faith and rebuked Charles Holland, who had been in command. The trouble behind the tragedy was soon brought to light. They had been praying for meat, Frank learned. They had all "gone into Baal worship," he told them, demonstrating again that they were no more than fleshpots, longing for the leeks and garlics of Egypt, or the fried pork and roast beef of the farms. Well, meat they would have.

"God is lining us up to uncompromising faith," wrote Arnold in his diary. April 17 (1906): "Mr. S. said he would trust God for Elijah fare for dinner, and Mr. Holland for breakfast." A week later the battle was still on. "War to the *knife,*" wrote Arnold, with no comic intention.

Sandford had been an advocate of peas and beans (the "pulse" of the Old Testament), because Daniel and his friends had become "fairer and fatter" on such a diet. Meat, other than pork, was not taboo, since Elijah had been fed "bread and flesh" by the ravens. But meat was expensive. Actually, even the beans had been scarce of late. Wholegrain corn meal had become the dependable staple. Bought in 100-pound bags at a dollar a bag, a half-pound per person at a half a cent each was all that was needed for a daily meal of cornbread or porridge.

On May 5, Arnold recorded the delivery of a 1,425-pound beef from Boston, which was hung ceremoniously from a hook in the dining room for all to see. Everyone must eat meat twice a day, breakfast and dinner—stewed, remembered Arnold, without potatoes or other vegetables. As a consequence "bowel trouble" resumed it miserable tyranny until the meat was gone.

Perhaps it was the conviction that things were bound to go wrong in his absence that led Sandford to the next step—to take the entire community of some six hundred people back with him to Jerusalem for the fall Feast of Tabernacles. He began scouting for a boat big enough to do so. When God's timetable still appeared not quite right for the ocean liner, at the end of April Sandford and Austin Perry settled for a three-masted barkentine freighter large enough to hold one hundred people. The *Rebecca Crowell* was brought to Rockland, Maine, and renamed the *Kingdom.*

Since the freighter's space was unsuitable for passengers, the richly appointed staterooms of the *Wanderer* were removed and refitted into the below-decks of the new boat, providing men's and women's cabins, a large dining room, and a chapel. The *Kingdom* would be registered now as a yacht to accord her the privileges of maritime law not permitted a commercial vessel under the American flag.

So not all of Shiloh, but a representative ninety people were chosen for the voyage. The Feast of Tabernacles was not the only reason for this two-ship excursion. Sandford had heard the command "Go around!" and was hoping to start a round-the-world trip in the *Coronet* as soon as the legal slate was wiped clean. The company for that trip, to be chosen out of the people on the two boats, would be named once they arrived in Palestine, so as goodbyes were said at the end of April no one sailing on either ship knew with certainty when he or she would return to America. As it turned out, some would not see their families for three years, and Sandford himself would not reside again on the hilltop for more than a few weeks at a time.

Four teenaged boys were among the ninety, to represent Shiloh high school. Everett Knight, Sandford's nephew (son of his sister Annie, by her first marriage), was picked to travel on the *Coronet,* Herbert Jenkins and Arnold White on the *Kingdom*—Arnold to serve as a cabin boy and member of the band, and Herbert as galley cook. Herbert was alone now, the only black member of the Shiloh movement. His sister Maude, who with Herbert had escaped the smallpox, had succumbed to tuberculosis in 1904, and when their father left Shiloh soon afterwards, Herbert elected to stay.

The twelve students of the High School "A-Class," with an agenda to graduate in 1907, had become a tightly bonded little society, evenly divided between boys and girls ranging in age from Merlyn Bartlett's nineteen years to Arnold's sixteen. As the potential first college students in the University of Truth, they understood their responsibility to be a model for all students to follow and accepted that honor with all that it carried. Though they knew they were watched closely, they were able to see some of the humor in the contradictory life they led. Once, on a day's outing with their teacher, Wendell White, they were caught in a heavy downpour and forced to snuggle together, boys and girls, under horse blankets for protection. Any sexual fantasies were quickly subdued since they were not supposed to touch each other in any circumstances, but they got away with as much "clean" physical contact as they could.

That escapade resulted in no serious repercussions. Another party was less successful, a group of unchaperoned young people including Enid White and Sandford's nephew Everett Knight, who slipped away to boil fudge in an old shack in the woods. Discovered, they were disciplined by Sandford with a three-day fast alone in their rooms.

As students, the class worked hard. Their courses—in addition to Latin, Greek, history, and zoology, all taught by Wendell White—included a sophisticated class in "physiology," taught by Jean Dart, using the organs of a sheep. French was delivered with a roll of a Welsh tongue by a once wealthy woman who, it was rumored, "had never held a broom in her hand" before coming to Shiloh. Joseph Harriman, a favorite teacher until he returned to Jerusalem, combined math and geography in a project to survey the grounds. Boys as well as girls studied typing and shorthand. The school had its own half-acre garden and put out its own newspaper, *The Young Warrior.* Aside from the frequent interruptions Shiloh life inserted, it was as good an education as he might get anywhere, Arnold thought. A collector and a recorder by nature, his butterfly specimens were displayed under glass in the Natural History Room. His diaries were filled with neatly penned data—the kings of England from 1066 to 1901, Theodore Roosevelt's cabinet, the population of India, and dozens of birthdays: Herbert Jenkins and Alice Roosevelt on the same day.

Arnold still nursed dreams of a medical career, but in a new context. His teachers assured him he would get the education he needed to join Shiloh's medical force, perhaps in Jerusalem or some foreign land, a calling that transcended the traditional concept of "doctor," since it involved a partnership with a healing and health-giving Heavenly Father. "Thy will, 'tis the gladdest, most glorious thing/ That even Thy heart, Lord, could give," he and the other young people sang, feeling the freedom of having released forever their little private ambitions. "Thy will—how my soul leaps/ To do its behest/ 'Tis life from the dead, and I live." A sailing trip to the Holy Land at age sixteen? Could anything more exciting happen if he were living in the outside world?

Late in August the two boats were ready to sail. Once again most of the experienced leaders were going abroad, including Charles Holland, Almon Whittaker (with his family along with time), Ralph Gleason (Willard was already there), and Austin Perry, who had taken out captain's papers and was now commodore of the fleet. Sandford, impatient with how long the renovation of the *Kingdom* was taking, had left already for London by steamer with Merwyn Wakeman, the band leader, to buy another harp for the *Coronet* to take around the world.

Out on the Atlantic, after three days of nausea, the "arbitrary period landlubbers were allowed," Arnold was soon scrubbing floors, cleaning lamps, and making up bunks like a veteran seaman as the ship pitched and rolled. The company was congenial, though he chafed under the authority of George Higgins, his assigned superior, who was not inclined toward boyish idiosyncracies. Tiny potatoes, dug prematurely to provision the boats, were the main staple of the *Kingdom* diet. They came to the table boiled in their skins, a plateful both delicious and filling, covered with a fish sauce. Made hungry by the work and the sea wind, Arnold ate his dinners with gusto, until Higgins remarked to him, loudly enough for everyone to hear, that he "ate as if he wished his gullet were as long as a hoe-handle." The comment, as Arnold perceived it, was not made in fun. If respect for elders, particularly a Shiloh minister, had not been so entrenched a part of his behavior, he would have proclaimed the truth of Higgins's statement. In spite of every effort to control his hunger as a good soldier of the cross, it stood over him like a king, waiting to be appeased, starting at about thirty minutes after the last meal, and to that king he bowed and scraped through the long table blessings, while his heart tried desperately to focus on the giving of thanks.

But just now, as they launched on this pilgrimage, Arnold was given enough to eat. He awoke each day to the smell of frying fritters. The galley was producing Down East food—beans and brown bread, tapioca and donuts, while he knew that back at Shiloh they seldom ate anything of the kind, since they had given up food stores to outfit the ships for the months ahead.

By plan, both boats were to arrive at Jaffa by October 3, the date the holy days began in 1905. The *Kingdom* lagged hopelessly behind schedule at the end of two weeks, having not yet reached the Azores, though Arnold confidently noted in his diary on September 4 that "a blessed powerful savior will get us to Jaffa on time." They had not seen a trace of the *Coronet* since they set sail. She had blown out of sight in an hour. The bulky *Kingdom*, lumbering along behind, anchored at Gibraltar at the end of thirty days, to discover that the *Coronet* had beaten them by a week and a half, had gathered up Sandford and Wakeman (and the harp), and shot ahead into the Mediterranean. The *Kingdom* paused only long enough to pick up its mail.

On deck in the sun, they read some of their letters from home aloud to each other. One bore bad news. The wife of Fred Caillat, a sailor and engineer, had written to inform her husband that she and their three children were leaving Shiloh for good. No one on the boat predicted the significance of this letter—that in another month Fred's wife would set off one more gale of bad publicity for Shiloh—but Fred slipped into a state of depression. He became sullen and indifferent in his work. One day the first mate chided him ("none too gently," observed Arnold) for his pokey responses to orders, saying they would never get to Jerusalem on time if everybody was as as slow as Fred. Angered, Fred responded, "Well, I don't care if we never get there!"

This outburst was reported to Charles Holland, and Fred was disfellowshipped. He hid himself away among the sails and ropes in the lazaret, talking to no one, refusing to eat. He remained in the sail locker for a month, then came out, triumphant over his pain and ready to cooperate. His wife was a rebel, he announced, and he planned to give her up along with the children if she followed through with her plans.

Other than Fred's drama, there was little excitement from Gibralter to Jaffa, neither craft making it on time for the Feast of Tabernacles. Sandford was deeply disappointed and disgusted with the performance of the new boat. But word had come from America that every legal charge had been erased. He was free at last to move on the next step in God's plans. "Mr. S. has had the message: Prepare for the great deep, and he is in a hurry," wrote Arnold in his diary. Still, things continued at a leisurely pace. For two months the boats sailed together (with the *Kingdom* always behind), first south along the coast of Palestine, then north. In recognition of the American Thanksgiving almost the entire party set off on an all-day jaunt into the mountains of Lebanon. Caught in a rain shower, the group laughed and sang in an abandoned manner that delighted the younger members. Arnold never forgot his amazement when the men were asked to each lend an arm to the women of the party, who had trouble walking on the rough terrain in their long skirts. Two by two they climbed to heights where views of great cultivated areas spread out to the horizon. As they marched, one hundred strong, they shouted in unison, "All this glorious land is mine!" while a gang of small boys ran alongside, jabbering in French.

All the while potential personnel for the trip around the world were being observed. As they were anchored off Beirut, Arnold was chosen to act temporarily as Sandford's valet on the *Coronet*. Arnold knew it was an experiment, and in his own estimation not a good choice. He was inclined to be absent-minded and had not learned to be punctual.

He had other problems as well. For one thing, he was preoccupied with blood-control to the face. As a redhead, he blushed readily, and blushing was thought to indicate a bad conscience or even carnal thoughts. He had heard Mr. Sandford bluntly declare to other men, "I don't like your face, brother." As a further complication, Arnold worried that his obsession with the "right look" might prove to be vanity. He was most anxious to feel and to act in a 100-fold manner, but often found himself blocked by self-consciousness or uncertainty. An entry in his diary at age fifteen read:

> O Lord please give me spunk enough to be the third to pray and possibly once in a great while help me to be the second and then give me enough spunk to possibly once in a great while to be the first.

He meant prayer out loud in front of others, as demanding as an extemporaneous speech. The answer, he knew, was to not think about it, to just do it, to "cast down reasonings and every high thing that exalteth itself"—casting down self-protection, that is, and his sense of what felt natural. Mr. Sandford, just as he had done with Wendell, had once laid hands on Arnold's head and prayed "powerful prayers" against his brain, which was prone toward "independent thinking and reasoning."

The word "feeling" was often substituted for "thinking" in Shiloh's struggle with the roles of the head and the heart. "We are feeling about what we should do next," someone would say. The phrase "Listen with the heart" was a favorite. Arnold was confused by such parlance. As a result he stifled alertness in many situations, far from helpful in practical pursuits of life. Yet Mr. Sandford was patient with him, "not too hard a taskmaster," not even in regard to punctuality. Arnold knew what that meant to him. He waited for no one. Captain Benjamin Sellick, at his recent wedding, had been forced to say his vows through the keyhole of a locked door when he arrived late for the ceremony.

In those days in Mr. Sandford's stateroom at close proximity to the man, Arnold never once questioned what he saw or heard. It was an honor to serve in this way, to be summoned by a pearl-headed button on a velvet wall, to handle his leader's possessions, polish his boots, carry messages, carry his books (dampened by the sea air) up to the deck to sun—those wonderful books, astronomy, geography, the story of the Mediterranean—the only collection of books Arnold had seen at

Shiloh other than his father's texts. If in his role as valet he overheard someone being scolded, he supposed there was a good reason. When he was asked to deliver to that same person some kindly message, or perhaps "some delicacy" from Sandford's room "at mealtime from his tray," it seemed merely a comforting gesture, a sign of restored approval. Far from "reasoning," he accepted the man's judgments totally, even when they led close to disaster.

Such was the visit to the Plain of Issus, at the most northeast corner of the Mediterranean. Alexander the Great had defeated the Persian troops there in 333 B.C., and Sandford wanted to see it. It meant sailing into the Bay of Issus, only thirty miles wide, with no charts or beacon lights. Fair winds bore them into this neck of water, while they listened to the story of the famous battle, then prayed that God would inject them all with the spirit of Alexander the Great.

Their return depended on a change of wind at the right time. Instead, as they waited, the wind continued from the same direction and soon blew more than a pleasant, smacking breeze. The sky to the southwest turned an ugly black. Water swept over the bow. Arnold stayed on deck as long as he dared, hanging on to the rigging well aft of waves, watching with fascination as the yacht "dipped into each trough in the sea as if reaching for the bottom," then rose again, slowly, to shed the water over the rail.

Several of the men, shortening sails in terrible haste, were out on the bowsprit struggling with the wet canvas of a jib billowing in the wind. As a wave engulfed them, Everett Knight, out on the footropes, lost his grip and fell overboard. One man managed to grab his hand and pull him to safety. He was carried, half-drowned, to the forecastle, where Arnold rubbed him down with towels and covered him with blankets in his bunk.

The storm continued far into the night, as the yacht slowly crept out of the Bay, sounding for depth in the darkness. All those not needed on deck were called to the saloon where, as the waves crashed over their heads, they were told that Satan had "his arm of steel against the yacht" and they had better search their lives for any thought, word, or deed which might hinder their rescue. By daylight the storm subsided and they sailed safely into Beirut Harbor.

Arnold could not recall later being able to "work up much of a feeling of terror. I knew this man was destined as one of the witnesses of God to die on the streets of Jerusalem, not to drown in the dark waters of the Bay of Issus." But he was scared enough. In his diary he wrote that day, "My life has been changed forever."

By now the new *Coronet* thirty had nearly all been chosen, for physical endurance, compatibility, and spiritual purity. Of the teenaged boys, Everett Knight and Herbert Jenkins were now considered worthy. Both had shown the fearless spirit Sandford liked, Herbert especially demonstrating "courage aloft in storms" in that one particular storm, high on the ropes above deck in gale winds. Others were being selected to maintain the Jerusalem quarters. Arnold was considered too young to remain away from his family, yet the two small boys of Rose and Willard Gleason, who had been left at Shiloh, would not see their parents for three more years. Sandford had decided that he needed the Gleasons in the Holy City, where both Willard and Ralph would share administration.

At the end of January 1907 the *Kingdom* left the *Coronet* at Jaffa and crossed the Atlantic to America under Holland's charge. Once home, Charles Holland, a widower for a year, announced his engagement to Gertrude MacDonald, a pianist and teacher who had also been a passenger on the boat. The two had handled their courtship at sea so discreetly no one was aware of it. The wedding was performed in an outdoor ceremony in the pine grove. Sandford, hearing of the marriage by mail back in Palestine, was appalled that "Moses," his second-in-command, would take such a step without consulting him. His return letter demanded that Holland and his bride be separated. They were not to live together or have anything to do with each other until they had received permission. Holland, obedient as always, acquiesced. Avis White, six years old, was intrigued to see the newlyweds walking "together," one on each side of the wide foot path from Olivet to Shiloh Proper, neither of them speaking to the other.

But the reproof did not stop there. The entire personnel of the *Kingdom* for that voyage home had obviously given way to the "natural life." Arnold never understood what that meant, since when Mr. Sandford's letter was discussed at a meeting of the *Kingdom* party, he was "ushered out." But he was present long enough to see Mrs. Sellick "hopping about the room, hands on her hips," supporting Mr. Sandford's charges by "screaming her rage" at the carnal. Arnold was amazed at her language, though the words she used were largely from the Bible.

Something more important than anyone could yet realize had taken place. The aberrations of sexuality were far broader than individual behavior. Throughout the entire excursion, new priorities had shaped themselves—the standard for Shiloh-on-the-sea. This had found an odd focus. The *Kingdom*—that is, the boat itself—had not proven herself worthy. A shadow had fallen over the slow, bungling barkentine and her various personnel, in the same manner that it had fallen over the hilltop. It was almost as if the impurities of the *Kingdom*'s marine architecture rendered her an unsuitable sanctuary for God's people. Life on that boat lent itself to natural pleasure. She could not measure up to the "white light of eternity" which shone on the *Coronet*. The day was coming when that difference would matter very much.

20

The Black Horse
1907

In reality two Shilohs were in operation in 1907—the one on land in England and America, and the one in Frank Sandford's mind. While the *Coronet* lingered for months in the Mediterranean, Shiloh on land struggled to keep its vision steady in the routine and extremity of day to day life. The hilltop in Maine especially was becoming a place full of both soreness and bonding. Staying there was often painful, but it was more painful to leave.

The romance of Arnold's excursion abroad was quickly reset against a somber background as he became aware of how much his family and the Shiloh community had endured in his absence. A new gust of criticism from the public had begun to blow even before the two ships had sailed in 1905. It could be said there was yet a third Shiloh—the one the world outside thought it saw. Tales of defections spread abroad, with little concern for accuracy of detail. A girl ran away over Shiloh's fields, barefoot. A woman "escaped" with her baby, leaving two small children behind with her husband, who refused to go. A woman visiting from Missouri found her suicidal daughter strapped to her bed in Bethesda and removed her in a catatonic condition to the State Hospital.

Then, as the *Kingdom* raced to Jerusalem, the story of Fred Caillat's wife was given major space by the *Journal*. The people of Shiloh were slowly starving, she said. Children often waited up until ten o'clock for their dinners and not infrequently got none at all. Shiloh gardens were improperly cared for; most of the fish caught in Casco Bay had been salted away for the boats; the cows and horses were in poor condition; and only those who were eligible for "extra food" had enough—the sick, or expecting mothers or the ministers themselves. She had seen the children of one minister sitting in their high chairs at the family table in the Extension dining room "look longingly" at the trays of food set down around their father's plate.

In November and December, while the two boats were touring the Palestinian coast, Shiloh had been beseiged by inquiries and inspections. George Allen, the agent for the county SPCA, and a representative of the Humane Society paid a visit to the Shiloh barns, examining in total seventeen horses and twelve head of cattle. The two men found nothing amiss. After dropping in at the High School, they were served dinner at Olivet: no cornmeal mush—instead, baked salmon, hard-boiled eggs, mashed potato, warm biscuit, baked apples, grapes, and cocoa. Agent Allen complained wittily of being given too much to eat.

Local pastors swung into action again and helped to prepare a petition to Governor William Cobb to institute a proper investigation of Shiloh. Cobb responded by sending over County Attorney Ralph Crockett, along with a physician, a nurse, a reporter, and two pastors. Reports back to Cobb varied all the way from gushingly positive to Crockett's conclusion that Shiloh was "a menace to the State." The visitors were escorted through every building, viewed a fine healthy newborn with its mother at Bethesda, dropped in on one hundred children in Olivet, all of them plump-faced and clear-eyed, and interviewed a dozen people, every one of whom denied hunger or unhappiness.

In the kitchen steaming loaves of bread just out of the oven were spread on the tables. In the storeroom the flour supply was sufficient for one more day (three barrels of it), one hundred baskets of fragrant grapes waited to be made into juice and jelly, a veal hung from the ceiling, and the shelves contained rice, oatmeal, canned goods, and sugar. The vegetables of a recent harvest overflowed the root cellar.

Nathan Harriman, in a published letter to Cobb, found the idea of such an investigation "laughable." The leaders had managed to throw "clouds of dust" in their visitors' eyes, he said, and had "Shilohized" their way through questions, never telling an outright lie, but simply answering questions with a different, deeper truth than they were asked for. To the question, "Do you have enough to eat?" the answer "I certainly do" meant simply "I have as much as God wants me to have."

The stories continued for months after Arnold got home in the spring of 1907. The sense of their hectoring penetrated far into his memory, yet he did his own "Shilohizing" on the pages of his diary. From November 1907 to May 31, 1908, he recorded not a word of unpleasantness. World events and the weather were crammed together among an assortment of facts. Good sliding was spoiled by a thaw. King Oscar II of Sweden died. A bunch of boys played football down by the river.

He made a napkin ring for his mother, went ice skating, popped corn on somebody's birthday, and made a New Year's resolution which he quickly broke: "No more tardiness." At age eighteen he did any job he was asked to do. He chopped green wood, now the main fuel for all Shiloh's kitchen stoves, and performed miracles of his own as he found ways to ignite it. The corn bread, made often with only corn meal, water, and lard, was baked in sheets in huge iron pans in the Extension kitchen, with portions transported to the other buildings. Arnold devised a wooden platform big enough for two of the pans, which he poised on his head as he walked to Bethesda.

In the tower tonight from 8–12. I prayed until I touched God for every true heart in the world.

Ladies Band [string] figured well today in getting our worship up to God. The river is frozen over.

Sabbath: I "blew up" a trumpet in Jerusalem turret at sunset.

Tardy or not, he was becoming one of the dependable people on the hill and was happily aware of approval, though he was not aware of the feelings of a particular member of his class. Working in the Bethesda kitchen, Merlyn noticed his blue-cold hands as he delivered the corn bread, and knitted him a pair of mittens. Apart from appreciation, Arnold thought nothing of it. Women at Shiloh did things like that.

Merlyn was not sure how she felt herself. Since Arnold had returned from the Holy Land there was something about his demeanor that disturbed her. When he gave a testimony or led in prayer, he often blurted out grand words that had no connection to the person he was at all other times. He was terribly eager to please. She understood that, but sometimes it seemed like a weakness, now that she was beginning to recognize her own strength. She knew strength was required to live at Shiloh, and live at Shiloh was what she wanted to do. She saw no other future for herself.

She had been told often enough that she was *not* strong. She was "delicate," someone said. Her headaches took her to bed two or three times a month. She was not a spiritual warrior like Enid White, and lacked the "Davidic exactness" of her friend Hazel Housler. She thought of herself as a rather hapless, fly-away person, her hair and clothing not always just right, making people laugh with remarks that popped out of her mouth without much thought. But she knew what she could bear, and lately she had been finding out what she could do.

In the year Arnold was gone she had begun to help in the kindergarten, working under two women who had taught in Boston with the Montessori method. It made her enormously happy to be with these children. She saved bits of her own food for them in case they were hungry. If a boy needed a haircut, she got out her scissors and did the job. If a girl needed a warm dress, she made her one—cut it out of a discarded garment in the sewing room and ran it up on one of the machines.

Merlyn had also discovered that she could speak her mind in a way that was not offensive. Once, tending Mr. Tupper's children, she found the two-year-old covered with bruises so ugly it made her cry. To her horror she was told that the child had been beaten "to break a stubborn spirit." Her heart thumping wildly, she confronted Tupper—a man who in the past had been as kind as a father to *her*—with the opinion that parents who whipped their children "whipped more devil into them than out of them." He accepted her comment and had not beaten the child since.

But of course as a member of the A-Class she was in a position of respect. The class had graduated in June (with Arnold standing on the hem of Merlyn's dress, tearing it) and since the University of Truth still lay vaguely in the future, they had become the honored nucleus of the new Bible School, taught by two of the ministers.

Arnold, in spite of skipping his senior year, was given academic credit for his year overseas. Herbert Jenkins and Everett Knight, now on the *Coronet,* were missing from the graduation picture, as was Clara Ferguson, the daughter of the artists. Just before graduation the Ferguson family had departed in a cloud of tension and anger. Clara, who wanted to stay and at age eighteen had the right to do as she pleased, wept in Merlyn's presence and slipped away with her parents. Her name had since been avoided in conversation.

Many people had gone recently, some hardly missed as the ranks closed in. But it was hard to forget the Fergusons. They had spread their color everywhere on the grounds in life-like reminders of themselves. Wendell felt their absence keenly. Doris White, who was fifteen at the time, witnessed a scene that struck her as curious. "I don't know how it came about but a while before [the Fergusons left] Dad had been talking with him. I didn't know that Mr. Ferguson was leaving but I noticed that he walked very fast, different from before, appearing as though he was almost driven crazy, and that my father did the same after Mr. Ferguson left, but that stopped after he saw he must stay."

At the time Wendell and Annie were running the Shiloh dairy at a farmhouse in the Bowie Hill section of Durham, several miles from the hilltop. Arnold was overseas. Years later his father told him the following story.

One day Wendell rode home in a wagon to Bowie Hill after a meeting at Shiloh Proper, feeling discouraged and, as he put it, certain there was "no good" in himself. Suddenly it occurred to him that "there *were* two worthy things" about him, after all. "Why, Lord," he said with surprise, "I have stuck to Shiloh."

A voice "seemingly outside him" answered: "Ah, but you would have gone a dozen times if I had let you."

". . . Oh," said Wendell, recognizing the truth. Then, turning to the "second thing," he added, "but, Lord—I chose *you.*"

"*You* did not choose *me,*" came the answer. "I chose you."

One of those "dozen times" occurred in 1905 when Wendell's friend Albert Field, the jeweler from Brunswick, disappeared from the hill with his family. The decisive element in Field's defection, as he finally told the newspapers, was an episode earlier that winter, while Frank Sandford was still at Shiloh.

Sandford's sister Annie and her second husband, Nat Brown, had lost their one-year-old son to what was thought to be cholera infantum, a digestive problem not uncommon among infants. Sandford apparently tried to revive the baby, remembering perhaps that the Elijah of the Old Testament had brought to life the young son of the widow Zerephath. But the baby named Brown did not revive. Its body was taken to one of the cold turrets and kept there for sixty days, while the Browns and Sandford and the ministers continued to pray for its restoration to life. One night the child was finally buried, the funeral held in the dark.

The *Enterprise* got wind of this while it was happening, and though the source was not given, quoted Sandford as saying, "If I don't bring that child to life, I'm a false prophet." And since he had failed, the *Enterprise* wanted to know, would he not deny that he was a "genuine, unadulterated, gall-soaked, brazen-faced religious humbug?"

The incident was kept a secret at Shiloh with only partial success. Wendell, if he knew of it, may have classified it as an unfounded rumor. Or did he, like Field, take it seriously and find himself almost smothered by the denial required to overlook it? If the resurrection of Olive Mills had been claimed as the seal of apostleship, did this failure then mean the unsealing? Or did it throw the miracle of Olive Mills into the shadow (or light) of a completely natural event, without extraordinary overtones?

Whatever means God used on this occasion to keep Wendell at Shiloh, when the Fergusons left, it was Annie. As Doris remembered it, her father wanted to go, but "Mama wanted to stay." Annie, who had not wanted to come to Shiloh in the first place, had since made a commitment. As a woman who never argued, who quietly and slowly made up her mind and then never went back on her word, she would have been as immoveable as a rock.

But in the end it was the children who made the final difference. When Arnold returned from overseas in the spring of 1907, a member of the Kingdom as an accountable adult, Wendell's book of options shut itself with a resolute clap. Not only Arnold, but Enid too, was thoroughly a part of the Shiloh fabric. So determined were they to be "true" that if Wendell and Annie had moved away they would have found themselves in the dreadful position of choosing between their children and their own freedom. It went against every perception of rightness. Wendell and Annie had never cut themselves off from their own skeptical relatives, as so many others had; correspondence continued with all siblings and Wendell still acted as big brother to his remaining sisters. Split families did not belong in his sense of God's world.

None of this should suggest that Wendell remained at Shiloh as an unbeliever. He simply began a new reading of God's will. Many years after it was all over, asked why he had stayed until the end, he gave a cryptic, shaved-down answer: "God told me to go to Shiloh and he never told me to leave." In other words Wendell remained at Shiloh not because of circumstances, but because of God. Living at the center of God's will was all that mattered, and all those times when he had wanted to leave were *not* God's will. God had not "let" him go.

Perhaps Wendell would have been honest enough to admit to the operation of fear as well. It made no difference how sensible and sane a person might be. Albert Field confessed to the newspaper that in order to escape from Shiloh he had scaled a terrible wall of apprehension. The first thing he had done was to "go and have a picture taken of the entire family, in case the judgments called down from God annihilated us." They had survived. Back in Brunswick, the Field family was doing just fine. Wendell could see that as well as anyone. But to let logic and evidence influence him even that far was risky—acquainted as he was with all the devious tricks of reason locked in his own "poor brain," as Sandford had once called it, with his tendency to expect God to act in the same way rational human beings ought to act.

In his memoirs Arnold tells one more revealing 1907 story, though his diary makes no mention of it. Annie's father had died the year before and in the spring of 1907 she received $350 from the estate. Though it was expected that any inheritance would be turned in to the Shiloh treasury, Annie and Wendell agreed to keep it. The children needed shoes badly and Annie had been praying for months for materials to make dresses for the girls.

But before the money could be spent, Wendell fell ill with terrible back and abdominal pain. When it persisted, he sent for the minister then in charge on the hilltop to ask for prayer. The pain eased before the minister got there, but Wendell and Annie had already determined the cause of the attack. They confessed their plans to use the money for themselves and instead turned it over to the Kingdom. Wendell's attack of pain did not return.

If Wendell wondered what kind of a God he worshiped, who could convey one message through a gentle conversation on a country road, and the next through intense pain, he would answer himself by saying that God had the right to speak anyway He chose. After all, the pain was not so different from a spanking on one's more fleshly parts— hurting but not harming. It was not God he feared, but himself—his own continuing penchant for failure.

He was not the only member of the family dealing with fear. Doris, now fifteen, still feared the consequences of not "squaring up" to the standard. She feared the possibility of committing the "unpardonable sin" (though no one knew for sure what that was). She feared the possibility of demon possession, a danger if one "got out from under protection." She feared being unprepared for the return of Christ, like the foolish virgins and their unfilled lamps. As one grew older and the expectations increased, so did the ways of losing favor with those above you, or of making some irreparable mistake.

Avis had survived the fear of abandonment that controlled her first year on the hill. She had adapted to being alone. One summer she kept a daily watch on the activity of a large grey spider in a web under the Extension veranda. Anything soft or gentle attracted her. A caterpiller became a pet; she collected cocoons to keep secretly in her doll trunk.

Secrecy was a good idea, she was learning. She was in school now, with teachers and friends she loved, but she was finding it best to keep her feelings to herself, even the good ones. Skipping down the path to Olivet one day, holding her limp right hand in her left, she was taken aside by someone and told to "walk to school like a little lady." When she and her "best chum" Madeleine were seen with their arms around each other, the friendship was curtailed by the leadership, lest they form too much of a natural bond. One Christmas season, taken by Annie to Peck's Department Store in Lewiston, she had evaded the store Santa Claus, ashamed to tell him where she lived.

Pinching back, pulling in, saving her smiles for safe situations, she often appeared to be a perverse and uncooperative child, which could not have helped her cause.

Avis was eight when the family moved back to a suite in the Extension. Annie had set up her sewing machine in the sunny bay window, where women joined her to do the institutional sewing. One afternoon three visitors were working there when Avis came home from school. With one "good arm" she had learned to do almost everything other children could do, but removing her heavy coat by herself was always a chore. As she was shaking herself out of it impatiently, she glanced up to see two of the visitors watching her with "an awful look." Suddenly both of them turned to Annie and began to reprimand her. The child was having a tantrum, they cried. She was not being "handled," she was spoiled, they scolded, their voices rising into shrieks. Then as Avis and her mother watched in disbelief, the two women tore the room apart. They yanked down pictures, smashed a china lampshade, threw over furniture, cracking the wooden cover of the sewing machine, spilling ink across the floor and scattering the contents of Annie's mending basket. The third woman had run out, perhaps to get Wendell, as he soon appeared at the door and ordered the other two out of the suite. They left immediately, but by this time Avis was sobbing uncontrollably and when she could not bring herself to stop, she was spanked. Apologies for the attack were made in due time, but not to Avis, and no one ever explained that the fierce anger displayed was brought on by the same inner strain shaping her own set of perceptions.

This incident, like Wendell's story, was not recorded in Arnold's cheery diary. Nor does he intimate any hunger that year, though often even the half cent per person per day for cornmeal was hard to come by. His only references to food were two items regarding "the year's supply." Reminded of the Black Horse of famine in Revelation by national panic and depression in 1907, the hill began to lay aside storable food, including white flour, against the threat that the mark of the beast—666—would soon begin to control commercial trade, a devastating feature of the Tribulation. In another several months the hilltop was forced to dig into that special stock, and for days Shiloh ate loaves of soft white bread, ordinarily considered a luxury.

THE LAST SOLEMN MESSAGE OF THE AGE

The A-Class at graduation. Standing left, Enid White, with Stuart Wolfe next to her; Arnold White, second from right. Seated far left, Marlyn Bartlett. Hazel Housler, second left.

Ladies' String Band. Merlyn Bartlett with mandolin seated far right.

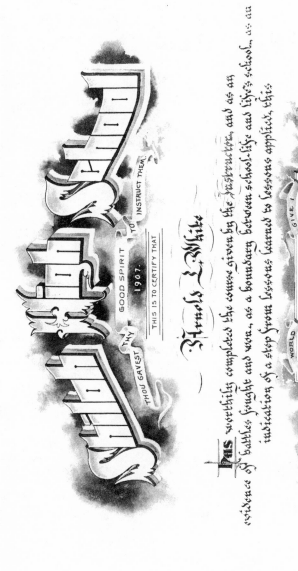

SHILOH SCHOOL

THOU GAVEST THY GOOD SPIRIT TO INSTRUCT THEM

1907.

THIS IS TO CERTIFY THAT

— Ernest L. White —

Has worthily completed the course given by the Instructor, and as an evidence of battles fought and won, as a boundary between school-life and life's school, as an indication of a step from lessons learned to lessons applied, this

NOT AS THE WORLD GIVE I DIPLOMA UNTO YOU GIVETH

with the approval of the Divine Teacher, is given this eighteenth day of June, A. D. 1907.

Shiloh, Maine, U. S. A.

Ernest F. Taylor

Wendell P. White

A-Class diploma, 1907. Note Wendell White's signature.

21

The Blind Horn's Hate
1908–1909

The barkentine *Kingdom* had left the *Coronet* in the Mediterranean in January of 1907. It was summer before the yacht was ready to begin the long-planned journey around the world.

Late in July, with the necessary money cabled in from Maine, the words "Make ready for the great deep," rose once more out of the sea, a sound to Sandford like "the noise of great waters," and they were on their way towards Gibraltar. The journey was to begin by crossing the Atlantic to the Caribbean and would continue down the eastern coast of South America, around Cape Horn, into the Southern Pacific all the way to Australia, then westward to the Cape of Good Hope, and up the west coast of Africa back to Gibraltar.

The ship held a full complement of thirty: nineteen men, six women, and the five Sandford children. Austin Perry, age forty-three, served as captain, with forty-eight-year-old Thomas Marshall, an experienced seaman, as first officer, and Lester McKenzie, twenty-four, as second mate. Six sailors included two in their late teens—Herbert Jenkins and Roland Whittom. Everett Knight, also not yet twenty, did double duty as a sailor and as Frank's stenographer, with another young man as his valet. The remaining male staff was comprised of the cook, the ship's carpenter, a seventy-year-old sailmaker, and a taxidermist from England. William Hastings, a musician and school teacher from Canada, filled posts as the children's tutor and as band leader (a large percentage of the men had learned to play instruments in the months of waiting), and two men in their forties, one of them Almon Whittaker, sailed as spiritual leaders. Of the women, Jean Dart went as nurse, Hama Perry as general domestic manager, and three single women as governesses and household help.

William Hastings had left behind at Shiloh a family of several small children, and Almon Whittaker was again separated from his family, who had remained in Jerusalem, his wife expecting their sixth child.

The voyage was not a missionary endeavor in any way conventionally understood. On this journey the personnel would not go ashore to distribute the Gospel or teach. The trip was archetypal, but real. This little band ("David's band") sailed to "subdue the world for Christ" by a tiny white presence against the horizon, in the way that Joshua had marched around Jericho. Standing off shore, they meant to "take" the world by prayer, for only by prayer could the "covering" which blinded the eyes of humanity be removed.

In 1897 Sandford had dreamed of the Four Horses of the Apocalypse, the white, the black, the pale, and the red, galloping at top speed. In Revelation, the white horse, the first, is mounted by a fearful warrior in white armor. In Sandford's dream the white horse was riderless. In 1901 he had believed that the Shiloh movement was the missing rider of the white charger, whose mission was to go out "conquering and to conquer." Now, complicating the metaphor even more, it seemed that the *Coronet* herself was the horse, with the company aboard her the rider. Combining the Syriac translation with Rotherham's, he read Revelation 6:1-2 as "Go! And I saw, and behold, a white horse, and he that sat thereon had a bow, and a *coronet* was given him, and he went forth conquering and to conquer."

As they advanced about the world, this body of saints would "come along side" the parts of the globe where Satan held full sway—intrude directly into his territorial rights. Such a confrontation was risky in every way they could suppose, vulnerable as they were in a small craft in merciless seas, with an Enemy able to control the forces of nature. Prayer was both their safeguard and their weapon of warfare, on the boat and back at Maine. Arnold, one of the prayer warriors there, brought with him on his turn in David's Tower a notebook into which he had copied words from Mr. Sandford's letters. God had made Sandford know, read one quote, "that He would empty heavens of all its contents to back me up in my mission to a lost globe, and that He would crush, as He would crush a spider, everything that stood in my way."

But if prayer back at Shiloh cut through time and space to free God's power in points at great distance, then why was the yacht needed at all? Not a soul on the boat or back at Durham could have admitted that anyone's craving for high adventure was entailed, particularly Frank Sandford's, but in another of Shiloh's pretzel-like twists, that superlative game of chance, played out on a watery stage far away, was owned vicariously by the hundreds on land—the danger and romance and tests of seamanship, all the more because they were sacrificing to pay for it.

Seamanship was no more than a small percentage of the requirements for success. Each passenger and sailor must be a "nucleus of the Bride of Christ . . . spiritually lovely, free from any ill-will and grudging." After Christmas in the Mediterranean, the *Coronet* company had spent a week in prayer, supplemented by the style of examination now familiar to the older members, bringing to light in private and public each other's weaknesses and strengths. Wrote one woman, "the white light of His presence made it awful for sin." From the beginning, the mix on board was good, Lester McKenzie remembered. At the worst moments of the trip a deep sense of purpose never wavered. Everything they did was to hasten Christ's coming. "You could have beat my head with a stake," remembered McKenzie, "and you couldn't have gotten it out of my head that I was going to see Jesus come back in the clouds."

Their battle began immediately, along the coast of Asia Minor, where they prayed for the overthrow of Islam, and a few days later, off Crete, someone had a vision in which the Turkish Sultan's head was "pressed slowly to the ground." Claiming each country and coast in the name of Jesus as they passed it, often sounding their brass instruments and playing hymns as they met other ships, they proceeded to Malta. There they bought provisions and faced another kind of reality—the size of the ship.

She was already filled to capacity. The deck, under the two low-slung booms where the men ducked each time they passed, left barely room enough to move among the coils of rope, the two brass signaling cannon, the anchor windlass, the wheel and binnacle, the three smaller boats (one a motor launch, probably twenty feet long) and the skylights and hatches. Below, in the saloon—the size of a one-room schoolhouse—a long table set in sockets on the floor, a piano bolted to the ceiling, and the huge harp (secured how?) claimed precious cubic feet of space. The four unmarried women, two of them small, fortunately, slept in one cabin; young John shared a room with Almon Whittaker, the girls and David slept with Helen, the Perrys and the two older sailors occupied the two smaller staterooms, the officers and ministers in the "after cabin," and the remaining crew bunked in the tiered canvas cots of the forecastle. Clothing and belongings were stored in every possible way in these areas, under the beds and hanging from both walls and ceilings. In the forecastle, extra sail canvas draped overhead.

Now places must be found for firewood and coal for the galley stove. The pantry shelves were jammed with food: 100 pounds of olives, 42 dozen eggs, 440 pounds of sugar, 8 cases of evaporated milk, 500 pounds of potatoes, 162 pounds of beef, 12 pounds of butter. Hiss claims that all this was needed just to get to Gibraltar.

Cracks and crannies had to be found for storing personal supplies such as razors and soap. To complicate matters, the company needed clothing for all weather, both the tropics and, as they rounded the Horn, a cold equal to that of Greenland. Oilskins, boots, blankets, and long woolens must be kept dry and easily available.

They reached Gibraltar on Sandford's forty-fifth birthday. More supplies were purchased, including "a complete set of eyes for stuffed animals and birds," and in one week's time the ship was scraped and painted and fitted to a new set of sails, while the women sewed the new white uniforms in a Drive. Then, cannon firing a farewell, they turned north to Palos, Spain, in order to start the journey from the port of Columbus's embarkation. From there faced out into the Atlantic, moving toward the West Indies as Columbus had done, in the arms of the trade winds.

Throughout the next month life on the *Coronet* was not much different than it had been for the rich mariners who had previously owned her, a month alone with waves and spray. The children attended school, the band rehearsed, Sandford worked at his writing and took lessons on the harp from William Hastings. Those not on watch slept well at night, "to the creak of woodwork and straining sails," and the children, waking for a trip to the bathroom, heard the reassuring feet of the night crew on the deck above.

In early November, safe at San Salvador in the West Indies, they found the *Kingdom* waiting, as had been arranged, with supplies and family members. For the remaining two months of 1907 they cruised together around the Caribbean, restoring the islands to God. One day, hiking on St. Thomas, they climbed a hill, where after preaching for seven hours, Sandford strode down the hill "like David with the head of Goliath," announcing, "I've got North America by the hair."

Before separating, still feeling uneasy about the spiritual status of the *Kingdom,* he anointed and set aside as holy two of her on-deck cabins, where only the most spiritual of the crew were to live. The harp had been transferred to the barkentine to be brought back to Maine. It was apparently not suitable. Plans were in the works for another better one.

The ships parted on January 15, the *Kingdom* heading north, the *Coronet* south, crossing the equator three weeks later. The "uttermost part of the world" lay ahead. There would be "no help or anchorage" for almost 4,000 miles, all the way around the bottom of the continent through antarctic storms to Concepcion, Chile, on the western side. Two American boats had already gone down off the Horn in 1908, and the year had hardly begun.

The "blind Horn's hate," as Rudyard Kipling had once phrased it, represented the apex of this ritualistic voyage. One hundred miles north of the Antartica peninsula, the rock-faced headland stood 500 feet high, often enclosed in fog and unseen by countless sailors who had fought their way around it in fierce westerly gales. For months the *Coronet* had been flying two flags from her topmast, one depicting a lion, the other a lamb. It was the lamb flag that fluttered aloft as they tacked down the coast of Argentina. They were "making a way for every human being on this globe to compass every hard thing" with victory "through the Lamb of God," wrote a crew member. The Straits of Magellan, the easy way around, would not do. They must pass the "roughest test" possible.

It began sooner than they expected. On April 14 in the Gulf of St. George, still more than 600 miles north of the Horn, the barometer began to fall in the morning, and by evening black clouds gathered in the southwest. Lester McKenzie had taken over as captain. "Before the yacht can be snugged down, the first force of the storm has struck us," reads his log. Throughout the night all hands were on deck, while sail after sail was blown from the ropes as fast as they could be rigged and the vessel virtually stood still against the head wind. By morning the gale had increased, with the yacht shipping dangerous amounts of water. The madness continued into the next day until 5 P.M., when McKenzie wrote: "A sea boards us amidships, smashing the stern of our life-boat but the fierceness of the gale seems to be abating."

Just a moment before, down in the saloon where all but the crew were praying, Sandford had suddenly shouted, "I put the Lamb of God into the teeth of this gale!" At the same instant McKenzie, up on the deck by the wheel, said to the helmsman, "Something has taken the teeth out of this storm." The "raging" had stopped. In the miracle play they were enacting together, there was no room for coincidence.

But the storms assaulted them without let-up for almost two weeks, with thunderous headseas and winds that screamed incessantly through the rigging. The process of lowering the enormous wet sails and hoisting new ones in gale winds was brutally exhausting. "For days we hardly knew where day ended or night began," remembered one sailor. They were encased by grey fog, sky and sea blending together. Below, in the darkened cabins (the skylights covered with canvas) six-year-old Marguerite Sandford watched "the water dripping down constantly, soaking the carpets," felt the boat rolling and lurching beneath her feet, and for the first time understood what trust meant when you were helpless. "All hands on board!" rang out three or four times a day, for the adjusting or hauling in of torn sails, to be mended in the saloon and returned to deck. Still, unless the tossing of the craft made it impossible, all who could be spared came together for prayer and study every day at 9:00 A.M. and then again at 3:00 P.M.

Starting at midnight on April 15, they gathered for communion—and continued to do so at midnight for the next seven days, rousing themselves from sleep at the ringing of the bell. The crew took turns, descending wet and cold into the saloon. "Behold, the Lamb of God," was the text for each of those nights. One year before, while still in the Mediterranean, Sandford had slaughtered a lamb on board the yacht to symbolize the restoration soon to take place all over the world. As the blood of the animal spilled into the blue water, he had "felt the wrath of God rising up," and thought of Revelation 13:1, when the "beast" of the anti-Christ lifts itself out of the sea. On that marvelous balmy day, such a possibility had seemed remote, but not now in the heart of this fury.

They were still 200 miles from the Horn. "Snow falling all day," McKenzie wrote on April 19. "Heavy seas heaving in from the south. Salt water thrown on board as we pound into a heavy head-sea makes the work on deck very cold and disagreeable. The penetration of the bitter cold had been hard to anticipate while they gathered supplies in the tropics. One day on deck Sandford wore leather boots, two pairs of woolen socks, two pairs of heavy "under flannels" covered by a woolen shirt, a vest, a sweater, a woolen coat and over all a fur coat. Even with his back to the wind, the "blasts" pierced those layers. In the saloon, wet woolens and rubber slickers steamed over chairs drawn up close to the saloon stove. The children found space at the big table for their lessons. When they could, they scurried into the smoky kitchen to check on the welfare of a canary moved there for warmth.

As if there were nothing else to think about, at the midnight meetings Sandford began a study of the life of Allen Gardiner, one of six missionaries who had died of starvation in 1848 while attempting to reach the Indians of Tierra del Fuego. Esther Sandford, who was ten, was gripped by their heroism, for their diaries had recorded nothing but praise in the last days of their lives. Every soul on board the *Coronet,* except the youngest children, was consciously facing death just now. On the sixth night, with the sea pounding the deck above, where the helmsman was lashed to the wheel for safety, Sandford said, "The Lord's Supper is eaten this night to take the fear of death out of us— the dread of the last enemy of every child of God throughout America."

On the eleventh day, Helen's forty-fourth birthday, the helmsman caught a rare sight of Cape Horn as the clouds momentarily parted. They had reached the Pacific. Rejoicing, adults and children climbed up to the deck, hanging on to the lines as the boat dipped and pitched, while Sandford restored the Pacific Ocean and the band somehow managed to play "All Hail the Power of Jesus' Name" out into the howling wind. In Helen's dark stateroom later the children gave a party, with the two youngest catching imaginary sunbeams in their hands as gifts for their mother. Before the day was over, the sailmaker, a man who had spent his life on the sea, saw a "shimmering white" angel on a rock, with a drawn sword held over the water. The Apostle John, on Patmos, had seen four angels at "the four corners of the earth," and what was Cape Horn if not one of those corners?

In the fine weather the next day Sandford shot an albatross, as easily, he said, as if he were plucking a "fowl from the roosts" for dinner at the old farm back in Maine. It landed in the water, still alive, and several sailors obligingly took to the smaller boat to retrieve it. Despite a wing span of over ten feet and a body as big as a sheep (observed three-year-old David Sandford) it was carried into the crowded saloon to be dressed and mounted by the taxidermist and hung from the ceiling. David was thrilled at the softness of the bird's feathers under the wings and all were awed at its whiteness.

Ishmael, in *Moby Dick,* felt deep emotion when he "beheld the Antarctic fowl," and decided that "in the wondrous bodily whiteness of the bird chiefly lurks the secret of the spell." Maybe no one on the *Coronet* had read about the "white of the white whale," or if they had they gave no credence to a novel's assertion that white was "the crowning attribute of the terrible," of unarticulated evil, including the "White Squall" of the Antarctic. White was God's color, not Satan's and here they were, a pure white company in a pure white yacht.

Melville aside, surely even the children knew "The Rime of the Ancient Mariner"—and knew better than to believe the superstitions of the sea (in spite of the sailmaker's angel). But that night chaos hit the deck. A powerful gale plowed into them shortly after nine o'clock with such force that it snapped the iron fitting attaching the foot of the main sail to its boom and broke the main sheet, or rope, which controlled the sail's position. The boom swung free in the gale and crashed into the rigging, breaking off about ten feet from the mast in a tangle of rope, canvas, and wood. The giant main sail, almost ninety feet high and seventy feet at its widest point, flopped loose, while the great boom, sixteen inches thick, hung over the ship's side, its broken end swinging like a mammoth club. McKenzie ran to cut it away before it could knock a hole in the boat, but Sandford shouted, "Stop!" In the midst of the chaos he began to pray that God would show them how to save the boom and the sail. Working in the dark against the wind, the men managed to lower the sail, roll it, and handle it down to the saloon. Throughout the night they cut and sewed the essential sail to fit the shortened boom. Up on deck, Sandford worried about continued damage from the broken-off section. It had been tied to the rail, but heavy waves were shooting it along the deck, perilously close to the motor launch. Remembering that the beautiful launch had cost $1750, he insisted on sawing away the jagged end of the boom, taking a good six inches. When, an hour later, a wave drove the boom to within three inches of the launch, he was sure the Holy Spirit had dictated that six-inch cut.

The disaster was taken in good spirits. In fact, the men sang as they worked through the night. For two days the sail was spread under their feet in the saloon as its repair continued. Meetings were conducted on top of it. When it was ready, Sandford had another idea. "Well, now," he said, "what I'd like on that sail is 'COUNTED ALL JOY.' "

"That sorely tested my faith, I'll tell you," McKenzie remembered. "But we did it"—two-foot-high letters painted on the sail: "ALL JOY." When the carpenter had finished repairing and fitting the boom, the mainsail with its message was bent to it with shouts of praise.

They could see the snow-capped Andes now, not far away. They had left the worst danger behind, though storms continued up the coast of Chile. On May 9 a Spanish steamer gave them their position by signal flags. They were near the Gulf of Penas, and the next day took refuge there, in a spot they named "Good Shepherd Beach." The weary crew enjoyed unbroken rest for the first time in a month. While others slept, John Sandford rather precociously recorded the new silence in his diary. After weeks of roaring, creaking, and shouting, there was not a sound "save the soft whir of wings, the gentle splash of water as the dove-like sea-birds feed upon the fish at the mouth of yonder brook. . . . No rolling of the vessel. No wild alarms as some sea sweeps the deck. . . . Nothing but a dead silence."

During the next week the laundry was done in fresh water from a stream on shore, the clothes hung on bushes to dry. Fresh water was carried to the yacht's tank, and Sandford and John—who had been given a new .22 rifle for his birthday—shot geese for a bonfire dinner.

They had just headed out again into deep water when first Mate Thomas Marshall suddenly died—not a victim of the blind Horn's hate, but of Bright's Disease, the recurrance of a kidney ailment. The ship turned back and he was buried in a sad ceremony on Good Shepherd's Beach. Marshall was the third death among the crew since the Thirty had been chosen. Two others had died of fever in the Mediterranean.

The strange telegram to Shiloh on June 20 from Concepcion, Chile, was surely not meant to belie the loss they felt: "Marshall dead, boom broken, life-boat smashed, need three thousand dollars, Jehovah reigns." Shiloh's reply contained only $400, but it covered present needs. The return cable from Maine also held comforting news—"the most costly Erard harp obtainable, a No. 7, Louis XVI Model," sheathed in gold leaf, had been purchased for the *Coronet* and was waiting for them in Australia. It had cost $1,000.

With the Horn and all its treachery behind her, the yacht moved gracefully out into the Pacific. Her company had successfully frightened off the white whale. But they had not beaten it. It had gone on ahead, to show itself later at a different pole.

Throughout the summer and fall of 1908 the *Coronet* eased her way through the South Pacific. Well-established churches welcomed the Thirty on many of the islands, where missionaries such as John G. Paton had spent lifetimes—Tahiti, Samoa, Fiji. Nevertheless, Shiloh "restored" all the islands within sight of the boat, including one occupied only by seals and birds.

Exploits now began to involve more than prayer. Back in the Mediterranean one year ago God had said "Go straight," which the group had interpreted to mean no idle, tourist-like expeditions along the way, but apparently that did not exclude hunting. In America the sport had lately gained new respectability and charm, enhanced by the expoints of President Theodore Roosevelt. A few years earlier, after hearing that Roosevelt had gone on a bear hunt, Sandford had taken John into the wilderness of New Brunswick, Canada, where John shot and killed a bear caught in a trap. Now at lush, green Mas a Fuera, a mountainous island one hundred miles from San Fernandez, the women waited in the boat while a party of twelve men, with John along, spent five days chasing wild goats on the precipitous heights. Fresh meat was the acknowledged purpose, and meat they got—if tough and stringy—along with another test of prowess and endurance among the cliffs and chasms. Nights were spent under the sky after suppers of goat meat roasted on sticks over an open fire. They returned to the ship utterly exhausted and pleased, giving credit to God for their own surprising physical strength, their safety, and their good aim. "How many did you get?" asked the women, as the carcasses were passed up onto the deck. "How many did you ask God for?" Sandford replied. There were twenty, the goal they had set on the first day.

At the end of November they reached the harbor of Sydney, Australia, to a cool reception. Frank Murray insists that Nathan Harriman had wired ahead to all the major ports with warnings of the *Coronet's* approach, but the Sydney newspapers tell a different story. First of all, there is no mention of the yacht's arrival or departure in their quite extensive maritime records. In a ludicrous coincidence, issue after issue of the *Morning Herald* was featuring the name of Sandford—a businessman, William Sandford, embroiled in dispute with the government. Only one paper paid attention to the *Coronet,* the *Daily Telegram.* When Sandford refused an interview, their reporter, miffed, asked in his headline, "Are They Holy Rollers?" then wired back to the States for data. A week later he reprinted an article that had appeared in *Harper's Weekly* the previous February, the most wretched nonsense that had yet been published about Shiloh, complete with naked men and a raving, wild-eyed prophet. Since this was the first the Shiloh visitors had seen of the article, they assumed the reporter had vindictively made it up. Undaunted, they rowed one of their small boats up the river as far as they could go and claimed the continent of Australia for God. Wrote Almon Whittaker:

The inhabitants of that land were not aware of what was taking place in their very midst, but . . . faith in the power of Jesus Christ will see it answered, and anything that opposes it will be subdued until Australia stands for God and His right to rule.

Whittaker, right at that time, was reeling under his own personal problems. Mail at Sydney had confirmed that his wife Florence, back in Palestine with their five children, was openly "in rebellion." The letters he found waiting for him were desperate and bitter. In the year and a half since her husband had left Jerusalem on the *Coronet,* Florence and their sixteen-year-old daughter had nursed each other through serious bouts of fever; the younger children (four boys aged three to eight) had suffered eye infections which threatened their sight, and an infant daughter (their sixth child) had been born and died. The family had been turned out of the Shiloh residence in Jerusalem, without funds, and was now in Jaffa in strained circumstances. Mrs. Whittaker wanted to go back to America as quickly as possible, and she wanted her husband to provide a home for the children.

Florence Whittaker, a mellow woman in her early thirties (married at seventeen and only twenty-five when she and Almon joined Sandford in 1897), had been fully in accord from the first with whatever sacrifices were required for the work, but both had been wounded by the long separation while Almon was in Jerusalem and Liverpool between 1900 and 1904. In 1906 Harriman had written in a letter to the newspapers, "that before coming home the last time [1904] he [Whittaker] came near breaking away altogether. After his return he was in retirement most of the time and all last winter he occupied a hut in the woods with his family, for discipline."

However much of that was true, Whittaker's dilemma never seemed to end. Yet those who knew him best were not surprised when he agreed to be part of the *Coronet* Thirty, though it would mean further years away from his family. He had spoken often of his vow in 1897 to go wherever God sent him without "shrinking," even if that meant what he dreaded most and expected would happen, leaving behind those he loved. If he doubted for a minute his call to be part of this voyage, that doubt might have centered in his role. His presence was not essential in practical terms. He was not a sailor nor a cook nor a teacher, though he often helped on deck; he was there as spiritual ballast, as a prayer warrior and a counselor. Even for a ten-year veteran of Shiloh, there must have been times when that definition felt vague and spongy.

Florence's problems were complicated by a quarrel between—of all people—the Gleason brothers, who were finding it impossible to cooperate in leadership in the Holy Land. They had, in fact, split completely, Willard taking a house in Jaffa and Ralph remaining in Jerusalem. The Holy Land company of about 70 persons had split along with the brothers, the smaller of the two groups going to Jaffa with Willard. Others, such as Gordon and Emma (Barton) Murray, moved without difficulty between the two men. Shiloh, meanwhile, raised and sent the rents for two houses, rather than one.

Florence Whittaker was now living at Willard's house in Jaffa, having been banished there by Ralph when he found it impossible to win her back to the Kingdom. Willard had taken her in, though it was obvious that he had not the room for six more people, and when it became apparent that his own persuasive powers were also ineffective, it nettled his conscience to feed and provide for a family that was at enmity with God. To all practical purposes Florence had no home and certainly no income. She was bumping into the same reality that shocked so many of Shiloh's disenchanted. To "forsake all," a state they had gladly elected, meant total dependence on the institution, a picture which came sharply into focus only when they wanted to leave and hadn't the means to do so.

Florence's plight did not change God's schedule. The yacht received a new suit of sails at Sydney, and late in December, without a pilot, beat her way against the tide up the Narrows at the entrance to Port Phillip, famous for its danger, and into the harbor of Melbourne. There they were received with warmth and adulation. Melbourne appreciated, as Sydney had not, the miracle of the *Coronet's* presence. Ship after ship had foundered or been wrecked by bad seas in 1908, eight in total around the Horn.

The yacht was dry-docked for repairs and paint in these last weeks of the year. By early 1909 she was nosing out into the Indian Ocean along the western horn of Australia. Here, in what the men named the "Happy Hunting Grounds," she was anchored frequently while the hunters went ashore. At Sydney room had been made on board for the new harp. No one has mentioned where that was kept, yet where else but in the saloon? Now, incredibly, two more albatross were added to the collection of trophies, along with four black swans and several ducks and penguins. At night, in the glow of the swaying overhead lantern, glass eyes winked from every corner of the room.

But birds had become too easy for Shiloh's marksmen. They were eager to try their skills with bigger game. Seeing wild cattle on an island, they stopped to bag fresh meat and were charged by a bull, which they dropped in his tracks, and coming upon five "monstrous sea elephants" in a cove, they shot two from the deck of the boat.

It was April before the *Coronet* docked at Capetown in South Africa. The mail waiting there informed Whittaker that his wife, still stranded in Jaffa, had contacted the American consul, who was helping her make arrangements to return to America by steamer. Almon's brother Rufus in Presque Isle, Maine, who had left the movement after the Black Winter, was sending her money for food. In her desperation Florence was flinging one of the worst possible insults at Shiloh. She was going to a defector for help.

Five months had passed since Whittaker had first heard of his wife's distress and anger. If he agonized over the delay, or if there was any discussion of his taking a steamer by himself back to Jaffa from Capetown, it is not a matter of record. He stayed on the yacht, and he did not, as Fred Caillat had done, break fellowship with the others or hide himself away in the lazaret.

The mail waiting at Capetown also held news of the bad press back home, stories of desertions and threatened suits coming in waves, as they always seemed to do. Charles Mann, angered by reports of hunger, was renewing his campaign against the "institution of humbuggery and damnfoolery," and a self-acclaimed "psychic clairvoyant" from South Paris, Maine, had attended chapel and seen the room full of "black-haloed earthbound spirits rollicking around."

The yacht left Capetown immediately after provisioning. Convinced that God had given the orders to take off, the crew proceeded to raise all sails—to the sound of laughter from nearby vessels, for there was no wind. In fact, it could not have been calmer, in a harbor noted for its frustrating calms, and when the yacht began to drift dangerously close to other ships, her sailors found it hard to maintain faith. Sandford called them down to the saloon for prayer. They returned to deck determined to try again, and in a smacking breeze that blew on their side of the harbor only, maneuvered clear of the breakwater.

But why did God want them to leave Capetown against such odds? They might as well have waited for an unsupernatural wind, because in spite of the pressing reasons to return to Palestine, the yacht ambled slowly north, seemingly in no hurry. Hugging the coastline of the Dark Continent, they studied the lives of African missionaries, in particular

David Livingston and Robert Moffatt. Meanwhile, the very real future of Shiloh was being determined by Florence Whittaker's circumstances.

Portugese West Africa offered the *Coronet* company hunting opportunities of great variety, including a "seven foot pelican" which several of the men chased on foot down a beach while the marksmen sailed along in the rowboat shooting. At Cape Three Points off the Longo River they hoped for tougher game. Taking the smaller boat ashore at dusk, they planned to sleep overnight and hunt in the morning on a spit of beach where tracks suggested the presence of animals. An eighth of a mile from shore the boat capsized where the river water met the sea. Swimming or grabbing onto oars, all made it to land, except the ship's carpenter, John Harrod, who could not swim. To their great relief, when the boat washed in, Harrod was under it, clinging to the seats, his head in a pocket of breathing space.

Their rifles, blankets, and food were gone. One man had lost his clothing to the tearing surf and all of them were chilled. Without matches to light a fire, they raced all night up and down the beach. The day before, exploring, they had seen the results of a fight between what appeared to be a huge lion and a crocodile. In the morning light they were "awed" to find fresh lion tracks along the edge of their spit of beach, but not a single track upon it. They were rescued at last by a *Coronet* sailor, who rowed ashore to find them.

Further north, off the mouth of the Congo River, when Lester McKenzie became ill with African fever and Deborah Sandford almost died of sleeping sickness, the yacht retreated to Annabon Island for fresh food and good water. They remained there deep into June.

Somewhere along the coast of Africa Sandford had a vision. John R. Mott, one of the young men who had played an influential role in the Student Volunteer Movement, suddenly appeared before him with a great troop of African converts.

Amazed, Sandford asked, "Mott, how did you do it?"

"Your prayers made it easy for me, Sandford," John Mott answered.

It was a vision full of irony. Mott's lights had not led him into the kind of missionary endeavor that would produce an army of converts in such a literal sense. He was still traveling about the world recruiting missionaries in behalf of the Student Volunteer Movement, acting as an ambassador for ecumenism and cooperation among denominational mission boards, an endeavor Sandford could hardly condone. Rather, he would have been shocked to learn how far apart he and Mott now were in their thinking, and that many of the young men he had admired back at Northfield twenty years ago had been making it a point to span the theological differences in the Protestant Church throughout the world. There would have been no room in their enterprise for Shiloh's exclusivism, if they had so much as heard of Shiloh.

On July 18, 1909, the *Coronet* crossed its own course beyond the Canaries, the "chain of prayer" completed. On deck for a cannon salute and a band concert, Sandford suddenly realized that it was twenty years "to the minute" since he had signed the pledge at Northfield (actually it was twenty-one years). Finding among his papers below deck a copy of the pledge, "I am willing and desirous, God permitting, to be a foreign missionary," he wrote under it, "I am that. So much so that what was home is now foreign, and what was foreign is now home."

July 18, 1909, says Frank Murray, also "seems to have been the same day that light came to the man of God that he should turn toward America." He had heard the words, "The conquest of America afresh." If Jerusalem had been for a moment their intended destination, it was now behind them, along with Florence Whittaker, who was now not just a complainer, but a traitor. A month later, after an uneventful voyage, they arrived in Portland harbor. In all, the *Coronet* had been gone three years and had traveled 51,924 nautical miles, 30,000 of that "going around."

22

Bring My Sons from Far
1910–1911

It was three weeks before they set foot on land. The *Kingdom* came out to meet them in the harbor and the two yachts moved back and forth together along the Maine coast. Shiloh residents were confused and a little hurt. "Thank you for your letter of welcome," Sandford wrote to Merlyn Bartlett. "I expect to have the Bible School come on board soon, and you are among the number. The Bible School is very precious to my heart. God has a great future for you, my child." He was waiting for God's directions, he told reporters. For three years they had not sailed into any port without seeking God's will.

Then, for the first time in more than three years, he appeared on the hilltop. While the entire flock waited out on the terraced lawns, he stopped first at the farm of a Mr. Curtis near the foot of the hill and paid for some cabbages Shiloh cows had "stolen" from his garden. At a meeting the next day to which townspeople were personally invited by house-to-house contact, the *Coronet* company sat on the platform in new white clothing, each telling part of the story of the voyage.

It was an important public relations measure, even apart from honoring God's protection and power. Earlier in the year Durham selectmen had been petitioned to institute a sanity hearing for Sandford when he returned. Nothing came of it, but the climate in the neighborhood was thick with hostility. Yet those who climbed the hill for the *Coronet* meeting to see for themselves if Frank Sandford was crazy found a genial, well-tanned gentleman on the platform, his blue-eyed gaze as direct and composed as ever.

The press treated him moderately, printing an interview and a letter he wrote to his dentist in Lewiston, a big-game buff, describing the *Coronet's* hunting exploits. The dentist was a well-known and respected man, Dr. Ezra White, Wendell's cousin, who, though not a Shiloh sympathizer, had provided Sandford with several gold fillings before the voyage began.

Behind the scenes the same old scenario played itself out. The leaders left in charge, George Jewell and Lester McKenzie's brother Frank, were blamed once more for failing to maintain a unified front and demoted. In the fall convention, which began immediately, Sandford called for a rebaptism of the Holy Spirit for the entire Kingdom, bringing, says Murray, "a new infusion of life and courage" and a new enthusiasm for active missions throughout the world.

In view of that, the next move was puzzling to many. Within a month Sandford was at sea again, sailing to Jaffa on the *Kingdom,* with a plan to close down the remaining work overseas, the Jerusalem headquarters, and bring everyone home, including the disputing Gleasons and Florence Whittaker. Almon did not go with him. It may have been entirely his own decision, if any decision at that point was independent. Murray says Sandford viewed the Whittaker affair as a domestic quarrel and had been trying to stay out of it himself.

At Gibraltar, a "bushel" of two-year-old, unforwarded mail explained much of the confusion between the Gleasons. Neither of the brothers had lost faith in their leader. The dissension was entirely between the two of them and how they construed their assigned roles. According to Murray, Ralph was largely at fault. As a supplement to Holland's identity as Moses, Ralph had been named after Moses' brother Aaron, the High Priest, though little was made of this at Shiloh. Ralph had supposedly become obsessed with this "priestly function." His turn at being "high priest" was over, Sandford told him when they met. It was time for him to try being "low priest" for a while, and then maybe "no priest."

Both brothers and their families had suffered in Jerusalem. Ralph and his wife Christine had seen two small children die of fever, ten months apart. Rose, Willard's wife, the pretty, good-natured girl from Chebeague Island who had been one of the first students, had lost her eyesight. All of the Jerusalem workers, some the original Twelve who had been there for eight years, had seen much hardship, but they were convinced that their presence in the Holy Land was a successful fulfillment of prophecy. Strife aside, hunger aside, it seemed like defeat or "backsliding," as Joseph Harriman said, to pull up stakes and move out of the "homeland."

Joseph had made Palestine his home in a way few westerners had ever done. While planning the trip around the world, Sandford had suggested that Joseph and Ralph Gleason "go around the Holy Land." They did so in the course of the next year, in a manner far beyond Sandford's expectations. Following Scriptural boundaries already established, they spent several weeks walking 1,300 miles through the hazardous desert wilderness, largely without a guide, driving their own pack donkeys. Worried American officials insisted that they travel with a military escort, but there was no money to do so. After days of canyons, cliffs, and maze-like cul-de-sacs, drinking at Bedouin waterholes and shooting birds for food, they spent eleven days on the Dead Sea in a canvas boat and arrived safely back at Jerusalem.

Sandford still believed that Jerusalem would become the center of world evangelism and the events of the End Time, and still believed he was to be martyred on its streets. He assured Joseph and the others that vacating the Holy Land was temporary—that the regathering of all members at Shiloh was no different than any other occasion when he had called everyone home for purposes of unity and revitalization. As a matter of fact, Shiloh never set foot in Jerusalem again and the mission was never reopened.

Florence Whittaker had begun her plea for help in the summer of 1908. By the time the *Kingdom* arrived, it was January 1910. She had just received money for passage on a steamer from her home in Aroostook County and she was not in the least interested in Sandford's offer of a free ride home. She had determined never to set foot on a Shiloh boat or Shiloh property again. Sandford was reasonable. He promised her private quarters on the yacht and good care; her present funds could be saved for her future needs in America and as soon as they arrived home she would be free to do as she pleased, he said. After seeking the advice of the American consul, Florence agreed reluctantly to his offer.

The trip home was very long, lasting from the end of January through early May. Aboard the ship every effort was made by the eighty-five passengers to live in harmony and good spirits. The children grew brown in the sun, food was sufficient, and Mrs. Whittaker was treated with courtesy. Almon was in Portland to meet her. They spent two days together on the *Kingdom* and then sailed on the boat to South Freeport.

But no arrangements had been made for even a temporary home for the family, as Florence had hoped and expected. Both Sandford and her

husband attempted to persuade her to go with them to Shiloh until
other housing could be provided. She refused. It was exactly what she
could not bear to do and had said she would not. The next day, May
11, the *Kingdom* weighed anchor and sailed off among the islands of
Casco Bay, with the Whittakers aboard, prisoners to all practical purposes.

A week later, on May 19, Sandford gave an interview to the Associated
Press. If the concentration of local press coverage had been astonishing
before, now it was as if Shiloh had become the area's daily soap opera,
with everyone waiting for the next installment. But no one knew yet
about Florence Whittaker. While she was crossing the Atlantic, her
husband, running the Durham farms, had been arrested on grounds that
the animals were starving. Though the case was dismissed, with Shiloh
given two weeks to correct the matter, the gathering momentum of
oppression was becoming almost intolerable. The avenues of inside
information were now multiple, with no possible way to plug the leaks
or quell the rumors.

Neighbors had formed a kind of confederacy to keep an eye out for
Shiloh's "victims." There had been widespread talk for years of an
underground railroad of sorts, which began at the nearby home of Elisha
Beal, where a sign in the front yard read TEMPORARY HOME FOR
ESCAPED SHILOHITES. Beal was known as a "tight, stingy man,"
but he was thoroughly generous in feeding Shiloh's children and loved
to tell the story of the boy who stood up halfway through a meal to
make room for more before he went back to the hill.

Sandford met this latest line of fire in his old style of chin-out
confrontation, by sharing Shiloh's far-reaching plans with the Associated
Press. A "chain of one hundred missions" would soon be established
"in the western hemisphere," he said, with one at Cape Horn and one
in the North Pole. The present fleet of the Kingdom Yacht Club would
be "doubled" to accomplish this.

Admiral Peary had claimed to reach the North Pole in April of 1909.
While Sandford was fighting sea lions on the way to Capetown, Peary
was being acclaimed as Maine's own adopted hero. Although not a
native, he had graduated from Bowdoin and owned a summer house at
Harpswell Neck in the Casco Bay. As Sandford explained in his interview
with the Associated Press, he had often talked in the past of taking the
Gospel to the North Pole, if he should learn that it was inhabited by
a single living soul. He had actually hoped to be the first to explore
that region, he acknowledged with a touch of humor, but Admiral Peary

had beaten him to it. Now, said Sandford, he hoped to open a missionary station in Greenland, from which all of the northland could be reached.

Asked for his estimate of the future of Shiloh generally, he replied, "I should say in a word it is sublime." Earlier he had told the papers that "the tide has already turned" in Shiloh's favor and soon disciples would be coming not "by the hundreds but by the thousands." When trouble hit the world, as it would soon, he would "yet be a popular man."

The remark was almost self-destructive, almost a deliberate attempt to widen the gap between himself and his opponents. Those who had been listening to him over the years expected him to boast, but it was not the boasting itself that bothered many people. Arrogance was not objectionable to the general public unless you failed to deliver the goods. Sandford would have said that he was boasting for God, and that God would do the delivering. The problem was that by now "God" had failed too many times. A line had been crossed while Sandford was gone these three years. There was nothing now that he could do or say in defense of himself or God that would not react against him.

After talking to the press, Frank sailed out in the *Coronet* to join the *Kingdom* and once more face Florence Whittaker. In another week Florence sent the following letter to Almon's brother Rufus and his wife in Aroostook County:

> The children and I are still here on this ship and they simply won't let us land. This is what I was afraid of when I was in Palestine. One of the reasons why I didn't want to come this way and chose to come on a steamer was because I felt sure they would never let me get ashore but get Al on board and put out to sea or something of this kind and they would never let me land until the children and I were straightened out, as they call it, and back into the movement again.
>
> Oh, you should have heard the promises Mr. Sandford made to me if I only would come with him instead of the other way; he said he had taken me to Palestine, now he wanted to land me again in my own country . . . ; and when I got here I was free to do as I pleased, take my train immediately and go home if I wanted to [to Aroostook].

She had avoided "rash steps," she said, because above all she wanted her husband to "live with us now and make a home for his family and provide for us. I would be glad and willing to work hard and live anywhere if he would only come but I cannot live any longer as I have the past thirteen years." Even that could be endured, she said, if it had been a "necessity," but "to fold one's hands" and watch one's children "lose their health," to be ordered about by "men who have no rights over you whatever—for God's sake, what could a mother be made of to stand this kind of actions the year round?"

But, you see, Al does not realize the truth of these things, for all he does is to be one of the chosen ones, to sail around in that beautiful yacht of Mr. Sandford's with every luxury dumped into it that Mr. Sandford can scrape up at other people's expense and you can well imagine how Mr. Sandford lives. He is ten times worse now than when you knew him.

Florence had been to Sandford three times, she said, asking to be taken ashore, and "he utterly refuses to allow me to go, until, as he says, I am adjusted to my husband: then, whatever God wants my husband to do, he is willing. Ah! But there never was any such agreement made as this when he was trying to get me to come on board in Jaffa! This is just what I felt he would do."

Almon, she continued, had flatly rejected her pleas that he leave Sandford and join his family, insisting that he would never allow the children to get off the ship in her custody.

Rufus, on receiving this, appealed to Nathan Harriman, who sought legal counsel for Florence. On the morning of June 6 the sheriff of Cumberland County boarded the *Kingdom,* now anchored off Chebeague Island. Whittaker himself was there to receive the writ. He raised no objection. His resignation was interpreted by a reporter as disinterest. He wore the "austere, inexpressive countenance" so common at Shiloh. Reporters had never learned, and never would, that the "countenance" was a mask for public purposes. Whittaker was crushed, says Murray, and undoubtedly he was. He was losing his family. He was also letting them go. Had he conquered his natural affections at last? If so, it was a singularly selfish victory, his alone, one he had opted for regardless of the needs of those he loved.

His family was taken to housekeeping quarters at the Cumberland County jail for several days. At a Supreme Court hearing in Auburn, Florence was given custody of the children. Whittaker's only comment to the press was that he felt he had acted within his rights as a father and a husband and wished to make it plain that whatever he had done was of his "own free will and accord" and not by direction of Sandford. Later, some years after he and Florence had divorced, he wrote for Kingdom members only, "It is a wonderful thing to deny oneself not only a selfish life, but self-existence."

While all this was going on, Austin Perry had been busy recruiting new passengers for both the *Coronet* and the *Kingdom,* concentrating particularly on the younger male generation at Shiloh who had reached adulthood in the years Sandford had been gone. Though the hill was not absolutely "depopulated" by malcontents, as the *Journal* claimed, more and more of these young men were going off on their own, one of them Arnold's friend and classmate, Arthur Shaw, who never returned from an errand in Boston.

Exactly where the new sailors were destined to go had not yet been decided. For the present they were to be trained in navigational skills and seamanship, giving Sandford and the officers the opportunity to observe at close hand their suitability for a longer voyage. Others were invited aboard the boats simply for recreation and pleasure. Four wag-onloads of men and women passed through South Freeport on June 7, reported the papers, believed headed for the *Kingdom.* They were.

Florence Whittaker's story, including her letter, probably sent to the paper by Nathan Harriman, had hit the outside world just the day before. Sandford, on the *Coronet,* did not see it. He had sailed to Boston on the first day of June while Florence was still on the *Kingdom,* and by now he was on his way south to the Virginia Capes. Above all, he had no idea that the woman was suing him for $15,000 for forcible detention. But outside Boston, on the verge of coming in to dock, the *Coronet* ran into a gale. With a premonition of trouble, Sandford heard the word "Sent." Instantly he gave a message to someone to take to the captain on deck: "Continue south!" The message was somehow never conveyed, but in a sudden gust of wind the yacht turned completely around and headed south "by herself"—or so the story was told.

On June 8 Captain Perry raised the sails of the *Kingdom* in South Freeport harbor and headed north. Perry knew more than Sandford, but only that Florence had departed the boat in the company of the sheriff and was suing for the custody of her children. He was not aware of the suit against Sandford, or that he himself had been named as an accessory.

The *Kingdom* had hardly disappeared out of sight of Freeport when authorities began to watch the ports, seeking to serve the papers. Sheriff Trefethen of Portland and an attorney were "keeping a close watch," said the *Journal,* suspecting the boats of hiding out in the thousands of tiny coves along the Maine coast. Days later, learning of this in Virginia, Sandford remembered the words of Jesus to the disciples, "When they persecute you in this city, flee to the next." He saw no reason to face false allegations. He also knew that Florence Whittaker's suit did not presuppose a criminal trial. But he had already been interrupted enough by the red tape of the courts and could not abide another day of it. Florence Whittaker might win the skirmish with her husband, but he was determined she would not win one with him. Let the process servers dash from port to port. The white sails of the *Coronet* would evade them until God directed otherwise. So the chase began.

The *Coronet,* on her cruise down to Virginia, carried twelve of the original Thirty, including the Sandfords, and about a dozen of the young student trainees. Their instruction was to be spiritual as well as nautical, of course. None of this generation had sat under Sandford's teaching for a concentrated period. For the next two months sessions of prayer and study were almost continuous, often throughout the night, in a crash program of preparation for the next venture.

During that same period, June and July, the *Kingdom* shuttled back and forth from South Freeport to Browns and Georges Banks, favorite fishing grounds off the coasts of Maine and Massachusetts, offering as many Shiloh members as possible a chance to vacation and pray for the northern regions of the continent. Arnold was among the young people on the *Kingdom* in those summer days. A white-bearded fisherman from Casco Bay, affectionately called Ole Man Day, was their tutor, teaching them to use 100-fathom cod lines baited with herring. Mr. Day had recently joined Shiloh with his daughter and grandchildren, the Campbells. His daughter, widowed, had turned a sizeable estate ($59,000) over to the Kingdom treasuries, money which was helping importantly in planning the new moves.

On July 25 a startled Austin Perry was arrested at last as he went ashore at Portland on business. He raised bail the next day, then hurried on north in the *Kingdom* to meet the *Coronet* at Browns Bank. After a week of conference, two decisions were made, one certain and one pending. A mission station was to be opened immediately on the west coast of Africa, and following that, possibly one in Greenland.

The *Kingdom's* destination now was Portland, Maine, to get supplies, an errand not feasible for the *Coronet,* since at all costs she must stay beyond the three-mile offshore limit, out of the jurisdiction of port authorities. The yacht darted north and in a month had gone as far as Mindon in the Strait of Belle Isle at the northwest tip of Newfoundland. As this was the most regularly used route to Greenland, eight hundred miles away, the purpose may have been to gain some experience in the navigation of those waters. But late in August winter had already come. Noting that the Indians had left their coastal houses and gone inland for the winter, the boat turned south.

One night early in September, hove to in the Gulf of St. Lawrence as the crew repaired a tear in the mainsail, Sandford lifted his face to the Labradorian chill and received a peculiar and unmistakeable message: *"Give up."* Not for one second did he wonder if it meant he should "give up the chase." Instead, he thought instantly of Isaiah 43:6: "I will say to the north, Give up; and to the south, Keep not back; bring my sons from far and my daughters from the ends of the earth." These were the words of assurance he had been waiting for. Africa was the first objective, and Greenland was the next. With a new certainty of God's backing and blessing, they sailed out of the Gulf of St. Lawrence to meet the *Kingdom* again at Browns Banks, off the Maine coast.

There, several members of the A-Class Bible School, including Arnold and Enid, were transferred to the *Coronet*. They had been brought to the Bay of Fundy to pray for the "capture" of another kind of "Big Fish," a wealthy man at Eastport, Maine. He had not been hooked, in spite of repeated sorties into land to hold meetings he might attend.

Chesapeake Bay was designated as the next point of rendezvous. At that time final selections would be made for the passengers and crew on both boats, which would sail to Africa together, where the personnel on the *Kingdom* would stay while the others moved on to Greenland. With most of the A-Class on board, the *Coronet* reached Lynnhaven Roads (off the Virginia coast) in early October.

Things were going badly already. The *Kingdom* had not arrived. Directly after the separation, lingering to fish south of Cape Sable, Nova Scotia, she had lost her way in the fog and ran aground Big Mud Island. The women and children were removed in a heavy sea and taken to the shacks of lobstermen, presently unoccupied. The ship's false keel was torn away, a large hole ripped in her port bow, the heel of her rudder damaged, and much of her copper torn off. Rising tides flooded "between decks," causing further damage. It was ten days before the boat could be towed to Yarmouth (at the southern tip of Nova Scotia) for repairs. Perry, who so often seemed to be the person faced with solving complicated problems, set about making arrangements to remove passengers from Mud Island and pay the unexpected bills.

The *Chronicle* of Halifax, the salty voice of a fishing populace, blamed Perry for the accident, clearly implying that any experienced seaman would not have run aground the shoal. (Actually, Charles Sellick was acting as captain.) None of the *Kingdom's* officials carried "certificates," diplomas of experience, as American shipping regulations did not require such certificates for yachts. "So those who travel have their lives at stake," surmised the *Chronicle,* adding that the *Kingdom* would soon be abandoned as no longer seaworthy.

But Halifax knew nothing of the determination of the barkentine's owners. In two weeks she was ready to sail again, though the cost of the damage was over $2,200. After loading $4,500 worth of supplies at Portland, she at last made her way south to meet the *Coronet.*

The yacht, while waiting, sailed quietly about in the Chesapeake area. Writes Arnold: "We anchored under Fort Monroe [at the mouth of the James], where we remained in great secrecy, the smaller boat beaching at unpopulated areas when it went in for mail and supplies." Nevertheless, Sandford took the risk of yielding to an old desire. On October 3, 1910, Arnold noted in his diary, *"Coronet* up Potomac to pray for President Taft." They prayed with a "great sense of danger" of impending war. While the president slept, Shiloh's prayers continued throughout the night.

Arnold's diary also contains reference to a circumstance that may have settled his own fate for the next year and a half, and perhaps forever. Mr. Sandford had insisted that no correspondence from the boat should give away their location. Arnold had written to an uncle, the Rev. Nathan Brackett, a Free Baptist minister who had co-founded Storer College, a school for black students at Harper's Ferry. Hoping for an answer, Arnold had given him a mailing address, which was a post office and did not entail the actual location of the boat. Since mail was being examined carefully as it arrived on board, Sandford was aware of it when a reply arrived from Uncle Nate.

Arnold had often listened in pain as others received the anger of the prophet full blast. Now it was his turn. He had been careless and disobedient, heedless of orders and stupid as well. To apprise a Free Baptist minister of their whereabouts was the same as notifying the maritime authorities. "I have half a mind to ship you off to your uncle!" Sandford roared. It did not occur to Arnold until much later that it might be a good idea. Instead, he was disfellowshipped and sent to the forecastle to fast and pray. He was not to socialize with anyone until given permission.

Arnold was now almost twenty-one. Like all of the members of the A-Class, he was fully committed to Sandford. If he was allowing himself to feel any complaint, it was only that the promised college course was so long in materializing. He had gone about his chores at Shiloh with an ache for further schooling, listing in a notebook subjects he hoped to study.

He had just recuperated from a bout with typhoid, which he had caught while nursing a patient at Bethesda. He had not been desperately sick, but the weeks in bed had left him enervated. Someone had arranged a vacation for him at Elim, the house in Boston, where the food tended to be more plentiful than at Durham, and he had worked himself back into shape by sawing and chopping firewood from trolley ties that had been pulled up from a neighboring street and abandoned. He felt good and would have gone to sea in a minute.

Perhaps there was little chance of that after all, even apart from the Storer College mistake. Sandford was not satisfied that Arnold had yet "thrown away his head," his "reasoning mind." Seeing the high school graduation picture of the A-Class, he had remarked before the school that Arnold's conceit was evident in his face. The remark was repeated several times on other occasions, followed once by an apology of sorts— a hope that Arnold's feelings had not been hurt. Arnold did not know how to answer. He had supposed that was exactly what Mr. Sandford had meant to do, to hurt his feelings, and he had supposed he must need it.

The disfellowshipping, however, seemed unjust. He had not disregarded instructions or been insensitive to the need for secrecy, though in fact, he had not been told the reason for it. At the end of three days he decided he had done penance long enough and emerged into society without permission, to find himself totally ignored by everyone, including Enid. On that tiny ship, where it was impossible to turn around without bumping into someone, he did not exist. Still, hungry, he went to dinner and sat down at the table across from one or two of the ship's officers. His appearance was met with sudden silence, the clink of spoons in the soup bowls the only sound. Then in a moment the conversation continued. To break his embarrassment Arnold contributed a comment. He was interrupted by Roland Whittom, the first mate, a man younger than himself, who said: "Arnold, as a company of men we have no fellowship with you, and we do not wish to have your conversation mixed with ours." The pompous words were familiar; it was what one said on such occasions to the ostracized. Whittom was simply doing what was expected. He himself, though an honored member of the *Coronet* Thirty, had recently been disfellowshipped. Now fully reinstated, he remained on the *Coronet* while Arnold went back to Shiloh by train, still in disgrace.

The *Kingdom* arrived in Chesapeake Bay on the first of November, now with a broken rudder post. After weeks of attempting to fix it, the crews gave up and the boat was hauled out of the water once more for expensive repairs. During this wait the final choices were made for the companies on both ships for the Africa-Greenland trip. Selections for the *Coronet* were completed quickly, but no combination on the *Kingdom* suited Sandford.

By now, through circumstances and choice, the *Coronet* had become the absolute focus of the movement. Even Jerusalem the Golden had been contaminated by disharmony. The yacht was the only spot on earth where Sandford felt completely happy, and now it also the only ark of safety. He would have preferred not to take the *Kingdom* abroad again anywhere. No matter who sailed her, she failed—in her performance as a craft and as a sanctuary. An attitude of self-service thrived under her masts and in her low-ceilinged cabins. Yet she was indispensible to the mission and not everyone could be sent home. All were called to personal scrutiny on the deepest level.

John Davis, one of the new young sailors, remembered that at one of those Cleaning-out times Mr. Sandford reminded everyone that he himself was not immune to criticism. As they were sharing their observations of each other (an "uncompromising airing of faults"), Everett Knight, Sandford's nephew, spoke up.

"Well, Uncle Frank," he said, diffidently. "I guess I should tell you that I don't feel right about the way you slurp your soup."

A few people chuckled, certain that Everett would only make such a comment jokingly, but others sat in stunned silence. Actually Everett was perfectly serious, and so was Sandford.

"It might be best, Everett," he said, gruffly, "if you learned to honor an elder as a father."

But Everett had nevertheless proven himself essential as a crew member of the *Coronet*. Besides Everett, Herbert Jenkins and Stuart Wolfe had been chosen from the A-Class. Stuart, the only child of well-to-do farmers, had come from western New York State in 1904, "fairly breathing milk and good care," it seemed to Arnold and his Shiloh classmates. He and Hazel Housler were in love, a secret the class had kept successfully.

Of the other younger men on the *Coronet,* Floyd Clark and Guy Campbell were seventeen, John Adamson eighteen. Floyd, a studious young man, had been brought to Shiloh as a boy with his widowed mother in 1900, a member of the Tacoma party. Guy, the grandson of Ole Man Day, was from Barter's Island. Unlike Stuart and Floyd, he had grown up on the water. His father, a shipbuilder, had been lost at sea in a hurricane off Cape Hatteras in 1906. Guy had dropped out of high school to volunteer as a sailor.

John Adamson was apprenticing as a sailmaker. Round-faced and easygoing, he had already established a reputation for dependability and hard work on the hill. His parents, who had come from Sweden a few years back, were separated. His mother, who hated Shiloh, lived with the younger children on the River Road to Brunswick, while his father remained on the hill with John and a sister.

Charlie Jones, barely sixteen, was the youngest sailor on the *Kingdom,* with no prior experience on the water. He was one of nine children of the Aroostook family who some years before had been run out of town for their Shiloh associations. Although shy and soft-spoken, he had volunteered ("no coercion") for the trip out of a hunger for adventure, and was thrilled at the chance to live close to Mr. Sandford, whom he admired so much he even wished he might look like him. ("He had penetrating eyes.")

Altogether, sixty-six people were on their way to Africa, thirty on the *Coronet* and thirty-six on the *Kingdom.* An accurate count of the children is not available, but there were at least the five Sandfords on the *Coronet,* and at least six others on the *Kingdom.* Half of the original proven Thirty were on the *Coronet,* though Whittaker was back at Shiloh.

With all the delay and confusion behind them, Sandford was delighted when it appeared that Christmas would be the date to at last set sail. He sent out orders to both ships to prepare for the day with as much holiday spirit as possible. On December 24 six crew members and Lester McKenzie rowed to shore in a lifeboat for the last mail pickup before crossing the ocean. While Lester walked to the post office, the other six, in order to remain inconspicuous, rowed back out away from the wharf and anchored there as they waited. Caught unaware by incoming swells, the men were unable to pull up anchor before the boat was swamped. Five were swimmers; one was not. He and the man who attempted to save him were drowned.

A knife to cut the rope would have prevented the accident, but as it happened, no one was carrying a knife. The deaths were officially reported, and since neither man had known families, their bodies were returned to the *Kingdom* and buried at sea. Sandford held Lester McKenzie responsible and sent him below decks, making it clear that the tragedy offered further evidence of the *Kingdom's* unsuitability. Then he took to his own stateroom and did not come out for ten days. On December 27, under a cloud of gloom, the two ships set out for Africa.

They sailed directly into the teeth of an Atlantic storm. Two more storms followed in close succession. In the second of those gales the unbelievable happened. The strain of a broadside wave snapped the *Coronet's* forty-five-foot jib boom and the pandemonium of Cape Horn replayed itself on deck, the crazed boom thrashing in the gale, threatening everything in its path. In the emergency McKenzie was restored as sailing master.

When the worst was over, John Adamson began a daily record of the trip. The date of the first entry was January 1, 1911.

> Sunday. Sailed under trysails all night and day. Cleaned up some of the boom wreckage. Mended the staysail. Day of waiting on God. Storm is getting over, sun shining again . . . pumped ship.

Seams in the hull had begun to yield in the pressure of the storms. The yacht was admitting water for the first time in her history, and the main topmast had cracked from the strain of diving into head seas. On the second, John wrote:

> Calm all day. Sewed all day on the jib [remaking the sail to fit the shortened boom]. Had meeting from 3 o'clock until midnight. *Things* not very pleasant. Somewhat discouraged.

Sandford was still in seclusion in his stateroom. In the saloon the gathered company searched their hearts for whatever impurities had brought God's judgment. Ten days later, half-way across the ocean, after days of mending sails and "plenty of pumping," John wrote: "Mr. Sandford with us again." He had come out of his stateroom and the atmosphere cleared. Band practice began once more and voices were no longer hushed below deck. On the twenty-second, a meeting lasted "all day until midnight," said John, who had been up since 6:00 A.M., polishing brass and washing decks. "Mr. S. talked to us about 'The Truth'; read all about it in the first five books of the Bible. Did not eat supper." The next day the three o'clock meeting lasted until 10:30 P.M. "Fine meeting," wrote John.

On February 1, with great relief, somebody spotted the *Kingdom* just ahead as they approached the Canaries. Throughout the next two months they cruised in tandem, among the Islands and then south down the African coast, singing to each other across the sea and sharing dinners under the awnings. Cameraderie was excellent now. Floyd Clark's eighteenth birthday was celebrated with Guy Campbell and John Adamson in Sandford's stateroom, eating oranges and examining his books on the Spanish American and Russo-Japanese Wars. Everyone loved the presence of the boys on board, with their nonsense and horseplay tucked into the day's labor. Guy and Floyd were merciless in their teasing, quick to target self-conscious piety. "Well, glory to God, anyway!" Guy would repeat at the slightest excuse, in perfect imitation of one gentleman's sanctimonious bray. Sandford was making it a point to spend time with the younger crew. John Adamson, after several days of suffering with a bad toothache and some stomach trouble, had an "encouraging little talk with Mr. S." and felt much better. In mid-February, with the Dark Continent on the horizon, John wrote:

> Had a fine meeting on the missionary line for Africa. . . . God kindled a fire in my heart for to be a missionary. . . . I was all changed over, prayed for the heathen most all day.

Their destination was the British colony and protectorate of Gambia, on Africa's westernmost salient, the safest place to establish an initial station—under the aegis of Anglo-Israel. The Gambia River was navigable 175 miles into the interior. But still north of their goal, off the coast of French West Africa, the *Kingdom* ran into trouble once more. The ponderous barkentine had, as usual, taken dangerous chances in following the *Coronet* close to the shore. At the end of February, after moving together all night, the fat-hipped *Kingdom* was driven into a cove and could not get out. "Light winds and very changeable ones very near cost the lives of us all," wrote John, who was temporarily

acting as sailor on the *Kingdom* at the time. Twelve feet from the
rocks a wind caught their furled sails and they moved to safety.

But they had lost both anchors. So back they ran for replacements
to the Cape Verde Islands, some three hundred miles west. On Friday,
March 31, they set sail again for Gambia. Bathurst, the capital, was
located within the British colony on St. Mary's Island, at the mouth
of the river. Drinking water on the boats was low, so the *Coronet* raced
ahead and got there first, dropping anchor off port. As the crew prepared
for entry, they were interrupted by port authorities. The city was beseiged
by smallpox. Under no circumstances would anyone be permitted to
come in—or, to their greater dismay, to purchase badly needed fruit
and water.

Just as the *Coronet* officers were absorbing the meaning of this alarming
information, they turned to see, to their astonishment, the three small
Kingdom lifeboats full of people drawing near across the bay. The
barkentine had made her last clumsy mistake. In trying to find the
mouth of the Gambia, Perry, without charts, had requested instructions
from a Netherlands vessel. A simple miscommunication in a thick Dutch
accent led Perry to turn at the wrong buoy, and the *Kingdom* had run
aground on a sandbar three miles from shore. She was already filling
with water. Four men had been left aboard her to salvage as much as
possible, while the thirty-two others had scrambled into the smaller boats
in frightening breakers. In all, it was a dangerous, messy affair.

As soon as the port doctor could give them the bill of health required
for leaving port, the *Coronet* beat back out of the channel, towing the
smaller boats astern, to where the damaged *Kingdom* waited. Nothing
could be done to save her. For the next five days the crews ferried as
much as could be saved from the wreckage over to the *Coronet*. A
heart-breaking lot must be left behind—a piano, an organ, and the
opulent bequest of the *Wanderer's* interior. As they worked, the *Kingdom*
listed deeper and deeper onto her side. After a visit from French officials,
the ship's masts were cut away to prevent capsizing. Meanwhile, thirst
was a steadily increasing problem until a large steamer asking directions
provided the *Coronet* with water.

John Adamson was one of those who spent the last night on the
sinking boat.

> Got up at 2 A.M. and got some wire stays off the mizzenmast. I
> undressed and went below in the men's cabin (in the water) and got

the grindstone and a few other articles. Loaded the boats with the remaining things and got the spanker boom and gaff, and started.

At dawn the crew of the lifeboat set the *Kingdom* afire, a burnt offering for the continent of Africa, her bowsprit pointing toward the Sudan. With the glow of the conflagration in the sky at dawn, someone heard Frank Sandford pray that the boat would "burn to the ground."

The *Coronet* now carried a total of sixty-six persons, including twenty women and at least eleven children, in a space designed for thirty, and over half the number brought with them the stigma of the *Kingdom*.

"What now, God?" prayed Sandford in desperation. "What now, that we have this company on board?" The answer was "Continue."

Deck of the *Coronet*. Courtesy New England Society for the Preservation of Antiquities.

Below deck *Coronet*. Redrawn for publication by Spencer Lincoln based on a lines plan courtesy Smithsonian Institution and arrangement plan courtesy The Kingdom, as published in *Wooden Boat* (January/February, 1980).

Route of the *Coronet*, 1911.

23

Glad and Unafraid

1911

Four months later, on the third of August, 1911, the *Lewiston Daily Sun* carried a small page-one item, with an ominous headline.

CORONET IN DISTRESS
"Holy Ghosters" Yacht Reported
Off Cape Hatteras With
Sails Split and Torn

A week after that a second news item reported that two U.S. Coast Guard cutters, searching for the *Coronet* off the shores of Virginia, had found not "a trace of the vessel." On September 8 The *Sun* asked a question by then on many lips: "Where is the *Coronet?*"

Little by little the pieces of the story have gathered themselves into a record that can be called complete. The sources, multiple and sometimes at odds, include John Adamson's diary, the oral accounts of various sailors, extensive press coverage, and court testimony, particularly Sandford's own.

The story begins back on the African coast with the word "Continue." The word was an oddly serene one without the sharp force of other commands God had given, such as "Go!" or even "Give up." Only Frank Sandford heard the word, as was usually the case, but its interpretation belonged to the entire company on board, or so Sandford later alleged. No one doubted that God had spoken it, and no one asked if it had a basis in Scripture. For a long time that question had not been put to the words Sandford heard. The meaning was all that mattered, and it meant, everyone agreed, that the wreck of the *Kingdom* was not to change the business of the *Coronet*. A vote was taken—a vote, that is, premised on the meaning of the order already given. The vote was unanimously in the affirmative. No one voted to "Not continue" or "Go home." It was Shiloh's antinomian style tuned to its highest pitch.

Yet not quite all were in agreement. One voice, at least, had been raised in protest. Regardless of what "Continue" appeared to mean, it was unsafe to travel in an overloaded boat. George McKay, a Scottish sailor and navigator who had been acting as first mate on the *Kingdom* at the time of the accident, suggested that they go to the nearest American consul and ask for passage home for the *Kingdom* party. Even apart from the obvious danger and the discomfort of crowding (people were sleeping on deck and on the floor of the staterooms), the water tank on the *Coronet* held only 1,600 gallons, barely enough to supply thirty people for three or four weeks, and right now that tank was close to empty.

Furthermore, though everyone was polled, only the *Coronet* company had a vote. Sandford had written off the wreck of the *Kingdom* as the inevitable end to a ship "filled with humanity that had never gotten right in the first place." Everyone on the boat knew how he felt, that he begrudged hospitality to people who were less concerned with obeying God than they were with their physical comfort and who listened to their own thoughts ("silly spawn from men's brains—*thoughts*") rather than to what God had to say. It was widely understood that the *Kingdom's* crew and passengers were second-class citizens.

McKay's fuss was gratuitous anyway. If God wanted them to "continue," He would provide for such a simple need as water. The yacht moved south, the destination, says John Adamson's diary, Sierra Leone, another British possession four hundred miles away. Its capital, Freetown, the most important seaport in West Africa, promised not only a source of water, but a potential landing place for the *Kingdom* missionaries.

As it turned out, they did not get to Sierra Leone at all. Immediately becalmed for four days, out of reach of land, the entire group was rationed to three swallows of water a day by the time a British steamer heeded their signals. That ship stood patiently by for the transfer of five hundred gallons, a process that took three hours to complete and earned a salute from the *Coronet* cannon as a thank you.

Several days later they found refuge at last off the Republic of Guinea at the Isle de Los (also known as the Island of Idols), where they stayed for a week, rowing in for gallon after gallon of spring water to top off the tank, while the women washed clothes and went ashore to the town on various errands. Soon after their arrival French officials of the Republic boarded the yacht to offer help. "They were very pleasant," wrote John Adamson in his diary. But no help was needed. The officials were not informed about the circumstances. Nothing was said by anyone, not even McKay, about finding an American consul or seeking passage home another way, and no one made any effort to leave the ship. Sandford might have been glad if they had, but in this oddly perverse situation, leaving, even for the best of reasons, had become akin to deserting, a direct disregard of "Continue." The priority was to put up heroically with difficult and uncertain conditions. That, of course, was what Shiloh people had learned to do best and it posed a familiar and unquestionable alternative to getting out. On Helen's birthday everyone "togged out in white as much as possible in celebration," wrote John, and Mr. Sandford talked to them about getting "white oak" in their souls to stand the strain.

At the end of April, supposedly with everyone in accord, the African venture was abandoned. The yacht turned north and tacked back up the coast, intending to strike out across the Atlantic to Greenland.

Twenty-three days later, with the current consistently against them, a northern route was determined impractical. They had gone as far as the Cape Verde Islands. Without touching in to shore, by vote of the *Coronet* company, they turned southwest into the ocean, coasting with the trade winds. "Meetings to determine God's will," wrote John.

Crisis enough had been packed into that three weeks of tacking north. It began with the illness of Ole Man Day, who developed a high fever, complicated by the intense tropical heat. His grandson Guy took over his care, barring everyone from the room who might disturb the man with "a lot of noisy praying." Only Sandford, whom Day loved, was allowed to enter.

Shortly after the old gentleman's death, a crew member reported a disturbing dream. In it, one of their number wore a black sleeve band. Asked what it meant, he replied: "One has died and three more deaths will follow before the end of the voyage." Within days, the dreaded "African fever," a cholera-like menace picked up at the island, swept through the boat, striking at least forty among the now sixty-five on board. Sandford prayed for each and all recovered, some immediately, their fevers receding during the prayer.

Throughout this trauma, Sandford himself was increasingly bothered by an infected sore on his leg. He had fallen in some brush at the island, breaking the skin. Before the last case of fever had been conquered, he was nursing a bone sore deep and stubborn enough to raise the fear of amputation. Jean Dart dressed it again and again; still the ugly infection spread. "Had meeting all day," wrote John. "Prayed for Mr. Sandford's leg. Getting after things." Following another all-day meeting, Sandford appeared on deck, feeling much better. "He dressed up in silk," noted John. Someone took his picture standing by the wheel and binnacle. But in a few days the leg acted up again. As Sandford had great difficulty in getting about, the ship's carpenter made a pair of crutches. The next morning passengers and crew found the response strung in large cut-out letters across the saloon: LET US COMPROMISE. LET US WEAR CRUTCHES.

The warfare of prayer began anew, and this time, with Lester McKenzie's hands upon his head, Sandford felt a shot of "molten steel" down his spine and knew he was healed. There was no silk, but the sore soon disappeared completely.

After the decision to cross the Atlantic, John's diary lists long meetings, some all day or all night. They were "getting after things," ferreting out the cause of all that trouble. Charlie Jones remembered the period as a "month-long time of judgment." In groups of two or three they gathered in Mr. Sandford's quarters. After a period of confession each received a personal message of encouragement or instruction. Even directly afterwards, Jones could not remember what words followed his own interview, but he pondered with anxiety two other "messages" he overheard. To George McKay, Sandford said: "If you don't damn your soul by the time you reach the shores of America, you've only God to thank," and to John Bolster, "the confessions of a dying man." Bolster, like McKay, had belonged to the *Kingdom* crew. He and his wife had been two of the five missionaries in Alexandria, putting in years of stubborn, optimistic service. Charlie Jones had known him as a neighboring farmer in Aroostook County, a man with a "rugged constitution." There was no reason to think he was dying, and at the time Charlie was unaware of any dissension on the ship.

If John Adamson's notations are dependable, spirits were not low during this old-time Cleaning-out period on the Atlantic. Bible study continued. Dinner was served under the awning on deck. Hair cuts were given. The business of seamanship continued cheerfully, though the boat was leaking "very much" and food and water were again low. They were drinking what rain water could be caught in the sails. A partial fast—one meal a day for the next twenty-eight days—was instituted by vote, breakfast at 7:30 of cornmeal mush and bread, sometimes with fish soup, and the night crew offered a cup of steaming gruel at midnight. If there were vegetables or fruit now in any form, they were not eaten by the general populace. At the same time there was no shortage of work. "Much to do," wrote John. "Enough to make the head spin." It was extremely hot. The sun was beastly on deck. John was "feeling the heat in his head." One of his teeth was acting up again, a nagging pain.

June 7. Mended the main sail. Meeting lasted until 2:00 A.M.—good time, very tired, we don't get much sleep.

June 8. Cleaned up decks before 9:00 A.M. Mainsail carried away, took it in. Had an hour's rest. Mr. S. came on deck—had a good meeting . . . . Up till 2 A.M. next morning.

June 9. Got up at 5 A.M., had a busy day mending the squaresail, cleaning up the decks. . . . Had a few hard squalls during my watch. In one the squaresail was carried away. She tore in ribbons, seems so.

Three days later, nearing land, they washed down the decks (with salt water), "in case we enter port." The next day they sighted Trinidad.

June 13. Had a good look at the land—did not stop. Sailed along the coast of Venezuela. Beautiful scenery.

June 14. Had calm all day. . . . Sighted a little sloop. Hailed her. . . . Got some fruit from her.

June 15. Good breeze. Sighted Margarita, an island on the coast. . . . Saw a few towns, many trees. Sailed by it in the night. Had a fine meeting, read about Christ's crucifixion.

"Sailed on by . . . ," wrote thirsty and hungry John, without stating the obvious question. Why on earth were they not going in to ports of call to pick up water and supplies? Money was not a problem. Kingdom Yacht Club checks were backed by a bank in Boston. Charlie Jones, for one, did not know that Sandford was being sought by port authorities, and it was his belief later that only those closest to Sandford on the boat did know it. Everyone else attributed the reluctance to stop to the possibility of inspection. The wretched appearance of the yacht might invite curious questions. She needed paint by now, her sails were patched, her hull quite crusted. The crew, who could hardly keep out of sight, had obviously lost weight—and down in the hold were all those extra people. An inspection would surely mean a deterrance to "Continue."

On June 16 they "sailed away westward bound for Panama." John spoke of "good meetings" ("God anointed us all") and beautiful scenery. But the sea got very rough and soon they turned north for the West Indies. On June 21 they "hove to off an island called Aruba . . . after midnight. Ran in at daylight and sent two boats ashore for provisions."

Five days later fruit is mentioned again. It came from Haiti, where the Sandford family, Perry, Whittaker, and some of the women stepped ashore, to find themselves caught in the middle of a revolution. They were all arrested as gunrunners and locked up in the guardhouse. It took a day to straighten out the misunderstanding. Then loaded down with a wonderful assortment of bananas, pineapples, coconuts, mangoes, breadfruit, and yams, the yacht took off at sunset.

On the first of July, as they again headed toward Cuba, reviewing together the details of the Spanish-American War, John wrote, "Have been feeling very tired for a long time." After two more days he made no more entries in the diary for three weeks, until this summary.

> Sailed up the straits [passage between Cuba and Haiti] with a good wind and headed for an island ahead. Did not make it. Quite a heavy sea. Sighted Hogsters Island in the morning at daylight. Fine run all day. At noon sighted Aklins Island [in the Bahamas] and Castle Island and beat up to Aklins Island and dropped anchor. Got water there and had an outing ashore. Mr. McKay and Mr. Sellick have been taken very sick, one with fever, the other with sunstroke. Left there and sailed to Fortune Island and got some provisions there. From there we sailed northward toward San Salvadore [also in the Bahamas] but officials would not let us land, as we had sickness aboard.

Roland Whittom, now captain of the ship, had a different observation of that last affair. When they ran the yacht inside the three-mile limit to seek provisions at San Salvadore, it was boarded by customs officers who asked that they sign "the usual port papers." When Sandford refused, they sailed away without provisions.

But there *was* sickness aboard, though John did not mention the death of two-year-old Jabez Sellick, or the cloud of disfavor which hung over the Sellicks and George McKay. The issue was apparently the matter of going into port to release the extra passengers and get food. McKay had been in disfavor anyway since Africa, his prolonged illness in the after cabin termed a judgment. How openly Benjamin Sellick did his grumbling is not stated, but his illness, too, designated God's anger. He and his family, including their small children, were set to fasting for twenty-four hours. During the evening Jabez went into convulsions and was dead by morning.

More were in rebellion than McKay and Sellick. The exact order of events during these Caribbean days is fuzzy, but in Roland Whittom's memory the discontent was so serious that Sandford asked God in front of them all to "make the decks of the *Coronet* a slaughter-pen if the people disobey me." He was referring, Whittom thought, to "four men" he had "put out of the church for acts of disobedience." Besides McKay and Selleck, the third of these was George Huey, a sailor in his forties, who with his brother Charles had gone around the Horn as a member of the honored *Coronet* Thirty. Charles was not in rebellion. John Bolster was the fourth.

All this time the boat was leaking seriously. "Lots of pumping to do," wrote John, and lots of "mending sails and catching rainwater." They "hailed two different steamers for food and water." As they approached Chesapeake Bay, with provisions all but gone, he added,

July 26. Fixed up the launch with a cover [to catch rain water]. Got very wet while catching the water and did not get to change my clothes and took sick. Had very bad bowel trouble and some fever.

July 27. Felt some better. Able to work some. Had meeting all day, planning trip up North and praying about it. Felt quite mean at night . . . .

July 28. Set all sails and had to take them all in again. Foresail parted the leach rope. Mainsail tore badly. Baffling winds—set try-sails—made decks ready for Sabbath.

July 29 [Saturday]. Had a fine Sabbath. Sea very calm and not much pumping to do. Had a good rest. Had dinner on deck.

The Sabbath may have been fine, but the controversy had been refired. They stood one hundred miles east off Cape Henry on the Virginia coast, and Whittom, as captain, representing what he understood to be a "majority," once more requested a landing.

"How can we," Sandford responded, "with all these traitors on board?"

Approached yet again by the officers, he announced that God had ordered him not to put into port at any country for which they had already prayed, which meant the United States and Canada. "I intend to obey God and God alone, and I will sail the *Coronet* all the way to hell if God should so instruct."

There was more to John's diary entry for July 29.

> Had meeting after supper till 3 A.M. Talked of sending boats to Chesapeake Bay for provisions.

Since Sandford insisted adamantly that the *Coronet* remain far out to sea, the only way to pick up supplies without docking was to send smaller craft in to land. The threat of arrest was surely common knowledge by now on the boat, as the intricacies of avoiding it were discussed at length. Though three miles off shore put them beyond the jurisdiction of port authorities, Sandford worried about the possibility of meeting Coast Guard cutters, which might be under orders to stop him. The motor launch was the obvious choice for a long jaunt to land, except that the gasoline had been used up in setting fire to the *Kingdom*.

Finally a plan emerged. Four men would take the launch ashore with oars and a rigged-up sail. One of them, Austin Perry, was to somehow acquire another boat, if possible in the Norfolk area, which would later meet the *Coronet* at the Nantucket lightship off Massachusetts, remove the extra people, and take them home. The other three men—Lester McKenzie, Roland Whittom, and Bertram Dustin—were to purchase fuel and provisions, and come back as quickly as possible under motor power. Meanwhile the *Coronet* would move toward shore along latitude 37° between Cape Henry and Cape Charles. After the return of the launch, the yacht then would sail on north, meeting Perry and the new boat off the Nantucket Lightship on the Massachusetts coast in mid-August. Greenland was still the ultimate destination for the *Coronet.*

The arrangement was sticky with problems, the most obvious the intricacy of finding each other again, since it would be almost impossible for the yacht to hold her position in the currents. If they simply obeyed, Sandford insisted, God would guide them. After all they had been through together, He would not forsake them now.

So at two o'clock that morning, July 30, the four men quietly transferred to the launch for the long pull to shore. Charlie Jones, on watch, peered with envy over the side as they disappeared into the darkness.

"Would I like to be on that boat," he whispered to George McKay.

"Never mind," answered McKay. "You'll likely get all the rowing you want before we're through."

The launch, an open boat, about twenty feet long, represented a still rare sight at sea—a small boat run by a motor. The motor was very likely an encased two-cycle "one-lunger," with about two-and-a-half horse power and a top speed of no more than five miles an hour.

What distance the men rowed is in dispute. Twenty miles in the troughs of the ocean would be extremely arduous, but with four at the oars and a sail, their speed probably exceeded what the motor could have provided. However long it was, it gave Roland Whittom time to think. The further he removed himself from Sandford's presence, the more he found his frame of mind altering. He had been baffled by the fact that again and again when the officers talked alone they had vowed to "demand" of Sandford that "food be secured," but whenever they encountered him face to face they found themselves in "complete submission." It was not until Roland had left the yacht that he began to see "in an entirely different light," and then, he said, he "could not understand how we could have allowed the man to dominate us so."

The launch made land without trouble, and Perry, finding no suitable and affordable ship in Norfolk, boarded a train to New York City. Whittom, McKenzie, and Dustin nursed the motor back to life, piled on as many supplies as the boat would take, and chugged back into the bay along latitude 37°.

For the next two weeks the three separated groups worked desperately hard to rejoin each other. The *Coronet*, beginning in the very hour the four men left the ship and for the next eight days struggled to adjust and readjust her position against the current, which moved her as much as fourteen miles a day. The weather was fair. Day and night the crew maintained a lookout in the crosstrees, showing a light at half-hour intervals. John Davis, to his chagrin and horror, fell asleep in this perch one night, one hundred feet from the deck, rocked to sleep by the motion of the boat. His relief found him astride the crosspiece without a safety rope.

On August 3, as they were eating breakfast under the awning, a passenger ship, the *Alamo*, came around the *Coronet's* stern and politely offered to radio her position to shore. The *Coronet* answered, "No thank you." It was the very kind of help that was not wanted. The next day the *Coronet* moved up north along the coast, and twenty-four hours later sailed down to the lightship Cape Charles, where the long boat went in for supplies, but they saw no sign of the launch anywhere. "Felt the pressure very much," said John. "Had feelings of wanting to be at home. Provisions low."

So when the news story of the lost *Coronet* broke at Durham early in August, the yacht was still in Chesapeake Bay.

Soon after that notice appeared, the hilltop, previously unaware of anything except that the *Coronet* had arrived safely in the Caribbean early in July, was astonished to see Captain Perry at a hastily called meeting in the chapel. At New York City Perry had accomplished one of his feats of negotiation by purchasing the *Alsatia,* an iron "hermaphrodite brig," that is, a two-masted vessel with both square sails and schooner sails. About to be sold for scrap, the ship was nevertheless sound and equipped with a good steam engine. Perry paid $2,000 for her, renamed her the *Barracouta,* and hurried to Shiloh to collect a crew. Now it was Perry's turn to be surprised, for Whittom, McKenzie, and Dustin telephoned from Elim in Boston.

Failing to connect with the *Coronet* at the Cape Henry point of rendezvous, those three had toured back and forth several miles in each direction, searching for the yacht as they thought through their alternatives. They had exactly one dollar left after the purchase of supplies. There was a limited amount of gasoline for the engine. If they were spotted by another ship they would surely draw unwanted attention, so far out to sea in an open boat. If they returned to Norfolk, there too they might be required to explain their actions. Above all, they had been instructed, they must not get themselves into a position which made it necessary to divulge the whereabouts or condition of the *Coronet.* Spying two Coast Guard cutters, the three men chose not to return to the yacht *or* to shore. Certain by now that the yacht had given them up and gone on north to meet Perry off Nantucket, they dug out for Boston themselves, four hundred miles in the motor launch, leaving the *Coronet* behind.

In a week they had joined Perry on the *Barracouta* and were speeding toward Nantucket Lightship, where they cruised the area, watching for the sails of the *Coronet.* They had personal reasons to be worried, as well as Kingdom concerns. On the yacht were the wives of Perry and McKenzie, Dustin's wife and children, and Roland Whittom's brother

Harry and sister Ella (Lester McKenzie's wife). When the agreed-upon time for meeting, August 15, had long past, they took to the sea, heading north to Nova Scotia to continue the search. At Halifax, Roland Whittom left the *Barracouta* and the Shiloh movement for good.

Back in the Chesapeake the *Coronet* party, with diminishing supplies, waited for the launch until August 7 before they voted to head north to Nantucket Lightship.

That day, during his watch, John Adamson "pumped 2700"—gallons, that is—of unwanted water from the hold. Someone was pumping all the time now. They caught and ate dolphin, cleaned the decks, and polished the brass—and pumped. Mrs. Perry and others became ill with fevers and recovered. Mr. Cook, the English taxidermist, died of "natural causes" and was buried at sea. "Food rather short," said John. "Feel quite hungry some of the time." They saw bananas floating by in the water. Did they pull any aboard? If so, John made no note of it. He admitted to feeling "very weak. Had to go aloft on the squaresail— didn't have much strength. Praise the Lord. Had the Lord's Supper about 10 P.M." So they proceeded, frequently in sight of land and other vessels, fishing along the way, and still praying for various countries. Roland Whittom's brother Harry had taken over as sailing master. Everett Knight was still first mate and John Adamson second mate.

On August 16 they realized they had accidentally run by the Nantucket lightship and turned south again, without making much progress. Two days later, giving up on the arranged meeting, they ran east by north, past Portland. They had done their best to both acquire supplies and discharge the extra passengers—short of putting into port, that is. For some reason God had not allowed them to follow through successfully with their plans. There remained one course: continue on to Greenland.

As they had learned the year before, winter sets in early in the Bay of Fundy. They had not traveled far before the weather turned foggy and unpleasant. On August 23 John made one of his more extensive entries.

> Sailed all night, hove to for fishing in the morning—caught fish for breakfast. Had our breakfast served in five courses by Mr. S. Trawl was set—caught 13 large fish after 10 A.M. Had a meeting in the After Cabin at 3 P.M.; was set apart for the officers only and had a special dinner served for us of seven courses—fish chowder, baked fish, broiled fish, pickles, fried liver, coconut, limejuice, cup of cocoa

and popcorn and orange-flavored jelly. I moved to the After Cabin. Have been feeling sick for three days. Constipated.

Two days later Sandford gave a talk on "being 'Perfect.' " Off Sable Island, Nova Scotia, hot drinks and pop corn were distributed to the men as they worked. Meetings continued as usual. The big pump went "out of commission" for a scary hour until it was fixed. The smaller one was nowhere near adequate to keep the ship from filling.

At 7:00 on Monday, August 28, they spotted a fisherman and rode over in the longboat to buy provisions. "Very kind," said John. They were successful in catching fish themselves, but on Tuesday, hove to all night and part of the day because of heavy fog, they lost their fishing trawl, essential for any large catch. On Wednesday, as it "blew fresh," they came upon a fleet of French fishing vessels. At the yacht's signal, one came around. As Harry Whittom made arrangements to row over to meet it in the longboat, John Bolster asked to be taken along and put aboard the fishing craft. Bolster's wife Alma, one of the women below on the *Coronet,* was not in accord with her husband's wishes. Whatever took place between them and however the decision was finally made, John did not go. Charlie Jones did, though not to defect. Charlie was getting his rowing in at last. Through waves so high they tipped the longboat at an almost perpendicular angle, they managed to come alongside the other ship, crank out enough French to make themselves understood, and return to the yacht with a purchase of three barrels of hard biscuit. They were met with cheers. There had been no bread on board for days. By now everyone had lost weight very noticeably, but for some reason the Huey brothers, both muscular, thick-necked sailors, were particularly thin.

McKay also asked to be transferred to one of the French ships. While they were in the midst of the fleet, he wrote a note to Sandford making that request and received the answer that he was "a shipwrecked sailor" and as such had "no rights." McKay was far from an asset at this point and Sandford faced an unsolvable dilemma. More than ever before he did not want to go to Greenland with the rebellious on board. It was the kind of mixture he had always hated and mistrusted. But McKay and the others in rebellion were sore and hostile, too dangerous to release.

On the second of September they sighted Cape Pine and Cape Race, Newfoundland, and passed on by. The reason was never given. They "expected to secure an abundant supply of vegetables and fruit in Newfoundland," Sandford explained later, and "were disappointed." Yet there was no attempt to land. That night a heavy fog set in and lifted just in time to avoid running aground. Sailing north up the coast they tried for fish and caught none. On Monday, September 4, they sailed northeast. They were very near the Grand Banks, on the eastern side of the island. This was the longer way to Greenland, not the more commonly used route through the Strait of Belle Isle. The top masts were taken down with an eye to freezing winds. "Very cold working aloft," said John Adamson. "Got chilled through. Pumping keeps us fairly warm." They were sailing away from land now, out into the open wintry sea. They had missed the Grand Banks. On Wednesday the sixth John noted that exactly a year ago they had left the Gulf of St. Lawrence for the south. It was, in fact, the anniversary of the words, "Give up."

"Cold and disagreeable," wrote John on this day. "Still we must be glad and unafraid."

The words, notably expressive for a most matter-of-fact writer, leap off the page of the diary. Where did they come from? The ship's log for that day: "Glad and unafraid say the people." Whoever had originally spoken the words, they represented the prevailing intention on board to Harry Whittom, who was keeping the log. "At 6:00 P.M. we turn southward from 49 degrees 15' N., away from the Far North."

Harry himself was appalled at the decision. They had turned completely around and were heading south, approaching the Grand Banks from the north. As Sandford remembered it, Harry said to him as the decision was made, "I shiver at the thought of turning south. What have we got to live for if we don't obey God? If God . . . does not settle the accounts of some of those men and run them down to the finish, I am mistaken."

They had come within six hundred miles of Greenland, where, in Sandford's explanation, they "planned to spend the winter." Already their prayers for the north had seemed to "annihilate space," he said. It was the "Mount Everest of our movement." Yet he (and Harry and the unspecified number who wanted to go on north) "readily joined in the unanimous decision to put back to Portland."

It was not quite that uncomplicated, in actuality. Charles Jones, who had not been listening for subterranean disturbances, who had been "just following with the herd" without a great deal of thought, suddenly understood that a "quiet mutiny" had occurred.

24

Guilty as Charged

1911

No one intended to tie up the prophet and take over the ship.
That was not what "mutiny" meant. Physical violence was out
of the question. Not even the angriest rebel would have entertained it,
and particularly not toward Frank Sandford. No brawl broke out. No
weapons appeared, not even so much as a fist in the face or a finger
jabbed against somebody's chest. The violence that actually occurred on
the boat in the days that followed took on far more menacing dimensions.

There are varying views of exactly what happened. George McKay's
was simple. He wrote Mr. Sandford another note, he explained at the
trial, a note stating that he was against going on towards Greenland
in a leaking vessel with a "rotten suit of sails and no provisions." He
got no answer, but the next day Sandford told the people that God had
directed him to turn south.

Sandford's version of it was that they were "turned back . . . when
Satan used two puny men in an attempt to balk the Almighty." McKay
and Bolster both presented him with what amounted to an ultimatum.
However that ultimatum was worded, Sandford prayed for three days,
until his "duty read very plain" to him. There was a vote, and he
"readily joined in" the unanimous decision to turn the ship back toward
America, though it was against his will.

Mutiny, then, was by vote. But even that would have offered little
hope of success in itself, since the majority of people would have voted
with Sandford either way, even if it meant sure death. Some of those
were relieved to be able to join him in the decision to turn, regardless
of his motive; some believed as deeply as Sandford that it was an act

of disobedience to God that they could not avoid. Sandford himself swung the vote, and he knew that he did. He had prayed for three days, he said, "before *I* [emphasis added] turned the ship back."

As soon as they turned about, the word "Distress" was "very strongly impressed" on his mind. Gathering the crew, Sandford read to them from the Gospel of Luke: "And there shall be signs in the sun and moon and stars, and upon the earth *distress* of nations." The time of "the world's great ordeal had come," he told them, that as "judgment began at the house of God," the yacht was probably destined for "great suffering," and that "then the distress would go forth to every nation." To the old guard on board, those words must have had a familiar ring.

Nothing was added to John's diary for two days. Then he made two more entries.

September 9. Had a good day off. Have been very weak and played out. . . . All the crew are nothing extra. Sailing most of the time under storm trisail.

September 10. Fine day, sunny and bright. Quite cool. Had fine meeting today. Set the mainsail. Getting near the Grand Banks.

That was his last entry. They missed the Grand Banks, where they had hoped again to fish. They had been on short rations forty days, and the diary had not mentioned fresh produce since Haiti, at the end of June. The reference on August 23 to bottled lime juice, the standby of seagoing people for so many years, was the only one in the diary.

Yet, Sandford claimed later at the trial, "there were ample provisions on board for the return journey" to Portland, which was expected not to take more than ten days. George McKay reported a conversation with Sandford soon after they turned south, in which Sandford told him that they "had everything in common on the ship" and the Sandfords were suffering from lack of food "like everyone else." At this point, according to McKay, the Sandford family had begun to eat separately, in their rooms. There were odds and ends of food supplies in the ship's pantry, McKay said. He had watched the steward take inventory, but he saw no canned goods. The mystery of how food was distributed on the boat for the next month was never clarified, though no one would have begrudged the children aboard whatever they needed to maintain health. If there were extra supplies in the staterooms which the sailors never saw—jams, dried fruit, nuts (and maybe some more of that lime juice, or the communion grape juice)—there wasn't a man on the ship who wouldn't have expected it to go to the children. Roland Whittom gave Sandford credit for "never letting the children suffer," though he also claimed that Sandford himself "never went hungry" in the time he (Whittom) was on the ship.

Concern about hunger soon took second place to a far more terrifying reality. They were making no headway. They had *turned* back, but they were not *going* back. The winds were devilishly variable. They wanted to go west, toward the coast of America. With every calm they were at the mercy of the currents. First, the strong Labrador current, moving south between Greenland and Canada, carried them to a point just below Newfoundland where it joined the North Atlantic drift of the Gulf Stream. This, when no wind in the sails resisted, carried them east toward the ocean. For almost a month they sailed southwest no more than fifteen or sixteen miles a day, and were still east of the Grand Banks at the end of the month. In Sandford's words, they found themselves "in the grip of a power superior to ourselves and we were appalled at our situation."

On September 28, George Hughey died in his bunk. His brother Charles was also feeling ill, as was Ralph Merrill, one of the faithful. John Adamson was barely getting about. They all attributed this to hunger and weariness. (On September 24 the ship's log had read, "No sickness.") Earlier in the month, said McKay in testimony, George Hughey had gone to Sandford to ask him for prayer, as he was feeling uncommonly weak. Sandford, said McKay, reminded Hughey that he had "withstood him" earlier in the voyage (at Chesapeake) and that he should expect God to deal with him "severely. " But how then to explain the malaise of the faithful ones?

They buried Hughey at sea that night. The next day, to everyone's great joy, an enormous steamer appeared through the fog on the eastern horizon. Quickly the crew ran flags to the top of a mast, the "starving signals." The steamer hove to and promptly offered help. "We were almost in tears," John Davis recalled, "as we saw the food arriving in the steamer's lifeboat." On the decks of the liner, hundreds of passengers watched the precarious transfer of goods to the *Coronet,* which must have look very tiny and bedraggled below them. The offerings, as it turned out, were two quarters of beef, several hams, some salt pork, milk, butter, cheese, and flour—no fresh fruit, no potatoes. One sympathetic passenger, standing at the rails of the steamer, sent two boxes of cigars, which at least provoked a good laugh.

Gathering everyone together afterwards for a prayer of thanks, Sandford explained that he had asked God that morning what was to become of his own personal family. God had told him they would be cared for, they would not perish. It was for this reason, he said, that the steamer had stopped. "You may be thankful my family is here. If they had not been, you may all have starved to death."

Reports conflict about what happened to that food. McKay claimed he never saw any of the beef and finally went to Sandford's room and asked for a slice of the ham, which he ate uncooked. It perhaps was never served from the kitchen, and very possibly Sandford had taken control of it, as one sailor later insisted, in order to distribute it equitably. It must have been available, because some of the men, adhering to Shiloh's policy of abstaining from pork, refused to touch it, in spite of their hunger. Others did and were ill. John Davis, who below decks was not able to keep the pork on his stomach, was able to retain it by chewing tiny amounts at a time while on deck in the fresh air.

The steamer which came to their aid (an ocean liner like the one Shiloh had so often prayed for) was the *Lapland,* of the Red Star Line, on her way to New York from Antwerp and Dover. She stopped to give help on September 29. On October 3 both Lewiston papers picked up a report from New York which was both encouraging and disturbing in its details. It explained that the steamer had spotted the yacht, jury-rigged, "her signals fluttering," 225 miles east of Sable Island, but the "steamer's officers were unable to learn the circumstances which caused the *Coronet's* predicament." The yacht had on board, said the report, twenty-three persons, eight of them women and two children.

The count was way off, but Shiloh had no way of knowing that. More, by the time the *Sun* had reprinted that news item, six days had gone by since the *Lapland* had given assistance, more than enough time for the *Coronet* to reach Portland by ordinary expectations. It helped not at all that throughout the next two weeks story after story of disasters in the North Atlantic filled the papers, one barkentine sinking with all hands lost just off the Bay of Fundy. With no wireless aboard, the *Coronet* could not even give an S.O.S.

Shiloh's fears were on target. The very next day after stopping the *Lapland,* the yacht was swept out to sea in a gale. That night Austin Perry, on the *Barracouta* in Halifax Harbor, listened to the wind and said, "If the *Coronet* is out in this storm, she can never live through it." She did, only to be hit by another gale and then another, each many hours in duration, each blowing her away from her destination.

In the course of this, the main storm trysail, essential to any progress, was blown to shreds and the lifeboat broken up by waves. They had never been so helpless. The routine manning of the boat that had been so unremitting in the tropics now seemed a warm memory of child's play; even the Horn looked easy in retrospect. Sails, heavy enough when water-soaked, were coated with ice as the men handled them to the slippery deck to be patched, only to blow away again as soon as they were hoisted. It was one long terrible dream, Charles Jones remembers, forty-one days in which they lived and slept in wet cold clothes, falling into their bunks only to be awakened in what seemed but minutes to take the next watch, crawling up the ladder to the deck. Through it all the wind never quit—snarling, whistling, screaming—a hell of unrelenting sound, and under it the rhythmic clankety-whoosh of the pump.

Amazingly, no one was lost overboard. Charlie Jones was lifted off his feet by a wave as it smashed across the ship, washed beyond the rail and then back again, to be dumped in a heap along the scuppers. Hardly realizing what had happened, he picked himself up and returned to the pump, completing his watch.

Above all, it was the pumping that eroded their spirits, two men at a time on either end of the handle, up and down, up and down, for as much as four hours at a stretch, the hull filling as fast as the water could be brought up to the deck, spurting through the top of the pump and flooding over their legs and feet.

Protective clothing was in short supply—oilskins, gloves, scarves. John Davis's only footwear was a pair of galoshes. "We wore anything at all that we could get on, layers, anything we could find," remembered Jones. "It didn't matter what. We were benumbed." Below, only the galley stove provided warmth. Trunks floated in ankle-deep water in the staterooms. Water poured through the hatchways as the men passed back and forth to the deck, while the women walked about with wet feet, their skirts tucked up, hardly able to move anyway, more crowded than ever now that the weather forbade visiting the deck. Serving meals, at least, presented no problem. Food had been reduced to two sea biscuits a day and rain water. When the crew changed hands, the men were called to Sandford's stateroom for a hot drink and an eggcupful of popcorn.

At first there had been twenty-five persons among the crew and officers to man the four-hour watches. Now, in the midst of that interminable chaos, a strange, unspoken consciousness was spreading among them. "I was in a daze," recalled Charles Jones, "but I observed certain things. I began to notice a pattern of deterioration. How they climbed the ladder to the deck. That was the first sign. How fast they could go. How much strength." Soon those whose knees wobbled on the ladders were the ones who quickly lost their endurance at the pumps and who fainted as they worked. Next they were in bed, unable to move.

Something else was taking place, harder to name. "Some didn't care whether they lived or not. Some of these boys would rather die than endure the process of operating the ship." For Jones, looking back, in this acid test of character the lines fell in a division that was unexplainable. Men who were unquestionably sick continued to work, staggering about the deck, refusing to give up. Others, hungry and weary, but not ill, remained in their bunks, or on deck gave only half their weight in labor. They actually hid away in the lazaret when they were called to watches and then emerged for their food, whatever there was. They seemed to have lost all shame. The demarcation, as Jones saw it, had nothing perceptible to do with loyalty to Sandford or to God.

The hardest work began to fall to a reduced number, day after day. Now others not part of the crew began to take turns at the pump— Sandford himself ("pulling a longer stroke than anyone else," someone observed), William Hastings (the children's teacher), the cook, and one or two of the women. But above all, in Jones's recollection, it was Harry Whittom who kept them afloat. "He kept us in touch with where we were. He understood the wind and the boat." You might not even know who was beside you at the pump, but Harry was always a vital presence, smiling a gap-toothed smile, for he too had begun to lose teeth. If it was true that Harry believed God might run the rebellious "down to the finish," he was still doing his best to get everyone home first.

By mid-October six men were too ill to leave their beds. Three had been taken to the after cabin where Jean Dart and a nurse tried to ease their suffering. Prayer had no power. Ralph Merrill was covered with running sores. On October 16 Merrill and the first mate, Charles Hughey, died within hours of each other. Charles, an "atoning lamb," and "every inch a hero" in Sandford's eyes, said with his dying breath that he "would rather go down on the *Coronet* than sail the sea on any other vessel."

Somehow they held funeral services, singing into the fury of the wind as the men's bodies were lowered over the side: "Not now, but in the coming years/ Some day we'll understand." Way back on the African coast, before the *Kingdom* met her unhappy end, the two boats had come across the hulk of a French man-o-war rotting on a sand bar. For several days, in heavy breakers, the Shiloh crews had rowed to the wreck and stripped her of marine hardware—turn-buckles, winches, davits, copper, brass, and lead. They had been stored in a corner of the *Coronet* for future use. Now they were used as ballast to weight the canvas shrouds as the bodies were dropped into the sea.

Stuart Wolfe, John Adamson, and John Bolster ("the confessions of a dying man") lay in their cots in the forecastle, unable to rise. Two others, Floyd Clark and Ralph Paine, were too sick to work. McKay was weak and dizzy, depleted by diarrhea and muscular pain. Others had sore gums and loosened teeth. Charlie Jones began to feel that same emptiness in the knees that he had observed first in those who were now dead. John Davis, with an ulcer on his leg, dragged himself to the deck, where he kept up his spirits by chewing the tiny kernel ends off popcorn cobs he had pulled from the garbage. In the forecastle the worst of circumstances prevailed. The ten canvas cots, less than three feet wide, were shared by twenty sailors, taking turns. The toilet had ceased to function. With the sea beating its way across the deck, the hatches were screwed down tight and the stench was wretched.

One day, Jean Dart, studying her medical books, suggested hesitantly to Sandford that the men might be suffering not just from hunger, as originally thought, but scurvy. For centuries now the symptoms of scurvy had been common knowledge among sea-going people. Even its capricious nature was familiar lore, the way it attacked the spirit first, making the best of sailors indolent. Vitamin C had not yet been identified, but fruits and vegetables and bottled juices had been recognized as the key to prevention since the 16th century. Yet not even the seasoned sailors or the older women, no one who had listened to old captain's stories or who had grown up with the sea wisdom of Maine and the Maritimes, had guessed what was happening on the boat. Dart's observation came too late.

Two days later John Davis, about to climb the ladder for his watch, stopped to take a long look at his friend Stuart Wolfe in his bunk. For days Stuart had lain muttering, "Feeding on Jesus, feeding on Jesus." Now he was silent. Though Stuart had lost many pounds, it took six men, in their weakened condition, to lift his body, wrapped in his blankets, up the ladder to the deck for his burial. He died within a hundred miles of shore.

By now skylights had broken and water frequently cascaded into the saloon. Every sail but two was gone or useless. One more storm would finish them, they knew. In that derelict condition, paintless, encrusted with barnacles, dragging seaweed, her rigging shredded, ragged storm tri-sails fluttering limply from her mast, the yacht reached Portland at 8:30 A.M. on the twenty-first of October and anchored alongside House Island, the medical inspection station. Pulling into harbor, Charlie Jones heard Sandford say: "I feel like I am going into the mouth of the lion." Their forty-five-day return had encompassed his forty-ninth birthday and the annual Feast of Tabernacles, neither of which had been celebrated.

After a glance aboard, port officials ordered that a flag be raised to the top of a mast, and it was done—Shiloh, the waver of flags, hoisting not the lamb or the lion, nor anything resembling the flags of victory on the hilltop, but the square yellow flag of quarantine, the Q of the International Code. Inspectors, openly appalled at what they discovered on board, called the senior medical officer, who told the already hovering reporters that these were the worst cases of scurvy he had ever seen.

By late afternoon, haggard and limping, Sandford was arrested and taken to the Portland city jail by a sheriff who boarded the boat with Mrs. Whittaker's warrant in hand. At 11:00 that night, attorney Coolidge, Merwyn Wakeman, and another Lisbon Falls man, Samuel Sylvester, a self-proclaimed atheist who admired Sandford's character ("He likes my heart, but is not so sure about my head," Frank once joked) posted bonds of $5,000, witnessed by Holman Day, who had heard the news in Lewiston and rushed to the courthouse to be of aid. Sandford then caught a train to Durham and secluded himself at Hephzibah.

Earlier in the day, Shiloh men, having been phoned, had hurried to Portland to remove the passengers and tow the ship back to South Freeport. Some of the ill, still on board, were carried to Bethesda, hardly recognizable for weight loss: Floyd Clark, Guy Campbell, Ralph Paine, Herman Dunning, Everett Knight, Herbert Jenkins. The women and children, though in better condition than the crew, were thin and drawn.

John Adamson was considered too sick to be moved. He was nursed in the forecastle by his father. His mother, arriving to see John with a basket of fruit, was met on the deck by her estranged husband, who refused to allow her to go below. Distraught, Helga Adamson was rowed back to shore, where she arranged to have John, not yet twenty-one, removed from the boat. The final entry in John's diary was written by his father. "October 28, Saturday. Was taken from *Coronet* by Mrs. Mary Burnham [Children's Protective Society] and removed to the Marine Hospital against his will. John died at the hospital 6:00 A.M. November 1, 1911. God gave me St. John 12:24." Mr. Adamson then gave the diary to Charlie Jones.

John Bolster also died at the Marine Hospital in Portland two days later. His weight had dropped from 165 pounds to 84. Alma, his wife, who had grieved on the yacht as she watched her husband's physical deterioration and his growing hostility to Sandford, claimed he was restored to faith before he died.

Round-the-clock attendants were assigned to the scurvy patients at Bethesda, drawing the men back from death as they had approached it, inch by inch. Stuart Wolfe's father, who had lost his only child but believed firmly he had given his life to Christ's service, volunteered to nurse Guy Campbell. John Davis, in better condition than others, was sent to his own home at one of the Durham farms. His mother was boiling timothy to treat a sick calf as John walked into the kitchen. "That smells good," he said. "Would you like some?" his mother asked. So hay was his first food off the boats.

In a matter of a few days Sandford was arrested again by U.S. Deputy Marshall Fred Stevens on a warrant charging him with "the death of Charles Hughey, and related counts." Not George Huey, who had become a rebel and was the first to die, but Charles, who had stayed loyal to the minute of his death. Brought again to Portland, to the federal courthouse, Sandford was read a sixty-page indictment containing six counts for the death of six of his crew. He had "unlawfully, knowingly, and willingly" allowed a ship to "proceed on a voyage at sea without sufficient provisions" though opportunity was available, read the indictment. He pleaded not guilty.

As it was too late this time to arrange bail, Sandford spent the night in a cold jail, where for hours he rested under his overcoat, then arose and read in Genesis about the arrest of Joseph, the first prisoner in Scripture. As he prayed throughout the night, the ugly room with its foul air was "filled with the glory of God," transformed into a "palace," and he recalled a hymn he had heard his mother sing back home in the kitchen of the old farm: "And prisons would palaces prove/ If Jesus would dwell with me there."

After a preliminary hearing, in which Sandford declared he would employ no legal defense (Olive Mills had heard the words, "Retain no counsel") and refused the right to examine or challenge the jury, trial was set for early December, to be heard before Judge Clarence Hale at the Federal Courthouse in Portland. Meanwhile the Maine and Boston newspapers climaxed their fifteen-year Shiloh epic with every conceivable story they could scrape together, quoting each other in a long series of projections and speculations. Roland Whittom, George McKay, Ralph

Paine, all gave lengthy interviews to reporters before the trial began, saying much of what they would repeat in court. Whittom, says Frank Murray in his account, "unfolded a skillful tale of halftruth calculated to damn Mr. Sandford as a trickster and a tyrant." Sandford told the story from his own point-of-view to the Associated Press.

The trial lasted two days. The court notes have disappeared from the federal files, so we are dependent on the newspapers and the memory of those who attended. No one doubted that this time the prosecution would win, hands down. With six dead as evidence of negligence, it seemed a much more clear-cut case than that of 1904. U.S. Attorney Arthur Chapman, in his opening address, traced the journey from the Caribbean to Newfoundland on a map, showing that there had been many opportunities for the yacht to enter ports for supplies. Among the handful of witnesses he called were Charles Holland, Roland Whittom, Jean Dart, and George McKay. None was cross-examined.

Spectators who had been disappointed at the last trial when Sandford refused to speak in his own behalf were gratified beyond the stretch of their curiosity when he finally took the stand and spoke for over an hour. He began by explaining that his "whole motive in speaking" was "simply to give each official the light he ought to have in deciding this case." He believed, he said, "as much as I believe my name, that two courts are in session today . . . High heaven is watching this scene at this very moment, watching to see if justice is administered, watching to see if each man in his own heart is without prejudice in judging this case."

He reviewed the entire voyage in detail, emphasizing that from the very beginning everyone knew that the *Coronet*'s destination was Greenland, and that after the wreck of the *Kingdom* all on board had participated in determining God's meaning in the word "Continue." Under no other circumstances would he act, and for this reason they had hugged the coast of Africa before moving on. No one was coerced to remain on the ship, he said; at no point was anyone deterred from leaving.

He acknowledged that his attorneys had strongly advised him not to divulge to the jury that God's word "Continue" was actually the basis for the decision at stake before the court—that such an admission would set him up for "certain conviction." But he was bound to tell the truth. "I make this statement advisedly," he said, "knowing what I am doing. I received this answer: 'Continue.' " The jury must deal with that fact any way they honestly could, he added, but they must remember, as they did so, that they were dealing with God.

In the same spirit, he explained, the reason they had not put into an American or Canadian port was because "God told us not to. We were not to go back to the countries we had already visited." They would have made it safely to Greenland had it not been for "two willful men," who typified in their disobedience to God the attitude prevalent among the *Kingdom's* passengers—"a spirit of gratification of animal pleasure . . . while on the *Coronet* it was the white light of eternity." When the *Coronet* entered Portland harbor on October 21, "it was the first time she had ever come into a port with dishonor." She had been sent to Greenland and she had not "obeyed."

The starvation and pestilence on the board the ship was easily explained, he went on, by the twenty-sixth chapter of Leviticus. Opening his Bible there in the courtroom, he read the words of God to the Hebrews: "And if ye will . . . walk contrary unto me; then will I also walk contrary unto you, and will punish you seven times for your sins."

His audience listened in silence to a speech unlike anything heard before in the room. "At times his voice was low," said the reporter. Then "he thundered forth his statements, slapping the railing of the witness stand with his hand, and talking with a rapidity that was hard to follow. At other times his voice broke and he all but sobbed."

Finally, assuring the jury that he was willing to accept whatever verdict the court of man might give him, he offered a blessing to all those who had attacked him over the years and asked to be remembered as a man who was true to his convictions. He thanked the court for listening, and turning to the jury, said, "Gentlemen, there will be no squealing from me. I am here for the rough and ready of the football game," and sat down.

What had he said? He had admitted responsibility. In his estimation he had broken a particular federal law in failing to provision a ship at sea, with death resulting. He had done so, in his own interpretation, in order to obey the higher law of God. *He* had done it, he was saying, even though he claimed that every decision had been made by vote and God had directed every move except the final fatal decision to turn back. He had broken the law of the land. He had done it because God had led him to do so, and he (Frank Sandford) would accept the repercussions. But he was not guilty of the charges—that he had "willfully" refused to provision a ship.

"It is necessary to come back from the vagaries of religious fanaticism to the cold facts that must govern this court," said District Attorney Robert Whitehouse, at the close of Sandford's speech. Yet surely Whitehouse understood that all of the cold facts in the case could not be covered by a court of law.

Others were sensitive to this, too. Shortly after Sandford's arrest, the *Lewiston Daily Sun* had printed a terse editorial: "A devil of a Lord that led Sandford that gait! And a pitiful abdication of intellect that surrenders to such a fellow as Sandford one's property, one's liberty, ambition!"

If Wendell White's brother-in-law, George "Will" Wood, editor of the *Sun,* was the author of those words, as he well may have been, he wrote them not only with his own kin in mind, but Roland Whittom, too, and Harry Whittom and Austin Perry and Everett Knight—all sailing masters in charge of the ship, who did what Sandford did not do, steered the boat and manned the sails, with the possibility of entering port after port literally within their hands. They were guilty too—as were all who participated in the lie, from Africa to the North Atlantic, by their acquiescent voting, by concealing the facts from authorities and other ships within their reach, by not leaving the ship and asking for help in the half-dozen instances in which they were able to do so in the Caribbean. Roland Whittom, though the long row into Newport separated him from Sandford's "strange power" long enough to clear his thinking, nevertheless did not go to authorities and report the location of the yacht. Power lay in the hands of many. None were prisoners, none tied up in the brig. In the same respect no adult was ever held prisoner on Shiloh hilltop, and as for those who *were* "imprisoned" by age or health or miles of water, Frank Sandford alone did not decide their fate, any more than he alone had decided Leander Bartlett's fate nine years earlier.

Though once again only Sandford was on trial, his followers were also guilty, as they had been in the manslaughter trial of 1904. Yet they had *not* broken a law in the matter that really counted to them— not even the common law as it rested on the books—by giving a man their allegiance, nor had he by receiving it, for there was no statute to cover that. George Wood, an attorney as well as an editor, knew that here was an island where the law of the land could not specifically apply. A "pitiful abdication" perhaps, but executed by free agents within a free society.

Still, since as free agents, as adults, they had made the choice of that abdication, however "pitiful" it might be, Sandford, by accepting their allegiance (totally apart from insisting on it) had also accepted a special duty to the same higher court he was asking the jury to recognize. It was here that he drew the shades. He was admitting responsibility (in spite of the voting) for breaking the law of the land that did apply, because to do otherwise would deny his authority as God's prophet. But he did not acknowledge (or comprehend) that the federal law in question was based on a reality of universal spiritual proportions—that those who have agreed to obey a leader at all costs are at the mercy of that leader's wisdom, discretion, and pity. He had broken the law of good kings, good prophets, good apostles, good generals, good slave-holders, good parents, good captains and shipmasters, good shepherds, and good football coaches. By his own standard it was a failure of despicable measure.

Within an hour the jury brought back the verdict of guilty. Sandford was freed on bail again until December 18, when Judge Hale would announce the sentence.

Shiloh, almost in shock, spent that week in preparation for the worst. The maximum punishment would be sixty years—ten years for each death—as well as a staggering fine. On December 17 Sandford preached for ten hours straight to a large crowd at the Temple, using as his text the entire book of Revelation, which he went through, from Alpha to Omega. In the course of those thousands of words, broken only by intermittent singing led by two harps, he comforted and cajoled the hilltop, gave an old-fashioned Gospel message to worldly listeners, and again predicted world disaster, including war in Europe within the next few years. When trouble began in earnest, the world would flock to Shiloh for protection. "If I go down, North America will go with me. I'll be a man of God wherever I go and I'll turn this world upside down no matter where I go. I never had North America so much in my hand as I have since I stood before the bar in Portland." The smoke of the devil had not touched him. He invited everyone to file up front and sniff his coat as evidence.

The sentence, given the next morning, was confinement in federal prison for a period not to exceed ten years, to begin immediately at the penitentiary in Atlanta, Georgia. Shiloh took the measure calmly, Sandford himself with composure and relief. No absurdity could surprise them by now. It seemed unimportant that the more logical prisons for serving out his sentence—Auburn, Maine and Sing-Sing, New York, his wife's hometown—were full, while faraway Atlanta, recently built, still had "openings."

Goodbyes had already been said many times over. In the escort of a deputy marshall, Sandford left the night of December 18 from Portland, dressed, said a reporter, in a "natty blue suit with a sailing cap bearing his insignia of the Commodore of the Kingdom Yacht Club and a white cravat." Just before the train pulled out two handcuffed young men climbed aboard with another official and joined them in their car. Sandford's "whole being flooded with joy," said his first letter back to Shiloh, to learn that the men were "two thieves," on their way to serve time for robbing the post office at Waterville, Maine.

"Shackled" to common criminals, if not between them, as the train "whirled through" Maine, New Hampshire, Massachusetts, "thundered through Connecticut" into New York, and sped on into New Jersey, Delaware, Maryland, Virginia, and North Carolina, Sandford's exaltation continued unabated. "Every roll of the car wheel is a ring of triumph," he declared in his record of the journey. "When men are willing to suffer the 'loss of all things' for the absent King, then the Almighty has a clear field and conquest is certain."

Florence Whittaker's suit had been all but forgotten, overshadowed by larger affairs. It had shrunk anyway while the *Coronet* was at sea— the $15,000 reduced to $5,000, and since her charge went uncontested after all, right now Shiloh was finding a way to remit to her a court-designated award of a mere $2,500.

25

The Eye-of-the-Needle
1912–1916

On the first day of 1916, Wendell White began to keep a diary. "We are living in the log cabin," he wrote. The cabin, a quarter mile east of Shiloh Proper, was rustic but spacious and quite cozy. He and Annie were alone. Arnold was working and living at Bethesda. Enid lived and taught at Olivet. Avis and Doris had rooms elsewhere on the grounds, Avis attending high school and Doris working about the place in various jobs. Wendell was still teaching. Annie filled many positions, mostly domestic.

Wendell was a calmer person generally, ever since it had been settled for good: Shiloh was where he belonged. He had not felt the old undirected rage in years, had not even expelled it in prayer. He had never been one of the shouters in chapel. The disgruntled inner arguments were quieter. He had put his mental house in order, and if in the process he had mislaid a treasure, it was not something he missed. He was happy to be in the Kingdom.

He wrote his 1916 diary almost off-handedly, in brief penciled notes, not a conscious record for the world's eyes. On February 7 he noted casually that the hilltop buildings were up for auction because of overdue taxes; a thousand dollars "came in just in time," on John Sandford's birthday. "F'd scarce," he wrote on February 29, as if to spell the word out would lend it too much importance. Ten days earlier a package of "edibles" had come from his sister Neve in Massachusetts "just as we needed it." On March 14 f'd was "still scarce." They were down to thin gruel again, often with meals skipped entirely. From this point until spring, Wendell's comments, like any good farmer's, mostly concern the weather. It had been a mild season. In March snow fell at last, winter dumping its heavy wet surplus as it yielded to spring.

One afternoon, just after a storm, Merlyn Bartlett followed someone's footprints on the trail to the log cabin, crossing Pinkham Brook from stone to stone in the swollen water. She had walked this field countless times in warmer weather, gathering Queen Anne's Lace and watching little hop toads leap out of her way into the warm grasses. Today the sun slanted low from behind her across the breadth of cold white waste, rippling like sculptured waves in a keen wind. The white was not really white, she noticed. The Fergusons had taught her that in art classes, just as they had taught her to see beauty in weeds. White was actually a score of other colors, like the sheep she had once painted, faintly blue sheep standing in snow in the light of the moon.

Just ahead of her now the smoke from the log cabin stove rose straight up from the chimney before shredding out among the trees. Arnold opened the door for her. His parents were there—Wendell, with his droopy grey moustache, and Annie, a pretty woman yet, with swirls of auburn in her white hair, pinned into a soft, thick knot at the back of her head. Merlyn had always felt a little in awe of Annie, who seemed so entirely in possession of herself, like Enid. But she felt at home with Wendell, a man (Merlyn thought) not much in charge of his life. She liked that about him. Whenever they passed on the grounds these days, they evoked little smiles from each other, as if calling up sudden memories of high school nonsense years ago, when as the teacher he had enjoyed moments of stolen fun as much as the pupils. Once at recess she had tossed him a paper lunch bag half-full of water and he had caught it, to his chagrin.

Annie was mending at the table, working in the last light of the day. A pot steamed on the stove. They were burning pine cones, a brisk fire that leaked fragrant smoke into the room. There was no smell of cooking food, and would not be that night, Merlyn knew, unless money suddenly appeared from somewhere to pay for a distribution of corn meal. The pot was full of water, waiting. On the table, along with Annie's sewing paraphernalia, Arnold had neatly positioned on a clean handkerchief several tools of dentistry, a tiny mirror on a stem, a tamper, three wicked-looking barbs and hooks, a blue paper roll of cotton, a bottle of phenal, a glass of water and a basin. He stood, bronze-headed, beside a straight wooden chair and politely gestured Merlyn to sit. Wendell lit a kerosene lamp.

With one of Annie's aprons around her neck, her head tipped back on a rolled towel, Merlyn patiently endured the half-hour of scraping and probing required to clean the cavity in one of her molars. She tried not to think about Arnold and this intimate proximity. It was the only time they had ever touched in any but accidental ways.

She had perfect confidence in his ability. She had watched him a year earlier in apprenticeship for the two weeks Dr. Smith of Waterville gave his time to Shiloh teeth while he taught four young people how to treat the neglected mouths of hilltop residents. Arnold, still learning, had filled his own tooth and extracted one of his mother's, and had since assumed much of Shiloh's dentistry. Merlyn often helped, mixing the amalgam of metal with a catalyst of mercury for the fillings, and tightly gripping the hands of those who underwent extractions without analgesics. Dr. Cushing, the dentist at Lisbon Falls, she had heard, hated to treat Shiloh people because they refused to let him administer pain killers.

The filling completed, Merlyn stood and buttoned on her coat, feeling a little faint, mostly from hunger. Since it was now dark, Arnold lit a lantern and offered to see her home to the Extension. Back out into the night they went together, he walking ahead of her to shine the light on the path. They said little. At the brook he scrambled down the steep bank, turning to hold the lantern as Merlyn descended by herself, then preceding her across the slippery stones in the water, going slowly to give her time to find proper footing in her long skirt and ankle high shoes. (She owned no "arctics" this year.)

He never offered her a hand or so much as gestured to help, and Merlyn, who had maneuvered the brook many times, did not expect him to. Single men did not touch women, not even to help them in and out of wagons. It did cross her mind that it would be nice if he should, but knowing Arnold's circumspect adherence to Shiloh rules, she believed that if she were to capsize into the icy water he might not help her out.

So she made very sure she did not fall, or do anything at all that might be viewed as manipulative. She needn't have worried. He would not have suspected her motives, though he knew she was in love with him. He had known it since August. It had "leaked out." Someone had shown him several poems she had written. One was about "unrequited love" and in a moment of dawning he knew without a doubt that he was the subject.

Staring at the lines in her round handwriting (iambic tetramater, rhyming precisely A, B, A, B), he felt as if he had been socked on the jaw. They had been friends for years and he had never guessed. He faced her with it, afraid that the naturalness of their relationship would be marred if the secret developed a double life. She admitted it openly, quietly but without embarrassment; lying was unthinkable. He acknowledged with regret that though the startling information had "drawn music from this harp," he did not return the feelings. Instead, he confided—not meaning to be cruel at all, only meaning to share what he could, giving Merlyn at least the gift of his trust if not his passion—that he was doing a little suffering of his own. For a long time he had been drawn to Helen Merow, who quite obviously did not return his interest, but he was praying that she would—if it should turn out to be the will of God, that is.

Merlyn sympathized wholeheartedly. They began a strange, warm shift in their friendship. Letters and notes flew back and forth, getting things straight. She reassured him that she had not the slightest "voluntary wish" that he would change in his feelings, and he must not ever misread anything in her manner and conversation. "My nature is naturally free and open, perhaps unwisely so, and I fear has often led to both my motives and manner being misunderstood." She had one goal—had long ago settled it: that "in it all . . . I am His own." Where God's will was concerned there would be no compromise. She was "a garden enclosed . . . a spring shut up."

Arnold, deep in his own romantic interpretation of matters, suggested the possibility that God might, after all, have a mysterious plan for them—"our lives given up together to the interests of mankind and the glory of God," he in his unfulfilled love and she in hers, mated in sacrificial service. Merlyn shot that one down in a flash. She had been watching such extreme tendencies in Arnold for a long time. The words, "I can't trust him," had been repeating and repeating in her head, she told him. His spirituality was something he turned on and off, she thought, and had not yet integrated with the rest of his personality. "You are sincere, but you do not know yourself," she told him. He was all mixed up in his feelings, she said. He wasn't yet ready to really love.

He thought she was wrong, but he accepted the criticism with humility. He would have been glad to acknowledge that he tried not to give in to his feelings for Helen Merow, and succeeded much of the time. He felt critical of couples he knew who seemed too engrossed in their love (perhaps lust) for each other, and of a certain preoccupation he had noticed in some of the people. On one terribly cold winter day he and another man were hanging laundry on the long lines at the back of the

Extension. Struggling in the wind with the ladies' underwear, the man remarked, "I don't think it's right for us to be touching these garments, do you? Because of the feelings they raise." Arnold, conscious of no sensation other than freezing to death, could not imagine what he meant.

But other feelings were clearly right. To *not* feel love for Christ or a burden for the lost or sympathy for another person's pain was a deep sin and he fought against such apathy. As for Merlyn, he unquestionably felt something good, a special bond, a warm rapport—but that was all.

So, nothing was any different between them except the relief of the secret unlocked. Merlyn was twenty-seven and had loved Arnold for ten years. She had "given him up" a thousand times before, had "gone all the way" with it, once (long ago) even getting safely through a ridiculous phase in which she had promised God she would marry a certain other person at Shiloh, a limp, grinning young man who was mentally deficient—if that served God's purposes best. The silly games were now over. Reality—that is, life without Arnold—had moved in like a cold roommate. He was as surely lost to her as Stuart Wolfe, buried four years ago in a northern sea, was lost to Hazel Housler. It was finished.

"Overcomers never think," Merlyn had once written in the back of her Bible. That was long ago, in the midst of her confusion and grief after Leander's death, which she had finally deposited in God's care under "Things we will never understand." She had learned to not reason, to not persist in "figuring things out." But lately she had been doing a kind of instinctual thinking. It was as if she saw the word LEAVE slowly spelling itself in her mind. Something would happen and a letter would form. Crossing the brook by the light of Arnold's lantern, water rushing under her feet, she knew she was close to the end of the word. She thought her heart would burst at the idea of saying goodbye to everything she valued on earth, the mature friendships, her kindergarten children, and—how could she even consider it?—her place in the Kingdom of God. Defectors were punishable by hell. But that was not the point so much as the fact that Shiloh was her home. Maybe, she hoped intensely, the final E would never appear.

Whatever Merlyn thought was wrong on the hilltop, she was sure it would not be wrong if Mr. Sandford were there. Yet the Kingdom Frank Sandford left behind in 1912 as he went off to prison was virtually the same as it had been for a very long while. Aside from the brief period after the *Coronet* tragedy, he had spent only a few weeks on the hill since 1906. It was a case of going on as they always had, full of determination to survive without his presence. But like a big weary bird that flapped its wings and could not quite leave the ground, nothing Shiloh did in the years of Frank Sandford's imprisonment seemed to get it into flight. Everything turned out to be little more than a parody of its earlier self.

More than ever, the need for money hung like a weight around the Kingdom's neck—monthly, weekly, daily. Besides the workers in Boston and the small churches about the country and abroad, over six hundred people still resided in the Durham area, most of them on the hill. These must be fed and kept warm, the buildings must be repaired, tax deadlines met, and the mortgage on the Boston properties regularly paid. Even without houses to maintain overseas, Shiloh was encumbered with real estate, and selling any of it was out of the question. Both harps were retained, and the *Coronet,* though she could never be used again for long sea voyages, was totally renovated at a cost of $5,000.

Before leaving for Atlanta, Frank Sandford had appointed seven ministers to share the responsibility of leadership. Charles Holland, as usual, was in general charge. The others—Almon Whittaker, Willard Gleason, George Higgins, Ralph Gleason, Ernest Tupper, and Austin Perry— moved about in various positions of authority. Helen Sandford was also prominent, as the person most apt to know the mind of the absent Shepherd. The spicy girl Frank had once so admired was long gone, but she had found a badge that bespoke her old courage and compassion and gave her entry into the action. She was a Red Cross worker of sorts, gently applying bandages and offering hot drinks on the battlefield. Yet she played this role, as she always had, without the slightest intimation that she disapproved of the wounds and the trauma. Of everyone at Shiloh over the years, no one was more faithful and believing than Helen. Asked by her husband after the trial if she had ever been sorry about her original commitment to a life of trust and risk, she had answered with a little laugh, "Certainly not!"

But roles in Shiloh's upper echelon had never been lastingly defined, and certainly no one had ever proved able to take the true leader's place. Everyone knew that. All eyes turned wistfully south. Writing to Mr. Sandford was now a regular part of Shiloh curriculum; to receive an answer was like getting a purse of gold. Many of his letters were printed and distributed, even some addressed to his family.

As a rule prisoners were allowed to send only two letters a month. Under a "dispensation for business correspondence" Sandford mailed many more, but every word he wrote passed under the eye of censors, who must have often wondered at the nature of the "business" of prisoner #3479.

When a new warden reverted to the old rules, a Shiloh member moved to Atlanta and became a weekly visitor to the prisoner. Through her secretarial labors, messages continued to flow north.

From the moment his sentence had been given, Sandford embraced his imprisonment as the will of God. He expected no delivering angels; he would not have escaped if the walls had come down. Yet his first reaction to prison life, he wrote, was a terrible "tightening of the skull." He was almost ill at the patience the adjustment required. "At times I suffer the awfulness of being immersed in IRON as it seems; the law of iron—iron rules, cold, relentless, and in a sense, merciless." He felt the tragedy keenly of those who were "buried" there for life. "It is like watching swimmers on a wild, stormy, violet sea—struggling for life— and one after another going down."

Nevertheless, in a daily regiment of hearty meals, sleep, and enforced exercise Sandford's health improved steadily over the months. In time he was honored with two jobs he enjoyed. Mornings he was the gatekeeper on the east portal, with a freedom pass that offered a daily chance for fresh air and a view of the surrounding countryside. In the afternoons he taught a small group of near-illiterate prisoners to read and write— the same job he had held at age sixteen. But his greatest joy was teaching a weekly Bible class, which began with one student and soon grew to over a hundred regular participants.

Those he taught admired and respected him. His cellmates became genuine friends. Other prisoners, some of whom had picked up rumors of Sandford's history, tormented him badly. He had never been good at taking personal jibes with a sense of humor. Now he found it absolutely necessary to do so and it tired and bored him. But in time he accepted the sneers as harmless teasing. Out on the prison baseball diamond, where he could still smash a home run, spectators on the sidelines would holler, "There's one for the Lord, Elijah!"

In 1913, Sandford turned down an opportunity to apply for a pardon, telling Austin Perry, who had worked hard to arrange it, that the president ought to be asking *his* pardon. By now he had adjusted enough to prison life to write, "the lines have fallen unto me in pleasant places." In fact, one of the harps had been shipped to Atlanta. He was allowed to practice on it and gave at least two Sunday concerts in the prison auditorium.

In spite of his choice to remain in prison, Sandford worried about

Shiloh constantly. Aside from scattered followers, the entire movement was now concentrated in Durham and Boston. No small band of perfect warriors operated in the glow of his favor. Though his letters often expressed tenderness, his admonitions persisted.

Once he had discovered, through enforcement, the benefits of daily physical exercise, he decided that this was the answer to many of Shiloh's ills. "Let your body have a blameless year," he wrote in 1914. He was convinced, he said, that many "in the movement . . . have a well-nigh chronic case of LAZINESS." He described his own regimen and wanted the hilltop to drop everything and exercise with him at 11:30 and 4:00. "If all my people would be *absolutely faithful one hour each day,* I know there would be far less graves in the grove hard by the bank. I wish half of you were as well as I am . . . I was referred to the other day by a powerful Virginian who brushed up against me, as a man 'like iron'—'Why,' said he, in telling others, 'he's one of the strongest men in here.' " Walk the verandas, he instructed, breathe deeply, get out in the sun.

Arnold was selected to teach a course in calisthenics. In the warmer weather hammocks were hung on the porches, and patchwork tents went up in the orchard and groves for outdoor living. Wednesday afternoon was set aside for sports appropriate to the season. Even the girls were permitted a softball team, with Esther Sandford, now sixteen, as the coach.

No one objected to such fun if Mr. Sandford requisitioned it. The trouble, as Arnold saw it, was that many found themselves too weak to participate with vigor. Some had to rest during the quarter-mile veranda hike. A friend of Merlyn's could hardly climb a flight of stairs without fainting, let alone touch her toes in a class of calisthenics. In a few months enthusiasm for exercise had waned and community recreation once again became a sporadic affair.

Yet, in this period of frailty and withdrawal, the Kingdom's thinking was more than ever worldwide. It still expected to embody the words of Isaiah: "And nations shall come to you for light, and kings to the brightness of your rising." In the spring of 1914 that seemed to be happening. The "king" was Chief Alfred C. Sam of West Africa. Chief Sam claimed to be the successor to the "throne" of a tribe on the Gold Coast. He had been converted by a former Shiloh student, Joseph Taylor, a member of the Fanti tribe who had returned to Africa in 1901 as a missionary. Chief Sam had visited Durham in 1911 and had been baptized by Willard Gleason in the Androscoggin. Now, three years later, he had come back with twenty new followers, seeking Shiloh's help.

One day on the *Coronet* off the coast of Africa, Sandford had prayed that an African chieftain might be saved and lead his whole tribe to Christ, the initial step in the salvation of the entire continent. Sam seemed a direct answer to that prayer. His father, the chief of the tribe, had died and his people were begging Sam to return and claim the throne. Sam wanted Shiloh missionaries to go with him and minister to the tribe. He had already raised the money and had bought a ship.

He had done this by establishing a back-to-Africa movement among the long-exploited black sharecroppers of the Southwest states. For $25.00 each the investors were to be carried to the Gold Coast on an old Cuban steamer, which he had purchased and renamed the *Liberia*. Once in Africa, Sam promised, they would build factories and begin a native industry in mahogany and cocoa on the twenty square miles of land he claimed to own.

Sam's followers provided the hilltop with "unexpected diversion," in Arnold's words. For three weeks they laughed and sang boisterously around the grounds. Their personal habits were shocking, their language startling. They all but took over in the chapel with "lusty" song and testimony. It was as if Shiloh's own style of enthusiasm was being returned to them in this coarse reinterpretation of Holy Ghost fire.

Somehow they managed to feed them. In spite of himself, Arnold resented the testimony of one "well-padded" gentleman, who praised God with a shout because he "felt so good." He might well "feel good," Arnold thought. "His stomach was full; mine was not."

On the third of June, 1914, when the *Liberia* steamed out of Portland Harbor headed for Galveston, where several hundred more passengers awaited, she was carrying twelve choice missionaries and sailors from the Kingdom, including Willard Gleason, Lester McKenzie, Harry Whittom, Austin and Hama Perry, Herbert Jenkins (who had never given up the idea of going back to Africa), and Jean Dart.

Sandford's letters expressed concern. Cultural differences meant little. Here was another suspicious mixture of spiritual levels. The project struck him as "Satanic trickery," he said. But it was already too late.

Capt. McKenzie is away—off—off—and I can see no reason why you all shouldn't blow far away in the same gale for you have no protection and no head and no obedience and no object or aim but to do as each little mind thinks best.

Perhaps McKenzie was doing as he had been taught so carefully—to find God's will with his heart, not his head. The ship arrived at Galveston on June 18, when hundreds of Sam's people "swarmed over it for days in riotous explosion of joy, drinking and smoking." While Sam went off to raise more money, the Shiloh group waited a full six weeks, fighting repeated attacks of dysentery. Galveston's consistent temperature of 85 degrees, along with a matching humidity, turned the hold of the iron ship into a steam bath. Outside their quarters the Shiloh personnel faced hostile threats from some of the black passengers. The project seemed doomed.

It was the war in Europe which settled matters once and for all. By August 3, with transatlantic waters hiding German submarines, Sandford sent an unmistakable order from prison: Go home. It was one thing to sail around the Horn with a company of absolutely pure people; it was another to sail into the path of danger in the company of those whom God could not bless with safety. Hadn't they tried that before?

But it was weeks before the Kingdom people made it home, and by then one of their men had died of dysentery. The *Liberia* crossed the Atlantic without their help and reached Africa, to find Sam's throne long occupied by another and all promises shattered.

The war in Europe also brought an end to any other thoughts of active involvement in foreign missions. So attention turned to a second postponed dream, the University of Truth. The idea had been initiated as far back as 1903 and had survived several abortive starts. Now Sandford insisted that the program be launched in the fall of 1915, when John Sandford could be one of the first students.

The first challenge to this plan was nostalgically familiar—finding the space for the new school. Since Olivet was no longer adequate for two hundred pupils plus a college, one corner of the unfinished Extension was chosen as the site of new school rooms.

"I have a plan," Sandford wrote to the youngsters in the spring of 1914, "that you all take your turn at the supernatural in preparing these great buildings for the opening of the University in 1915. . . . Why can't you boys and girls finish on the inside what we so triumphantly completed on the outside?"

The children were thrilled. They had heard stories of Shiloh Drives and Charges but many had never been part of one. Calling themselves the "Light Brigade," they began at 3:30 A.M. on June 20, every child from age five to eighteen working at fetching, painting, plastering, and carpentry until the job was done on August 18. In the middle of the drive typhoid broke out, but the children's crusade triumphed anyway. On the day of completion they all gathered for a victory picture on the steps outside and were rewarded with a twelve-page booklet—a letter from Mr. Sandford praising them for their help, printed in gold letters and tied with a gold cord. In tiny print at the bottom of the last page his instructions to the adult leaders were included verbatim. "Copy to each child in a fine envelope. Never mind cost—elegant." The little book looked good enough to eat, like a piece of frosted cake, and many of its honored recipients may have indeed wished it were edible.

The bright new rooms were immediately occupied by existing grammar and high school classes. The college program never got under way. Like the rest of the Extension, the superstructure for the University of Truth was there, up and ready, yet it remained a great echoing shell, a fine idea awaiting the birth of its own reality.

Soon after the Light Brigade, Merlyn Bartlett gathered up her courage and wrote a candid letter to Mr. Sandford. The drive to finish the school room had united the younger and older people in important ways, she told him. But life for the children at Shiloh was still far from satisfactory. Not only were those in their twenties, like herself, still "treated as children," those yet younger were "being maimed forever." Their sins were important, but their opinions were not. They were "suppressed by continual law and rebuke." There was a "stagnation" at Shiloh that would not change "until something moves out of the way and the young people move up and on into their places."

She was not sure Mr. Sandford ever got the letter, until four months later, when he returned it to the leaders with a note: *I endorse every word of it. . . . I hope Shiloh will have the wisdom to feel her letter KEENLY."* What happened subsequently was not what Merlyn had in mind.

In 1912 Sandford had arranged that his son John, then fifteen years old, would begin to assume the emotional focus of leadership that Shiloh so badly needed. John, a slender, brown-haired boy, very unlike his father in personality, had not felt the same confidence in himself. Since his dramatic role in the Black Winter, his place in Shiloh's affairs had been understated. But he agreed to begin by editing a new Shiloh periodical. With "F. Weston Sandford (Father)" and "John Sandford (Son)" as joint editors, *The Golden Trumpet* materialized immediately—on slick paper, with an air of expense. It turned out to be Shiloh's best publication to date. The writing, even Sandford's lead editorial, was quiet and professional, without the freshman rush of language that had characterized the earlier papers.

Other than *The Golden Trumpet,* very little else of a concrete nature set John apart as a leader for another three years. Then sometime in the fall of 1915 was authorized by his father to institute the "Eye-of-the-Needle." The "Eye" was a Sanhedrin of sorts, like the one-time tribunal of the Jews. It began at Shiloh as a process for screening enrollers in the University of Truth, but soon it extended to include every person on the hill. Like the Fair, Clear, and Terrible purge, it was meant to establish a new core of pure people. Its escalation may have been prompted by the growing number of defections that year. A total of thirty-two people had deserted, including Ralph Gleason, one of the seven ministers in charge. Ralph had quietly "disappeared," moving his family to a house in Lisbon Falls, address unknown. Word quickly spread at Shiloh that the man had "gone to pieces," and perhaps he had. It had been a long time since he and Charles Holland, wearing their citified bowlers, had appeared before Sandford in John Douglas's barn, the first of the young people to give themselves permanently to the movement. In the years since, Ralph had seldom been satisfied with his role, as High Priest or otherwise, and now, in his forties, he was working in a shoe factory.

His departure was demoralizing, one more sign that things were not going as they ought to on the hill. It was not that the struggle for an "uncompromising spirit" had abated. It was still essential to "square one's life right up to the plumbline of exact righteousness," and help others to do the same. "You have got to strike at anything that is not right and expect others to do the same by you," went someone's diary note. If a person "felt something" in another that was "not quite right," then everyone must "go after it," though sometimes the process was ludicrous. John Fuller, the superintendent of the gardens, thought to be godly, was singled out as he sat in a meeting one day and told that his face lacked the light of grace. He was asked to leave until he had straightened out whatever was wrong. Fuller went to his quarters and shaved, then came back to the chapel to be praised for having "done business with God."

Children were not excused from the responsibility of exactness any more than they had ever been. The Black Winter epidemic of beatings had never recurred with the same intensity, but isolated stories of severe treatment had multiplied and circulated over the years, a murky collection deep in the community's consciousness. What exasperated Merlyn was the enormity given to infractions which were innocent and funny. When two nine-year-old girls, who had "earned" several pennies selling some rags and old rubbers to a passing junk dealer, "held back" two cents of that money after they had been told to turn it in to the storeroom, they were warned that God had struck dead Ananias and Sapphira for the same sin. When Cal Higgins accidentally opened a bathroom door on a female visitor at the Higgins Cottage, his father made him fast and pray for days until he was sure he had been forgiven by God. Two boys were spanked in front of their class because, forbidden to pick apples from the trees in the old orchard, they had taken bites out of one and left the core hanging on the branch.

But something else was going on at Shiloh. While the machinery of judgment hummed and vibrated as noisily as ever, the community was becoming skilled in the art of humankindness. News of each other traveled the grounds constantly. All were aware of who was sick or bereaved, who was lonely and needed attention, or who needed a coat or other clothing. They worried about young August Marstaller, who went to work in the woods with burlap wrapped around his worn canvas shoes. They worried only a little less about Arnold, whose feet were pinched by a pair of donated second-hand shoes—orange, with dapper pointed toes, one size too small. Gladys Stacey, working in the lamproom, prayed for those she knew sat through dark evenings because they lacked the funds to buy kerosene. Even intimate details were sometimes shared, as when it was whispered about that a woman at Bethesda had her impacted feces removed with a silver teaspoon.

They did what they could for each other. Blind old Mrs. Boardman twisted hundreds of newspapers into long tapers used to "borrow fire." Arnold was delighted when sample tubes of Ipana toothpaste arrived for "Dr. White." Feeling rich, he gave them all away. Birthdays were important. Lists were published each month and celebrations held, in ways that were honoring, if not elaborate. Each year on Stuart Wolfe's birthday, young men who had been his friends spent time with his parents. At Sandford's urging, one meeting a week was given over to expressing appreciation for each other, a somewhat embarrassing time that was pleasant, nevertheless.

Maybe that was what made "Eye-of-the-Needle" seem pointless. It was a "mystery," remembered Doris White, "a strain." A committee of judges was chosen to assist John Sandford, all of them in their twenties—Enid White, Floyd Clark, Everett Knight, and Fern Brown. This band of five set up headquarters in Ebenezer, the same room in Jerusalem Turret where John had faced his symbolic whipping during the Black Winter. The young panel interviewed Kingdom members of all ages one by one. Those who passed through the "Eye" were "set apart," once again a pure group pulled out of diversity. Practically, that meant only that the holy held meetings with John as their leader. But the whole operation carried neither the terror nor the joyful purging of the old cleaning-out times. The load of authority for John, little more than eighteen, was cumbersome and awkward. The leader's son, said the *Lewiston Journal,* "has apparently incurred much resentment among the young people by his arbitrary measures and his dictatorship in trivial matters."

John hardly deserved to be called a dictator. In ordinary circumstances he was a young gentleman, a little too refined to be entirely "regular," but with a generous inheritance of Sandford whimsy and candor. He had once told a group of friends that he thought he could tell what God was going to say about a particular matter if he could find out just what his father wanted at the moment. It was an astonishing statement, as if the movement's best kept secret had suddenly been exposed, yet he said it with humor, and everyone knew he would go to any lengths to do what his father "wanted." But shepherding may have been beyond him. A young woman left "because she would not yield to the command of John" to report on another girl, and Avis White was wounded by a long list of offenses John read off to her as she appeared before the "Eye" committee. Mary Hastings, twelve years old, wrote a note, blithely expressing the confidence that she was safe in Jesus. John wrote back to warn her of "conceit."

Then, right in the middle of the "Eye," the two couples on the judging panel announced their engagements—Enid White to Floyd Clark, Everett Knight to Fern Brown. They had dutifully gotten the permission of the ministers. All four had proven themselves many times over as dependable young leaders. In fact, Floyd and Everett were cherished on the hill. They had survived the *Coronet* experience with their faith intact.

Sandford was outraged at this inappropriate gesture. He sent orders that each couple was to be "separated" for a year—that is, they were not to speak to each other or recognize each other's presence for that time—a stance not only impractical but almost impossible. The couples complied as well as they could.

The mandate from Atlanta effectively brought the "Eye-of-the-Needle," to a close. If it hadn't, it would certainly have been upstaged by the next startling event on the hill. While John was still doing his best to be a spiritual leader, Shiloh was brought to a state of whispered unbelief by the disappearance of his sister Marguerite.

The five Sandford children, except for their years abroad or at sea, had attended the Shiloh schools whenever they were on the hilltop, had mixed in daily activities and enjoyed close friends among the population. Yet they were different. They had been raised with the utmost control and protection. The "best" of the Shiloh unmarried "sisters" were chosen to assist Helen in the care of the family. They ate separately, with meals prepared by the family cook. It was commonly understood that they enjoyed a better diet. Shiloh children knew this with certainty if the adults did not. David Hastings, who was hungry much of the time, used to like to play with David Sandford after school, because there would "always be cookies." Yet he never questioned the difference between the Sandford cupboard and his own at home. The Sandfords were the most important children in the world. They deserved cookies.

Marguerite was now fifteen. For years she had been warning her mother that she could no longer stand to be told "every minute of the day what she should do and what she ought to be, spiritually." She could not measure up. At times she had wondered if she really belonged to the family. She even looked different, her skin dusky rather than fair. She had found it an enigma to know how to please her father. Once, as she was playing with a collection of shells by herself on the yacht, he had walked up to her, removed her shoes, and spanked her on the bottoms of her feet with them. He never explained why.

Sandford's way of honoring his children was often to project them "into the spiritual drama of the Kingdom," as William Hiss puts it. A letter to Marguerite on her thirteenth birthday became a letter to the entire Shiloh community when it was printed in *The Golden Trumpet.*

Addressing her as his "One Pearl of Great Price," her father apologized for forgetting her birthday and went on to explain how such forgetfulness could happen. It was all because of Marguerite's special role in the family. John, the firstborn, had been "with the Holy Ghost from his mother's womb." Esther was "God's little bugler to the young people." Deborah, like John, was "called of God to be a special character in spiritual things . . . to the ends of the earth." David was "davidic in every bone and his father cannot help loving him with the love of the heroic that fairly leaps and courses though his bones."

> But the young lady in the center of the family is entirely different from any other member of our little circle. I cannot detect the slightest trace of either of her parents or of grandparents on either side . . . in her makeup. For years, however, I have felt that you represented some foreign strain of blood like that of the brave daughter of Moab, and I have often called you mentally "our little Ruth."

He had forgotten her birthday, he said, because she represented "the great Gentile world almost entirely forgotten by Christendom." His forgetfulness was an object lesson, a reminder of God's love for every creature, "for the great thronging multitudes."

After explaining this at length in terms tender and hortatory, making both her birthday and his forgetfulness a matter of major significance, he concluded:

> Marguerite, your father congratulates you on your high, holy, world-wide calling. If you should die tomorrow your life has not been in vain. My precious little daughter, your father loves you.

A well-trod shortcut led west along the river on Shiloh property to the road to Lisbon Falls. One day in January 1916 Marguerite took a walk on that wooded path and never returned. Maybe she was acting out her identity as the rebellious gentile. If so, her wandering feet had already been spanked.

For days no one at the hilltop knew where she was. "Gloom fell over us all," says Cal Higgins, who was twelve at the time. Daily prayers concentrated on bringing her back.

She was safe and soon contacted her mother. At Lisbon Falls, without a cent and without a notion of how to find help she could trust, she had been recognized on the street by a former schoolmate who belonged to a recently defected family. Soon she was on her own in Lewiston, with a rented room and a job. She never went back to Shiloh.

Sandford, suffering "so deeply" he felt "like stone," encouraged his family to bear the tragedy bravely. It was just one more skirmish.

I know it seems as if it would never end, children, but we will laugh and dance for millions of years as we see multitudes worshiping our great God BECAUSE we 'didn't fail or get discouraged' while on earth. Let's clasp hands and ride like lightning on our family charger into the future *now*.

Nothing was said about what it could possibly mean for a child of the Shepherd to run away, the offspring of David, like Absolom in revolt—or what happened to leaders who fail to "handle their children." Marguerite had struck a hard blow at the chain of authority, but no one openly acknowledged such a frightening fact.

26

The Pale Horse
1916–1917

A few months following Merlyn's walk with Arnold across Pink-ham Brook, an outside physician examined a group of persons in Bethesda who were thought to be consumptive. Merlyn had come down with a persistent cough, and because of her past history she was scheduled for the exam. She was last on the list. The doctor was in a hurry to catch a train. Hearing something suspicious through his stethoscope, he put her "under consignment" with several other women in Bethesda until she could be examined more thoroughly.

The isolation of tuberculosis patients was fairly new in the world. Like the rest of society, Shiloh was dealing with a sudden increase of the "Great White Plague" since the onset of the European war. Until now the hill community had been no more knowledgeable than anyone else about the causes of contagion. Tuberculosis had been active at Shiloh since the very beginning, when young Maud Peacock enrolled as one of the Bible School's first students. Though half an invalid, Maud had lived until 1904, intermingling with the community much of that time. Flora Harriman, Nathan's daughter, had given cooking lessons to the High School while she was in the final stages of the disease.

In 1914 state authorities discovered TB among Shiloh's cows, after George Higgins's youngest son developed it in the bones of his face and hands. In the same year Higgins lost his oldest daughter to pulmonary tuberculosis. Now, as always, the infection seemed to catch hold among the strongest and most loyal young people, and no one was surprised when Merlyn appeared to be another victim.

After nine months in isolation at Bethesda, feeling perfectly well and without a follow-up exam to suggest otherwise, she was released by a friend of her mother's in Boston. Edythe MacIntire, healed of "brain fever" under Willard Gleason's ministry in 1897, daughter of the woman who had introduced Elvira Bartlett to Shiloh, insisted on paying for a diagnosis for Merlyn at Massachusetts General Hospital. There she was once again declared free of disease. The doctor at Shiloh had "heard" the residue of scar tissue from her condition at age thirteen, the first undeniable evidence that, by whatever means, she had been healed during her first months at Shiloh long ago.

Dismissed from the hospital, Merlyn found herself—now away from the hill and its hardships—unable to face a return. She went instead to Elim, thinking a few days there would give her the courage she needed to go back. Elim, as it happened, was in battle. A long Charge was in progress, prayer to meet the mortgage payment on the two Boston houses. One evening Merlyn joined the kneeling forms in the great double parlors. It was the same storming of the forts of heaven she had been part of more often than she could count. But this time something was different. Word had circulated that "certain people of means" were present in the rooms. She knew who they were, and realized that the prayers which rose fervently around her were not being addressed to God at all, but to those particular people, that couple there among them, who were also kneeling in prayer. That was not what was different. It had happened before, many times, and more often than anyone could estimate it had worked. It had brought in the money. Until tonight Merlyn had been a willing part of it, believing it was right, that it was God's way of speaking to people, and never seeing it as she did now, as a deceit, a sickening ruse, the exploitation of good and generous people. The difference this night was the sudden and frightening clarity with which Merlyn could see.

She stood up and walked out of the meeting. Composing herself in the hall (she was trembling), she scribbled a note and sent it back into the parlors, an urgent request that the minister in charge (Willard Gleason) step out and speak with her. When he appeared, they played out another familiar scene together. Merlyn "struck out" at the "wrong," as she had been taught to do, calling it a shameful charade. Gleason, though surprised, received the criticism in the proper manner, listening meekly and thanking her politely for the observation. Then he returned to the assembled group and continued to pound amens on his chair.

Humiliated and angry, Merlyn climbed the stairs to her room, where she remained alone for a day and a night, until she was ready to do what she knew was necessary. The word L-E-A-V-E was finally complete, but acknowledging it brought no freedom, only sorrow, regret, and guilt.

There was no place to go. Her mother, still a live-in housekeeper, had no home to offer, even temporarily. Back at Durham, Merlyn found a job through a young woman who had once lived at Shiloh and who now ran a secretarial school in Manchester, New Hampshire. Then she took the next steps, everything in order. She had no desire to sneak away. She wrote first to Mr. Sandford, then disclosed her plans to the ministers in charge, then said goodbye to her friends, one by one, and her kindergarten children. She experienced every kind of response, from tearful hugs to angry reprobations. Someone made her a dress. Someone else gave her a coat. At last, one early morning, her old valise in hand, she caught the mail wagon to the Lisbon Falls depot, going the way she had come at age thirteen.

At Manchester, Merlyn stuck it out for six months. Living at a boarding house for women, working as a stenographer in a shoe factory, she kept largely to herself—sleepless, eating poorly, and steadily losing weight, though for the first time in years she had all the food she could eat. Overcome with anxiety, unsure of herself in a world as alien as another planet, she saw no hopeful prospect for the future, no reason even to live. On two occasions in her life, when she had been given a sentence of death, she had felt perfectly well, and now, though nothing was wrong with her body, she felt quite sure she was dying.

Merlyn left Shiloh early in 1917, just before the United States declared war on Germany. Sandford had been following the war in Europe closely, exhilarated by it and impatient with President Wilson's neutrality. Far from sharing the popular notion that it would soon be over, Sandford saw it as the beginning of an unending conflict that would "lead on to Armageddon" and all that implied for the Kingdom. In spite of this— in spite of supporting America's wars and reading cosmic import into any military uprising in the world—Shiloh people had always thought of themselves as pacifists. Now they had a decision to make, whether or not their eligible men ought to apply for status as conscientious objectors. One day, finding a newspaper headline that read "In Time of Peace Prepare for War," all Sandford saw were the words Prepare for War standing out from the page in three dimensions. Soon after, asking God if America was "authorized to smite the Beast," he got the answer "Send." He wrote Shiloh to ask everyone to pray over the word and not to take a step until they were certain of its meaning. He was disturbed by the words in Revelation 13:10—"He that killeth with the sword must be killed by the sword"—which seemed to directly contradict the possibility of participation. Yet Scriptural history and prophecy both were full of wars initiated and supported by God—the enemies, therefore, unquestionable.

At Shiloh, Merwyn Wakeman, the band leader, saw exactly what that troublesome verse meant. Human aggressors "must be punished by human agents of the Almighty," he explained. When the Germans "killed with the sword," they "doomed themselves" to reciprocal treatment. Just as any criminal must "be fought" by the police, so nations and governments are "equipped by God" for the same purpose. Shiloh saw this familiar line of reasoning as a bright new revelation. Sandford wrote with excitement that he himself had come to the "same conclusion."

> I never had such a sense of unutterable greatness as at this time. . . . I almost felt the words of John, 'Behold, He cometh with clouds and every eye shall see Him. . . . Jesus is going to show Himself at Armageddon as a General, and all the world loves a hero. I suppose ten thousand corpses will lie on that battlefield when the charge of the White Cavalry is over. He can fight as well as pray and pray as well as die. What a Captain!

> It is sweet to die for one's country. . . . I love a hero. It's a joy to watch a martyr carry the banner to the end. . . . Shiloh's sons will show all men—how to live, and then if necessary how to die. It may be new boys, this way; but our brave ones have long been showing us the way.

He would have denied that he was a warmonger, but so would a multitude of others who were translating the war into their loftiest ideals, among them some of the country's more respected church leaders. Lyman Abbott, a well-known Congregational clergyman and a liberal theologian who would not have allied himself with Frank Sandford in any way, viewed the war as a "twentieth century crusade," more "Christian" than the crusades to the Holy Land of a thousand years ago.

If any of the young men at Shiloh eligible for the draft sensed a disparity between the new word "Send" and the old word "Go," they gave it little thought. Both words had come from God, and it disturbed them not at all to be "sent" by superiors who stayed at home. Rather, like a pack of restless horses, they were anxious to be off and running. Even Arnold, as unmilitaristic as it was possible for a person to be at the time, acknowledged his duty without regret.

Though most of his friends volunteered, Arnold decided to wait for the draft. Young men were badly needed at Shiloh; so few people were well and strong. For years he and Charlie Jones had constituted most of the male staff of nurses at Bethesda, a duty with a wide definition. They attended male patients in every way necessary, emptying bedpans, changing linen, cleaning and fumigating the rooms with clouds of disinfectant, carrying trays, running errands, filling and pulling teeth, and—lately—preparing bodies for burial. In 1917 one funeral followed after another, monthly, sometimes weekly. It was as if they had gotten good at dying, Arnold thought, and therefore were doing it more. In July, in fact, Mr. Sandford wrote: "Our people die well; I've never seen one quail yet."

Harry Whittom, who had evaded scurvy on the *Coronet's* last voyage, had been fighting TB ever since. He survived the record-breaking cold of the early months of 1917 to die in April. In 1914 Gordon Murray, another honored sailor, had developed tuberculosis of the bone after cutting his foot with an ax. He and his wife, Emma Barton, now lived in one of the "camps" in the grove with their seven children. The "camps," built years ago by families who came regularly to Shiloh summer conventions, allowed separate quarters for families who needed privacy. In August 1917 Arnold was assigned to the Murrays as Gordon's nurse and general aide.

Later that same month, Merlyn returned to the hill. She had quit her job in New Hampshire and come back. Arnold made no effort to contact her, or she him. Repentent defectors were placed on probation, and it would not have been appropriate anyway for him to seek her out. Besides, he had not really missed her, or only "normally," he told himself, as you might miss anyone who cared for you. But one day early in September, as he crossed the grounds, he found himself walking toward her on the same path. There was no way to avoid an encounter, and he was deeply relieved. He had been wondering if he ought to send her a note. That morning he had written in his diary, "Merlyn's birthday. Praying for her safety."

He felt himself blush as they met, and Merlyn colored too, or her face brightened, perhaps. She was very thin and white. He had heard that she weighed no more than ninety pounds.

"Happy birthday," he said.

She thanked him for remembering. They talked briefly. She confided that she might not stay, though she had been back only a week. "Things are not pleasant," she said.

He answered that he understood, but he hoped she would be careful to do God's will, and he believed it was God's will for her to remain at Shiloh.

"If it is, I'm sure He will show me," she said, and they each went on their way.

Merlyn had come back to Shiloh in a kind of quiet joy, not caring that she faced hunger or cold or disease, wanting only to be home again. She knew what happened to returning defectors, so she was not surprised when she was placed on probation, "sent under the hill" to live at the Higgins cottage. What surprised her was the cold manner with which she was treated, the somber glances and expressions of disapproval. She was banned from chapels, refused contact with her former kindergarten children. Old friends, embarrassed, retreated quickly from her presence. Returning was itself a form of repentance, but she would receive no forgiveness until she had proven herself.

More than anything else, she felt stifled by the atmosphere of disapproval at the Higgins house. She had always respected George Higgins, and been a little afraid of him. One of the toughest and most independent leaders, he was the only member of the Kingdom who had ever been physically attacked—tarred and feathered in Aroostook County in the early days of the movement. It was well known that Sandford had never completely trusted Higgins since the Black Winter. His "compromise," as Sandford saw it, with his brothers in the matter of his inheritance had not helped his reputation. Higgins had shared his resources generously with Shiloh again and again, but the legal arrangement he had agreed to made it impossible to turn large amounts over to the movement. When George's daughter Mary died in 1914, word got around that Mr. Sandford had written from prison: "It's a wonder all of your children aren't six feet under." Yet Higgins was still a staunch and faithful member.

He expected the same kind of loyalty to the movement from others. He saw it as his duty while Merlyn was in his house to help her face up to her failure and give it a name: self-pity. Unwelcome anywhere else on the hilltop, she was subject to his sermonizing.

On the night of Merlyn's birthday, September 5, Arnold walked under the pines outside the Murray's camp, asking God to take over in her heart. On October 7 he made another entry in his diary: "Terrific battle—conflict for Merlyn's soul." There had been special prayer for her in chapel that day. Ten days later, he added: "Merlyn left again."

He had not said goodbye. No one did. On the morning she was to catch the mail wagon once more for the train, she descended the stairs of the Higgins cottage to find the floor of the hallway below blocked by a group of adults and children, stretched out on their faces, praying aloud that God would restrain her. The only way out was across their prone bodies. Then, seating herself on the train at Lisbon Falls, she turned to see George Higgins and another minister entering the car. They had followed her. Both wore formal black suits, as Shiloh ministers had taken to doing when on official business. All the way to Brunswick they reasoned and cajoled and scolded, Higgins calling her a "harlot and a whore" in a voice so loud other passengers turned to stare. Merlyn had heard a lot of women at Shiloh called harlots. Frank Sandford had more than once called his wife a whore. The appellation was borrowed from Old Testament references to Israel's sin—"awhoring" after the idols of the world. But it occurred to Merlyn with both horror and humor that no one else in the car knew the allusion was spiritual. From Brunswick she continued on to Boston, while the men returned to the hill, giving her up forever.

A month later she wrote Arnold from a resort in Florida owned by the parents of another Shiloh defector. She wrote just to let someone at Shiloh know that she had arrived safely and had found employment. She expected no answer and got none. She believed she would never see Arnold again. He supposed the same, but as a compulsive keeper of records, he jotted down her address before he destroyed the letter.

One morning in the following winter, 1918, too uncomfortable and restless to kneel any longer on the floor of the cold chapel as the company prayed for Patagonia, Arnold retreated. He seldom abandoned the fort, but affairs on the southernmost tip of South America seemed not even remotely important, and in his state of mind he was a detriment to the success of the prayers. He had recently helped bury Gordon Murray, a man he dearly loved. Without a thought to where he was going he ran down to the kitchen of the Extension, laughing at himself with a sense of despair as he escaped to that strange station of hope. How many times had he fled there to get warm by the great brick ovens or had stuck his head in diffidently to see if there was "anything doing," as people would say, as they checked on the prospect of a meal. He had even slept there, not to keep warm, but to keep alive the flames under the copper mush kettles, just in case God sent cornmeal for breakfast.

There was nobody else in the kitchen right now, and not a lick of fire anywhere. There was *nothing* on those all shelves, not even salt. There had been no breakfast that day. Arnold paced back and forth, the heels of his ill-fitting orange shoes making clicks on the floor.

He had never once before considered leaving Shiloh. He had seldom had a wistful thought about the outside world—except once long ago on a visit to Lewiston, when seeing a young man with a pocket full of change, it had occurred to him with a twinge that he had never had that and probably never would. It was certainly not the lack of loose change that tormented him now, and it was not hunger—though there in the bare room with a faint smell of cooking lingering in the air, thoughts of food flew unbidden into his mind. He had to admit the constant hunger made him angry. It was the fact that it made no sense. Here they were, people experienced in "putting food by," with generations of training behind them in preserving, drying, pickling, smoking, and salting, with the knowledge of how to seed early (and a greenhouse to do it in) and harvest late, of how to raise beef and poultry, how to fish in every season, how to rotate crops (and acres for the purpose), how to develop seed, how to keep hens laying and cows from going dry, skilled in the art of using leftovers and scraps. Then why on God's earth were they hungry?

He knew all the usual answers—apart, that is, from the failure of faith. He knew that work was often interrupted by sudden calls to the chapel, and that long-range gardening plans were often abandoned because the human chain of responsibility broke at some undetected point—or the "animal chain," for a horse must be well fed to be useful. He knew, as everyone did, that often there were supplies enough in the store room on the good-credit "loan" from Lisbon Falls grocers, but they could not be touched until there was cash in hand. Cash came in only as God chose to provide it, and if He didn't, it was because He had something to teach them. But sometimes it seemed that every lesson that could possibly be taught by hunger had already been given long ago. And what were the small children learning by hunger? Or the animals? The horses were so thin their bones almost showed. His father had shot one last spring, a mare he had inherited from a cousin, because he could no longer bear to see her suffer.

But it was not the hunger that agitated Arnold now, nor even Gordon Murray's death. What appalled him was the realization that he was twenty-eight years old and "nothing was happening." So many things were not "working out." It was 1918 and the college course that he had been told was to be the "crown of school life," the top of the "long climb up the highway of education and character building," had not materialized. The stairs had led nowhere. The winter ahead looked very long. He knew, of course, that he might be "called up" anytime as a draftee, and for a moment he welcomed the prospect—and at the same time realized that if he went to war he might very well not come back. He rejected both thoughts instantly and with shame: war as an escape from a personal predicament and the fear of death in any circumstances. Why on earth should he fear?

Then, as if it had suddenly been shaken loose in his brain, an idea slid down that chain of thought and fell into his hands. There was no God. It was as simple as that. He had never actually believed that there was one, or not one who cared a shred about his own existence. For just an instant he stared at this, a recognition so bright he thought it would blind him. Then he dropped it. Brought to his senses by the peril of acute doubt, he began to pray, and then everything was all right. It was just the same old test of waiting and patience that Shiloh had endured for years and, above all, must not fail now.

When noises overhead indicated that the chapel had been dismissed, he slipped out the back door and took himself to his parents' present home. In their fifteen years at Shiloh Wendell and Annie had been moved a total of fourteen times to various locations on the property. Most recently, they had been moved out of the log cabin back to the Extension. Unwilling to face the chill of winter there, they had taken things into their own hands and transformed a shed in back of the Extension into a cozy one-room home. It had once been the pen of Isaac, a deer, kept as a pet for Shiloh children years ago. Wendell had insulated the shed with newspaper, covered the floor with pine needles and installed a heater which burned brush from the woods. On the stove simmered a pot of water, in it some beef bones, acquired for a penny or two from Mr. Shaw, who still bought supplies for the storeroom. Six times over Wendell and Annie had boiled those bones, and now Arnold, saying not a word to his parents about his experience in the barren kitchen, sat in the tiny room full of piney smells and drank a cup of the thin, pale soup and thought it marvelously delicious.

That summer Arnold was one of twenty-four Shiloh men joined to war-related services in America and Canada. The first soldier to go had been "shot" off the terraced arrow point while the band played a march by John Phillip Sousa. Wendell's diary records March 29, 1918, as the day Arnold and Herbert Jenkins returned from the draft board in Auburn. "Drafted, examined and accepted but not yet called." On May 29 Arnold departed to Camp Devens in Massachusetts, and on July 9 he shipped overseas. "Somewhere in France," Wendell noted in his diary in the middle of August. "Health good. On top body, soul and spirit. Praise be to Jehovah."

The Kingdom schools, August 1914. Merlyn Bartlett stands back row far right. The three men seated center are Joseph Harriman, William Hastings, Ernest Tupper.

John Sandford, August 1914, age 17.

Marguerite Sandford, age 15.

White family, about 1916. Standing, l. to r.: Enid, Arnold, Doris, Avis. Seated, Wendell and Annie.

The draftees. Standing, far left, Charles Jones; third left, Arnold White. Next to Arnold is Herbert Jenkins. Middle row, second right, Floyd Clark. Front, far left, Guy Campbell.

27

The Red Horse
1918

Throughout the summer of 1918 Shiloh hilltop shook itself out like a carpet in spring cleaning, opened its windows for an airing, and took a deep breath of relief. Mr. Sandford was coming home. His sentence had been shortened by three years for "good behavior."

Down in Atlanta Sandford faced his freedom with mixed feelings. Even apart from accepting Atlanta penitentiary as the exact center of God's will for him, he had found a space in the prison world that was more comfortable than he had dreamed was possible, almost like a vacation for the soul. With someone else setting the limits, without the awesome responsibility of "leading" every moment of every day, by being neither Elijah nor David, by being not number one, but number 3479, he had fallen into a role and a ministry that were as natural as breathing. "Does a man have to leave here just because he behaves himself?" he asked the warden on the day of his departure.

What the years behind bars can do to or for a person, in the best or worst of circumstances, can be only partially assessed by those who have never been imprisoned. Without making assumptions, one story Sandford himself eventually told sheds an interesting light.

Years earlier he had instituted at Shiloh what some called "closed communion"—that is, the ceremony could be shared only by those in full fellowship with Shiloh's creed and principles. In the prison, communion served by the chaplain, was "open" indeed, shared not only by persons of mixed religious beliefs, but with murderers and thieves and rapists. For this reason Sandford had never gone to communion in prison. Then one Sunday in 1917 he saw the matter in a new light. In that mixed group were many of his own Bible class students, who might be confused by his detachment. As he filed out of Sunday service with the other prisoners, God said "Turn," and he entered the room designated for communion. It was the first ecumenical gesture he had made in almost twenty-five years.

But did he still think of himself as Elijah and David, as the forerunner of Christ's return? If he had changed his mind about that, he was not saying so. More than anything else, as Shiloh's people faced Mr. Sandford's homecoming, they understood what he wanted *them* to be. Only a year earlier he had written, "I never wanted a man around who failed me once, and when I get out I expect to have nothing there but what we had in the first place—the same quality that stood the tests then. . . . I can have nothing on that hilltop that is not the hundredfold life— the very highest quality that there is!"

He was released in September. When he got off the train in Boston, his family was waiting for him at Elim. They enfolded a man no longer young, but healthy and firm, his moustache iron grey in a face browned by the southern sun. He enfolded a little group that startled him with their changes. Helen had aged beyond her years, was "wrinkled and atremble," says Murray, with "shattered nerves." John who had come from Fort Devens in uniform, also seemed "burdened" for one his age. Esther, no longer a girl, was a blond, willowy young woman, animated, but too thin and pale. Red-haired Deborah, fifteen, had grown quiet. David alone had thrived with the years—at thirteen a sturdy, cheerful youth. Margerite was not there. They did not expect her.

With the Feast of Tabernacles convention soon due, Sandford began by drawing together and addressing the Kingdom church members of the Boston environs and visiting the replenished *Coronet*. Then he and the family drove to Durham in a brand new Cadillac, dark green with a mahogany interior and curtains, presented to him by a Chicago follower, who also acted as chauffeur. In this, the "Land Coronet," the returning prophet "swept up the hill of the Lord in triumph," said the *Journal*. Shiloh, heeding his request for a low-key welcome, expressed its joy by opening the Gates of Praise and serving a sumptuous meal that belied the long months of want. Hazel Housler, one of the last remaining members of the A-Class, never forgot how strange it seemed to spend hours in the Extension kitchen preparing a chicken dinner when she could hardly stand up for hunger.

With the aroma of that feast filling the halls, Sandford greeted group after group of his people pressing in to shake his hand, some of them in tears. It was as if the place could hardly contain the resurgence of the old magic. Small children, who had never seen him but had been hearing about him all their lives, stared in wonder. Alice Miller, who was six, was awed at both the vigor of the man and the phenomenon of the chicken. "He sat on some steps above us and he had a chicken leg in his hand that he was eating at and waved it around to emphasize whatever he was saying. I remember wondering what it would taste like."

The next day chapel was jammed with those from the outside who came to hear him speak for the first time in seven years. David Wiley, age four, joined a group of a dozen or so young boys brought up to the platform to sit on the floor around him. "As young as I was, I was enormously impressed by the magnitude of the man. His presence was powerful, like an electric current in the room."

In that two-hour message Sandford related in detail his ministry among the prisoners and the process of faith and determination by which a penitentiary had become "the house of God." If reporters were listening for remarks such as "I shall yet be a popular man in Maine," he did not quite disappoint them. Part way through the address he produced a "little volume" in which he had written "from time to time" while in prison. From it he quoted, observed the newspaper, "the remark of a prosperous Boston businessman." The words were these: "There is only one Christian in the U.S., and he is in Atlanta."

"And yet," said Sandford, "I have been hounded for years because I am a Godly and righteous man."

He concluded by praising his people, who had so patiently endured the years of waiting. They had proven that they were willing to "pay any price for loyalty."

He did not add that the needs of some of those people were already crushing against him: hunger, broken families, spiritual confusion, illness, the loss of loved ones. Wasting no time, Sandford swung into this mountain of horrors by praying for a carpet for the chapel, the room they all sat in at that moment. It was a remarkable touch, like a pail of cold water on the head. On their own no one would have dared to suggest spending $150 on a carpet when the taxes were falling due and there was no coal or food for the winter ahead. Ah, yes, *but*, said Sandford, reading their minds, there was a great deal of praying to be done in the coming months, and they would all do it better if they were not kneeling on the bare cold floor. The money came in instantly.

A crew of volunteers cut and laid the rug. Spirits soared. God still cared about the little things.

What amazed Doris White, who helped to install the new carpet, was that she suddenly had enough to eat. It was largely corn bread, but it materialized in quantity. They were eating a steady two-meal diet again after years of uncertainty. Within days it was announced that the money needed for coal had come into the treasury. Not only that, a great mass of visitors was expected for the convention at the end of the month. They must be fed something besides cornmeal. A railroad carload of potatoes and other items (including a pair of oxen to be killed and roasted) totaling $800 were ordered, cash in hand.

Sandford was back at work with the old verve—though he was already beginning to feel the first wave of adjustment from the protected and regulated life of the prison to the chaos of responsibility and decision-making. Things at Shiloh were far worse than he had imagined, so bad he could hardly assess the damage. The movement he had come home to was a long way from the valiant, determined institution he had left behind. The place seemed full of walking dead, suffering from what he termed as "spiritual shellshock." The elated response to his presence had masked only temporarily the absence of vitality. Something had gone out of the movement that new carpet could not restore.

The first proof of this was delivered through one of the children—his own. Three days after Frank's arrival on the hill, Deborah ran away. Like Marguerite, she had been feeling discontented for years. In fact she had told her mother at the time of her sister's disappearance that she would go too when she was old enough—or so some rumors claimed. Even if that was true, and even if she had continued to be open about her intentions, no one could have predicted the terrible timing.

Mary Campbell, a close school friend of Deborah's, was not surprised. Shortly after the Sandford family returned from Boston to Shiloh she was asked to spend time with Deborah at one of the farmhouses. She was "terribly down," said Mary. She confided in tears her "deep disappointment" in the father who had come home; "he did not show affection or act like a father." Whatever Deborah's perceptions, something sparked the waiting tinder and two days after her father's return speech in the chapel, the girl was gone, walking to Lisbon Falls, as Margerite had done. A letter arrived the next day to assure her family of her safety. She had taken a trolley to Lewiston and had joined her sister.

By the time Sandford himself arrived at Margerite's rooms, Deborah had fled. Since there was no way Margerite could provide for her, she had gone to stay with another family, the location a secret. In time, both girls traveled to Worcester, Massachusetts, where Sandford's nephew, Alton Lancaster (the same who had raced with him to the depot at Bowdoinham) was a practicing physician.

It was Marguerite who apprised the *Journal* of her father's visit and of his expressed "determination to have his family together again."

"But I know better," Margerite said. She wore, said the *Journal,* "a winsome little smile which is characteristic of her when she is talking."

Now eighteen, she evidenced "no bitterness" or "rebellion." When she left Shiloh she had been "activated solely by the longing for companionship and a craving for normal pleasures."

"And Deborah is like me," she added. Or so the newspaper said.

The Sandfords could have pressed their legal right to see Deborah returned, as they could have done earlier with Marguerite, but once it was clear she was safe and had made up her mind to not come back, she was viewed as any other dissenter. Months later, her mother, taking a walk with Doris White on the street outside Elim in Boston, lapsed into a rare moment of confidence. She had gotten a letter from Deborah, she said, but "Mr. Sandford" would not permit her to answer. Doris, overwhelmed at Helen's apparent suffering, had no idea what to say, though she thought with wonder at the words in Malachi that had been pressed on them again and again, that Elijah shall "turn the heart of the fathers to the children, and the heart of the children to their fathers, lest I come and smite the earth with a curse."

Deborah and Marguerite Sandford were the only minor girls to ever run away from the hilltop.

Although he could not reassemble his own family, Sandford's power was not limited elsewhere. Of all the circumstances he had found waiting for him at Shiloh, the amount of sickness distressed him most. Among those ill, ten of the unmarried women, ranging in age from early twenties to mid-forties, lay close to death with what had been diagnosed as pulmonary tuberculosis. Sandford had visited them all, all long-time loyal members, one of them Margaret Main, that feisty first student who so long ago had defied her parents to join the school, and one—of all people—Jean Dart, herself such an important part of Shiloh's medical staff, as well as other trained nurses. Some had been "consigned" to Bethesda with Merlyn in 1916. Several, prior to the onset of the disease, had gone to bed with exhaustion and "nerve trouble."

Shiloh's attitude toward illness as a manifestation of evil had modified considerably over the years. The most victorious warriors, those closest to God, had been desperately sick at times and some had died. Even if they died "well," as Sandford put it, they had lost the battle to disease. How that was interpreted depended on the person and the circumstances. Arbitrary views did not apply. Sometimes God "took" the faithful, for His own reasons. Sometimes individuals were refined or instructed by suffering. In some cases, God still demonstrated judgment by striking people down.

But poor health might also be an attack of Satan, to be overcome by prayer. The ten tuberculosis cases at Bethesda fell into this category. Feeling intense anger at the forces which could so undermine the lives of such valuable persons, Sandford was determined to see them whole, though each one had been given up as "hopeless."

What happened next is how Frank Murray tells it and how it was retold on the hill many times. On October 3, a warm, sunny day, with the entire Shiloh community following behind him, Sandford led the way down to Bethesda and, setting ten chairs in front of the building, sent up word asking the ten women to leave their beds and come out. Slowly, one by one, they came, not ten but nine—walking on the arms of attendants, some still in their robes and wrapped in blankets, sweating and panting with the exertion. As they sat in the chairs, Sandford anointed each one with oil, laid hands on their heads and invited others to do the same. Then turning to Frankie Pulford, one of the more gravely ill, he asked her to walk to Shiloh Proper, some two hundred yards away, much of it uphill. He followed her closely with the chair, allowing her to sit when necessary. Though lightheaded and nauseous, she covered the distance successfully and never went back. Gradually the others followed, with the "cloud of witnesses" watching. All nine, soon fondly called "the nine lepers," recovered, some quickly, some over a period of months. All nine lived for many more years. The tenth, the one who had refused to leave her bed, soon died.

That confrontational style of healing—"Get up as if nothing is the matter"—had not worked with others in the past, such as Edward Doughty, ill with typhoid in Jerusalem in 1902. From a medical standpoint it had probably killed him. But whatever was wrong with these women, the approach was exactly what they needed, and a marvelous triumph of heroism, for them and for Sandford.

It was just now that the ravaging worldwide epidemic of influenza reached the community. One hundred thirty Shiloh residents fell ill, entire families laid up together for two and three weeks of helplessness.

No one died, though Lisbon Falls and Durham were hard hit, reporting death after death. Shiloh nurses, men and women, as quickly as they could be freed, volunteered their services in the surrounding towns.

Avis White, receiving communion and prayer, was one of those healed of the flu at Shiloh. Feeling the symptoms almost fly from her body, she never doubted it. But a few short weeks later, the same power failed to operate for her most crucial physical need.

Prayer had been offered many times over the years for the restoration of Avis's crippled right arm. It had remained the same, hanging limp at her side, thinner and shorter than the left. Meanwhile, she had grown tall and slender, with a grace of movement that was particularly her own. She stood straight, her shoulders back, an indication of the same strength of will that had insisted over the years on doing exactly what everyone else did. She had succeeded so well, as a child and as a young woman, operating with a kind of legerdemain in the kitchens, the laundry, the sewing room, at school, at play, on the farms, handling animals, gardening, that no one guessed the energy she poured into not giving up. Once, asked to braid a girlfriend's long hair, she agreed without hesitation, taking one strand of the hair in her teeth, to her friend's astonishment. Yet "doing up" her own heavy hair (auburn, like her mother's) was often exhausting, her "good arm" aching before she was finished.

She was now eighteen. After a childhood that, looking back, seemed like "one long fear," she had drawn from a few people she loved a devout sense of God that, perhaps, like her one good arm, had grown strong simply by determined use. But at the same time she had watched the community around her with a skepticism that seemed to grow up by itself alongside her, a strange weed she hardly knew how to name. She knew only that very often "two and two didn't make four."

The idea of being healed had never completely left her mind or the family's. It was as if her arm was a piece of unfinished business that had been regularly postponed by the predominance of other matters, and Avis had become skeptical of the possibility. One winter day when she was about ten, she broke the forebone of the paralyzed arm by falling on it as she slid down a bank of snow. For some reason God was "not expected" to heal broken bones at Shiloh, except on rare occasions. Avis's arm was set in a splint. At the end of two weeks, almost crazy with the itching, she conveniently remembered that her friend Charity Brown, who had once broken her arm, had gone to Dr. Miller claiming

God had healed her when she was tired of the bandage, and sure enough, the bone had knit.

Avis tried the same thing and, oddly, was allowed to go home and remove her own splint, which she did. She felt the bone give. It had not healed. She never told anyone. The ends eventually mended, leaving a bunch.

Sometime during the fall of 1918, as Sandford was cleaning out the illness on the hilltop, Avis was selected for healing. A large group had gathered in the chapel of Olivet to pray, just for her. On the wall hung the Fergusons' painting of the children welcoming the Second Coming of Jesus, with the tot in the lower center, arms upraised, whom Avis had always thought was herself. In another smaller room Mr. Sandford and several of the ministers were praying separately. In time, feeling shy and self-conscious, Avis was called to join them. There was some dialogue, some questions about her readiness, then more prayer. At last, Mr. Sandford put his hands on her arm.

"Do you feel anything?" he asked. Did she feel life in the arm, he meant.

She felt nothing. The process was repeated, several times, the prayers, the laying on of hands, and the same question. Then, suddenly, she "felt something"—a consistent "prickling," a sensation she had never experienced before. The men in the room became "very excited." Sandford hurried across the hall to the chapel and heralded the news. By the time he returned to Avis, the feeling had left the arm. No amount of praying from that point brought it back.

Apart from the awful letdown, Avis was overcome with embarrassment. Worse, she knew she had made Mr. Sandford feel foolish. Following on the heels of the long series of recent victories, the failure was almost ludicrous. Sandford sent Avis to Peniel, the prayer room in Jerusalem Turret, to fast and pray for three days alone to determine for herself why the feeling had disappeared. Each night she was to report back to him to tell him what she had learned. The interview was always short.

"I've got nothing," she reported, hardly able to raise her voice.

"Nothing at all?"

"No, nothing."

One evening as she left Peniel, Helen Sandford was waiting for her out in the hall. "Don't get all strained up, Avis," she said, in her soft voice. It was an honor to receive a moment of kindness from Helen, but the words to Avis in this moment of supreme tension were merely a platitude. She *was* "strained up." She knew Mr. Sandford blamed her for the failure and that what she was supposed to "get" in her session of prayer was light on her own shortcomings as a person of faith. She had often been intrigued by a Shiloh axiom: "Unless you take all He holds out to you, you will lose all you've got." Now God had held out this miracle, this powerful change in her destiny, and she had not been able to "take" it, as if she would not have known, after all, what to do with two good arms.

Yet she harbored her own unspoken version of what had happened. *He,* Mr. Sandford himself, had gotten "in the way," rushing out so elatedly to make that premature announcement to the waiting group in Olivet chapel. She had felt like an exhibit, like a performer alone on the tightrope who had lost her balance and toppled to the floor. But she never told Mr. Sandford that. It never occurred to her to tell him. She had learned long ago to keep her "mouth shut." Three nights in a row, "I've got nothing," was all she ever said. The matter died away and was never raised again.

Sandford had already moved on to other kinds of housecleaning. Soon after arriving he had learned the shocking news that several of the Durham houses had been mortgaged in his absence in order to meet other expenses. Late in October he initiated a program for the remaining seventy days of the year, a prayer drive to eliminate those debts. The agenda was breakfast, then prayer without interruption until midnight, then supper and bed, the process repeated until New Year's Day. To his displeasure, the response was less than enthusiastic, but eventually a sizable group agreed to participate.

Doris White recalled that Mr. Sandford spent much of the time during those days rallying their spirits.

One time he had us shouting praises to the Lord and kept at us as we shouted "Glory to God!" We shouted until we were tired but had to keep on and on and put more into it than we had in us. One day he had every one of us arise and say, "I will never be selfish again." Some seemed to think that a strong statement and added, "By the grace of God." He said, "You don't need to say that! You *have* his grace." . . . We were very tired, but some of those meetings turned out to be wonderful, God so real and near. At midnight we went down to the Extension kitchen and got a large piece of cornbread, maybe three by five inches, nothing with it or on it, and took it to our rooms and ate it. It was almost impossible to get up the stairs, we were so weak and tired. One time . . . I told him how I ached in the last few hours before twelve. He listened but didn't say anything

or change anything. One time he spoke of possibly making Saturday
an exception—a day's respite, and he said the Lord has said to him:
"Sacred endurance."

But they continued to fast on Saturdays as well. Meanwhile they
were rising early to fit in their regular household duties before breakfast
at 9:00.

> One time there were very few of us in the meeting in the daytime,
> because we had to be out doing necessary work around the place.
> He had us (those who had gathered) go out and sit on the front steps
> for a change and some fresh air. He made a comment about how few
> there were and said, "We ought to do the work between midnight
> and 9:00 A.M. the next day." No one responded and nothing more
> was said. It gave me an awful feeling. How, I thought, could that
> be done? How could we stand it with so little rest as it was?

Still, they would have done anything that was necessary to keep him
there among them after the long absence. Some things were harder with
him at home, but life was never without excitement. In the end their
lethargy aside, the money for the mortgages rolled in.

On November 10, in the midst of the "Seventy Days," John Sandford
and Theodora Holland were married, the first and second children born
to the Kingdom. Sandford was openly eager for the union. Neither of
the young people would have disobeyed him, however uncertain they
might have been about their feelings toward each other. Theodora, who
was twenty years old and much like her mother Caroline had been in
beauty and spirit, was not ready for the step. In sobs, she told her
girlfriends that she did not want to get married, she would "rather be
with them," and word circulated that she was in love with someone
else. The wedding was arranged in haste, since John, who had been
trained to join a machine gun battalion where the casualties had been
consistently high, expected to be shipped overseas very quickly.

As it turned out, there was no need for either worry or rush. On
the day after the wedding, November 11, factory whistles and church
bells at Lisbon Falls rang out across the river. The war was over.

"Germans licked, Arnold safe," wrote Wendell jubilantly, in his diary.
Both statements were true, but their juxtaposition could in no way
suggest that Arnold had done any of the licking. When he had sailed

to France on the transport ship *America* in the previous July, he fully expected the war to accelerate into the horror of Armageddon, with "blood to the horses' bridles," as Revelation described it. He carried more baggage than most other buck privates, among his possessions notes on survival in the wasteland of a world under the domination of the anti-Christ. What a remarkable course of events, then, that he should be virtually untouched by the incomprehensible slaughter and destruction of this most humanly oriented crusade. Blood to the horses' bridles, indeed. Arnold, like any one of the Shiloh draftees, would probably have proven to be a courageous and resourceful soldier under fire, yet like all the others, he saw no heavy action—in spite of Sandford's expectation.

Arnold had crossed the Atlantic as he had on the yacht *Kingdom* fourteen years earlier, tooting an E-alto horn in a band, playing some of the very Sousa marches he had played for Shiloh listeners. After arriving at Brest, he had been motored for three days to a point well behind front lines, where he repaired telephone wires and dug cable trenches for the 317th Field Signal Battalion. He survived a mild case of the flu and survived the chow (which seemed to him remarkably good and unbelievably plentiful, though others scorned it). He survived with only a hint of nervousness two heavy barrages by German shells. He felt wrapped in a blanket of protection in every way. Jean Dart had written that God had given her Isaiah 27:3 for him. "Lest any hurt it, I will keep it night and day." At no point was he required to do violence to another. Though he had gotten the highest marks in target practice, his eye and hand steady in spite of Shiloh's diet and schedule, he was not issued a revolver until just prior to the Armistice. He never used it.

He tried hard to be a good soldier, never complaining, never once late to any drill or inspection. At Shiloh, tardiness had continued to be his prevailing fault, sometimes a serious one. His most inexcusable blunder had been in preparing Gordon Murray's body for the funeral. He had done it in great love, but belatedly, putting off a job he dreaded to do. Emma Murray, in her grief, had scolded him mercilessly.

He supposed he was growing up in the Army. In many ways he knew he was already more adult and composed than some of the other men in the battalion—those who drank too much and wore a dapper air of carelessness that fooled no one. Yet he was intrigued to notice that he felt a unity with even the most wordly—not different or set apart, as he had supposed he would feel. No one made fun of him because he read his New Testament, or because his language was "clean." Only once did anyone engage him in a discussion of religion, and then it was the battalion "intellectual," who found it a matter less for debate than simple curiosity.

After the Armistice, Arnold was billeted at St. Mihiel in what was left of the shelled university buildings, once more playing in the band and using his Shiloh conversational French in the homes of hospitable residents. He was aware that only weeks before the American forces, with terrible loss, had shattered the German salient at St. Mihiel. He knew with certainty that Shiloh had been praying hard throughout the war for an Allied victory. He had still been home in Maine when Mr. Sandford wrote from prison to ask the hilltop to join with him in secret prayer to "control" events overseas. As well watching as the Expeditionary Force in Europe, Shiloh was following British movements in Palestine with vigilance and excitement, seeing the long-admired English armament as "God's Israel and scourge." The defeat of the Ottomans at Jerusalem and the Balfour Declaration, determining the boundaries of the Jewish nation, were thrilling steps in God's control of history. It was during the Tribulation that a great number of Jews would turn to Christ.

Arnold did not know, as he waited at devastated St. Mihiel, that Mr. Sandford was crediting the fall of the Hindenberg Line to his very own specific prayers. By June first, the Germans had moved to within thirty-seven miles of Paris, and Sandford, feeling the presence of this unquestionable enemy in an almost palpable way, had prayed (as he himself later reported it): "Father, that Hindenberg Line has stood there for four years. You said in the Bible 'They that war against thee shall be as nothing,' and they have been *anything* but nothing. *I demand that you put a dent in that line!*"

When, on the following day, the Allies blocked the German advance, he cried, "Now, Lord, I want a dent that can be *felt!*" By the end of the summer, the German front had given way, the forces of the anti-Christ yielding this skirmish to Ephraim and Manasseh, the savior nations. In September, soon after Sandford's return, Shiloh entered into one last Charge for a "cave-in all along that line." Thus the Allied victory was won, singlehandedly.

The war had sent Shiloh's heart blood coursing once more, not only because of its infinite proportions, but its finite ones. The building enterprises and the sea adventures had lent a concrete outworking of the abstract qualities of the movement. The danger and necessity entailed in manning the boats had made the restoration more comprehendable, tying it to a thing to "do." In the last seven years there had not been that kind of extenuating involvement. With the stations closed—England, Africa, and Jerusalem purified out of existence—with no campaigns and no university, the war offered a new undeniable reality as justification of Shiloh's purposes.

Armageddon *had* begun in Shiloh's eyes—both as the long series of wars Sandford was predicting, and in the strategic fighting that had occurred at Megiddo and the Plain of Esdraelon between the British and the Turks. Nevertheless, Arnold was going home, and that meant back to Shiloh. He entertained no other plans, and this was particularly significant in view of the circumstances. He and Merlyn Bartlett, with three thousand miles of water between them, had decided to be married.

When Arnold entered the Army, he had no idea where Merlyn was living. In France he had mailed a card to the Florida address he had jotted in his book in 1917 after her second departure, though to send even a postcard to a defector was a gesture of defiance. His letter, moving from post office to post office on a tenuous thread of information, followed her to Rockfish, North Carolina, where she was teaching in a rural schoolhouse. The outcome was a trail of long letters across the Atlantic. Away from the need to spiritualize every emotion, Arnold had discovered he was in love.

Far from disillusioning him about Shiloh, Merlyn wrote that she would go back if that was what he wanted, but it must be what he wanted. That is, he must know it was exactly the right thing for *him* to do. She had been through those waters again and again, and free at last of dependence on Shiloh, she was ready to go either way without humiliation. Mr. Sandford had written to offer her welcome, and she had told him she was undecided. She had not mentioned Arnold, but from Arnold's point of view in France there was no decision to make. Shiloh was their home.

Shiloh certainly expected him. Like all worried parents, it watched eagerly for news of its military sons. A telegram from August Marstaller in Germany, which read "Entering His gates with Thanksgiving," somehow was misread in the hilltop's anxiety to mean that August was dying. Passionate prayer went up throughout a day and a night before the mistake was discovered. August, in perfect health, was at that very time sailing home to Durham, Maine—all the heaven he figured on needing at the moment.

August, like a half-dozen of the twenty-four Shiloh men who had entered the war, was still a sound and loyal member of the Kingdom. But others, rounding out their various commitments to the country, were thinking different thoughts. In winning the Great War, Shiloh lost an important skirmish, for most of its drafted children, survivors of the onset of Armageddon, never returned.

28

The Holy Ghost Dethroned
1919

At the signing of the Armistice things looked wonderfully hopeful at Shiloh. The new year began "Gigantic with Possibilities." The mortgages on the farms had been paid off with $7,000 raised in two months, and a new Bible School had been formed. The "Forty" who comprised it were a select group of young people, mostly between the ages of eighteen and twenty-five. Among the students were John and Theodora Sandford, Doris and Avis White, Esther Sandford, some of the Holland children, several of the Marstallers, and some of the returning veterans. This was a logical opening class for the University, but college courses had been set aside once again by the war, and Sandford was eager to prepare these young people spiritually before they went on to other education.

The new school proved a disappointment. If ever there had been a ragged mixture of students, it was now. Some, like Doris, had made it through the "Eye" with John two years earlier. Others appeared shallow and self-absorbed. Some had slipped through the cracks in Shiloh's educational system and were ill-prepared as students generally.

Worse, the spirit of lassitude and failure seemed almost like a mindset. Throughout the fall, in spite of the victories of healing and funding, Sandford had bucked against this frustrating lethargy many times over. He had challenged, rebuked, prayed, comforted, preached; he had humored, praised, scolded, shouted and whispered, and often wept. No one seemed "right," not even the long-standing faithful.

Those accustomed to Sandford's volatile style of leadership took the artillery in stride: today things might be unpleasant, tomorrow they would be fine. But some were unprepared. Gladys Stacey, a young woman who had joined Shiloh in 1912, was astonished at his scathing verbal attacks, particularly those directed at Charles Holland and Helen before gathered assemblies. Mr. Holland, she noticed, quietly hung his head when the ammunition was targeted his way; Helen sat with her head up, chin lifted, wearing her little smile.

The high school age group was shaken by its own experience. They had been brought up during the prison years to adulate the absent shepherd. When he showed an interest in them they were thrilled. Fifteen or twenty of them, both boys and girls, were invited to Ebenezer one day for a private devotional talk. It lasted only fifteen minutes. Mary Campbell was "horrified" when Mr. Sandford stopped speaking and after a moment of deadly silence dismissed them with a shout. "All right! That's it! We're done! I never want to see any of you again!"

For weeks there was no further explanation. Mary, unable to bear the tension, asked for a hearing. Mr. Sandford explained that a boy in the class had been "making eyes" at a girl, neither of them listening. Mary interceded for the others, those who had done nothing wrong. At last they were "all forgiven," and Mary Campbell left Mr. Sandford's presence sure now of what she had been suspecting, that the prophet was fallible, as truly imperfect as David and Elijah.

Prison had changed Sandford more than he could guess. In the company of convicted criminals, sinners without question, there had been no onus of leadership. Returning to Shiloh meant reassuming transcendant roles every day, with Shiloh like a dead weight on his back. One day in January 1919, Sandford abruptly announced to the hill that God had settled the matter. He had spoken the word "Remove." This time he asked for no shared interpretation. He knew what it meant. He and his family were going. That is, they were going *permanently,* to live at the Boston headquarters. The "Holy Ghost has been dethroned on Shiloh Hilltop," he said. He saw no possibility of reviving the old-time vigor. In this tired body of people no David's Band existed, no purified Twelve, no fearless Thirty. He did not care whether any of the Forty followed him or not. If they wished to, they could, but they must find their own transportation. He would not help them in any way.

Most of the hilltop took the abandonment as yet another fiery test. He would come back when he was ready. He always had. He had withdrawn so many times in the past, to his room in the Turret, or to David's Tower. He had gone off in a rage during the Black Winter, after "plunging" them all into hell. On the *Coronet* he had retired to his stateroom for days on end, seeing no one. He had abandoned them again and again, wayward children who knew they deserved it, but he always rejoined them, finding a way to begin again.

Others understood that this time things were different. To some it seemed he was defecting, in fact. They had waited for him for seven years, sticking it out through hunger and illness and boredom. And now, after six months among them, it was *he* who was unable to "stick," quitting, like so many others, when things were not to his liking.

In fact, those who thought Mr. Sandford would come back were partially right. He had not abandoned them entirely. He soon returned for visits, most often at night, somewhat furtively. The hilltop did not shut down. Yet it was altered deeply. "The Kingdom is exactly what you are," Sandford had said many times. But it was true only to a degree. Shiloh was his. It was not just his "lengthened shadow." It was himself. The movement could not exist without him.

At Boston Sandford immediately began a new periodical and initiated a small new campaign of evangelism in New England. Willard Gleason, now grey at the temples but untiring, traveled through Massachusetts, starting out with $2.00 in his pocket and no destination, as if to revive the early spirit of abandoned faith. In Hartford and Providence and New York State new little fires of interest had sparked. When a woman in San Francisco asked for baptism, Sandford decided to do it himself and traveled to the West Coast, stopping in Chicago to renew contacts.

While he was gone, most of the Forty managed to straggle to Boston, where Jean Dart was in charge. Arnold sent train fare from France for Doris and Avis. Enid, though not a student, was also at Elim. She and Floyd, married in 1917, were the parents of a baby girl. Floyd was enrolled at a training school for naval officers in Boston. He and Lester McKenzie, who was also not planning to return to Shiloh, had chosen the sea for their future.

On the day before Mr. Sandford's return from the West Coast, Doris White began her first diary, at age twenty-seven. For over a decade, like Merlyn Bartlett Doris had endured unexplained headaches. Since aspirin or analgesics were out of the question, there was nothing to do but bear up, applying a wet cloth in a darkened room. She had been prayed for mightily, once with the ministers lined up behind her, "laying on hands" in a chain, a pageant that fascinated Doris but did no good. She blamed herself. She was not an overcomer. Her constant illness demanded a self-absorption she knew was wrong. It drained her of a sense of God's presence. She was disgusted with herself much of the time for yielding to the pain and tried to compensate by absorbing herself in the needs of other people.

On March 25, 1919, she made the first penciled entry in the journal that was to continue through May of the following year. It began with an outpouring of misery that she would never have aired aloud.

> Pressed beyond measure, most extreme suffering for a week or more, felt as though I could not possibly go on. Made up my mind I would have to go and wrote Aunt Neve. Awful night, head paining fearfully. Awful step to take, seemed like stepping into hell.
>
> March 26: Left while they were at dinner [noon]. Arr. Worcester about 8 P.M. Aunt Neve and Uncle Ed away until midnight. Landlady said she had no room for me. I went to Aunt Neve's room to wait. Felt horrors of Tribulation and no protection, no shepherd. Aunt Neve and Uncle Ed came about 1:00 and Aunt Neve took me into bed with her. Awful night, worry and pain.

Enid phoned the next morning, telling her that she and Avis and Mr. Sandford had prayed until after midnight for her return. Enid had been instructed to tell Doris that God had given Mr. Sandford the word "Bring." He wanted her to come back. "He felt I was not a quitter," wrote Doris in the diary, "but stolen by the devil, true to the heart's core."

Neve, Wendell's younger sister, had always been loudly outspoken in her disapproval of Shiloh but had done all she could to help the family. She had already paid for two pairs of glasses for Doris, neither of which had helped the headaches. Now she made an appointment with a specialist at the local hospital. For two weeks letters flew back and forth between Worcester and Boston, while Neve and her husband treated Doris to restaurant dinners and banana splits and bought her a jaunty sailor hat. The doctor concluded "that nothing was physically wrong," that Doris's trouble was "nerves," and she ought to have "lots of self-confidence" and "live a normal, natural, happy life and not worry." There were referrals, another eye exam, sleepless nights.

Finally, on April 12, after reading one more letter from Mr. Sandford, Doris apologetically thanked her aunt and uncle for their kindness (now she was failing *them,* too) and returned to Boston. Sandford welcomed her warmly in the presence of the school.

He talked at length about the difference between a quitter and one captured by the devil, as he felt was the case with me. Spoke of my integrity and love for him and so it was natural that Satan should charge on me while he was away and pick off the finest warrior.

Doris asked him to forgive her. Nonsense, Sandford said. There was nothing to forgive. Not a word out of her about being sorry. At the end of two more days of meetings and fasting, in which the Bible School surrendered and "melted," Sandford addressed Doris again. "Told me that whatever my weakness was that caused me to do as I did it was all laid on Jesus. . . . Did not need to fear ever failing again." Three days later they talked once more. There was "one point" she had "gotten off on," he said. "Got off in going to hospital without consulting *him.*" She had not wanted "to know what God wanted. . . . Made me feel that was an awful thing to do etc." She had turned instead to relatives outside. "Said I should be thankful I got back. Just the mercy of God. He prayed for me and I cried . . . and then I got through. . . . I stayed and the Holy Spirit and Calvary were very real."

In the next several days Sandford exhibited some of his own weariness to the students. "He cried as he prayed," wrote Doris, "and felt as tho he didn't have it in him to do anything . . . or help anyone. Seemed all worn out and broken up. He talked to us about keeping close to him."

Throughout these weeks he expressed increasing concern for the people left back in Maine. His anger toward the hilltop had abated. Early in May he asked the Bible School to return to Durham. Shiloh needed them, he said. He had had a day of "fearful pressure," wrote Doris, "as if the devil had a grip on him. Shiloh was like that only much more. He spoke of how good we would look to the people down there all tired and be-deviled. It would do Shiloh good just to see us smile. Called us kittens. Told us to magnify Jesus, talk just as big as we could about Him."

Brought back gradually, this time in the green Cadillac, the Forty took up housekeeping at Shiloh Proper. Jean Dart was their teacher now; John and Theodora acted as houseparents. If any of them had dared to ask what was happening, they might have at least suspected that for the second time in four months their teacher had made a discovery about himself. The presence of young people had never bothered him before. But forty of them, housed at Elim and the twin brownstone next door—forty seemed a lot, more than they had seemed at Shiloh

where they were spread out among the hundreds of others on the
premises. As quiet as they tried to be—and the lovely old Victorian
rooms with their dark varnished woodwork induced quietness—the voices
and laughter and movement of forty active bodies, forty extra chairs
scraping in the dining room, eighty extra feet on the five flights of stairs
was hard to take. Their chatter disgusted him, and their obvious spiritual
needs were overwhelming.

The hilltop may have needed more smiles, but it did not need forty
additional appetites. The temporary spurt of food had ceased—as if it
had also followed Sandford to Boston. Throughout the winter some of
the men drawing pay in the armed forces had been sending what they
could spare, though a large portion had gone to help pay off the mortgages.
Aware of the shortage, the Bible School ate its meals separately, not
touching Shiloh stores. Meals were more erratic than ever, never a
certainty. John and Theodora, who had access to food, shared as well
as they could.

Enid had also returned to Shiloh, where she awaited the birth of a
second child and wrestled silently with her thoughts. At the end of May
Wendell sadly drove her to the Lisbon Falls station. She and Floyd had
found an apartment in Quincy, Massachusetts. Their separation from
the Kingdom was final. It was not a sudden decision for Enid, though
it seemed that way, especially to Sandford, who just months earlier had
prayed with her for the regathering of the scattered A-Class. Wendell
knew Enid's nature. Like Annie, decisions came slowly, but once she
had made up her mind, it was settled. "Well, I commit her into the
hands of One who is "able to *subdue all things* unto Himself," he
wrote on the day she left. There would be no estrangement. But this,
the first splintering off of the family, filled Wendell and Annie with a
sense of impending trouble. Doris was so ill she could not get up to
say goodbye when Enid drove away.

But Arnold was expected soon. He had written to assure them that
both he and Merlyn were coming home. His last letter to Merlyn had
expressed only a little less confidence. "I will come and get you if I
have to, but perhaps you will be there [meaning Shiloh] waiting for me
when I arrive."

Instead, she was at the ship when it docked in New York, more
beautiful that he had remembered and so slender she was almost nothing
in his arms. "Oh boy!" he wrote in his diary that night. Merlyn wrote
nothing. Her face pressed against his khaki shirt, her one thought was
that at last she "belonged."

She belonged to Arnold, not to Shiloh. Her freedom made him uneasy. If she married him, she would go with him, wherever he went. That commitment was no surprise. Both of them understood marriage in those terms. But Arnold found the responsibility of being the one to determine to their fate unnerving. They decided together that he would go back to Maine alone, stopping first at Boston to talk things out with Mr. Sandford, who would surely convince them to stay—or so Arnold thought.

When he and Sandford met at Elim that June day 1919, they had not seen each other for eight years. Arnold expected to find Sandford looking older—but perhaps Sandford was unprepared for Arnold's new leanness, the mature lines in that boyish face. Was he still "conceited looking"? It never entered the conversation. Not much of importance did. Arnold spoke of his impending marriage and the decision that lay before himself and Merlyn, but nothing got thrashed out. For the next two hours, in Arnold's report of it, instead of engaging themselves in the issues at stake, their dialogue was diverted to "petty things." Sandford did "most of the talking," referring to one and another of those who had failed him, including Enid and Floyd. Arnold, remembering the terrible strain it had been to keep Shiloh alive during the prison years, spoke of how much the people had loved him and had suffered in his absence. Sandford answered darkly that he had also suffered in prison.

"Why one day," he said, "we had nothing to eat but turnip tops," adding "of course, we had bread with it."

Arnold stared, unable to reply. No one at Shiloh had ever spoken resentfully of the three meals a day Sandford was getting in prison, nor had they been surprised that the Shepherd would be fed when the sheep were not. After all, he had often told them that he had "never missed a meal" other than voluntarily since he began the life of faith, that God had always fed him and would feed all who had the faith to trust Him to do it. What shocked Arnold now was the apparent distance between the sheep and the shepherd. He was on another hillside altogether.

Sandford gazed back at Arnold, with his clear eyes steady and strangely "blank." It had never occurred to Arnold before that something was wrong in the man's mind. He brushed the thought aside, but the chill remained. The conversation ended. Neither was able to reveal what each was masking—Arnold's warring emotions, the need to talk about his confusion, and Sandford's painful suspicion that he was losing one more loyal member.

Arnold stopped next at the *Coronet,* then visited his sister Enid in

Quincy. Floyd was home. He was feeling poorly—a low-grade fever and night sweats. He expected to return soon to the ship, headed for Mexico, hoping the sea air would help him. The three talked all night, with Enid and Floyd taking care not to influence Arnold's decision. He left them no more settled in his mind than when he had arrived.

The adulation that waited at Shiloh almost undid him. He and two other returning soldiers were honored in a decorated chapel, then at a picnic on the Marstaller farm, with ice cream and victrola music and a game of "killer croquet." Arnold remained on the hilltop for a total of twenty-one days, most of which were spent in deliberation. After drawn-out talks with his parents, he visited friends in Bath and Brunswick—defectors: the Field family, Roland Whittom, Arthur Shaw, Charles Jones and his new wife. Back on the hilltop with the faithful, Arnold sought out those he respected—Everett Knight, Jean Dart, Mr. Holland—all the while probing his own reactions.

Late one night he walked up and down the dirt road near Shiloh's "Old Ladies Home" where his parents lived and worked. That day had been hot, the fields sizzling already with the buzz of locusts. Tonight the air was filled with an orchestration of cool nocturnal sounds from the fields and ditches. Almost frantic with the pressure of the decision, he called on God for an answer and, getting none, called (a little sheepishly) on the spirits of his Aunt Louella, who had died of cancer five years before, and Gordon Murray. Praying to the dead was hardly a Shiloh custom. He had never done it before. But both of these admirable people had died absolutely loyal to Shiloh in spite of prolonged and terrible pain. What did they know now that they had not known before?

Arnold had been using his head like a lawyer all these days, gathering the evidence, turning it over and over, tallying up sides—yes, no. In the end he did as he had been taught for seventeen years. He listened to his heart. His heart said something was terribly wrong at Shiloh and had been for a long time, perhaps always.

His decision that night was the first major one he had made in his life totally on his own, without Mr. Sandford, without his parents, without spiritual superiors, without the U.S. Army. Even God had refused to bail him out.

At the end of June Doris wrote in her diary: "A. told me he was going to skip the coop. Said he could not possibly stay. Expressed his doubts about Mr. S. I talked with him but nothing would take." Doris's world was falling apart. She felt "condemned and troubled." On the morning Arnold left she was again "too weak" to get up. Two days later the Bible School, with Doris and Avis included, went to Jerusalem Turret and wrote a letter to Mr. Sandford, pledging their eternal loyalty. They signed it "Yours forever." Wendell and Annie had no words. There is nothing in Wendell's diary for that day. The children who had once been his only reason to stay at Shiloh were gone.

Anxious to convey the news to Mr. Sandford directly and not disappear without a word, as so many had done before him, Arnold stopped in Boston on the way back to Philadelphia, where Merlyn was waiting with friends. Sandford, knowing already what Arnold had to say, refused to give him audience, and they never saw each other again.

29

Eva Beane Looks Forth
1920

If it took "two puny men" to turn the *Coronet* around in the North Atlantic, it was a "puny woman" who delivered Shiloh's deathblow. She was not only puny, but close to the day of her own death. Her name was Eva Beane. Not a hero and not a villain, she was, perhaps most accurately, just the person who was there when the time and conditions were right.

That time did not come until the winter of 1920. In July 1919, on the eve of Arnold's and Merlyn's wedding in Pennsylvania (at the home of Shiloh defectors, with no family present), Wendell was in the green Cadillac on his way to Boston with Frank Sandford. Throughout the summer Shiloh had been raising $14,000 to pay off the longstanding mortgages on the two Boston houses, the last remaining hurdle to financial freedom. Selected people were to spend the final seventy days of the campaign in Boston. It was Wendell's first long auto ride, the excitement only a slightly dampened by Sandford's insistence that the shades in the rear of the car be drawn all the way down the windows.

On October 2, Sandford's fifty-ninth birthday, Wendell gave a little shout in his journal. "Victory! Both houses now freed!" Wrote Sandford to his sister Annie, "I am tremendously *gone* in my feelings, but so is Satan." It was a crown on his first year out of prison, what Murray calls "twelve solid months of unceasing conquest." With all back debts eliminated, it was possible now to turn attention to the real work. The next year, from October to October, the eighteenth anniversary of the restored Kingdom, was declared to be "The Great Evangelistic Year."

More than ever Sandford felt the presence of evil powers around him, gathering and waiting for orders. Not only were the shades in the Cadillac pulled, they were drawn at Elim too, right to the sill. He was snappish about it, nervous about unexpected visitors, reluctant to go out in daylight. Only a few of those closest to him knew he had been receiving threatening letters.

Maybe it was the need to escape that initiated a brand new acquisition. They had no sooner laid to rest all the back debts, when it came to Sandford's attention that Center's Point on Merrymeeting Bay, not far from his birthplace in Bowdoinham, was for sale. The property consisted of one hundred acres of "Mr. Center's duck-hunting paradise," as Frank Murray calls it, and a large farmhouse with a stone fireplace and a magnificent view over the water. A single long cart path into the peninsula insured privacy. The price was $2,500.

Sandford first intended to buy this for himself and his family, a private purchase. Shiloh would be excused from another exhausting Drive. But by early November, with $2,000 still to be guaranteed, he decided that the place must be Shiloh's. It was a perfect vacation spot that everyone ought to be able to share. He had already named it Hachilah after the hill fortress where David hid from King Saul's murderous intentions. Perhaps the Bible School, the Forty, would be willing once more to "fight the good fight of faith," until they had a "spiritual consciousness of standing victoriously upon the Hill of Hachilah." Of course they would, they told him, and they did.

Late in December, with most of the funds assured, Sandford was given permission to use the place and invited the Forty to join himself and Helen in a retreat of "roughing it" on the new property. The week turned out to be a farewell party.

Typical of Shiloh affairs, it began with obstacles to be hurdled. Though the temperature was seventeen below zero, most of the men walked the eighteen miles from Shiloh. The more "weak" of the women were driven in what was meant to be the first of several trips in the car. When a cracked radiator put the car out of commission, the remaining students, determined not to be thwarted, caught the electrics to Brunswick and a train to Bowdoinham, then walked the remaining four miles, arriving at 4:00 A.M. Emma Marstaller, the Sandfords' cook, sleeping on the floor of the kitchen, got up to make hot oatmeal. After spending the rest of the night stretched horizontally five and six across the available beds, they woke at 8:00 and went out to gather wood for the fireplaces. "Mr. S. greeted some of us from his window," wrote Doris, "and his face fairly beamed with love." They had done exactly what he loved to see Shiloh do, beat the odds.

The plan was to spend the week studying Revelation, but Sandford was more in the mood for outings. The entire week was spent in hikes around the property and across the iced-in bay, with evenings of pleasant chatter before the fireplace, eating native apples and salted peanuts, a wonder produced from the Sandfords' personal supplies (though the students tried not to notice when he ate a box of chocolates in front of them). On the whole, he was in top form, teasing, full of stories and jokes and boyish ideas, keeping them laughing.

On their last day at Hachilah they gathered around a fire on a small island they had named "Patmos." That forenoon Mr. Sandford "wrapped" them in "the light of life, threw it over the young women like a shawl and over the young men like a cloak," wrote Doris. At the house they "prayed a long time" and Sandford "retook the colors, the white and the gold, Shiloh's colors that had been trodden down so long and he commissioned us to see to it that they forever remained at Shiloh. He prayed the white and gold into our lives. Gave it to us as a Christmas present."

The Forty were back at Shiloh the next day, while the Sandfords returned to Boston. Later in the spring, 1920, at the end of a winter of impassable snow, Hachilah burned to the ground, the blackened stone fireplace all that remained.

The snow did not start until the end of January, though record-breaking cold continued unabated into the New Year. The hilltop was out of coal again. A charge of prayer brought no results. One evening the students were told to go to bed because the wood was gone. So was the food. The feast at Hachilah on Merrymeeting Bay was the last steady provision the Bible School saw that season. Most of the others at Shiloh had not enjoyed even that small spate of good things.

Doris's diary in 1920 is sprinkled with references to the lack. No breakfast, no supper, waiting for supper, nothing since yesterday, praying for breakfast. Avis kept small packages of powdered cocoa, raw oatmeal, and sugar under her bed. When things got unbearable, she took a mouthful of all three. Doris's headaches, which had lessened during the fall and had disappeared at Hachilah, began again with a rage.

By the middle of January things on the hill had slowed to a crawl. Only the necessary chores were done—finding scraps of wood, fighting to keep the fires alive, milking the cows, doing a minimum of laundry. No one had the energy even for that. Annie, aroused from a nap by

Doris to help with the washing, burst out with, "Why can't they give us something for strength!" Doris had never heard her complain before.

Doris herself was spending hours of every day at the home of the Hastings family. Elma Hastings was dying, and Doris had been doing what she could to help with the eight children, most of whom were still small. Elma's husband William, one of the Kingdom ministers, the teacher and musician on the *Coronet,* had sometimes counseled Doris, giving her "light" or "comfort" when her headaches grew unbearable. "Feel like a different person after a little talk with Mr. Hastings," she had noted several times in her diary. The ability to suffer heroically, he said, was the secret to Shiloh's purpose. Suffering without self-pity was the sign of a true heart.

Elma and William Hastings had joined Shiloh at the turn of the century. Both had grown up in a community of Amish in Kitchener, Ontario. William, a brilliant young man, had begun teaching in the local school in his late teens. Elma Beane was one of his students. After their marriage, dissatisfied with the Amish style of life, the two had moved from church to church until they discovered Frank Sandford.

Elma's parents, never happy with the marriage (they considered Hastings unstable), were much less happy with the move to Shiloh. But the Beanes knew very little of what went on at Shiloh, for Elma seldom answered their letters and pointedly returned gifts of money.

In 1917 William joined the Canadian forces and was sent abroad. While he was gone, his oldest son, Ford (christened Sandford), ran away. A boy of sixteen, he was working for Wendell White on a farm at the foot of Shiloh hill when a friend who was leaving stopped to bid him goodbye. "I'll go with you," said Ford. He set down his shovel and walked off, without notification to anyone, going the usual way, along the road to Lisbon Falls. Feeling a moment of panic at the corner of the River Road, he "took the Lord's name in vain for the first time." When nothing happened—"a hole didn't open in the ground"—he figured he was safe and found his way to Kitchener and the grandmother he had never known, Eva Beane.

His brother Solomon followed a year later. By now their mother was bedridden. The influenza epidemic had left her with pneumonia and then pleurisy. She was hospitalized at Bethesda, while Shiloh women assisted with her children. William was still in Europe. The news of her daughter's illness was more than Eva Beane could bear. In poor health herself, believing this to be her last opportunity to see Elma again, she traveled to Durham.

At Shiloh her worst fears and suspicions over the years were confirmed. She found the children in one of the camps in the grove above the river, six of them and their housekeeper crowded into two rooms, sleeping on mattresses on the drafty floor. The children were pale and scrawny. They had been so long without solid food they threw it up when it was available. Frank Sandford had returned from prison not long before and the new carpet had just gone down in the chapel. Eva was not impressed. Convinced Elma was dying, she returned to Ontario and rewrote her will with two provisions: to protect her daughter's inheritance from going to Shiloh and to provide a fund to be used to care for her grandchildren at Elma's death.

Elma, unaware of her mother's measures, improved in health that spring, enough to leave Bethesda and go back to her family. Mary, the oldest girl, now fourteen, took over the domestic management, getting herself and the younger children ready for school in the morning and coming home to do the wash and prepare whatever food was available. Shiloh friends dropped in to help. Born at Shiloh, Mary had never questioned hunger. You had food if God wanted you to have it, and if you kept your eyes on God, an empty stomach mattered little. It upset her to hear the youngest, who was only two, cry for meals that never materialized, climbing in and out of her high chair, but somehow it was all God's will. They were managing together.

In the summer of 1919 William Hastings rejoined his family and Elma became pregnant. Her health declined again and soon there seemed little hope of her recovery. That fall, with the mortgages paid on the Boston houses and hundreds of dollars being raised for Hachilah, Shiloh entered its most prolonged period of hunger. The Hastings children went in search of berries and leaves, anything that looked edible. Old Mary Robinson, the cook for the first Bible School, whose exactness forbid her to pick an apple in the orchard, was found sound asleep under a tree, waiting for one to fall. Hunger continued into the winter. The week the Forty vacationed at Hachilah there was no food whatever on the hilltop. It was restored erratically after Christmas. Doris, who was now recording day by day what she ate, was sick one night because she devoured four small pieces of corn bread, two helpings of gravy, and two cookies. She vowed she would never eat so much again.

One day in January, climbing through drifts of snow, she joined the Hastings children in a choir around their dying mother's bed, singing "Joy, oh joy, behold the Saviour," as she slipped away. The next day

Doris helped prepare the body and cleaned up the house. The day of the funeral was "stormy and drifting," says her diary.

In Ontario, Ford and Solomon received a telegram from their father: "Dear Mama has gone to be with Jesus." Their grandmother, Eva Beane, had died the previous autumn. The boys did as she had instructed; they contacted their Uncle Melvin, Eva's son, who was managing the estate. The three came to Durham, confronted William (the first the boys had seen their father since he had gone to war) and explained their intentions. In another month Hastings was in probate court in Auburn, facing a suit brought by Melvin Beane in behalf of Solomon and Ford, charging their father with non-support and petitioning for the guardianship of the children.

That was how the end came about. After all the clamorous efforts over the years to shut Shiloh down, all the exposures and investigations, the inches of headlines and oceans of published words, all it took was a gentle push from Eva Beane to set in motion the chain of events that would empty out the hilltop.

By the end of January the Kingdom had been alerted to the danger. At Elim, Sandford arranged the assistance of Henry Coolidge, the Lisbon Falls attorney who had represented or advised him at other trials. There was little else Sandford dared to do. Living daily with the portent of trouble, he had been giving informal talks to Boston members, warning of days just ahead full of enormous hardship. God had now launched Shiloh into "a Martyr Movement," he said. "We have all got to be like a rubber ball—a ball that you can kick as long as you please and it will come up in shape again. . . . That is the way we have got to be."

By the day of the hearing it had begun to blizzard again. In spite of almost total preoccupation with calamitous weather, with trains and trolleys buried on the tracks and milk being delivered by sleds to houses snowbound to second story windows, the *Journal* still found a little space on page six for this new phase of the Shiloh story. Yet no one seemed to expect much from it or take much interest. It was not Frank Sandford who was on trial, but one of his followers, a man whose name no one knew.

The proceedings were quiet and unsensational. Few people were there, other than a reporter and one or two people from Shiloh called by Henry Coolidge as witnesses. Nathan Harriman had no part in this affair. Holman Day with his sentiment, Charles Mann with his poignant sarcasm, Rev. Weiss and his "inside story" were all gone from the scene. No one was paying attention. The few testimonies were given without rancor. Solomon, describing conditions at Shiloh as he had known them from his childhood, excused his father from blame. He referred often to "my Dad" with affection, and Hastings asserted his love for his runaway sons. Melvin Beane asserted that his brother-in-law was not necessarily a neglectful father, but that Shiloh's conditions forbade proper care of the children.

Henry Coolidge did his best to counter this soft-spoken attack.

"Do you doubt that boy is well and healthy?" he asked Beane, pointing to red-cheeked David, William's ten-year-old son, who was, said the *Journal* reporter, "an exceedingly bright-looking little fellow."

David, "exhibit A," as Beane's attorney later called him, looked much younger than ten. He was naturally round-faced, and his red cheeks may have been attributable to the fact that he was very hot. Someone at Shiloh had made him a heavy new wool suit just for his court appearance, the first new clothes he had seen in a long time. The temperature in the well-heated courtroom seemed almost tropical to him, so much so that in his adult memory of the event, he thought the trial took place on a warm day in May or June.

At ten he was old enough to be baffled at much of what he heard. Though frightened almost speechless at the idea of being taken away from his father, he was aware of evasiveness in the remarks of Shiloh's witnesses. Asked if the children ever went to school without breakfast, Hilda Smith, a nurse who frequently helped out in the larger families, said, "It has been the talk." David could not have named the day he had last eaten breakfast before going to school.

"Do they have butter on their bread?" Miss Smith was asked. They seldom had butter, she said, but they were given "fat." That David could remember. He had been given lard on his bread on Christmas Day.

"Do you know of the children going without supper?"

"I know the children are cared for," murmured Miss Smith.

Mary Hastings, too, listened with shock at this interesting way of telling the truth. She was recalling a time when county agents had appeared at Shiloh and she had been taken for a walk, out of sight of the inspectors, because she looked small and unhealthy. Only the plump, rosy-cheeked children were exhibited. She was also remembering another day, when fresh loaves of bread and other items had been delivered to outlying homes by the Shiloh "mush-wagon," with instructions to display the food if authorities arrived—but not to eat it. She had heard of

"Shilohizing" the facts at other investigations. So this was how it was done.

Hastings, speaking always in an "even tone," said the newspaper, described his work at Shiloh as a combination of teaching and preaching. He had no intention, he said, when asked by the court, of taking on manual labor for pay—unless God should so direct him. He saw no reason to forsake his calling because of "the irregularity of a meal or two."

"When there was no food for your babies, why didn't you go and earn some?"

"God told me not to," he said.

A self-educated man, one of the more intelligent people at Shiloh, Hastings was capable of doing any number of jobs, though he had an admitted distaste for physical labor. He was forty-six. His hands, which he rubbed together gently as he spoke, were long-fingered and manicured, the skin uncalloused, his face gaunt and sensitive under blond, wavy hair.

Couldn't he, or wouldn't he, take up carpentry, for instance, as Jesus had done? he was asked. Not unless God told him to, he answered. Oddly, in the eyes of the questioning attorney, Hastings's willingness to take on manual labor seemed to be the key to determining his responsibility as a father. No one suggested he might give piano lessons and make music for a living, or teach English for a salary. But if they had, he would still have given the same answer.

"Suppose," pressed the attorney, "the food should become continually scarcer, that it got down finally to one meal a day, then less than that, do you mean to say that you would not work unless you received a direct communication from God?"

"I can't say what I would do, but I would walk with God as I do now."

The message had not yet gotten through to the prosecuting lawyer. The hypothetical "one meal a day, then less than that" was not a case for the future. It was real now, that day, yesterday, last month, last year. Hastings knew exactly what he would do, because he had been doing it.

Solomon and Ford, realizing Coolidge would marshall out the strongest witnesses he could find in defense of their father, had spent the previous weeks bringing their own evidence up to date. Among those who agreed to testify was Elisha Beal, the Shiloh neighbor who had been feeding Kingdom children for years.

By the time he was called as a witness, another twenty inches of snow had fallen, bringing the record for the two months to sixty-one inches. Beal would have tunneled all the way to Auburn, if necessary, for the chance to tell the world at last what he had known so long. The story swung to page one of the paper, with headlines heavy enough to topple the hill into the river. William Hastings's quiet little day in court was now framed in "famished children" and "horses worked to the bone."

Throughout the proceedings Doris made constant notations as reports were brought back from Auburn. The judge made his decision on February 28. Doris wrote: "Case went against us. Mr. H. absolutely victorious. Coronet all over. Riding the waves." Hastings had lost his children but was trusting God to take care of everything.

By now the Children's Protective Society had joined the action, filing a complaint with the state and proposing that all Shiloh minors be removed from their families. Henry Coolidge, not known as a man of prayer, and also not one to yield to defeat or wink at reality, immediately went into conference with Sandford. Melvin Beane, who had been granted the guardianship of the children, had agreed out of court to give Hastings time to find employment and prove his intention to feed the family. If he did so to the court's satisfaction, Beane would withdraw the suit and not take the children. Hastings, Coolidge knew, would get a paying job only if Sandford so directed. Otherwise, he would lose his children. A precedent was being set, argued Coolidge. Shiloh now faced a long series of expensive, time-consuming, damaging legal entanglements, as relative after relative brought suits for non-support. There was only one way to stem the tide.

Living in the shadow of his own alleged culpability, Sandford was in no mood to face the courts about anything. Since his release from prison, he had been hearing of efforts to resurrect the indictments in the remaining five *Coronet* deaths which had been "continued" in 1911. There were people who hated him enough, he was certain, to bring him to trial again and send him back to prison for the rest of his life.

God's directive came in two messages, delivered officially to the hilltop by letter on March 9, 1920. The first, addressed to the household heads responsible for minors, particularly those who had never been considered 100-fold, was "Work." The second, intended for all other remaining male adults, was "can work"—if they chose to do so, that is.

The new order was read aloud in chapel by Charles Holland. The letter was simple, unaccompanied by rhetoric or lengthy apologetics.

Each wage earner would turn over a tithe to the Kingdom; some who were able could contribute more. Those who were needed full-time in the maintenance and care of the institution were free to perform that service. Nobody was preaching on I Timothy 5:8—"If any provide not for his own, and specially those of his own house, he . . . is worse than an infidel"—but the implication was understood. There had been too much laziness at Shiloh all along, Mr. Sandford was now saying, too many who had sponged and loafed while others picked up the slack.

As early as March 12, the hill was reporting a daily income of over a hundred dollars. Twenty-five men, including William Hastings, had been hired for construction work at the new Worumbo Mills just over the bridge into Lisbon Falls. Others had moved off the property to take more distant jobs.

Of all those surprised at what happened next, Henry Coolidge must have been the most unprepared. His intention had been to save the Kingdom from disaster. It made every kind of sense to him, a working man, that heads of Shiloh families should get employment—or that some should—and that the children should be supported and fed. To his way of thinking, Shiloh could go right on as it had, better than ever before, in fact, with the terrible problem of money dealt with once and for all.

But in a matter of a few days everything stopped. The prayer vigil ceased in David's Tower, without enough men available to keep it going. The Bible School was depleted of male students and word came from Boston to close it. When the message to work was brought to the hill, there were 370 people living there, by the state's census. In another month the population had dropped to less than a hundred. Even the leaders were vacating. Willard and Rose Gleason took their family back home to Reading, Massachusetts. John and Theodora moved to Lisbon Falls, as did the Hastings family. Some were returning to the far-off places they had come from—Tacoma, Chicago, Kansas City. Families such as the Marstallers and the Wolfes, who owned farms, stayed in Durham.

For Jean Dart, who had been fighting poor health again, the shock was overwhelming. One night she had a dream of dying which she related to some of the girls. The next day the wood stove in her room exploded. Men smothered the flames and tossed the stove into the snow, but Jean collapsed. Her arms and legs became paralyzed, her breathing and her heartbeat barely perceptible. In another day she had recovered, and Olive Mills, an old hand at death, interpreted the dream as a "warning," a foreboding of great trouble.

Many of those who were leaving the premises did so as staunch members of the Kingdom. Others were thrown into consternation by the new directive. For twenty-five years Shiloh had operated on a "strictly faith basis," with hundreds relinquishing every worldly possession, committing themselves to a principle so unbreakable as to threaten deportation and hellfire to those who turned aside. This was the 100-fold life, the highest attainment in faith, to *not* work for money, for "the meat that perisheth," but to trust God for every need.

Now, with all that behind them, had God changed His mind? If the meaning of "faith" had been a mistaken one all along, confused with laziness and sponging, why was God only just now pointing that out? How come it was now acceptable to join the ranks of Mammon?

But of course Shiloh had always belonged to Mammon. Money had been in control all along. Their suffering, their heroism, their victory in battle, their estimations of themselves and each other were centered in the lack of it. When their prayers for funds were answered, it was the world's money that God sent, the product of the industrial age. Shiloh, the hungry and unclothed, had been a great consumer from the start—and like everyone else in the country, fooled by the power of capitalism and its illusory twists.

But the belief that they were transcending that had bound them together. It was part of the view of reality that had hardened years before, unshaped then and afterwards the only way it could be—by questions, re-evaluations, and simple observation. They had always obeyed to the letter a limited reading of the challenge Jesus issued to the rich young ruler, to give up their possessions, but they had ignored the larger message. Poverty-stricken by choice, they had never hammered out a philosophy of poverty. The sacrifice alone had become their strongest rationale.

When their men went off to the mills, everything changed. With the risk gone out of the "safe place," with the assurance that they would never be hungry again, that needs would be met the way everyone else did it, there was no reason to stay. They could be ordinary Christians anywhere.

Day after day wagons rolled to the depot filled with families. Unable to express the unsorted tangle of emotions, to pull out even one strand that made sense, people said their farewells with odd understatements.

Frank McKenzie, Lester's brother, had shared the administration of the hilltop for fifteen years. "Things just didn't pan out," he said simply, as he shook hands with William Hastings.

Doris was present and heard the remark. She had been walking over to Lisbon Falls each day to be with the children. Mary, who was now sixteen, needed to be relieved from the constant care. On the day her uncle left to go back to Ontario she had impulsively tried to go with him, making it as far as the depot. Her father had caught up with her there and, weeping and ashamed of herself, she had returned to the house.

As attached to her father as Mary was, she was finding it hard to deal with his behavior. "He was desperate, would not even speak to the children at times," she said, in her memory of this time. He had always been inclined to "bait the boys," provoke them to back-talk and inevitable punishment. Now he "broke up a buggy whip every week on them," it seemed to Mary. Once he had beaten eight-year-old Marshall "all over his feet." That night when Mary sneaked into the boy's room to comfort him, her father caught her and bawled her out. She had yelled back at him: "This wrath of God you talk about isn't anything but your own nasty disposition!"

Doris knew none of that. She knew only that her presence gave Mary a chance to get out of the house and get a job on her own. Doris herself felt better than she had in years. "So good to feel like working and enjoy it and feel like waiting on God and be able to and feel like living, some heart in life and something to live for. So strange when it is such a blessing to me to be there and such a blessing to them." She had never been in love. Her feelings for William Hastings were tender and respectful and confusing. But she knew exactly how she felt about those children.

Even beyond the emotional tie, her job at the Hastings house had become her one point of practical stability. Floyd Clark had been hospitalized in a port in Mexico after hemmorhaging from the lungs. He was dying of tuberculosis. On April 10, Doris rose early in the morning to see off her parents and Avis at the Lisbon Falls depot. Avis was headed for Worcester to board with Aunt Neve, and Annie planned to stay in Quincy to assist Enid, while Wendell found a job in order to support them all.

As had always been true in Wendell's life, he made his decision on the basis of exigency—which meant however he was clearly needed, and Enid needed him. He was neither depressed nor elated at going. He was sad and accepting. Long ago he had worried about his "manliness," and manliness, as it turned out, was a matter of endurance, of "sticking." He had stuck to the end and God was not just "letting" him go now, He was sending him. Loose ends, if there were any, could wait to be tied up at a later time.

By May the exodus had been given a name. "Scattering all through the air," Doris wrote. There was no longer a choice. Everyone must go. The hilltop was to be vacated, closed down completely except for caretakers. On May 11 those of the Forty who agreed to stay on until the last day listened as a letter from Boston was read aloud.

> Precious little band—my heart goes out to you. . . . We can never forget each other; life will always be grander because of our association! We have walked the highway of absolute righteousness; we have sought to live the separated life—"undefiled"—and not only separate from sinners, but made "higher than the heavens."
>
> . . . I asked God for something the other day when the flames seemed hotter than I could endure, and I opened to this statement— one that seemed to bring this hemisphere and the other one before me—America and the "Land of Beulah." These were the words: "Instead of the thorns shall come up the fir tree."
>
> You've been such a true little Bible School—indomitable—true blue. God be with you as you CLOSE, gradually, wisely, orderly, and loyal to the interests of the Kingdom to the last.

That night the windows of Jerusalem Turret fell dark for the first time in twenty years, the last vigil taken by the woman who had held the first. The goodbyes "seemed myriad," writes William Hiss, not just to people but to objects, holy places, to customs and traditions. "The arrowhead in the front lawn, the long verandas, the various workshops, the natural history museum, the olive wood pulpit in Olivet Chapel, the devotional paintings . . . , the great dining hall with its murals and mottoes. . . ."

Doris's last diary entry was May 13, her twenty-eighth birthday. The Shepherd himself had remembered. He wrote her a note to tell her she had been "pure gold." That afternoon, after the Forty sat for a picture under one of the Gates of Praise, they were served a "big supper" of beef stew, raised white bread and real butter, beet pickles, and lemon pie. Then all who could be "gathered together," some two dozen or so, walked over to Olivet to sing. "Came home after eleven to have ice cream and cake," wrote Doris. "I come to my room and find cake of chocolate, banana, orange, bunch of Mayflowers." In the morning she received a gift from Esther Sandford, a "satchel bag her father had once given her with the words 'A Sweet Savor of—.'" The missing word is "Sacrifice." It was torn off, ripped out accidentally when Doris removed the next page of her diary at some point in the future. On the discarded page, shortly after her birthday, she married William Hastings.

The *Lewiston Evening Journal* gave the hilltop one more spread on May 14, including a large picture of the already deteriorating buildings. CITY OF MYSTERY AND HOME OF RELIGIOUS DEVOTION WILL SOON BE NO MORE. The place was eerily silent, thought the reporter. He had found one woman available for comment. "It is the dearest place on earth," she told him.

"Have you loved it so much, even when you were hungry?" he asked.

"Soldiers when they go to battle do not have pies and puddings," she answered with a little smile.

The next day a Miss Haines of the State Board of Charities and Corrections gave a "painstaking" report to the *Journal*. Her investigation "bore out the stories of conditions of Shiloh," she said, and went on to describe the premises, rehearse the history of the movement, and proclaim its idiosyncracies as if she were the first to tell the world all about it. Maybe Miss Haines was new. By the time the public read her remarks, they rang like an empty echo through the deserted grounds and across the river.

The article carried Frank Sandford's photo, the same one he had seen through the falling snow on the front page of the paper the night he was arrested in the death of Leander Bartlett. He missed it this time. Ten days earlier, on May 6, the Feast of Pentecost, God had whispered, "Retire." The word, says Murray, was comparable to the ones God had given Elijah before his dramatic confrontation with the prophets of Baal: "Go hide thyself by the brook Cherith."

In other words, Sandford was about to enter a period of waiting and preparation. So on the tenth of May, after writing dozens of final messages to the Bible School and other faithful members of the movement, Frank and Helen Sandford disappeared, leaving the remaining fragments of business in the willing and steady hands of Charles Holland.

30
Underground Shiloh

Back in the days when as a child I was shutting out Shiloh Talk, one question, impossible to ignore, hung in the air. Now and then it would get an answer. In 1936 the *Portland Press Herald* announced, "Elijah of Shiloh Durham Still Alive, Says Son." Well, if alive, then where, doing what? To that there was no answer, or at least not a public one, for a long time to come.

Soon after the directive to retire, Frank and Helen Sandford, with David and Esther, settled into the home of friends on a farm in a tiny rural town in the mountains of the northeast. Frank Murray identifies the spot only as the "Holy Hills." From this seclusion Sandford soon began a slow and scrupulous regathering of his flock, with centers developing in the homes of various followers around the country. Off and on he appeared at baptisms and various meetings—without warning, as Elijah had done—but his work was accomplished largely through other people or by correspondence. He spent much of the rest of his life farming, raising sheep, praying, writing, teaching small groups at the Hills, and studying astronomy and nature. In time he traveled to one center of the movement or another, and vacationed, successfully anonymous, at beaches and resorts on the east coast.

At the beginning Sandford's messages to members, which were not signed, were sent to Elim or other clearinghouses to be posted, or were delivered by a trusted person. During the first year of the hide-away, that person was apt to be Almon Whittaker. When Whittaker died in 1921, Jean Dart took over as courier and go-between. The inner circle was very tight, no more than two or three dozen. People were chosen on the basis of absolute dependability as loyal members, those who would be "not passive sheep," but "forceful, spiritual and powerful

personalities" (Sandford's words) in themselves. It required strict separation from "quitters," who now by far outnumbered the faithful.

With his usual genius for impounding Scriptural symbols, Sandford
saw the new David's Band as represented by the "Little Shiloah," the
stream in Jerusalem which, says Isaiah, "goeth softly," fed by a spring
under the Temple area and flowing out of the old Pool of Siloam. This
"river," usually little more than a trickle, on occasion had swollen to
a rushing brook, and would, says Isaiah, speaking metaphorically, someday
overflow into waters which were "strong and many . . . reaching to
the neck."

Underground Shiloh, going softly, was made up almost entirely of
women, many of them unmarried, some of them former members of the
Coronet Thirty. Appreciating their warrior strength and willingness to
endure hardship, Sandford organized them into a growing body of workers
who soon would form an unwavering core of stability. The dearth of
men was a problem at first. After Whittaker's death, only Holland and
Willard Gleason remained of the early ordained ministers. Holland
continued to live in his Cottage on the Durham grounds. Gleason
worked as a traveling salesman, with his base in Reading, Massachusetts.
Austin Perry, following his defection in 1919, had moved to Florida;
Ernest Tupper, though still in the Durham area, became neutral in his
affiliation; George Higgins sold his Cottage and at last cut his ties to
the Kingdom. Among the younger men only a handful remained, Joseph
Harriman for one, and August Marstaller. Lester and Frank McKenzie
both had become outspoken defectors.

Lester, Tupper, and Perry returned in later years. Meanwhile, those
who had been only boys at the time of the Scattering, growing up in
families of the faithful, moved into places of leadership. The old, men
and women, with no notion of giving in to age, seemed to grow more
determined and vigorous as time went by. Some motored about the
country in the most arduous circumstances, rounding up new members
and establishing churches, while others—without a printing press, with
only a couple of typewriters—got out multiple copies of the messages
and Bible lessons which circulated among them.

Though many members earned a living, all were starting from nothing,
and the new movement remained poor for several years. The Sandfords
and the Hollands and many of the unmarried women continued in the
100-fold life, supported by the tithes and offerings of working members.
Things got better before the Depression, enough to provide two new
Franklin touring sedans in 1926, one for Sandford and one for Holland,

and to invest in two more working farms, one in Pennsylvania and one near Washington, D.C. Because of the farms and the preservation and distribution of their produce, few Kingdom members were hungry during the Great Depression—one last little twist in Shiloh's history of economic incongruity.

These years, as Murray describes them, were remarkably satisfying and serene ones. The household at the Hills was full, with visitors coming and going, and children always present. Old age favored Sandford—or "retirement" did. Maybe he had retired from himself, the many selves that had become too great a burden. Rested and relaxed, he was something of a loveable curmudgeon, teasing people, insisting that the middle-aged women join in the games of baseball, calling everyone out into a freezing night to look at something he had just found through his telescope, holding a contest for the discovery of the first spring bluebird and winning it himself. The schedule of prayer went on as intensely as ever, yet days were moderated in a healthy way by hard physical labor and congenial social activity. Messages from God still predominated in all major decision-making, and in some minor matters as well. One day a lost baseball was found in a field because the Holy Spirit whispered, "Farther ahead."

In 1932 over a hundred people were invited to the Hills to celebrate the Sandfords' fortieth wedding anniversary. The secret location, now shared by so many, remained a secret nevertheless. A year later a *Journal* reporter, describing the difficulty of getting information out of the faithful, said, "It will be as though the other were a mute, as though you had not spoken." My grandmother, Elvira Bartlett, at our home in Massachusetts, spoke of "Mr. S." with a hush, though there was not a soul within proximity outside the family who knew or cared where he was.

By this time the Sandfords had bought their own home on adjacent land in the Hills. A fire had swept through the farm house where they had originally lived, and in time another fire would flatten the second home as well. Neither fire was suspicious in origin. Both were totally destructive, in each case entailing the loss of Sandford's journals and collected writing. He accepted the second fire as he had the first, with remarkable aplomb, telling Jean Dart that at least she never need worry again about a certain mouse that had frightened her. Within a year a crew of workers had erected another home on the same foundation, designed by Joseph Harriman, who was now employed as a structural engineer at a Boston firm.

Throughout these years neither Marguerite nor Deborah was reconciled to the movement, though I understand they established contact with their parents and remained in touch from a distance. Both had married. John, earning his living in various ways, still resided in the Durham area and along with Tupper and Holland participated in a local ministry of care among the sick and neglected of the area. David and Esther stayed close to their parents at the Hills, until in his mid-twenties David established an outpost for the Kingdom in New Hampshire.

In November 1941, Helen, who had been in failing health for several years, died at age seventy-seven. She was buried in the old Shiloh cemetery, with a stone bearing an epitaph by her husband: "Little Helen Kinney, with her sweet and quiet ways. . . ." Sandford never completely recovered from the loss. But she died only two weeks before Pearl Harbor, and like a soldier pulling his boots back on for one more campaign, he threw himself into the world conflict. The war in Europe had already absorbed him, arousing not only his "fighting blood," but his old paranoia. He was more nervous than ever about leaving his hide-out. To the wave of public uneasiness ("Loose lips sink ships"), he added his own "well-founded apprehensions" (Murray's phrase) about his personal enemies. Both Hiss and Murray resort to veiled language here. Sandford's concern for his own safety seems to have overlapped with the threat of German subterfuge, the fear that Satan might use "German sympathizers to stir up his [Sandford's] old religious enemies."

Armageddon now took center stage once more. Sandford felt, as he had at the onset of World War I, "almost a sense of relief that Anglo-Israel's die was clearly cast." He had abhorred President Franklin Roosevelt's policies in general. Now he supported him in his pro-British position. For several years Bible students at the Hills had been relating passages in the book of Daniel with Mussolini (see Daniel 11:42,43) and had predicted that Italy would invade Ethiopia and Egypt, measures which could severely affect events in Palestine.

There was no question this time about the involvement of Kingdom men in military conflict. On Armageddon Day (August 18), 1942, Sandford told the prospective GIs that as Shiloh had gone to war in 1917 as "police," now they were to go as "executioners," particularly so because they were men of God sent by God. A score of them entered the armed services, this time with serious casualties.

Once again Sandford moved the clashes in Europe along from crisis to crisis with his prayers. This war, like the last one, was part of "removing the veil" from the world, the order God had given back in 1898. Throughout the year 1943 the Kingdom prayed for the Twelve

Tribes, one each month, for the raising up of the 144,000, which Sandford had concluded were "God-appointed missionaries for the final harvest" in the uttermost parts of the earth. He now saw his own work as part of a "Great Ground Swell." He said nothing that I am aware of about a new voice calling itself Fundamentalism, nothing about the famous "monkey trials," or such charismatic leaders as Aimee Semple McPherson. He despised the work of the Jehovah's Witnesses. It was almost as if they had stolen the rights to the name Jehovah, the idea of the Kingdom, and the 144,000. But he included in the army of which he himself was a part many he would once have excluded—D. L. Moody, the Booths of the Salvation Army, A. B. Simpson. All these, he said, formed "a sort of Book of Acts in modern days," and if everyone would "get into the 'One Church' the Master instituted, that the man of God [Sandford] has restored, and stay there, you will see the omnipotence of the Great I AM let loose. . . ." He was confident of victory. "The devil is as good as in the pit now," he told someone. In the Japanese surrender he saw a positive sign of God's final victory in the world.

At the same time he reasserted his imminent martyrdom, his own and Charles Holland's, and still talked about that coming event in Jerusalem in high-flown language. Nevertheless it was a mistake, he warned, to attempt too close an interpretation of the book of Revelation. Better to just read and watch God work.

He often remarked in these days, "Don't look at me. Look over your own shoulder and you'll see Jesus Christ." But the very fact that he needed to say it—that he *did* say it—is transparent. The rider on the white horse was himself. He still believed he was Elijah the Restorer and said in one of his later writings that the world might well have been annihilated already "were it not for someone living so as to merit divine approval," adding, "he who betrays Elijah in our day and generation—nothing too awful can be meted out to him."

Yet, struggling once with his continuing anger toward Nathan Harriman, he acknowledged that the mercy of God was greater than the sin. In fact, at the close of 1941, when God gave him the word "Remit," Sandford declared a remission of all past sin for Kingdom people. The cleansing applied only to those who repented, of course, and Charlie Jones, survivor of the *Coronet* tragedy, listened in vain for some sign of remorse on the part of the man he had once emulated—remorse, specifically and publicly stated, as Jones meant it—for the deaths of the sailors on the yacht thirty years earlier.

The priestly act of remission is even more quixotic in view of Sandford's continuing repudiation of the hilltop in Durham, from which he had once found it necessary to "Remove." In his last program of writing he quoted the prophet Jeremiah: "Go ye now unto my place which is in Shiloh, where I have caused my name to dwell at the first, and see what I did to it for the wickedness of my people Israel." Since 1920 the hilltop had been falling into ruin. The *Coronet* had been overhauled again, but nothing had been done to preserve the Durham buildings, other than Shiloh Proper, and they had been robbed and vandalized and rotted by rain and snow. A woman living nearby told of waking at night to the awful tear and roar of Bethesda, once the manifestation of perfection, collapsing in upon itself.

The word "Remit," suggests Murray, may have been a conscious gesture on Sandford's part to prepare the movement for his death. Like any father who senses his waning physical powers, he was tying up a bundle of possessions for his children. If so, it was as mixed and disparate as any such collection, the jewels and china tea cups in with the worthless mementos, the sterling qualities of spirit all mixed up with abandoned projects, unkept promises, and unresolved tensions. While he tried to prepare his flock for the hard realities they would face at his death, at the same time he could not quite let go of the dream himself. To do so was to fail. Never able to accept failure, he had made his own failure impossible by binding his will inextricably with God's. If he failed, then God failed, and God could not fail, therefore he could not fail. So the only conclusion to draw was that he had not. Just as one way to fulfill prophecy is to say that it has been fulfilled, one way to avoid failure is to declare success. The covering had been removed. They had obeyed and God Himself would "finish the job."

At the close of the war Sandford gradually withdrew himself from personal contact with all but a few of the church's members and arranged for Charles Holland also to "go apart." In 1944 Austin Perry, along with others, took over general administration from the aging Holland. In 1946 Perry died, leaving his post unfilled. The matter of secondary leadership had never been settled in a satisfactory way, and Sandford had been openly looking to see who would "run things after I am gone." Both John and David Sandford had worked hard in the ministry, but it was "clear," says Hiss, that Elijah's mantle was to fall on neither son.

On the day after Perry's death in 1946, Frank Murray, Gordon and Emma (Barton) Murray's son, lately home from the war, was anointed as president of the incorporated Kingdom. Another young man had already slipped into a key position in Kingdom affairs. In 1928 Victor Abram had joined the family at the Hills to serve as Sandford's personal aide. His own father had died at Shiloh in 1913, and Abram had once said he would be willing to have his years cut in half if they could be spent at Sandford's side.

As time progressed, it was Victor Abram on whom Sandford learned to depend day by day. In the fall of 1947, shortly after his eighty-fifth birthday, Sandford's health took an acute turn for the worse. By Christmas he was eating almost nothing and was wearied by any activity. During the next two months he seldom left his armchair, though he played with the children and retold the familiar old stories. During meetings he asked over and over for the hymn "Brighten the Corner Where You Are," a favorite of his mother's in her aging years. "Everything's all right, from the south pole to the north pole," he told his son John.

After March 2 he ceased to speak. Early in the morning of the 4th, a dozen people gathered around his arm chair, where he sat with his eyes closed, but still looking as if he were "about to rise," observed Frank Murray, holding Sandford's head against the pillow. The room was silent—no singing or crying or audible praying. At 7:00 the Seth Thomas clock in the room rang the Westminster chimes, then struck the hour. As the last bell faded into the silence, he was gone—without pain or panic, without bullets or stones or swords. He just died, carried off by "natural causes" in his arm chair, surrounded by those who loved him.

Victor Abram prepared the body for burial. Legal obligations were handled with privacy, recording the death of a man who had lived in the town for twenty-eight years without a record of his presence. Everything was done, says Murray, without breaking the law and without the involvement of "any outside person."

More than twenty years before, Sandford had one day climbed a favorite maple tree on the Hills property, rolled up his sleeve to bare his right arm, as God would someday bare His own, and vowed that "every sheep that wants a shepherd *shall have one!*" The tree became known as the "Shall Tree." He was buried just beyond it on March 6, 1948.

The funeral ceremony was not only simple, but secretive and performed with haste. This was the moment the scornful had been waiting for, irrefutable proof that the man had been a false prophet, the whole movement forced into admitting it had been based on a delusion. The fifty followers at the funeral, particularly those who had been with Sandford at the end, had already transcended their doubt and anxiety. But as yet no one else had been informed of his death. Murray gives credit to Victor Abram as the person whose assurance carried the entire movement safely through the crisis.

There by the grave, honoring Sandford as apostle, priest, and prophet, Abram admitted to the difficulty the word "prophet" presented, in view of all their expectations. But their questions had already been answered in the 55th chapter of Isaiah, he said: "My thoughts are not your thoughts, neither are your ways my ways, saith Jehovah." God was telling them, said Abram, that they were "bound to get it wrong." But He was also telling them that "His word will accomplish what He pleases. . . ." It was not the end. "The next thing I want to say this morning," continued Abram, "is that I loved him so! . . . I just loved him, that's all. . . . I have told him over and over again the past days when I don't know that he could hear me—'I can't get along without you. I can't possibly get along without you—but I will.' And we all will. We can't, but will; and we are doing so this morning."

The announcement of Sandford's death was made at the annual convention in Boston a short while later. Though what the gathered company experienced, says Murray, would have seemed to the outside world as "nothing but a poor denuded flock trying to adjust to a crushing disappointment," that "was not the case." They were all of a mind. Their leader might be dead, but his movement was not, and the work that lay ahead of them had nothing to do with what had *not* happened, only with what had. They hardly needed Abram's clarification, that "if God decided to spare him that last awful thing [martyrdom in Jerusalem] he was facing so bravely, why should we weep for him? Our tears are for ourselves."

The newspapers were notified of Sandford's death six weeks later, without the rush of persecution that had been feared. By Murray's reckoning, out of the present one thousand members of the Kingdom, only a half dozen or so walked out. As for a "successor," there was none, and there never would be. The future leadership of the Kingdom would be shared and custodial.

Charles Holland, relieved of his appointment with destiny in Jerusalem, died the next year, and within a decade nearly all those who remained of the first faithful ones were gone. Typical of many movements, today's members of the Kingdom church know relatively little about these pioneers and warriors. Apart from their belief that they are carrying on the process of Restoration commenced by their prophet and founder at the turn of the century, their creed differs in no major way from that of other groups who share identity as Christian fundamentalists. The younger members at least are apt not to be familiar with the details of Shiloh's history, but their historian, Frank Murray, is careful to defend and, in fact, to champion Sandford as a man led by the Spirit in every phase of his life.

To William Hiss, whatever the contemporary Kingdom believes about its past or its present, "those ideas seem a pale and bloodless reflection of the people," the ones he grew to know well in the course of his own research, who exhibited consistently in their lives a combination of courtesy and kindness, personal discipline and simplicity. With reservations about the full import of Hiss's statement, I underscore his appreciation of the character and demeanor of many Kingdom people. But, then, I saw the same qualities in many of the defectors, and in my own family. It was not long before I understood that those closest to me functioned as tested people, in touch with their own resources in a way that made them sturdy and honest. They would not, I knew without articulation, "go to pieces" in the worst of circumstances, and they had ample opportunity to prove it. Yet both their hardiness and their ability to love generously were scarred by what they sometimes called "the Shiloh complex," a painful absence of self-confidence. My mother often yielded to its tyranny. My father overcame it almost fiercely as a door-to-door salesman for twenty years, ringing 50,000 doorbells by his count, a daily challenge to his ego.

Yet their diffidence never silenced them, and as tired as I grew of the Talk, at least it was healthier than denial. Good memories were rehearsed as well as the bad ones. My parents enjoyed a storehouse rich with inside jokes, and they never lost the company of those hundreds of persons they had known so intimately. "Wasn't Helen Sandford a lovely person!" my mother would suddenly say, apropos of nothing. Or my father would speak of a kindness Charles Holland had once shown, or either one of them would once again recall the gingerbread, warm from the great brick ovens, its aroma filling the halls on those occasions when things were going well.

The repudiation of Shiloh seldom entailed bitterness. Certainly I heard none of that from my grandparents. I don't know how long it took Wendell and Annie to decide they were no longer in sympathy with those who chose to rally around Sandford in the post-Scattering days. I suspect the break was as slow as the joining. After all, God had never told them to leave—rather just sort of dumped them out of the wagon. In 1934 Wendell wrote a letter to a distant relative who was gathering data on the White family. "I left Shiloh in April 1920, 63 years of age and penniless, yet I would not have those years taken out of my life if I were offered many times what they cost me." He meant what it cost him economically. Maybe that was the only cost he was aware of, or could admit. The Bowdoin College alumni office lists Wendell's occupation after 1903 as "None." He and Annie both spent the rest of their lives in menial labor, but with dignity and pride. "God has been pleased to bless my labors," added Wendell in his letter, "and now at 76, I own this 4-tenement house and double garage and have enough laid by to 'burry us dacently,' as the Irishman said."

So God's blessing continued to be measured by the provision of material need and gain, by property. I am not faulting my grandfather. I can still see the grime in the cracks of his hands that no soap would remove. God blessed the labor of those hands, he was saying. In the end that was all he asked.

My grandmother, Elvira Bartlett, also never indicated bitterness, though she was rejected by Shiloh to the close of her life. While she was staying with us in Holliston she tried on two or three occasions to be permitted by those in charge of the new Kingdom to live among the women at Elim or be cared for at the home for the elderly at Durham. Willard Gleason wrote to suggest that instead she learn to be happy "right where she was." Though I understand now how keenly she felt the disappointment, I heard no words of resentment.

Of those I knew who became outspoken critics of Frank Sandford, most maintained a core of Christian faith, so that the delineation of loyalties as they talked together was full of complexity and ambiguity ("neither wholly in nor wholly out.") My father was the noticeable exception. To him any religious allegiance came from the same package, the same deluded mind-set. In every other way, politically, socially, as a parent, as a businessman, he was the model of moderation and openness. But he had given Shiloh something he could never regain. So he tutored himself, like a determined teacher with a recalcitrant schoolboy, in the science of religious unbelief. It was a life-long project, and its public nature (for he talked about it freely) crowded my mother into deeper privacy. She had gathered her faith at Shiloh as naturally as an armload of field flowers and had learned to see beauty in weeds. Why throw the whole thing away?

Actually, my father, too, found it hard to let it go entirely. Late in his life, his mind still clear and reliable, he admitted with humor to a repeated dream that woke him in the night with its enchantment: a great choir of voices at a distance, as if across the sandy wastes of Shiloh hilltop, singing the stirring old hymns.

Though he decried the egotism and tyranny Frank Sandford represented to him, he never hated the man, and as children we were not taught to hate him. But hate or not, my father's memoirs were a vendetta against his years at Shiloh. That was the way he had to tell the story, as Frank Murray has told it his way, without including a line, as he says, from Sandford's "vindictive critics." It could be told in half a dozen other ways, by historians and sociologists, psychologists and theologians. I am none of those. My intention has not been analytical, but rather to see the story whole, from inside Shiloh's skin as well as out.

Let me try to explain a part of what that has meant. In my early teens, only half understanding the fire it would kindle, I "started" as a Christian, much as Wendell did, openly, happily, aggressively and, in my zeal and drive, no doubt obnoxiously. My older brother and sister had joined a church, but it was the church our family attended casually, a safe society of largely unspecific creed. Not satisfied with that, I struck out on my own. With no idea of what fundamentalism meant, I entered the Christian faith through a door into the fundamentalist subculture. In spite of the similarities to Shiloh, the context was very different. In fact, it was now that I discovered the exercise of inner freedom. Yet if I had consulted with the devil to find a way to make those I loved feel betrayed, I could not have come up with a more diabolical scheme. I was an A-Class all by myself, reading the Bible in plain sight (deliberately), going to prayer meetings and "separating" myself from worldly activities. I devoured *The Christian's Secret of a Happy Life* (with no inkling that Frank Sandford had once done the same thing), entered a deep and extended affair with holiness, and prepared myself to die an early death in some obscure corner of the foreign mission field. I report this somewhat facetiously, but I make light only of the self-importance entailed, certainly not the commitment or the solid core at its center.

My father, as much a missionary as I, and filled with anxiety for my future, saw it as his duty to deter me. A constructive exchange was never possible, not even later, when my soul moved into a larger house, one, to borrow Emily Dickinson's words, "More numerous of Windows." I doubt if it ever occurred to my parents that my allegiance would enable me to understand their past, any more than I could have imagined that someday a study of the Shiloh movement, the source of the dreaded Talk, would give me the forerunning history of my own pivotal experience, something I had been aware of in only a fragmentary way.

But apart from that and the probing light it sheds, apart from the fact that the exploration has involved my family and the gamut of emotions that is bound to exact, what has it meant to me? While I draw back from an overarching thesis, of course the story has raised questions far beyond the confines of itself. None of these questions are new. Other people have spent their lives pondering them. If I add anything fresh in the thoughts that follow, it is simply to present them against the scrim of Shiloh.

On one of my visits back to the hilltop in the early sixties, I brought along my five-year-old daughter. Standing in the front hall of Shiloh Proper, gazing up the staircase that led its five flights to Jerusalem Turret, she amazed me by exclaiming, "I like this place! Why don't we live here!" She knew nothing of the significance of the building, or that those were the stairs her grandmother had once washed down on winter mornings. Maybe she was enchanted by the smell of gingerbread, for the hall was full of it. It floated up from the kitchen below, where the caretaker's lunch was waiting, but for me it came charging straight out of the past, that symbol of the "good times," with all the appeal and challenge that Shiloh represented, and along with that its danger. I want to talk about the danger.

I have asked myself on scores of occasions, "Why tell this story?" Why bother with such a tiny movement, one that will appear to the world as just another skeleton in the overloaded closet of the Christian church, another example of a hierarchical, patriarchal style of religion, anti-intellectual and repressive, led by a man who may have suffered a personality disorder? Nothing is original here. Shiloh was neither the first nor the last of its kind—though it thought it was, as all others have and still do. But that dismissal itself underscores the danger. In our present-day fascination with the surface of things, we tend either to denounce a religion like Sandford's or sentimentalize it or tolerate or ignore it—unless some tragedy results. Too often we fail to understand it, and understanding it means two things—to recognize its unparalleled potential for both supreme evil and supreme good, and to realize that its impetus is common to us all.

More than anything else as I have studied the movement I have seen a body of people struggling with the same old things that all of us have trouble keeping straight. I am amazed by the heap of confusions that can pile up in one small corner of history—the blurred lines between liberty and responsibility, between authority and tyranny, between goodness and self-righteousness, between righteousness and being right, right and narrow of heart, between faith and piety, prophecy and prognostication, obedience and mindlessness, passion and sentiment, heroism and bravado, self-sacrifice and self-destruction, success and the absence of failure, being perfect and being forgiven, between union and unity, unity and harmony, harmony and agreement. In the cracks of the differences our most threatening dangers hide.

Shiloh longed, as most people do, for human qualities that seem less and less common in the world—courage, endurance, faithfulness, personal discipline, ardor and fire, and the magic of transcendence. We want our lives to be significant. Yet our most transcendent moments are filled with peril. Entering them is like entering a frontier where the borders of excess and distortion are seldom clearly marked and all the terrain looks the same. We need guides and shepherds very much, so much that we grow irresponsible in our choices. In our romanticism (and both Christianity and democracy have always lent themselves to romantic treatment), it is the "lonely hero" who catches our admiration more than anyone else, the one who dares to go it alone.

Shiloh tried to do this as a body. It trained itself in the hardship of lonely heroism. Frank Sandford taught his people that it is hard to be a Christian and to do it right, and so it is. But Shiloh's brand of Christianity (or humanity) was the easy one. The lure of the gingerbread is this—the appeal of what purports to be justified hardship.

In all appreciation for the sacrifice Shiloh entailed, the fact remains that it determined the boundaries of its own reality. It eliminated uncertainty. It is easier to be dualistic than to deal with ambivalance, easier to cast out demons than learn to live with them, easier to read the Bible as a series of answers than to hear the questions it asks, and easier to read God's voice in scattered words of Scripture than to heed the larger import of the whole Scriptural record.

It is easier to insist on unexamined authority than to engage in dialogue, and easier to give up freedom than struggle with its problems. Frank Sandford, says his biographer Frank Murray, was "as fine a Christian gentleman as America ever produced," a man "who breathed out goodness," whose presence "was a rebuke to anything ungodly," and that those who followed him were "pure, honest" and "trustworthy." However true that apologia may be, it tells only part of the story, as does William Hiss's conclusion that Kingdom beliefs seem "pale and bloodless," a mere shadow of the people themselves. The aroma of gingerbread rises again. "I am not a man who is trying to harm you," Sandford said publicly, just before the Black Winter. "I am not a man that is trying to blight your morals." Yet he followed those words with the threat of everlasting destruction for all who disregarded his message. The manipulation of blind, unquestioning loyalty, by whatever means, is a moral blight of the worst order, an atrocity against the human spirit, and it is not made "bloodless" by the passage of time or the finest display of character.

Shiloh, setting itself apart from the world, sidestepped the harder necessity of carving sense *out* of the world, of making sense *in* it. In spite of its consummate intentions, as a movement it never affected the course of history, not in any perceivable way. But it did reflect history, or rather, appropriated it, picked it up and ran with it like a football, winning sometimes, but at the world's game—not a radical, prophetic movement, after all. That one revelation has continued to surprise me. Shiloh was not just someting that *happened in* America, but something that *belongs to* America. Born out of a force that deplored the spiritual union of church and state, it nevertheless echoed and re-echoed the popular mood of the country. While it thought it was acting and speaking prophetically, it was actually aggrandizing the ideals of a nation with a messianic, perfectionist, and military vision of itself.

Shiloh never started a war. It incited no violence in the world, other than the violence it did to itself. Yet it contributed to a spirit of violence wherever it took its message. The dispensational, premillenarian view today feeds on expected worldwide cataclysm—"wars and rumors of war." The apocalyptic vision is more than ever at large, religiously and politically. It is always centered in violence—if not the "anger of the Holy Ghost" then someone else's. It invites war by presupposing it, by creating an enemy when none is at hand—for it must have an enemy to validate its own righteousness. We have been so universally conditioned by apocalypse that we are able to go on entertaining our greatest insanity, the mutal destruction of each other, an alternative that—appallingly— is easier to imagine than renounce.

Our world is far more evil than Frank Sandford envisioned it to be. Everything is *not* "all right from the south pole to the north." But we can't afford any more heroes who wield heroism as power, and we can't afford any more chosen people—unless that includes us all.

"I dwell in Possibility—," wrote Emily Dickinson, "A fairer House than Prose—/More numerous of Windows—/Superior—for Doors." She was speaking of poetry, not theology. But Possibilities, as she would say in her ironic voice, go hand-in-hand with limitations, and only then become possible. "May you portray the earthen, crackpot truth of Christianity," a friend said not long ago. Is there any other kind? Of all the windows in the house of faith, one of the most important is actually a door, opening out into the world. If being a Christian, or a Jew or a Moslem, American or Russian, male or female, or any other identity, means separation in spirit from the rest of humanity, something is perilously wrong.

Well, I have lived at Shiloh, I could tell my five-year-old daughter now, and perhaps I have made it possible for her to do so too, for a little while. It is for her that I tell the story after all, as she stands in my memory at the foot of the staircase in Shiloh Proper, looking up, claiming her share of the inheritance. I tell it for all the innocent, for those who, like Leander, are bound to be the victims, destined to fall from the cliffs of someone else's ascent toward the highest and the best.

Merlyn and Arnold White, shortly after their wedding in 1919.

Frank Sandford, at the Hills, under the Shall Tree.

Bibliography

This book is not a definitive history of the Shiloh movement. Nor is it an extensive treatment of the religious and cultural context from which Shiloh emerged. The story brings us in touch with areas of history that have been the subject of wide and expert study during the last generation. The scholars represented here have been my instructors and mentors for over a decade of research. I am indebted to them beyond measure for the light they have provided and regret that the size of the project makes it impractical for me to include them directly in the text. They should not be held responsible for the distilled use I make of their work.

For facts regarding Frank Sandford's life and the history of Shiloh, I must thank Frank Murray for the years of compiling which have given me access to a full chronology I could not have gained by myself. To that, William Hiss's excellent dissertation adds insight and balance—and it was Hiss, as well, who did the grueling exploration of newspaper coverage on which I have been able to build.

My father, Arnold White, has been the obvious major source for White family data and the collected stories of many Shiloh participants. His memory of fact and nuance, enduring and quick throughout his life, has no substitute as a primary source.

Most of Shiloh's history is verifiable beyond reasonable doubt. Yet the substance of rumor, gossip and hyperbole—when they are noted as such— have a legitimate place in the total story, for the Kingdom was a reality of many kinds. So I have used every source available to me, sleuthing out the facts, but recognizing the value of biased accounts and faulty memory. Those are history, too.

Published Sources

Books and Articles

Abram, Victor P. *The Restoration of All Things.* Amherst, N.H.: The Kingdom Press, 1962.

Ahlstrom, Sydney E. *A Religious History of the American People.* 2 vols. New York: Doubleday and Co., 1975.

Anderson, Frederick I. "The Man Who Heard Voices." *Harper's Weekly,* (15 February 1908); pp. 10–12.

Arrington, Leonard J. *Brigham Young: American Moses.* New York: Alfred A. Knopf, 1985.

Barron, Hal S. *Those Who Stayed Behind: Rural Society in 19th Century New England.* New York: Cambridge University Press, 1984.

The Bates Student, 10–14 (1882–1886).

Baxter, Norman. *A History of the Freewill Baptists.* Rochester, New York: American Baptist Historical Society, 1957.

Becker, Ernest. *The Denial of Death.* New York: The Free Press, 1973.

Berger, Peter L. *The Sacred Canopy: Elements of a Sociological Theory of Religion.* New York: Doubleday, 1867.

Berman, Jeffrey. *The Talking Cure: Literary Interpretations of Psychoanalysis.* New York: New York University Press, 1987.

Boardman, William E. *The Higher Christian Life.* Boston: Henry Hoyt, 1858.

Brodie, Fawn M. *No Man Knows My History: The Life of Joseph Smith.* New York: Alfred A. Knopf, 1971.

Brooks, Van Wyck. *New England: Indian Summer, 1865-1915.* Boston: E.P. Dutton and Co., Inc., 1940.

Bumsted, J. M., and Van de Wetering, John E. *What Must I Do to Be Saved?: The Great Awakening in Colonial America.* Hinsdale, Illinois: The Dryden Press, 1976.

Bundy, David D. *Keswick: A Bibliographic Introduction to the Higher Life Movements.* Wilmore, Kentucky: B.L. Fisher Library, Asbury Theological Seminary, 1975.

Burther, Robert W., and Chiles, Robert E., eds. *A Compend of Wesley's Theology.* Nashville: Abingdon Press, 1954.

Carpenter, Joel A. "Fundamentalist Institutions and the Rise of Evangelical Protestantism, 1929-1942." *Church History* 49 (March 1980), 62-75.

Carter, Paul. *The Spiritual Crisis of the Gilded Age.* Dekalb, Illinois: University of Illinois Press, 1971.

Carter, R. Kelso. *The Atonement for Sin and Sickness.* Boston: Willard Tract Repository, 1884.

The Christian and Missionary Alliance Weekly, 27 December 1890, p. 395.

Cox, Harvey. *The Seduction of the Spirit: The Use and Misuse of People's Religion.* New York: Simon and Schuster, 1973.

Dakin, Edwin Franden. *Mrs. Eddy: The Biography of a Virginal Mind.* New York: Charles Scribner's Sons, 1929.

Daniels, W.H., ed. *Dr. Cullis and His Work.* Boston: Willard Tract Repository, 1885.

Davis, David Brion, ed. *Ante-Bellum Reform.* New York: Harper and Row, 1967.

Day, Holman F. "The Saints of Shiloh." *Leslie's Magazine* 101 (April 1905): 682-691.

Dayton, Donald W. *The American Holiness Movement: A Bibliographic Introduction.* Wilmore, Kentucky: B.L. Fisher Library, Asbury Theological Seminary, 1971.

——. *Discovering an Evangelical Heritage.* New York: Harper and Row, 1976.

——. "The Theological Roots of Pentecostalism." *Pineuma* 1 (Spring 1980): 3-21.

de Tocqueville, Alexis. *Democracy in America.* 2 vols. New York: Vintage Books, 1945.

Douglas, Ann. *The Feminization of American Culture.* New York: Alfred A. Knopf, 1977.

Dublin, Thomas. *From Farm to Factory.* New York: Columbia University Press, 1981.

Fellman, Anita Clair, and Fellman, Michael. *Making Sense of Self: Medical Advice Literature in the Late Nineteenth Century.* Philadelphia: University of Pennsylvania Press, 1981.

Fitzgerald, Frances. *Cities on a Hill: A Journey Through Contemporary American Cultures.* New York: Simon and Schuster, 1986.

Fogarty, Robert S. *The Righteous Remnant: The House of David.* Kent, Ohio: Kent State University Press, 1981.

Frank, Douglas W. *Less Than Conquerors: How Evangelicals Entered the Twentieth Century.* Grand Rapids: William B. Eerdmans Publishing Co., 1986.

Gaustad, Edwin Scott, *The Great Awakening in New England.* New York: Harper and Brothers, 1957.

Gordon, A.J. *Ecce Venit: Behold He Cometh.* New York: Fleming H. Revell Co., 1889.

Gordon, Ernest B. *Adoniram Judson Gordon.* New York: Fleming H. Revell Co., 1896.

Gosse, Edmund W. *Father and Son: A Study of Two Temperaments.* London: William Heinemann Ltd., 1907.

Grose, Peter. *Israel in the Mind of America.* New York: Alfred A. Knopf, 1983.

Gundry, Stanley N. *Love Them In: The Proclamation Theology of D. L. Moody.* Grand Rapids: Baker Books, 1982.

Handy, Robert T. *A Christian America: Protestant Hopes and Historical Reality.* New York: Oxford University Press, 1971.

Hardesty, Nancy. *Women Called to Witness: Evangelical Feminists in the 19th Century.* Nashville: Abingdon Press, 1984.

Hareven, Tamara K., ed. *Anonymous Americans: Explorations in Nineteenth-Century Social History.* Englewood Cliffs, New Jersey: Prentice Hall, 1971.

Hatch, Nathan O., and Noll, Mark, eds. *The Bible in America: Essays in Cultural History.* New York: Oxford University Press, 1982.

Hays, Samuel P. *The Response to Industrialism.* Chicago: University of Chicago Press, 1957.

Helmreich, Louise R., ed. *Our Town: Reminiscences and Historical Studies of Brunswick, Maine.* Brunswick, Maine, 1967.

Hiss, William C. "Shiloh: Frank W. Sandford and the Kingdom, 1893-1948." Ph.D. Dissertation, Tufts University, 1978.

Hofstadter, Richard. *Anti-Intellectualism in American Life.* New York: Alfred A. Knopf, 1963.

___. *The End of American Innocence: A Study of the First Years of Our Time, 1912-1917.* New York: Alfred A. Knopf, 1959.

Hopkins, C. Howard. *The Rise of the Social Gospel in American Protestantism, 1865-1915.* New Haven: Yale University Press, 1967.

Horton, Rod W., and Edwards, Herbert W., eds. *Backgrounds to American Literary Thought.* New York: Appleton-Century Crofts, 1967.

Howe, Daniel Walker, ed. *Victorian America.* Philadelphia: University of Pennsylvania Press, 1976.

Hudson, Winthrop S. *Religion in America: An Historical Account of the Development of American Religious Life.* New York: Charles Scribner's Sons, 1973.

Hunter, James Davison. *American Evangelicalism: Conservative Religion and the Quandary of Modernity.* New Brunswick, New Jersey: Rutgers University Press, 1983.

Hutchison, William R. *Errand to the World: American Protestant Thought and Foreign Missions.* Chicago: University of Chicago Press, 1987.

Jaher, Frederic Cople. *Doubters and Dissenters: Cataclysmic Thought in America, 1885–1918.* Glencoe, Illinois: The Free Press, 1964.

Jewett, Sarah Orne, *The Best Stories of Sarah Orne Jewett.* 2 vols. New York and Boston: Houghton Mifflin, 1925.

Kazin, Alfred. *An American Procession.* New York: Random House, 1984.

Kelley, Dean M. *Why Conservative Churches are Growing: A Study in Sociology of Religion.* New York: Harper and Row, 1972.

Larcom, Lucy. *A New England Girlhood.* Boston and New York: Houghton Mifflin, 1889.

Lewis, R. W. B. *The American Adam.* Chicago: The University of Chicago Press, 1955.

Lowen, Alexander. *Narcissism: Denial of the True Self.* New York: The Macmillan Co., 1985.

Marini, Stephen A. *Radical Sects of Revolutionary New England.* Cambridge: Harvard University Press, 1982.

Marsden, George M. *Fundamentalism and American Culture: The Shaping of the Twentieth-Century Evangelicalism, 1870–1925.* New York: Oxford University Press, 1980.

___, ed. *Evangelicalism and Modern America.* Grand Rapids: William B. Eerdmans Publishing Co., 1984.

Marty, Martin E. *Pilgrims in Their Own Land: 500 Years of Religion in America.* New York: Viking Penguin Inc., 1985.

___. *Righteous Empire: The Protestant Experiment in America.* New York: The Dial Press, 1970.

May, Henry F. *The Enlightenment in America.* New York: Oxford University Press, 1976.

McCullough, David. *Mornings on Horseback.* New York: Simon and Schuster, Inc., 1981.

McLoughlin, William G. *The Meaning of Henry Ward Beecher: An Essay on the Shifting Values of Mid-Victorian America, 1840–1870.* New York: Alfred A. Knopf, 1970.

___. *Modern Revivalism: Charles Grandison Finney to Billy Graham.* New York: The Ronald Press, 1959.

___. "Pietism and the American Character." *American Quarterly* 12, part 1 (Summer 1965): 163–187.

___. *Revivals, Awakenings, and Reform.* Chicago: The University of Chicago Press, 1978.

Mead, Sydney M. *The Lively Experiment: The Shaping of Christianity in America.* New York: Harper and Row, 1963.

Miller, Perry. *Errand into the Wilderness.* New York: Harper and Row, 1956.

Moody, William R. *The Life of Dwight L. Moody.* Chicago: P. W. Ziegler and Co., 1900.

Murray, Frank S. *The Sublimity of Faith: The Life and Work of Frank W. Sandford.* Amherst, New Hampshire: The Kingdom Press, 1981.

Murray, Timothy. *"Coronet:* Whither Away?" *Wooden Boat* 32 (January-February 1980): 20–27.

Noll, Mark A. *Between Faith and Criticism: Evangelicals, Scholarship, and the Bible in America.* San Francisco: Harper and Row, 1986.

___, et al. *Eerdmans' Handbook to Christianity in America.* Grand Rapids: William B. Eerdmans Publishing Company, 1983.

___. "Common Sense Traditions and American Evangelical Thought." *American Quarterly* 37 (Summer 1985): 216–238.

Numbers, Ronald L., and Amundsen, Darrell W. *Caring and Curing: Health and Medicine in the Western Religious Traditions.* New York: Macmillan Co., 1986.

Parker, Robert Allerton. *The Transatlantic Smiths.* New York: Random House, 1959.

Penney, Will, and Penney, Minnie. *Eighty-eight Years on a Maine Farm.* Farmington, Maine: The Knowlton and McLeary Co., 1970.

Pierson, Arthur T. *Forward Movements of the Last Half Century.* New York: Funk and Wagnalls Co., 1900.

Plummer, Francis W., Sr., and Plummer, Charles W., ed. *Lisbon: The History of a Small Maine Town.* Lewiston, Maine: Twin City Printery, 1970.

Ruether, Rosemary Radford, and Keller, Rosemary Skinner, eds. *Women and Religion in America: the 19th Century.* Vol. 1: *The 19th Century.* San Francisco: Harper and Row, 1981.

Ruether, Rosemary, and McLaughlin, Eleanor. *Women of Spirit* (New York: Simon and Schuster, 1979).

Russell, Howard S. *A Long Deep Furrow: Three Centuries of Farming in New England.* Hanover, New Hampshire: University Press of New England, 1976.

Sandeen, Ernest R. *The Roots of Fundamentalism: British and American Millenarianism, 1800–1930.* Grand Rapids: Baker Book House, 1970.

Sandmel, Samuel. *The Hebrew Scriptures: An Introduction to Their Literary and Religious Ideas.* New York: Oxford University Press, 1978.

Schlesinger, Arthur M. *Political and Social Growth of the American People, 1865–1940.* New York: The Macmillan Co., 1941.

Seymour, Harold. *Baseball: The Early Years.* Vol. 1. New York: Oxford University Press, 1960.

Shanks, T. J., ed. *A College of Colleges: Led by D. L. Moody.* New York: Fleming H. Revell Co., 1887.

Sherman, Ivan Cecil. "The Life and Work of Holman Francis Day." M.A. Thesis, University of Maine, 194.

Simpson, Albert B. *The Fourfold Gospel.* New York: The Christian Alliance Publishing Co., 1925.

Sizer, Sandra. *Gospel Hymns and Social Religion.* Philadelphia: Temple University Press, 1978.

Smith, Gary S. "Calvinists and Evolution, 1870–1920." *Journal of Presbyterian History* 61 (Fall 1983): 335–52.

Smith, Hannah Whitall, *The Christian's Secret of a Happy Life.* Old Tappan, N.J.: Fleming H. Revell, 1966. Original edition, 1870.

Smith, Timothy. *Revivalism and Social Reform: American Protestantism on the Eve of the Civil War.* New York: Harper and Row, 1957.

——. "Righteousness and Hope. Christian Holiness and the Millenial Vision in America, 1800–1900." *American Quarterly* 31 (Spring 1979): 21–45.

Stewart, I. D. *The History of the Freewill Baptists for Half a Century.* Dover, N.H.: Freewill Baptist Printing Establishment, 1862.

Stinchfield, Ephraim. *Some Memories of the Life, Experience, and Travels of Elder Ephraim Stinchfield.* Portland, Maine: privately published, 1819.

Stoeffler, F. Ernest, ed. *Continental Pietism and Early Christianity.* Grand Rapids: William B. Eerdmans Publishing Co., 1976.

Strachey, Ray. *Group Movements of the Past and Experiments in Guidance.* London: Faber and Faber Limited, 1934.

Thomas, Robert David. *The Man Who Would Be Perfect: John Humphrey Noyes and the Utopian Impulse.* Philadelphia: University of Pennsylvania Press, 1977.

Thompson, A. E. *The Life of A. B. Simpson.* New York: The Alliance Publishing Co., 1920.

Todd, Mabel Loomis. *Corona and Coronet.* Boston and New York: Houghton Mifflin and Co., 1899.

Tuveson, Ernest Lee. *Redeemer Nation: The Idea of America's Millenial Role.* Chicago: University of Chicago Press, 1968.

Wacker, Grant. "Are the Golden Oldies Still Worth Playing? Reflections on History Writing and Early Pentecostalism." *Pneuma* (Fall 1986), 81–100.

——. "The Holy Spirit and the Spirit of the Age in American Protestantism, 1880–1920." *The Journal of American History* 72 (June 1985): 45–62.

——. "Marching to Zion: Religion in a Modern Utopian Community." *Church History* 54 (December 1985): 496–511.

Warfield, Benjamin Breckinridge. *Perfectionism.* Edited by Samuel G. Craig. Philadelphia: The Presbyterian and Reformed Publishing Co., 1958.

Webber, Timothy. *Living in the Shadow of the Second Coming: American Premillennialism, 1875–1979.* New York: Oxford University Press, 1979.

Weiss, C. S. *Sandfordism Exposed: A Warning and a Protest.* Lisbon Falls, Maine: privately published, 1899.

Westbrook, Perry D. *Acres of Flint: Sarah Orne Jewett and Her Contemporaries.* Metuchin, New Jersey: The Scarecrow Press, Inc. 1981.

White, Arnold L. *The Almighty and Us: The Inside Story of Shiloh, Maine.* Ft. Lauderdale, Florida: privately published, 1979.

___. "The Tragic Voyage of the Shiloh Schooner 'Coronet.'" *Down East* 20 (May 1974): 54–76.

Williamson, William. *The History of Maine.* 2 vols. Hallowell, Maine: Glazier, Masters and Co., 1832.

Wilson, Harold Fisher. *The Hill Country of Northern New England: Its Social and Economic History, 1790–1930.* New York: Columbia University Press, 1936.

Winslow, Ola Elizabeth, ed. *Jonathan Edwards: Basic Writings.* New York: New American Library, Inc., 1966.

Woodward, E. P. *Sandfordism: An Exposure of the Claims, Purposes, Methods, Predictions and Threats of Frank W. Sandford, the "Apostle" to Shiloh, Maine.* Portland, Maine: Safeguard Publishing Co., 1902.

Ziff, Larzer. *The American 1890's: Life and Times of a Lost Generation.* New York: The Viking Press, 1966.

Newspapers

The Boston Herald, 13 February 1957.

The Lewiston Evening Journal and *The Lewiston Saturday Journal,* 1895–1948. More than 200 items and features regarding Shiloh and the Kingdom.

The Lewiston Daily Sun, 1 July 1911–31 December 1911, and selected features.

The Lisbon Enterprise. Clippings, circa 1896–1912, from the private files of Arnold White.

The Maine Sunday Telegram, 6 July 1969.

The Maine Times, 14 April 1972.

The New York Times, July 1897–November 1967. A dozen articles related to Shiloh and the Kingdom.

North Shore, 27 January 1968.

The Portland Press Herald, 21 August 1936.

The Providence Sunday Journal, 8 February 1959.

The Shore Liner, June 1952.

The Daily Telegram (Sydney, Australia), 26 November–2 December 1908.

The Morning Herald (Sydney, Australia), 26 November–2 December 1908.

Public Documents

State Board of Health. *The Secretary's Report,* 1902–1903. Augusta: State of Maine. Pp. 14–29, 105–111.

Supreme Judicial Court. State of Maine vs. Sandford. *Atlantic Reporter* 59 (3 January 1905): 597–601.
Trial Transcript. Supreme Judicial Court. Franklin County, May Term, 1904. State of Maine vs. Frank W. Sandford.

Shiloh Publications

Periodicals

The Everlasting Gospel, 1–2 (January 1901–December 1902, with Special Issues 1903).
The Golden Trumpet, 1–4 (October 1912–September 1916).
The Glad Tidings of the Kingdom, 1–3 (October 1902–October 1905).
The Glad Tidings of the Kingdom of God, January 1919–May 1919.
Kingdom News, April 1905–June 1905.
Tongues of Fire from the World's Evangelization Campaign on Apostolic Principles, 1–5 (January 1895–December 1900).
The Truth, 1–6 (January 1917–December 1918).
The Young Warrior, 1:4 (July 1902).

Books and Pamphlets by Frank W. Sandford

"Around the World." Great Falls, New Hampshire: F.S. Shapleigh, 1980.
The Art of War for the Christian Soldier. Amherst, N.H.: The Kingdom Press, 1966. Original edition, 1904.
The Golden Light Upon the Two Americas. Amherst, N.H.: The Kingdom Press, 1974.
The Majesty of Snowy Whiteness. Amherst, N.H.: The Kingdom Press, 1963. Original edition, 1901.
"Mr. Sandford's Account, Written from the Federal Prison at Atlanta, of His Arrest and Journey South." Pamphlet reprinted from the *Portland Express Advertiser,* 7 February 1912.
"Scriptural and Authoritative Baptism." Durham, Maine: Shiloh Bible School, 1902.
Seven Years With God. Mt. Vernon, N.H.: Kingdom Publishing Co., 1957. Original edition, 1900.
"To the Future Students of the University of Truth." 1912.
Prison Letters. Random copies, 1912–1917.
Compiler, original edition, 1897. *Warrior Songs for the White Cavalry.* Amherst, N.H.: The Kingdom Press, 1972.

Other Shiloh Publications

Gleason, Ralph E. "Wilt Thou Be Made Whole?" Durham, Maine: Shiloh Bible School, n.d.

Harriman, Joseph B. *Israel and the World Crisis*. Mt. Vernon, New Hampshire: The Kingdom Press, 1952.
Harriman, N. H., and Harriman, J. B. *Shiloh As It Is*. Durham, Maine: Shiloh Bible School, 1904.
Funeral service, Mary Higgins
                Evelyn White
Daily Bible Readings for the University of Truth.
"A Sacred Tribute" to Stuart Wolfe.
"Rebecca," a poem by Merlyn S. Bartlett.
(For a complete list of the extant writings of Frank W. Sandford and other titles published or printed by Shiloh and the Kingdom, see Frank S. Murray, *The Sublimity of Faith*.)

Unpublished Sources

Diaries and Notebooks

Wendell White, 1916
Arnold White, 1905–1907, 1916, 1917
Merlyn Bartlett, 1916–1917
George White, 1865–1930
Doris White, 1919–1920
John Adamson, 1 January 1911–10 September 1911. Property of Charles Jones. Typescript of the original in the files of Arnold White.

Interviews (in person or by correspondence)

By the author:
Helen Curtis Brown
Brother Ted of the United Society, Sabbath Day Lake, Maine
Gordon Campbell
Mary Campbell
Avis White Carr
Arlene Clark
Gladys Stacey Davis
Isaac Gleason
Phyllis Hassen Gleason
Frances Gunnell
David Hastings
Doris White Hastings
Cal Higgins
Miriam Higgins
Alice Miller Holmes
Charles Jones, taped interview, February, 1984.
Louise Marstaller
Marion Marstaller
David Wylie

Arnold White (for which notes and tapes have been preserved):

Dorothy Barton
John Davis
Ford Hastings
Leslie Hutchins
Alton Lancaster
Marguerite Sandford Linde
Almeda Baily White
Marjorie White

By Robert Hine, Department of History, University of California at Riverside:

Mary Hastings Thomas

Correspondence

Frank and Helen Sandford to Mary Jane Sandford: seven letters, October 1890 to April 1893.
Frank Sandford to Merlyn Bartlett: September, 1809; 29 February 1919; March 1919; 12 May 1920.
Frank Sandford to Wilhelm Marstaller: 18 January 1904.
A. Guptil to the high school at Shiloh: 7 December 1903.
Everett Knight and Herbert Jenkins to the high school at Shiloh: circa 1908.

Other

Sandford family records, in the private files of Edward Webber.
White family records, in the private files of Shirley Nelson.
Bartlett family records, in the private files of Shirley Nelson.
Bibles (marginal entries): Merlyn Bartlett, Arnold White, in the private files of Shirley Nelson. Frankie Pulford, in the private files of Arlene Clark.

Acknowledgements

One advantage in taking a long time to write a book is that the circle of support widens and grows delightfully large. How could I have proceeded from year to year on a project that sometimes has seemed endless without the encouragement and help of so many? The disadvantage is in building up a collective debt that can never be properly repaid. But if saying thank you in this manner depreciates that at all, I offer my warm appreciation to the following people.

Extended family and old Shiloh friends, most especially my two aunts, Doris White Hastings and Avis White Carr, for the dozens of times over the years when I have poked and probed and squeezed their memories. Those who gave prolonged interviews—David Hastings, Mary Campbell, Louisa Marstaller, Isaac Gleason, Helen Brown, Cal Higgins, Charlie Jones. Those who wrote as well, in some cases many pages of memories—Cal Higgins, and again Mary Campbell, Phyllis Gleason Hassen, Gladys Davis. My cousins, Arlene Clark and Marion Clark Marstaller, for days on end of hospitality when I needed it badly. Edward Webber, who typed up Sandford family records for me and made gifts and photos and old correspondence. Charles Plummer and David Graham, for providing photographs. David Wylie, for stopping by twice with whole armloads of Shiloh publications. Robert Fogarty, for sharing his own work on Shiloh. John Sawin, for sharing his knowledge of the Kinneys and A. B. Simpson. Those who have read—sometimes consecutive and mountainous drafts—Jan and Tom Bourne, Patricia and Ned Trudeau, Bill and Anne Averyt, Harold and Mary Fickett, Bobby Garber, Mary Arensberg, Jerry Gill, Jeff Berman, Barbara Wheeler, Margaret Mirabelli—all bringing to the book new eyes and much personal wisdom.

Donald Dayton opened a whole world of research to me in a package like a Christmas present. Joel Carpenter knew just what to say at a crucial time. Mark Noll and Grant Wacker read bumpy drafts and pushed me over a difficult spot with their expert advice and warm encouragement. William McLoughlin and Dean Kelley wrote letters of response I will always treasure. Tom Allen increased my knowledge of small sea craft. And the historical societies, who actually seemed pleased to help—Androscoggin and Freeport, and Hobart Holly at Quincy, Massachusetts. The librarians—at Bates and Bowdoin, Mary Riley at Batesiana, Sally Stephenson and Gwen Dieber at SUNYA, and the reference desk at Albany Public, almost my second home.

To Bill Hiss, for cutting the way along several paths. To Scott Nelson, for giving me time when I needed an artist. To Yaddo, for six winter weeks of confrontation; to Nancy Nicholas, for believing in the book before it was anything but an idea; to Judith Jones and Maxine Groffsky for professional guidance. And to all those at British American, for their patience and enthusiasm—Susanne Dumbleton, Kevin Clemente, Bernard Conners, Kathleen Murphy, Margaret Mirabelli (again), and Stephanie Fisher and Ed Atkeson, for their visual imaginations.

Spouses are always last in Acknowledgements, on purpose, so the world will remember them better. Mine is also a writer, one who manages to confine his work to the area of a desk, while I spread papers on every flat surface in the house. The book could hardly have materialized without that gift of space (outer, inner), without that good mind to listen and interact so unfailingly, or the generous hours of reading and *connecting,* or—to be completely down-to-earth about it—without the open-ended, on-going, no-questions-asked Rudy Nelson "grant," collaboration of the highest order.

Far now from all the bannered ways
Where flash the legions of the sun,
You fade—as if the last of days
Were fading, and all wars were done.

Edwin Arlington Robinson
"The Dark Hills"

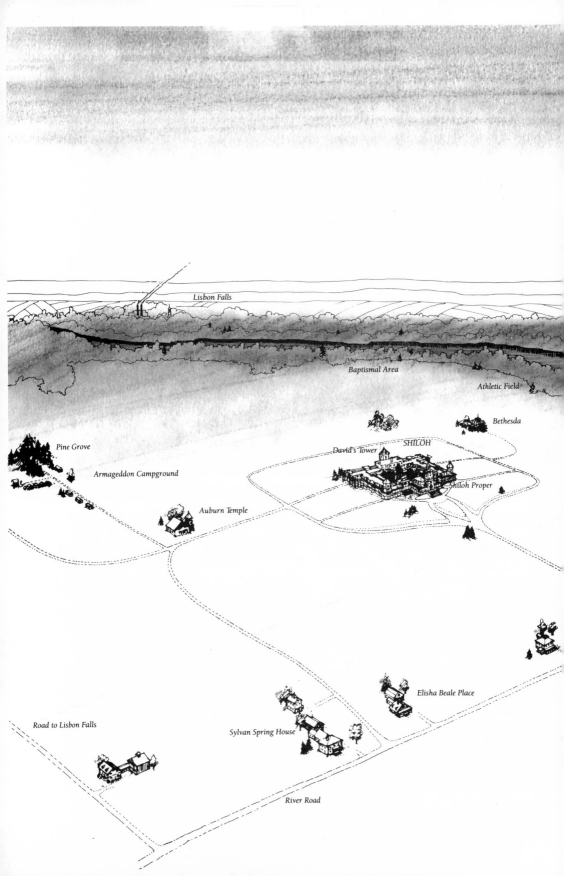